THE DAWN OF A NEW LIFE

After the painting by Thomas Shields Clark

COMPOSITION AND RHETORIC

BY

WILLIAM M. TANNER

INSTRUCTOR IN ENGLISH IN BOSTON UNIVERSITY

GINN AND COMPANY

BOSTON · NEW YORK · CHICAGO · LONDON
ATLANTA · DALLAS · COLUMBUS · SAN FRANCISCO

The Athenæum Press
GINN AND COMPANY · PRO-
PRIETORS · BOSTON · U.S.A.

PREFACE

This book aims throughout to promote self-cultivation in correct and effective speech and writing. Better English for immediate use, rather than the futile attempt to "develop writers," is its goal.

The capacity, the needs, and the interests of the average student have at all times been considered in the preparation of the text. The specimens of composition, selected from both standard and contemporary writers, have been chosen for their attractiveness to modern students as well as for their illustrative aptness. The subjects suggested for oral and written composition afford boys and girls, country-bred and city-bred, opportunity to use material familiar to them through everyday observation and experience. Numerous exercises in oral narration and exposition, frequent assignments in letter-writing, and definite practice in the writing required of students in other school subjects,—note-taking, translating from foreign languages, and the writing of reports and examination papers,—all furnish specific motivation for the study of composition and render the instruction immediately usable. The twenty-one full-page illustrations, which are made the basis of a number of exercises, include a rather wide range of subjects that appeal to the present generation of boys and girls.

Besides the usual equipment found in the average manual of composition, the present book contains a large amount of important supplementary material commonly available only in handbooks. This additional material enhances the value of the book for purposes of recitation assignment and makes it useful for frequent reference after it has been completed as a class text.

iii

Though the arrangement of the first three parts indicates the relative order in which each topic may be profitably taken up, the entire book is readily adaptable to a variety of conditions and special needs as well as to the particular pedagogical ideas of the individual teacher.

Part One consists of an introduction to oral and written expression. Practice in oral composition and in the retelling of another person's thought constitutes a natural approach to the writing of original compositions. Detailed instructions and well-planned exercises in the proper choice of a subject, the selection and orderly arrangement of material, the making of a simple outline and its logical development, and the thorough revision and careful rewriting of each composition furnish the student necessary guidance in his efforts at original expression. Letter-writing affords valuable practice in the most natural and familiar type of written composition.

Part Two deals with the units of composition : the paragraph, the sentence, and the word. The writing of paragraph compositions provides considerable drill in paragraph development. The four chapters devoted to the sentence include a more extensive treatment of sentence structure than is to be found in most text-books of composition. Punctuation and grammar as they function in sentence construction are treated in a practical way. The chapter on cautions in grammar and sentence structure supplies the student with the means of correcting many faults in his everyday speech and writing. The four chapters devoted to diction will help him to overcome errors in his diction and will arouse in him an interest in word study.

Part Three contains a concise discussion of the four forms of prose discourse. As many illustrative selections are included as space permits. Though formal argument receives its share of attention, greater emphasis is placed on oral debating and free informal discussion. In each of the first four chapters in this section there are appropriate exercises in letter-writing. A special chapter on the short story is added to the discussion of narration.

Part Four is intended for frequent reference by the student, though each chapter may be profitably assigned for close, systematic study. The brief grammatical review supplements the chapters in Part Two dealing with sentence structure. Exercises in Chapters VIII and IX may be utilized for drill in parsing and in sentence analysis. The final chapter, containing the principal rules of spelling, a list of the common prefixes and suffixes, and more than six hundred words that are often misspelled, will have decided value for a majority of students.

The material included in the six sections of the Appendix will contribute appreciably to the student's equipment both in the study of literary selections and in writing.

From twelve years of experience in the teaching of English, and from association and discussions with progressive teachers in many schools, the author has evolved the plan of organization and derived a great amount of the material for the present book. As a teacher in the high schools of Texas, and later as instructor of a large number of freshman students in one of the state normal schools and in the University of Texas, the author had opportunity to observe closely the product of the high school and to study from both points of view the problem of composition-teaching.

For most valuable aid in the preparation of this book the author desires to acknowledge his special indebtedness to the authors of Lockwood and Emerson's "Composition and Rhetoric," by whose kind permission he has freely embodied in his text methods and material made familiar by a long acquaintance with that excellent book, which in its own day was probably the best in its field. If in the making of this textbook to meet present conditions and supply modern teaching needs the author has succeeded in catching something of the spirit of practical help-fulness to pupil and to teacher that characterized that book of an earlier period, his greatest desire will have been realized.

To the following persons grateful acknowledgment is made for their assistance in the preparation of this book: to Mr. Frank W. Cushwa, of Phillips Exeter Academy, Exeter, New Hamp-shire, and to Mr. A. B. De Mille, formerly of Milton Academy, Milton, Massachusetts, for a thorough reading of the manuscript and for many helpful suggestions; to Miss Caroline M. Doonan, of the Newton Technical High School, for valuable criticism of the proofsheets as the book was going through the press.

The selections from Hawthorne are used through the courtesy of Houghton Mifflin Company. The frontispiece, "The Dawn of a New Life," is reproduced, by permission, from the original painting, which hangs in the Berkshire Athenæum and Museum, Pittsfield, Massachusetts. The two student letters in Chapter VI (pp. 117–119) are reprinted by permission of the Committee on English of the Newton Public Schools, Newton, Massachusetts. The right to use other selections and illustrations has been duly acknowledged where the material appears in the text.

To the members of the editorial staff of Ginn and Company and to the members of the Athenæum Press it is impossible to express adequately the author's indebtedness and his sincere appreciation of their inestimable service and splendid coöpera-tion in the production of this book.

CONTENTS

PART ONE

PAGE

CHAPTER I. THE STUDY OF COMPOSITION 1

Composition defined, 1. Kinds of composition, 2. Essentials of effective composition, 2. Reasons for studying composition, 3. The mastery of English as a tool, 5. Self-cultivation in English, 6.

CHAPTER II. ORAL COMPOSITION 8

Importance of oral composition, 8. Knowledge of the subject, 10. Clearness of thought, 14. The value of an outline in planning a composition, 16. Clearness of speech, 22. Correctness of speech, 24. Vividness of speech, 26. Two devices for keeping attention, 28.

CHAPTER III. WRITTEN COMPOSITION : REPRODUCTION . . 32

Oral and written composition, 32. The proper form for written composition, 33. Requirements of learning to write, 36. The value of conscious imitation and emulation, 37. Self-cultivation in English through reproduction, 41. Retelling closely, 42. Translation a valuable means of retelling closely, 49. Retelling by condensing, 51. Taking notes on what we read, 53. Taking notes on what we hear, 55. Writing examination papers, 60. Retelling by expanding, 62.

CHAPTER IV. PLANNING AN ORIGINAL COMPOSITION . . . 67

Approach to original composition, 67. Requirements of a good composition, 68. Choice and limitation of the subject, 68. Choice of the title, 69. Point of view, 70. Selection of material, 72. Arranging the material by means of an outline, 74. The law of unity, 74. The law of coherence, 75. The law of emphasis, 78. The form of an outline, 79.

CHAPTER V. WRITING AN ORIGINAL COMPOSITION . . . 86

Developing the outline into a composition, 86. The beginning of a composition, 91. The ending of a composition, 92. Transitions from paragraph to paragraph, 94. Revising a composition before it is submitted, 95. Rewriting a corrected composition, 97.

PAGE

CHAPTER VI. LETTER–WRITING 104

Importance of letter-writing, 104. General form of letters, 104.
Parts of a letter, 106. Qualities of the friendly letter, 111. Informal
notes, 120. Formal notes, 122. The business letter, 124. Qualities
of the business letter, 126.

PART TWO

CHAPTER VII. THE PARAGRAPH 131

Definition of the paragraph, 131. Length of the paragraph, 132.
Unity in the paragraph, 133. The topic sentence, 133. Position of
the topic sentence, 133. Coherence in the paragraph, 140. Methods
of paragraph development, 140: (1) By repetition, 140. (2) By details, 141. (3) By definition, 143. (4) By specific examples, 144.
(5) By comparison and contrast, 144. (6) By supporting the topic
statement with reasons, 146. Connecting words and phrases, 150.
Emphasis in the paragraph, 152. Transitional paragraphs, 155.

CHAPTER VIII. THE SENTENCE GRAMMATICALLY CONSID-
ERED 159

Nature and purpose of the sentence, 159. The simple sentence, 159.
Phrases, 160. The compound sentence, 165. The complex sentence,
170. Noun clauses, 171. Adjective clauses, 173. Adverbial clauses,
174. The compound-complex sentence, 180. Kinds of sentences according to use, 181. Phrases and dependent clauses incorrectly used
as sentences, 182.

CHAPTER IX. THE SENTENCE RHETORICALLY CONSID-
ERED 186

Kinds of sentences, 186. Effect of different kinds of sentences, 187.
Unity in the sentence, 190. Coherence in the sentence, 195. Emphasis in the sentence, 201. Euphony in the sentence, 204.

CHAPTER X. PUNCTUATION 211

Requirements of accurate punctuation, 211. General directions for
punctuation, 212. The comma, 212. The semicolon, 221. The colon,
224. The period, 226. The question mark, 229. The exclamation
mark, 229. The dash, 230. Parentheses, 233. Brackets, 234. Quotation marks, 235. The apostrophe, 238. The hyphen, 239. The
caret, 239. Points and asterisks, 239. Italics, 239. Capital letters, 241.

PAGE

CHAPTER XI. SPECIAL CAUTIONS IN GRAMMAR AND SEN-
TENCE STRUCTURE 248

Agreement of subject and predicate, 249. Nouns and pronouns,
253. Case, 253. Number, 255. Agreement of relative pronouns,
256. Reference of pronouns, 256. Adjectives and adverbs, 259.
Expressions of comparison, 259. Adjectives and adverbs not to be
confused in use, 260. Verbs, 263. Principal parts of difficult verbs,
263. Six troublesome verbs, 264. Uses of *shall* and *will*, *should* and
would, 266. Additional cautions regarding tense, 271. Uses of the
subjunctive mood, 273. Reference of participles, 274. Reference of
verbal nouns, 275. Reference of infinitives, 276. Prepositions and
conjunctions, 277. Improper omission of words, 278. Double subjects and double objects, 281. Double negatives, 281. *When* and
where clauses wrongly used, 281. *Because* clause wrongly used, 282.
The *period fault*, 282. The *comma fault*, 283. Faulty coördination
in compound sentences, 285. Parallel construction, 287. Shift in
point of view, 288.

CHAPTER XII. THE CORRECT USE OF WORDS 292

The English language and its sources, 292. Diction, 293. Good use,
294. Violations of good use, 294. Barbarisms, 294. Solecisms, 295.
Improprieties, 296. Slang, 296. Obsolete and archaic words, 297.
Technical words, 297. A list of common errors in diction, 298.

CHAPTER XIII. THE EFFECTIVE USE OF WORDS 316

Effectiveness of diction, 316. Exactness, 316. Appropriateness, 317.
Expressiveness, 319. The suggestive value of figures of speech, 320.
Violations of effectiveness, 327. Needless repetition, 327. Exaggeration, 328. Trite expressions, 328. Hackneyed quotations, 329. Overuse of figurative language, 329. "Fine writing," 330.

CHAPTER XIV. THE IMPORTANCE OF A LARGE VOCAB-
ULARY 333

Poverty in words and thoughts, 333. Anglo-Saxon words, 333.
Classical words, 334. Idioms, 334. Synonyms and antonyms, 335.
How to acquire a large vocabulary, 336.

CHAPTER XV. THE USE OF THE DICTIONARY 339

Importance of the study of the dictionary, 339. Unabridged and
abridged dictionaries, 339. Arrangement of an unabridged dictionary, 340. Information about words, 341.

PART THREE

PAGE

CHAPTER XVI. SIMPLE NARRATION 345

Simple narration defined, 345. The three essentials, 345. Unity in simple narration, 348. Coherence in simple narration, 350. Emphasis in simple narration, 350. Oral narration, 351. Anecdotes, 353. Tales, 355. News stories, 356. Letters, 359. Diaries, 360. Biographies, 360. Autobiographies, 361. Travel sketches, 362.

CHAPTER XVII. DESCRIPTION 365

Description defined, 365. Expository description, 365. Artistic description, 366. Unity in description, 366. Point of view, 367. Singleness of impression, 368. The fundamental image, 370. Coherence in description, 370. Emphasis in description, 371. Vividness in description, 371. How to describe a place, 375. How to describe an object, 378. How to describe an animal, 380. How to describe a person, 382. Description by effect, 385. Principal aids in writing description, 386.

CHAPTER XVIII. EXPOSITION 388

Exposition defined, 388. The importance of clearness, 388. Oral exposition, 389. Methods of exposition, 390. Definitions, 390. Explanations of processes, 394. Discussions of facts and ideas, 397. Essays, 400. Expository biography, 405. Reviews and criticisms, 407. Newspaper editorials, 410. Expository letters, 413.

CHAPTER XIX. ARGUMENT AND DEBATING 415

Argument defined, 415. Conviction and persuasion, 416. Informal argument, 417. Formal argument, 421. The value of debating, 421. Subjects for debate, 421. Wording the question, 422. Exposition of the question, 423. Definition of terms, 423. Conflict of opinion, 424. Proof, 425. Refutation, 426. Burden of proof, 426. The brief, 427. Developing the brief into an argument, 431.

CHAPTER XX. THE SHORT STORY 434

The short story defined, 434. Characteristics of the short story, 434. Essentials of the short story, 435. Singleness of impression, 442. Plot, 443. Dominant incident, 445. Characters, 446. The complication and its resolution, 446. Setting, 447. Point of view, 447. Where to begin a short story, 448. How to begin a short story, 448. The title, 449. Aids in writing a short story, 449. Sources of short stories, 451.

PART FOUR

PAGE

CHAPTER XXI. A REVIEW OF GRAMMAR 457

Nouns, 457. Pronouns, 462. Adjectives, 466. Adverbs, 470. Verbs, 471. Prepositions, 483. Conjunctions, 484. Interjections, 485. Sentence analysis, 485.

CHAPTER XXII. SPELLING 487

Importance of learning to spell correctly, 487. Rules for spelling, 487. Helps in learning to spell, 490. Syllabication, 491. Prefixes and suffixes, 492. Spelling-list, 494. Words frequently confused, 498. Proper names frequently misspelled, 500.

APPENDIX A. SUGGESTIONS FOR STUDYING THE PRINCIPAL
TYPES OF LITERATURE i

APPENDIX B. SUGGESTIONS FOR USING A SCHOOL LIBRARY viii

APPENDIX C. VERSIFICATION xv

APPENDIX D. A LIST OF COMMON ABBREVIATIONS . . . xxv

APPENDIX E. MARKS USED IN CORRECTING COMPOSITIONS xxviii

APPENDIX F. MARKS USED IN PROOFREADING xxx

INDEX xxxiii

LIST OF FULL–PAGE ILLUSTRATIONS

	PAGE
The Dawn of a New Life . . . . Frontispiece
Robinson Crusoe opens the Chest	26
The Fight in the Rigging	54
A Marble Tournament	72
Putting the Shot	94
Camping in Colorado	116
A City Market	146
The Sagebrush of Idaho	172
Man's Conquest over Nature	198
Off !	220
Harvesting Ice	258
Flotsam Castle	296
The Skyscrapers	324
The Pirate	348
A May-Day Frolic	360
Yosemite Falls	370
The Village Censor	382
The Lights of Industry	402
Thrift and Prosperity	424
Strolling Players	448
The End of the Trail	476

COMPOSITION AND RHETORIC

PART ONE

CHAPTER I

THE STUDY OF COMPOSITION

1. Introduction. As we enter upon the study of composition we may ask: What is composition? Why should I study it? How can I master it? To give preliminary answers to these questions is the purpose of the present chapter. To provide a practical treatment of these and other related questions is the function of the remainder of the book.

2. Composition defined. Whenever we communicate with other persons, either by speech or by writing, we are *composing*; that is, we are putting together thoughts so selected and arranged as to convey our meaning. Expression by means of speech is termed *oral composition*. Expression by means of writing is termed *written composition*. In order to express ourselves clearly and well, we should learn to exercise care in the choice and arrangement of our thoughts and acquire skill in the use of words and in the construction of sentences, paragraphs, and whole compositions.

Composition, like any other art, is governed by established rules and principles. These have been discovered through practice by generations of speakers and writers before us. For our convenience and profit they have been brought together and clearly stated as the rules of grammar and the principles of rhetoric. Grammar is the science that deals with the forms and the constructions of words. Rhetoric consists of the study of the principles governing the clear, forceful, and elegant expression of thoughts. *Composition, therefore, is the expression of what we have to say in accordance with the rules of grammar and the principles of rhetoric.*

3. Units of composition. The whole composition, which is the largest unit of expression, is made up of three subordinate units; namely, the paragraph, the sentence, and the word. These four units will be fully discussed and illustrated in later chapters.

4. Kinds of composition. According to our purpose as speakers and writers, we may make our composition (1) *narration,* (2) *description,* (3) *exposition,* or (4) *argument.* By means of narration we seek to entertain our hearers or readers by recounting an experience, relating an incident, or retelling a story. By the use of description we attempt to represent vividly for them a scene, an object, a person, a mood, or an impression that has interested us. By means of exposition we endeavor to explain something to them. By employing argument we try to lead them to believe as we do and to act as we desire them to act.

5. Sources of material for compositions. Though the subjects on which we may speak and write are infinite, we derive these subjects, and the material for developing them, from a relatively small number of sources. The most common of these sources are personal experience, observation, conversation, lectures, and reading.

6. Essentials of effective composition. Before we can make a subject interesting to others we must understand it thoroughly ourselves and must learn how to present it clearly and effectively. The manner of expressing our thoughts is next in importance to the thoughts themselves. As speakers and writers we should constantly endeavor to make it easy for others to understand what we have to say. This we can learn to do by conforming to the three essentials of effective composition; namely, *clear thinking, adequate expression*, and *good form*.

Few of us are endowed by nature with the ability to think clearly. This ability we may acquire, however, by limiting ourselves to definite subjects which we are capable of handling; by forcing ourselves to decide what it is we wish to say about the subject and for what purpose we are going to say it; and by persistent care in making our words express exactly what we mean.

Adequate expression requires that our composition be properly adjusted to the subject and carefully adapted to the interest and understanding of our hearers and readers. Out of all the possible ways we may think of and experiment with in expressing our thoughts we should try to discover the one most effective way. Only by doing this can we attain to adequate expression.

Good form in composition is at all times essential. We should therefore make conformity to the following requirements habitual:

1. Effective oral delivery.
2. Proper arrangement of manuscript.
3. Strict observance of the rules of grammar.
4. Care in the choice of words and in the use of idioms.
5. Correct spelling.
6. Intelligent punctuation.

Violations of these requirements hinder hearers and readers in their attempt to get a clear understanding of our thoughts, and for this reason greatly detract from our efforts at clear thinking and adequate expression.

7. Reasons for studying composition. The ability to think and to convey his thoughts through speech to others of his kind distinguishes man from the lower animals. The ability to think accurately and to express his thoughts clearly and permanently distinguishes the educated man, who leads, from the uneducated man, who must be led. During our school life the mastery of the English language is of immediate importance, for our progress in every other subject is dependent on our command of English. In later life this mastery will prove of even greater importance in promoting our success and happiness.

Perhaps in other days a man who was too indolent to give attention to his writing might have avoided the necessity; crude expression might have served him. But today, under the influence of our quickened civilization, a man can scarcely hope to become an important factor in society unless he can express himself with some degree of adequacy. People will not stop to listen to him if he cannot explain his wants clearly and without unnecessary hesitation; and they will not do what he desires if he cannot convince them and move them to action. And if a man is unable to use his mother tongue accurately, he not only turns many away from him day by day because of his obvious habits of carelessness, but when the supreme opportunity comes, he is, through his lack of power, unable to reach a large part of his audience of readers. Unless he is content to be a third-rate lawyer, minister, business man, or scientist, and is willing to be forever classed as uneducated, he must be able to increase the value of his thoughts by expressing them skillfully.[1]

Interested, intelligent study of composition will enable us to develop greater skill in speaking and in writing. Some of us may discover that we have thoughts to which we desire to give literary expression. This desire we may ultimately accomplish if we first train ourselves in the clear, accurate, and forceful expression of the thoughts we now have. *Our immediate aim in studying composition should be the mastery of English as a necessary tool.*

[1] From "The Art of Writing English," copyrighted, 1913, by R. W. Brown and N. W. Barnes. Used by permission of the American Book Company, publishers.

8. The mastery of English as a tool. Every person who attains success either as an artist or as an artisan must first of all become the master of his tools or instruments. He must acquire such skill in their use that he can do with them exactly what he desires to do. Every user of the English language who attains success as a speaker or a writer must first of all become the master of his language, the tool or instrument of communication. He must acquire such skill in its use that he can say accurately and effectively what he desires to say.

If we allow our present inability to speak and write well to discourage us so that we make no effort to master our language, we shall condemn ourselves to a life of commonplaceness and inefficiency. Similarly, if we envy successful speakers and writers their mastery of English but content ourselves merely with dreaming of the time when we too, through some magical gift, shall possess an equal mastery, we shall never realize our dream. Mastery of English does not come in that way. It must be won through persistent, well-directed effort.

In our efforts to gain greater skill in expression we have many valuable aids. Sympathetic teachers and good textbooks will furnish us guidance. Association with the best speakers and writers will stimulate and inspire us. By improving our speech we shall acquire accuracy and readiness of utterance and increase our power over words. By listening to good speakers and by reading widely we shall add to our general information as well as to our knowledge of the correct methods of speaking and writing. Through frequent systematic composition we shall gain indispensable practice in clear thinking and in the accurate expression of our thoughts. Sir Francis Bacon, a man who rose to great political power and literary eminence because of his mastery of English, emphasized the importance of reading, speaking, and writing. "Reading maketh a full man, conference a ready man, and writing an exact man."

9. Self-cultivation in English. The mastery of English as a tool cannot be taught; it must be learned. That is to say, we must acquire it through self-cultivation. Others may advise and encourage us, but they cannot give us command of our language. It is our task, as well as our privilege, to obtain it by our own endeavor.

Early in our school career we should develop a real interest and pride in our speech and writing. We should learn increasingly to be our own guides and critics. A thorough knowledge of the principles of composition and the rules of grammar will enable us to overcome the habits of careless and incorrect expression into which we have fallen. We should constantly watch our everyday speech and should take advantage of every opportunity that we have for learning to write. Conversation and the writing of letters and school exercises afford us daily practice in composition. In all our efforts at self-cultivation we shall find the companionship of the best speakers and writers a most valuable stimulus to improvement.

EXERCISES

I

Devote at least two hours to becoming acquainted with this textbook. First, examine the table of contents. Notice the plan of arrangement by parts and by chapters. Next, turn slowly through the book, pausing to study the pictures and to read wherever you become interested. Try to get a general idea of what each chapter contains. Notice particularly the chapters dealing with sentence structure, grammar, words, spelling, and punctuation. These you will find valuable for close study as well as for frequent reference. Though you will be assigned particular topics and sections as your teacher may see fit, remember that the entire book is yours, to be used as you need it. Begin self-cultivation in English at once. Try to discover for yourself the means for improving your speech and your writing.

II

Come to class prepared to answer the following questions: Do you find the pictures in this book interesting? Which do you consider most interesting? Why? Which chapters do you think will be of most value to you in your study of composition? Why?

III

Read carefully George Herbert Palmer's "Self-Cultivation in English" (Riverside Literature Series, No. 249). Come to class prepared to discuss the five precepts that the author gives and to answer any other questions that your teacher may ask you about the essay.

CHAPTER II

ORAL COMPOSITION[1]

10. Importance of oral composition. If we desire to speak and write well, we should watch our everyday conversation. In this most of us are careless. We are content to express or suggest a fraction of a thought, and then, with the pitiable acknowledgment of our laziness "Oh, you know what I mean," we leave our friends to guess the rest. The result is that when occasions arise on which we wish to express ourselves well, we often fail to make ourselves understood or to get what we want, because we cannot say what we mean. We make a personal or written application for a desirable position, but fail to secure it for the reason that we are unable to set forth our qualifications adequately. We misdirect a friend from one place to another, not because we do not know the way but because we cannot express ourselves accurately. We may often make an unsatisfactory recitation in history, science, mathematics, or literature, not because we have failed to prepare the assignment but frequently because we cannot state clearly and in order what we have learned. Only by daily practice in speaking correctly can we make the expression of our thoughts accurate and clear. In this endeavor we should enlist the aid of our family and friends. Perhaps we may be able to help them in return.

11. General directions for practice in oral composition. Oral composition includes both informal and formal expression.

[1] At the discretion of the teacher certain parts of this chapter may be taken up in later assignments.

Almost all conversation is informal and spontaneous utterance which reveals the personality of the speaker. In familiar conversation we make free use of incomplete sentences, and of colloquial expressions such as *I'll*, *you're*, *can't*, and *don't*, which are not permissible in formal composition, either oral or written. But the informality of conversation does not warrant our making mistakes in grammar or in the choice of words, or otherwise violating good form in speaking. We should therefore, first of all, concentrate our attention upon the definite improvement of our everyday speech. Correct speech, we should bear in mind, lays the foundation for good writing.

Outside of your home you cannot find a better place to practice oral composition than the classroom and the school auditorium; nor shall you ever have a better audience than your classmates. Make every recitation in each subject, and every opportunity that you have of speaking before your classmates, an occasion for improvement.

When you talk, you should stand in the front of the room, facing the class. Remember that the effectiveness of what you have to say will depend in large part on your manner and bearing while you say it. You should therefore stand erect, hold your head up, and speak directly to your audience, instead of looking at the floor or out of the window. You should, furthermore, try to speak slowly, distinctly, and pleasantly, avoiding the quick, jerky speech which no one enjoys hearing. If necessary, you may refer occasionally to your brief outline, which you will find useful in helping you to select and arrange your material properly; but you should not, while speaking, depend on it too much. After you have taken your seat, the teacher and your classmates may offer criticisms on your talk. Suggestive questions for your guidance in preparing and criticizing these talks will be found with each general exercise.

12. The first necessary quality : knowledge of the subject. In the preparation of an oral composition our first concern should be the selection of a topic, or subject, that we fully understand and that we are capable of presenting interestingly to others in the time that we are given. Topics of this character we shall be able to secure from such sources as the following:

1. Occupations, interests, and amusements of our family.
2. Subjects studied in school.
3. School athletics and contests of various kinds.
4. Economic and social life of our town or community.
5. Nature and outdoor life about us.
6. Personal experience and observation.
7. Individual interests, ambitions, and hobbies.
8. Conversation and public lectures.
9. General reading.
10. Science and invention.

Suppose that we have the following list of topics from which to select a subject for a short talk before the class:

1. The Radio Telephone.
2. Costume Designing.
3. Baseball.
4. Motion Pictures.
5. Pure Food.

The question that confronts us immediately is, Which subject shall I choose?

This question we may best decide by answering the following questions, which should guide us in selecting every subject for either oral or written compositions:

1. With which subject am I most familiar?

2. Is the subject that I am considering properly limited to fit my information, my ability, and the time allowed me?

3. Can I make this subject clear and interesting to others?

As we look over the topics given above we may discover that we know something about each of them, but not enough about any one of them to deal with it satisfactorily in its present general form. From each of these, however, we may derive several limited subjects better suited to our present ability.

1. How to Install an Amateur Radio Telephone.
2. An Interesting Radio Concert.
3. How Father Uses the Radio Telephone in his Business.
4. Why I Wish to Be a Costume Designer.
5. How I Made my Last Party Dress.
6. How I Remodeled my Suit.
7. The Qualities of a Good Pitcher.
8. How to Throw Curves.
9. The Power of an Umpire.
10. The Use of Motion Pictures in the Study of Geography.
11. The Physiology of Motion Pictures.
12. The Animated Newspaper.
13. The Importance of Milk Inspection.
14. How to Pasteurize Milk.
15. How to Distinguish Fresh from Stale Eggs.

The short compositions printed below illustrate how such limited subjects as these may be dealt with in brief talks.

HOW TO THROW CURVES

In throwing the outcurve the pitcher usually grasps the ball with the first two fingers and the thumb. The third finger is sometimes used to steady the ball. The hand is turned downward, and the ball is allowed to pass between the thumb and the first finger. This imparts a rotary motion which causes the curve. The arm must be swung around the side of the body, a movement which is known as the side, or underhand, delivery. If the arm is swung over the body at about halfway between horizontal and vertical, the result will be an outdrop. If the arm is swung directly over the body, the result will be a drop. In throwing the incurve the pitcher grasps the ball in exactly the same manner as in throwing the outcurve, but the ball is allowed to roll off the ends of the fingers instead of passing between the thumb and the first finger. The incurve, may be thrown either with the side delivery or with the overhand delivery. A "spit ball" is a ball moistened on one side with saliva. It is thrown by gripping the ball and swinging the arm in the same manner as would be used for any of the curves just explained. Because of the moistened side the ball moves with greater speed, and the resulting curve is more uncertain.

INTERRELATIONSHIP OF LIVING THINGS IN THE SOIL

The different things living in the soil may prey upon one another quite as do things that live aboveground. The soil is often filled with a dense population of living things, some feeding upon mineral matter in the soil, some upon dead organic matter, some upon other living things.

An instructive illustration of the extent to which these interrelations may go is seen in the case of the roots of the corn plant and certain animals that may often be found upon or near these roots. Extremely small insects, known as plant lice or aphides, bite into the tender roots of the corn and suck out the nourishing juices. The aphides are almost stationary animals and cannot ordinarily make their way from one plant to another without assistance. When well nourished they excrete small drops of a glistening, sweetish solution sometimes called honeydew. This honeydew is an article of food for certain black ants which also live in the cornfields. It has been found that the ants will dig furrows at the side of the corn plants until they can reach the roots, and will then carry the aphides and place them upon younger and more tender roots. When food for the aphides becomes scanty, they are moved to new plants. The aphides thus secure abundant food, and the ants secure the honeydew as their own food. Both are parasites upon corn, one directly, the other indirectly. Corn and grasses are often killed by these animals, and the soil, rendered porous by the burrows, dries more rapidly than it otherwise would. This is but one of many illustrations of the interrelationship of animals and plants in the soil.—CALDWELL and EIKENBERRY, "Elements of General Science"

HOW THE MOSQUITO CARRIES MALARIA

When a mosquito of a certain kind feeds upon human blood, it injects a small amount of salivary fluid into the wound that it has made. If the person has malaria, the mosquito secures blood which may carry malarial germs; and if these germs are present, they multiply rapidly within the mosquito, really living in a way quite different from their life in the human blood. Some of the germs get into the mosquito's salivary glands. When the infected mosquito bites a second human being, germs may be injected into the wound with the salivary fluid. These may produce the disease in the person thus infected.—CALDWELL and EIKENBERRY, "Elements of General Science"

EXERCISES

I

In a short talk before the class, discuss one of the limited subjects in the list on page 11. Select your subject by means of the three questions suggested on page 10. Plan your talk carefully. Make brief notes to aid you, but do not write out what you intend to say.

II

Limit the following subjects:

1. School Games.
2. Vacation Trips.
3. Training Animals.
4. Insects.
5. Amusements.
6. Photography.
7. Domestic Science.
8. Manual Training.
9. The Red Cross.

III

Come to class prepared to discuss orally three of the subjects that you limited in Exercise II.

IV

Tell the class a good joke that you have recently heard.

V

Relate to the class a humorous anecdote that you have lately heard or read.

13. The second necessary quality : clearness of thought. Our success in speaking depends largely on the clearness of our thinking. If we are inexperienced, we are likely to fail, for one or more of five reasons, to make ourselves clear: (1) we do not give our audience a clear, concise statement at the beginning as to what our talk is to be about; (2) we fail to follow a natural or logical order in taking up the details or incidents of our talk; (3) we use too many vague, general terms instead of specific words; (4) we wander from the subject and bring in unimportant, if not irrelevant, details; and (5) we omit entirely some important details. What happens when we commit one or more of these errors is illustrated by the examples given below in Exercises I and II.

EXERCISES

I

Read the following examples aloud. Then answer these questions based on them: (1) How many of the five errors given above are responsible for the lack of clearness in the first paragraph? (2) What particular expressions are confusing? Why? (3) What particular expressions make the second paragraph clear? (4) What definite changes can you suggest in the first paragraph to make it as clear as the second?

HOW TO REACH MY HOME FROM THE STATION

1. I live about five or six blocks from the station. To get to my home you go down the street until you come to a street that goes over a bridge. This bridge was rebuilt a few years ago to take the place of an old wooden one that used to be there. This one is of concrete. My grandfather helped build the first bridge. Then go along the right side of the street till you come to a street with an old brick house on the corner. I live just about halfway up the block from the corner. The house has just been painted.

2. I live six blocks from the station. When you come out of the front door of the station, you will find yourself on Main Street. Walk up Main

Street one block to Magnolia Avenue. Here turn to your right and walk three blocks to a cross street marked "Sycamore." Then turn to your left on Sycamore Street and walk two blocks to the corner of Linden Avenue. The second house from this corner, on the right side of Linden Avenue, is my home.

II

For which of the reasons given above does the following answer of Mrs. Brown's lack clearness? What changes would you make in the order? How much of Mrs. Brown's reply is necessary to answer the lawyer's question?

LAWYER. Are you sure that the house was robbed on Wednesday?

MRS. BROWN. Yes, sir, I'd just stepped over to Mrs. Davis's a minute to borrow a bit of yeast for my baking. Her husband won't eat a bite o' bread that's baked with store yeast. You know, all the Davises are queer. His father was the one who wouldn't ever paint his house, though I'm not sure but that he was right, for an old building like his was hardly worth painting. Our woodshed is just about as bad as his house, if you come right down to it. Well, before I started baking I went into the shed to get Mr. Brown's old coat; he is always so absent-minded, leaving his things around everywhere. I 'most always bake bread on a Wednesday, you know. Yes, I'm sure it was Wednesday.

III

Come to class prepared to give some of the following directions. Do not write them out, but think over carefully what you will say. Try to avoid making any of the mistakes mentioned above.

1. Direct a friend from your school to your home.
2. Direct a stranger from your school to the railroad station.
3. Direct a visitor to the principal's office.
4. Tell your chum how to find your baseball glove.
5. Direct a friend to a certain picture in an art gallery.

IV

Explain orally how some simple game is played.

V

Tell the class how to train some pet animal to perform a trick.

14. The value of an outline in planning a composition. In our efforts to think clearly and to present our subject to our audience or readers in an orderly manner, we shall find that the first step in the proper arrangement of our material consists in the making of an outline. The plan of the short talks that we have given thus far we have been able to carry in our minds. For our longer oral and written compositions, however, it will be necessary for us to write out our plan in the form of a brief outline.

If we have chosen a familiar subject and have limited it properly, we should have little difficulty in choosing the necessary material and in discovering a natural or logical order of grouping the details. Since every composition should be a complete treatment of the subject selected, we should use care in choosing the points at which to begin and end. Few, if any, of our compositions will require a formal introductory paragraph. Usually a sentence or two stating what our talk is to be about will furnish sufficient introduction. Likewise, we shall rarely need a formal concluding paragraph, though a sentence or two rounding out and completing our talk is often felt to be necessary.

The three rules that follow will guide us in planning our compositions:

1. Select only material that belongs to the subject, but do not omit anything that is important.

2. Arrange this material according to its proper time, space, or logical relationship, so that your composition will be clear.

3. Begin directly, but naturally and clearly, and stop as soon as you have presented your subject.

The simple outlines printed below will furnish us models in preparing plans for our oral compositions. Notice that each numbered topic is a division of the subject stated in the title. Study these outlines closely, to discover the principle governing the arrangement of the material. You may refer to these outlines frequently in planning your own compositions.

AN UNUSUAL PET

1. How I acquired him.
   a. Place.
   b. Time.
   c. Circumstances.
2. His intelligence.
3. His unusual habits.
4. His one bad habit.
5. Tricks I have taught him.
6. His devotion to me.
7. His place in our family.

GETTING A VACATION JOB

1. Introduction.
   a. My desire to earn some money.
   b. My friend's advice.
   c. Father's advice.
2. My letters of application.
   a. Favorable replies.
   b. Unfavorable replies.
3. My personal applications.
   a. Reasons for my failure at first.
   b. Improvement of my method.
4. Securing the job.
5. The value of the experience to me.

A FRIEND OF MINE

1. Circumstances of our first meeting.
2. Her personal appearance.
3. Her interesting habits.
4. Her quaint personality.
5. Qualities that endear her to others.
6. The quality I most admire in her.
7. What her friendship means to me.

HOW OUR SCHOOL RAISED MONEY FOR OUR FRENCH ORPHAN

1. Introduction.
   a. The school rally.
   b. The committee's plan.
2. Domestic-science bazaar.
3. Tag day.
4. Box supper.
5. School play.
6. Success of the plan.

MAN'S THREESCORE AND TEN YEARS

1. From whom I heard the fable.
2. All animals summoned before Nature's throne.
3. Nature's gift to the donkey.
   a. The donkey's sorrow and plea.
   b. Nature's concession.
4. Nature's gift to the dog.
   a. The dog's sorrow and plea.
   b. Nature's concession.
5. Nature's gift to the ape.
   a. The ape's sorrow and plea.
   b. Nature's concession.
6. Nature's gift to man.
   a. Man's sorrow and plea.
   b. Nature's concession.
7. The effect of man's added years.
8. The result of man's greed.

The simple outlines that we have constructed will greatly aid us in making our subjects clear and interesting to others. When we have devised a satisfactory plan, more than half of our preparation has been completed. The student who made the last outline given above found little difficulty in retelling the following fable:

MAN'S THREESCORE AND TEN YEARS

My grandmother has often related to me the following story of how man received from Nature his threescore and ten years.

When Nature had finished her task of creating the earth and all living things, she summoned her creatures before her throne to assign to each his period of life. They made a motley array as they appeared before her to receive whatever she saw fit to bestow.

First came the donkey. "Well, my good friend," said Nature, "will twenty years of existence satisfy thee?"

"O mother, be kind!" pleaded the donkey. "Think of my sorrows! Men will abuse me. When I am old, I shall do nothing but hard work. Men will use me for their own selfish advantage, caring nothing for my sufferings. Dear Nature, do not make me live twenty years."

Moved by the donkey's plea, Nature allotted him but ten years in which to drag out his weary life on earth.

"And you, friend," asked Nature, as the dog appeared before her throne, "will you too be dissatisfied with twenty years of life?"

"How can I live so long!" answered the dog, in tears. "What pleasure will life hold for me? As I slowly but inevitably grow old and useless, my former friends will forget me. My toothless mouth will no longer be able to grant me the enjoyment afforded by tempting morsels of meat. What shall I do but sit alone in a corner and growl and sleep my life away?"

Again Nature heard the plea and cut her gift in half. Nevertheless, the dog turned away discontent with having only ten years subtracted from his allotted life.

Next in line came the ape. "Surely you will want twenty-five years," said Nature, "for what labor shall you have but sporting in the woods?"

But, to her surprise, the ape too began to weep. "Have you no pity?" he wailed. "You have made me a figure for men to scoff at. Must I sit in a cage all those years to gibber and grin for men to jeer at me and mock me? Nature, have pity on me!"

Again Nature yielded, though somewhat reluctantly, and took off fifteen years from the ape's original portion.

Last of all came man. Nature, wishing to have at least one long-lived creature, offered him thirty-five years. Again her offer was met with tears, but this time for a different reason.

"Alas," sighed man, "only thirty-five years! Why, within that brief period I shall have just made something to keep me comfortable. I shall have a home, a wife, and children. Just when I am about to enter upon the enjoyment of the fruits of my labors, must I die?"

Moved once more to kindness, Nature gave man the ten years rejected by the donkey, but man was not satisfied. Then she gave him the ten years spurned by the dog. Again man cried out at her injustice to him. At last, to appease him, she bestowed on him the fifteen years left by the ape. No more would she give. Grumbling even then, man turned away and left Nature's presence.

Thus it is that man lives thirty-five years happily and successfully. Then follow the years of the donkey, when man is driven by all till he is useless. These years are followed, in turn, by those of the dog, wherein man must sit toothless, friendless, and alone in a corner with nothing to do but complain and growl. Finally there come the fifteen years of the ape, which complete the threescore and ten. During these years man loses the respect and consideration of all his former associates. No one will listen to him. Mockery is his share. But as his years of wretchedness draw to a close, he actually complains because death and the grave are so soon to put an end to his misery.

Greediness and the fear of death have earned for man his own just reward.

EXERCISES

I

Study by means of the outline the fable you have read. What purpose does the opening sentence serve? the closing sentence?

II

Prepare an oral composition on one of the other subjects outlined on pages 17 and 18. You may modify the printed outline to fit your particular material if you find any change necessary.

III

Make a brief outline of some fable or folk tale that you know. Come to class prepared to relate the fable or tale orally.

IV

Make an outline for a talk on one of the following subjects. Select your subject carefully by means of the three questions mentioned on page 10.

1. Why I Like Manual Training.
2. Why I Like Domestic Science.
3. How to Organize a Civics Club.
4. My Most Interesting Experience Last Vacation.
5. The Trials of a Freshman.
6. My Home.

V

Make notes on some lecture or discussion that you have recently heard. Arrange these notes in the form of a brief outline, and come to class prepared to give a connected report of what the speaker said.

VI

Make an outline of the chief points in a short newspaper article, and come to class prepared to retell it in your own words.

VII

Outline some incident recorded in your history text, and come to class prepared to retell it clearly and interestingly.

VIII

Come to class prepared to place on the blackboard the outline that you made in Exercise IV. As you give your talk the class can see whether your oral composition and your outline agree. The following questions will guide the class in their criticism of your composition: (1) Did the speaker discuss his subject so that you thoroughly understand its main points? (2) Was his beginning clear and direct? (3) Should any topics have been arranged in a different order? (4) Should any topics have been omitted? (5) Were any topics mentioned in the composition which are not in the outline? (6) Was the ending natural and satisfactory? (7) Did the speaker omit entirely any necessary points? (8) Did he use and fail to explain any words that are not familiar to you?

15. The third necessary quality: clearness of speech. Although knowledge of the subject and clearness of thought are essential to success in oral composition, there are other important qualities that we must not overlook. However carefully we may have chosen our subject and planned our talk, it will not be effective unless we deliver it well. If we mumble our words, or hesitate in our speech while groping for words, we invariably lose the attention of our audience. In delivering an oral composition, therefore, we should pay particular attention to the clearness and effectiveness of our speech. The following suggestions will help us in improving our oral delivery:

1. Face the class. Your audience can hear you better, and you have the advantage of talking directly to it.

2. Enunciate distinctly. Do not slur certain words and syllables. Be sure not to omit final *g's, t's,* and *d's.*

3. Pitch your voice naturally, preferably low. A high, nasal tone irritates your listeners and does not carry well. Talk through your lips, not through your teeth. A tone which comes through half-shut teeth is indistinct and lifeless.

4. Pronounce each word correctly. If necessary, consult your dictionary for the correct pronunciation of each word in regard to which you are in doubt. Incorrect pronunciation distracts the attention of your audience from the thought you are trying to convey.

5. Do not memorize what you have to say. A speaker who does this is apt to talk in an expressionless, mechanical fash-

ion. If he forgets the exact word he has learned, he is at a loss for another. Be so thoroughly familiar with your subject that words come readily; but *do not memorize.*

EXERCISES

I

Pronounce aloud the following words distinctly. Be sure that each syllable receives its proper emphasis.

Cattle, bottle, children, round, arctic, can't, castle, difficult, going, Mary, very, public, coming, audience, gymnasium, Wednesday, little, pronounce, people, respect, battle, library, perhaps, usually, saw, chimney, sophomore, beautiful, absolute, recognize, hesitate, kettle, Tuesday, yesterday, what, liked, idea, fact, anything, government, something, history, doing, laboratory, soda, elm, creek, larynx, fire, salad, interested, forehead, Calvary, cavalry, February, surprise, tomorrow, candidate, athletics, Latin, grievous, mischievous, which, finally, sword, attacked, probably, when, while, program, geography, separated, quantity, calculate.

II

Pronounce aloud the following pairs or groups of words with such clearness of enunciation that the class may accurately distinguish each word by its spelling and meaning from the other word or words with which it is sometimes confused by careless speakers:

Affect, effect; air, are; sit, set; then, thin; real, reel; complement, compliment; elusion, illusion, allusion; tell, till; sense, since; pen, pin; council, counsel; cavalry, Calvary; ten, tin; partner, pardoner; poplar, popular; race, raise; rise, rice; cease, seize; device, devise; pillow, pillar; picture, pitcher; statue, statute, stature; irreverent, irrelevant; err, ere, ear; been, bean; white, wight; which, witch; wear, were; what, watt.

III

Find in your dictionary the correct pronunciation of the following words. Pronounce each word aloud several times until you are sure of yourself.

Abdomen, acclimated, address, applicable, automobile, chauffeur, clandestine, compensate, consummate, contemplate, decade, demonstrative, dessert, detail, elegiac, envelope, exquisite, finance, formidable, horizon, hospitable, illustrate, illustrative, incomparable, indisputable, inexplicable, inquiry, mischievous, portray, precedence, prestige, recess, renaissance, research, respite, restaurant, romance, superfluous, theater, vehement.

IV

Bring to class a list of words that you have recently heard mispronounced.

V

Make an outline for an oral composition on one of the following subjects. Come prepared to place your outline on the blackboard and to discuss your subject before the class.

1. An Experiment in Science.
2. How to Print a Kodak Picture.
3. How to Make a Butterfly Tray.
4. How Coke is Made.
5. How to Fill a Silo.
6. A Fashion that I Detest.
7. The Importance of Good Manners.
8. An Incident in the Early History of our Town.
9. An Ideal Camping Place.
10. How I Earned my First Money.

16. The fourth necessary quality : correctness of speech. If we would speak naturally and correctly, we should be careful in our conversation. Since, during all our life, we shall probably talk more than we shall write, it is important that we form the habit of correct speech, not only in all our oral recitations but also in our conversation at home, on the street, and on the playground. It is a mistake to think that we can talk in an ungrammatical, slangy, or careless way half the time during our school days and then easily and permanently assume correct speech when we grow up.

Although slang is often more vivid at the time it is uttered than accepted language, it is to be avoided, because it is seldom permanent or universal. The slang used by the English people of Queen Elizabeth's time is in many instances without meaning to the Englishman of today. Even much modern slang which is clear, let us say, to a person living in New York conveys little or no meaning to a resident of Wyoming, Oregon, or Alabama. A still stronger argument against slang is that those who use it are not likely to learn good English words with which to express their ideas. Such people can talk only with those who understand slang; when they go among others they must be silent, for they are at a loss how to express themselves. In giving an oral composition, then, we should never allow ourselves to make use of any slang term, but we should find its equivalent in good English.

EXERCISES

I

The following sentences contain errors frequently heard in the conversation of careless or illiterate persons. Read the sentences aloud, point out and explain the errors, and correct the sentences.

(In Chapters XI and XII you will find these and many similar errors discussed.)

1. Just between you and I, it don't seem right.
2. Who did you give the book to?
3. She slept good last night and is some better this morning.
4. The prof flunked me on the final exam.
5. That picture don't flatter you none, does it?
6. If I was you, I would lay down and get some rest.
7. I love to set by the fire and read on these kind of days.
8. We just had a hunch that they would come real late.
9. I like her best of the twins.
10. I can't seem to learn geometry.

II

Organize your class into a permanent "Better-Speech Club." Select each week a committee of three students, to whom the other members of the class may hand in, on slips of paper, errors heard in the classroom, on the playground, on the street, or elsewhere. No names need be mentioned. At a class period once each week these errors may be read by members of the committee, and others in the class may be called on to explain the errors and correct them.

III

Prepare by means of an outline an oral composition on one of the following subjects or on a subject suggested by your teacher. Be sure your plan is clear, your delivery good, and your speech correct.

1. The Protection of Bird Friends.
2. A Defense of the Motion-Picture Show.
3. The School Building as a Social Center.
4. The Influence of the Automobile on my Community.
5. My Favorite Winter Sport.
6. A Plan for Improving my Use of English.
7. Why I Desire to Go to College.
8. A Humorous Experience with the Telephone.
9. An Amusing Mistake and its Result.
10. My First Experience Selling Papers.

The following questions will guide the class in their criticism of your composition: (1) Could you follow the main points that the speaker endeavored to discuss? (2) If not, what point was obscure? Why? (3) Was any topic introduced which did not relate to the subject? (4) Was any important topic omitted? (5) Was the speaker's delivery effective? (6) Where did the speaker fail through lack of earnestness to be effective? (7) What words were pronounced poorly or incorrectly? (8) Was *and* used too often?

17. The fifth necessary quality: vividness of speech. Even though we speak clearly and correctly, we may fail to interest our hearers because we do not express ourselves vividly. Vivid-

ROBINSON CRUSOE OPENS THE CHEST

ness of speech is gained by choosing specific words instead of general terms and by carefully selecting details that make a clear picture or result in an accurate explanation.

Read the example given below. The italicized specific words are those in the original passage. Reread the passage, substituting the words in parentheses (which are general terms carelessly used by everybody), and notice the loss in vividness.

At the same moment, another pirate *grasped* (took) Hunter's musket by the muzzle, *wrenched* (took) it from his hands, *plucked* (pulled) it through the loophole, and, with one *stunning* (hard) blow, laid the poor fellow senseless on the floor. Meanwhile a third, running unharmed all round the house, appeared suddenly in the doorway, and *fell with his cutlass on* (attacked) the doctor. . . .

I *snatched* (took) a cutlass·from the pile, and someone, at the same time *snatching* (taking) another, gave me a cut *across the knuckles* (on the hand) which I hardly felt. I *dashed* (went) out of the door into the *clear sunlight* (air). Someone was close behind, I knew not whom. Right in front, the doctor was pursuing his assailant down the hill, and, just as my eyes fell upon him, *beat down his guard* (attacked), and sent him *sprawling* (flat) on his back, with a great *slash* (cut) across the face. . . .

Mechanically I obeyed, turned eastwards, and, with my cutlass raised, ran round the corner of the house. Next moment I was *face to face with* (opposite) Anderson. He *roared* (cried) aloud, and his *hanger* (sword) went up above his head, flashing in the sunlight. I had not time to be afraid, but, *as the blow still hung impending* (before the blow fell), leaped *in a trice* (quickly) upon one side, and missing my foot in the soft sand, *rolled headlong* (fell) down the slope.—STEVENSON, "Treasure Island"[1]

EXERCISE

Prepare a talk on one of the following subjects or on a subject of your own selection. Choose details that will make your talk vivid. Make the class see and feel what you formerly experienced.

1. A Spectacular Play.
2. The Bravest Deed I Ever Witnessed.
3. My Worst Scare.

[1] Used by permission of Charles Scribner's Sons, publishers.

4. An Exciting Ride.
5. The Last Five Minutes of the Game.
6. Our Burglar.
7. A Humorous Blunder.
8. My First Experience with an "Automat" Lunch.
9. My First Experience as an Actor.
10. Alone in the House.

The following questions will guide the class in their criticism of your composition: (1) Did the speaker succeed in his attempt to make you see the picture or feel the excitement of what he was telling? (2) What nouns, adjectives, or verbs can you mention that were particularly good? (3) Explain why one of these words was unusually clear. (4) Where can you suggest better words?

18. Two devices for keeping attention. Even though we plan carefully what we have to say and say it well, our talk may not be entirely successful unless we use some device to render it effective, to make our audience see the thing we are talking about. One helpful means is the use of objects, or small models of them, to illustrate our talk.

EXERCISE

Bring to class an object or a model to illustrate a talk which you will prepare on one of the following subjects or on a subject of your own choice:

1. The Distinction between a Mushroom and a Toadstool.
2. The Root System of a Plant.
3. The Mechanics of an Electric Bell.
4. How a Camera Works.
5. How to Group Objects for a Still-Life Picture.
6. The Law of the Lever.
7. How to Select Seed Corn.
8. A Hornet's Nest.
9. Something you have recently made in the domestic-science or manual-training class.
10. How to Tie Various Knots.

A second device for making a talk before our class effective is the use of a rough blackboard sketch. It may be made before the recitation begins or while the talk is being given. A perfect drawing is not necessary; the important things are that the sketch shall give some idea of the subject, shall have its parts properly lettered, and shall not contain too many details.

EXERCISE

Come to class prepared to explain orally one of the following subjects. Before you begin your talk, place on the blackboard your outline and a drawing to illustrate your explanation.

1. How to Play Tennis.
2. How to Make a Lamp Shade.
3. Modeling a Hat Frame.
4. A Trap Nest.
5. An Attractive Bird House.
6. An Automatic Poultry Feeder.
7. How to Use a Terracing Level.
8. How to Graft a Tree.
9. The Circulation of the Blood in the Human Body.
10. How to Lay Off a Baseball Field.

The following questions will guide the class in their criticism of your composition: (1) Was the drawing complete and properly lettered? (2) Did the speaker talk to the blackboard or to the class? (3) Were there any details that you failed to understand? (4) Was any part of the drawing unexplained?

GENERAL EXERCISES

I

Retell orally the incident from "Robinson Crusoe" suggested by the picture facing page 26 or the incident from "Treasure Island" suggested by the picture facing page 54.

II

Study the other pictures in this book and prepare a talk on a subject suggested by one of them. Make a brief outline of what you intend to say.

III

Prepare a talk on one of the following subjects or on some topic of local interest in politics, athletics, your school, or your home:

1. Training a Hunting Dog.
2. First-Aid Treatment in Cases of Drowning.
3. A Tastefully Furnished Sitting Room.
4. The Work of the Red Cross in my Community.
5. Ice Harvesting.
6. A Lobster Pot.
7. Blanket Weaving.
8. A Snake Hunt.
9. Unusual Traits of a Pet.
10. What the Boy Scouts Did in the World War.
11. A Needed Improvement in our Town.
12. Rice Growing.
13. Cranberry Growing.
14. A Local Indian Legend.
15. How to Secure a Patent or a Copyright.
16. The Uses of a Gasoline Engine on the Farm.
17. Salmon Packing.
18. A Process in a Cotton Mill.
19. What it Means to be a Camp-Fire Girl.
20. An Ideal Vacation.
21. Rope Making.
22. Characteristics of a Good Salesman.
23. My Grandfather's Favorite Story.
24. The history of some interesting invention.
25. What a Well-Trained Ford Can Do.
26. The Mechanics of an Artesian Well.
27. Irrigating Arid Lands.
28. The Latest Improvements in Dairying.
29. Fire Protection.
30. Fly Fishing.
31. The Usefulness of Dogs in the World War.
32. Ice Boating.
33. How the Schools of my State are Supported.
34. Our Athletic Schedule for this Year.
35. A Good Joke.

19. Summary. If we desire to speak and write well, we should improve our everyday conversation.

In oral composition effective delivery is next in importance to a good subject.

The five necessary qualities of an oral composition are

1. Knowledge of the subject.
2. Clearness of thought.
3. Clearness of speech.
4. Correctness of speech.
5. Vividness of speech.

The two greatest aids to clear thinking in oral composition are (1) the choice of a familiar subject that we are capable of making clear and interesting to our hearers and (2) the construction of a simple outline to guide us in our talk.

Two devices that we may frequently use for holding the attention of our audience and illustrating our talks are (1) the object itself, or a small model of it, and (2) a drawing that is properly lettered and not too detailed.

CHAPTER III

WRITTEN COMPOSITION: REPRODUCTION

20. Written composition. The ability to write exactly what we mean is one of the most important attainments in life. Almost every day most of us will have occasion to express ourselves in writing as well as in speech. During our school days we are called upon to write exercises, compositions, reports, examination papers, and minutes of club and society meetings. In addition, we write notes and letters to relatives, friends, and business firms. Many of us will desire to write stories, sketches, essays, and verse for our school and local papers. After we leave school we shall find the occasions for writing infinitely increased and the subjects on which we must write greatly multiplied. In learning to write well, as in learning to speak well, we shall find no better training than that afforded by the written work in our various courses. We should not make the mistake of thinking that our English class affords us the only opportunity that we have.

Many of us will at first find the effort to write our own thoughts difficult and uninteresting. A few of us may even say, "Some people are born to write, and they will write; other people, like me, are not born to write, and they cannot write." It is true that most great authors are born, not made. It is equally true, however, that anybody may acquire a certain skill in writing, and this skill is so valuable that no one should begrudge the labor necessary to attain it.

21. Oral and written composition. Written expression, since it is more deliberately composed, is almost always more formal than oral expression. Good conversation is apparently spontaneous, effortless speech. Good friendly letters, as well as many familiar essays and personal sketches, are characterized by much the same pleasing naturalness of expression, though they are rarely so informal as conversation. The oral compositions that we give before the class differ from the easy, familiar oral expression that we habitually use in talking with our family and friends. Likewise most of our written compositions, since they will represent the more permanent expression of our thoughts deliberately composed for a large number of readers, will be more formal both in plan and in expression than our friendly letters. But written composition, however formal, should never be impersonal or mechanical. On the contrary, it should at all times give evidence of the writer's personality and originality in his choice of subjects and materials for composition, as well as in his manner of expressing his thoughts.

22. The proper form for written composition. In oral composition, as we have learned, the success of our talk depends largely upon the correctness of our speech and the effectiveness of our manner of speaking. In written composition, if we are to attract readers and make the comprehension of our thoughts easy and pleasant for them, we must use great care in arranging on paper what we have to say. An untidy composition, like an untidy person, creates a bad impression and lays itself open to prejudice and unfavorable comment. Though we may have good ideas about our subject and may think clearly and express ourselves effectively, if our manuscripts are lacking in neatness and correctness of arrangement, persons who might otherwise enjoy reading what we have written will judge us slovenly in all our habits and put our composition aside unread. Whether we are composing a letter to a friend, writing a composition for our English class, or preparing a manuscript for an editor, *we should make our manuscript neat, correct, and attractive in every detail.*

The rules governing the proper arrangement of manuscript have become well established, though they may vary in some particulars, such as the manner of folding and indorsing the paper. *If your teacher gives you no other instructions, prepare all your written compositions according to the following directions:*

1. *Writing-materials.* Provide yourself with what is commonly called theme paper. This is usually ruled and has a margin at the left. Use black ink and a clean pen that does not scratch or blot. Keep at hand a good ink-eraser and a clean blotter. A ruler will often be found convenient.

2. *The title.* Write the title on the first line of the page. Arrange it so that the spaces to the right and to the left of it shall be equal. If the title is too long to be written on one line, put as much of it as will look well on the first line, and place the rest, centrally spaced, on the next line; thus:

HOW THE SCHOOLS OF MY STATE
ARE SUPPORTED

Begin with a capital letter the first word and all other important words in the title. The underscoring of each word in the title with three straight lines indicates that all letters would be printed in capitals. If you typewrite your composition, capitalize all letters in the title. No mark of punctuation should follow the title.

3. *Indenting.* Begin the first line of each paragraph about an inch to the right of the margin line at the left of the page. This is called indenting the paragraph.

4. *Margin.* If your theme paper has no margin line, rule off a margin of one inch at the left side of each page. Do not write in this margin. By care in the arrangement of words and in the division of syllables by means of the hyphen, try to avoid leaving long, irregular blank spaces at the right side of the pages. Do not crowd words at the end of the line. Make the entire page neat and attractive in appearance.

5. *Pages.* Write on only one side of the paper. Do not skip the first line on a page. If the last line is so near the bottom of the page that the lower stem letters cannot be made distinctly, leave it blank. Number each page in the upper right corner. Use arabic figures. Place no punctuation after page numbers.

6. *Folding.* Having arranged the sheets in order, fold them together once lengthwise. See that the edges are even.

7. *The indorsement.* Place the folded composition on the desk before you so that the loose edges are toward your right hand. Be sure that you have not carelessly turned your paper upside down. About two inches down from the top of the folded paper write the first line of the indorsement. The indorsement should include your name, your class and section, and the date, and should be written as follows:

> Helen F. Ames
> English 1 A
> October 17, 1922

8. *In general.* Observe the following suggestions:

a. Write neatly and legibly. Avoid flourishes, conspicuous shading, or any other peculiarity in penmanship.

b. If you discover that you have misspelled a word that you have just finished writing, do not draw a line through it or inclose it in marks of parenthesis and then write the correctly spelled word after it or above it. Erase the misspelled word neatly with an ink-eraser or a penknife and write the word correctly spelled in its place.

c. If you have omitted words, do not write them above the line when you can avoid doing so. It is better to rewrite the entire page.

d. Never present a soiled or blotted manuscript. Rewrite any pages that are not neat and clean.

e. Take pride in making every written exercise correct and attractive in its arrangement on the paper. Good thoughts make a better impression when they are arranged in strict accord with the principles of good form.

23. Requirements of learning to write. Three things are necessary if we would master English as a means of effective expression: (1) We must have something to say. (2) We must have some idea of how we wish to say it. (3) We must practice the different ways of saying it until we can say it well.

Many of us who express ourselves freely and naturally on a great variety of subjects in conversation and in letters to our friends have difficulty in finding something to say when we are given an opportunity to express our thoughts in writing for a larger number of readers. There are usually two reasons for our difficulty. First, we have acquired the erroneous idea that the subjects and materials that we use in oral composition are not suitable for written composition. That is a mistake. The subjects and the materials are usually the same. The chief difference between oral and written composition is that in writing we compose somewhat more deliberately and try to make the interpretation of our thoughts accurate and easy without the assistance of vocal inflection, gestures, and other aids that we naturally employ in speaking. If we will first give our composition orally, we shall rarely find very much difficulty in expressing the same thoughts in writing. A great part of our best literature is nothing more than good talk permanently recorded in writing.

A second reason why it is difficult for some of us to find something to write about, or even to talk about interestingly, is that we are not mentally wide-awake. We fail to make good use of our eyes and ears and other organs of sense. We do not exert ourselves to learn anything that is not assigned us or forced upon us. We fail to observe the scores of interesting things that surround us in our daily lives. More than that, we often fail to think about the things that we notice. The world is so full of interesting everyday things for everyday people that it should be impossible, for any person who sees and hears and thinks, to have difficulty in finding something interesting to write about. Observation of people and things about us, and a little care in discovering our own interests in life, will enable us to find as much material for written compositions as we naturally make use of in oral composition.

24. The value of reading. Though it is not the office of the writings of others to furnish us material for our compositions, the value of wide reading as a means of getting ideas and of furnishing ourselves with models of effective expression cannot be overestimated. Through books we become acquainted with new realms of thought. A book of travel acquaints us with new countries, new people, and new customs. A biography may introduce us to some person or group of persons worth knowing. An essay tells us what its author has thought and felt. Short stories, novels, and plays stimulate our imagination by presenting interesting persons in situations that reveal their character as well as the skill and ingenuity of the authors. If we read books thoughtfully, we gradually learn through unconscious imitation to improve our own writing, just as association with good speakers will enable us to improve the quality of our speech. It is important, therefore, that we read well-written books, for books are like people in their influence over us. Just as we unconsciously adopt a friend's mannerisms, so we imitate a writer's manner of expression, or, as we term it, his *style*. If we read books written in an interesting, pleasing style and filled with life and personality, our own manner of writing will necessarily be improved.

25. The value of conscious imitation and emulation. Unconscious imitation of good speakers and writers will, as we have observed, result in the gradual improvement of our own oral and written expression. But conscious imitation, plus emulation, will enable us to make much more rapid progress. That is, if we pay close attention to the thought expressed and the style employed by more experienced speakers and writers, and then practice retelling their thoughts in our own words, we shall learn much about the construction and the coördination of parts in a well-planned composition. If we later go one step further and emulate their style in expressing our own thoughts, we shall find our approach to original composition-writing natural and easy. From our infancy to the present time we have freely employed imitation and emulation in our attempts at learning to speak and to write. Heretofore the process has been for most of us an unconscious one. Henceforth it should become a conscious process.

Many of our greatest thinkers and writers trained themselves in clear thinking and forceful expression by consciously imitating and emulating other speakers and writers. Lincoln, Franklin, and Stevenson taught themselves much by this process, though they by no means continued to be imitators of others. They used the skill they had thus acquired as a means of more effectively expressing their own thoughts.

26. How Lincoln taught himself clear expression. Lincoln's Gettysburg speech ranks as a masterpiece of clear, effective expression. In Lincoln's own words we have the explanation of how he acquired this mastery of the English language.

I can remember going to my little bedroom after hearing the neighbors talk of an evening with my father, and spending no small part of the night walking up and down and trying to make out what was the exact meaning of their, to me, dark sayings. I could not sleep, though I often tried to, when I got on such a hunt after an idea, until I had caught it; and when I thought I had got it, I was not satisfied until I had repeated it over and over, until I had put it into language plain enough, as I thought, for any boy I knew to comprehend.

That is, Lincoln's desire for accurate knowledge and clear expression made it impossible for him, even in boyhood, to rest content until he had fully comprehended the "dark sayings" of his elders and had retold these sayings in language so simple that any of his boy associates could understand them. We see the result of this great passion of his for self-expression in the wonderful simplicity, directness, and power of all his later speeches, letters, and State papers. Lincoln acquired the ability to explain himself, and he possessed the courage to stand firm for what he believed to be right. These two characteristics made him a leader of men. He was able to command what he wanted.

27. How Franklin taught himself to write. Benjamin Franklin, another great American, second only to Lincoln as a statesman and public benefactor, owed much of his greatness to his ability to say exactly what he meant. In his "Autobiography" he tells us how he consciously imitated and emulated other writers, particularly Addison and Defoe.

About this time [at the age of fourteen] I met with an odd volume of the *Spectator*. It was the third. I had never before seen any of them. I bought it, read it over and over, and was much delighted with it. I thought the writing excellent, and wished, if possible, to imitate it. With this view I took some of the papers, and, making short hints of the sentiment in each sentence, laid them by a few days, and then, without looking at the book, tried to complete the papers again, by expressing each hinted sentiment at length, and as fully as it had been expressed before, in any suitable words that should come to hand. Then I compared my *Spectator* with the original, discovered some of my faults, and corrected them. But I found I wanted a stock of words, or a readiness in recollecting and using them, which I thought I should have acquired before that time if I had gone on making verses [as he had formerly done until his father discouraged him]; since the continual occasion for words of the same import, but of different length, to suit the measure, or of different sound for the rime, would have laid me under a constant necessity of searching for variety, and also have tended to fix that variety in my mind, and make me master of it. Therefore I took some of the tales and turned them into verses; and, after a time, when I had pretty well forgotten the prose, turned them back again. I also sometimes jumbled my collections of hints into confusion, and after some weeks endeavored to reduce them into the best order, before I began to form the full sentences and complete the paper. This was to teach me method in the arrangement of thoughts. By comparing my work afterwards with the original, I discovered many faults and amended them; but I sometimes had the pleasure of fancying that, in certain particulars of small import, I had been lucky enough to improve the method or the language, and this encouraged me to think that I might possibly in time come to be a tolerable English writer, of which I was extremely ambitious. My time for these exercises and for reading was at night, after work or before it began in the morning, or on Sundays.

28. How Stevenson taught himself to write. Robert Louis Stevenson, one of the most versatile English writers of the nineteenth century, likewise taught himself to write by means of conscious imitation and emulation. Here is a part of his account of the process.

All through my boyhood and youth I was known and pointed out for the pattern of an idler; and yet I was always busy on my own private end, which was to learn to write. I kept always two books in my pocket, one to read, one to write in. As I walked, my mind was busy fitting what I saw with appropriate words; when I sat by the roadside, I would either read, or a pencil and a penny version-book would be in my hand, to note down the features of the scene or commemorate some halting stanzas. Thus I lived with words. And what I thus wrote was for no ulterior use; it was written consciously for practice. It was not so much that I wished to be an author (though I wished that too) as that I had

vowed that I would learn to write. That was a proficiency that
tempted me; and I practiced to acquire it, as men learn to whittle,
in a wager with myself. Description was the principal field of my
exercise; for to anyone with senses there is always something
worth describing, and town and country are but one continuous
subject. But I worked in other ways also; often accompanied
my walks with dramatic dialogues, in which I played many parts;
and often exercised myself in writing down conversations from
memory.

.   .   .   .

Whenever I read a book or a passage that particularly pleased
me, in which a thing was said or an effect rendered with propriety,
in which there was either some conspicuous force or some happy
distinction of style, I must sit down at once and set myself to ape
that quality. I was unsuccessful, and I knew it; and tried again,
and was again unsuccessful and always unsuccessful; but at least
in these vain bouts, I got some practice in rhythm, in harmony, in
construction and the coördination of parts. I have thus played the
sedulous ape to Hazlitt, to Lamb, to Wordsworth, to Sir Thomas
Browne, to Defoe, to Hawthorne, to Montaigne, to Baudelaire, and
to Obermann. . . . Even at the age of thirteen I tried to do justice
to the inhabitants of the famous city of Peebles in the style of the
"Book of Snobs." . . .

That, like it or not, is the way to learn to write; whether I have
profited or not, that is the way.[1]

29. Self-cultivation in English through reproduction. In
three respects, at least, the experiences of Lincoln, Franklin,
and Stevenson are identical.

1. Each man discovered in boyhood his desire to learn to
express himself well, and definitely resolved to realize his desire.

2. Each set himself diligently to work in boyhood and continued to work diligently during manhood until he had accomplished his purpose.

[1] From "The Essays of Robert Louis Stevenson," published by Charles
Scribner's Sons. Used by permission.

3. Each taught himself, through conscious imitation and emulation, to express his own thoughts effectively.

All three men acquired their mastery of the English language through self-cultivation.

30. Additional value of reproduction. Retelling in our own words the thoughts of another not only provides a natural and helpful approach to original composition but also cultivates accuracy in hearing and in reading. If all of us heard correctly, we should be guilty of fewer inaccurate statements. If we truly read,—that is, "thought the author's thought after him,"—we should be much better informed, and the task of the author would be lightened. The person whom we like to employ in business, or to have as a friend, is the one who can be trusted to "get things straight." This "getting things straight" is not merely a matter of honesty or cleverness but is quite as much a matter of attention and of care in retelling. The habits of attention and of care in retelling can be and should be cultivated.

31. Methods of retelling another person's thought. There are three ways of reproducing another person's thought: (1) We may retell it closely. (2) We may condense it. (3) We may expand it.

32. First method: retelling closely. To retell another person's thought closely means to reproduce as nearly as possible his ideas in words of our own. If the passage to be retold contains figurative language, instead of a literal statement, we shall often find that a paraphrase in simpler language will render our version of the original more clear. The first four of the retold versions given below are literal reproductions; the fifth, however, is a paraphrase.

1. "To say nothing and saw wood" seems to me one of the most sagacious phrases passed down by our hard-working forbears.

RETOLD. I think that the expression "to say nothing and saw wood" is one of the wisest sayings handed down to us by our energetic ancestors.

2. It is not that the outside world is wearisome : the trouble is with the monotony of our own minds.

RETOLD. When we are bored, as we think, with life, it is not the world without that is uninteresting, but our own minds that are dull and commonplace.

3. There can be no doubt that for some people mathematics has flavor, even though for me it is as the apples of Sodom.

RETOLD. It is true that for some persons mathematics is a delight to their mental taste, but for me it is dry and insipid.

4. The world is so full of a number of things,
    I'm sure we should all be as happy as kings. — STEVENSON

RETOLD. There is such a variety of interesting things in our everyday lives that we should all be supremely happy.

5. "There is none like to me," says the cub,
    In the pride of his earliest kill.
But the jungle is large, and the cub — he is small.
    Let him think, and be still. — KIPLING

RETOLD. After his first achievement a young person is apt to believe that he can accomplish more than anyone else. He must discover, however, that the affairs of the world are much more important than his own, and must learn to be modest.

The value of retelling another person's thought closely lies in the fact that in retelling we are forced to realize how carefully the writer has worded his thought. Notice how inferior the retold version is to the original in the examples given above. Furthermore, in order to reproduce what another has said, we should thoroughly understand every word used in the original expression. To do this we must increase our vocabularies by looking up new words and discovering their exact meaning. Perhaps the greatest value of retelling closely is that it compels us to read carefully. When we read hurriedly we get only a general impression and therefore often miss important details.

33. General directions for retelling closely what is read. We shall usually find it easier to retell what we read than what we hear, for we can reread the passage we are considering as often as we wish. We shall need, however, to give careful attention to the work of reproducing closely what we have read. The following directions should be observed:

1. Read *aloud* the selection that is to be retold. Reread it until you understand clearly what the author has said. Make use of an unabridged dictionary to find the correct meaning of any words that are not familiar to you.

2. When you have become thoroughly familiar with the passage, reproduce as nearly as you can, in your own words, the exact meaning of the original. Use words and phrases that the writer has employed only when expression of the thought in your own words would result in a change in meaning.

3. Be careful *not* to make the process of retelling closely an exercise in the *mere substitution* of words. Get the author's thought and then interpret it in your own language.

4. It is not necessary to follow the original construction of a sentence. Variety may be secured by changing from indirect to direct discourse, or from a declarative sentence to an interrogative or an exclamatory sentence. There will be a greater number of changes of construction in retelling poetry than in retelling prose.

5. In changing poetry to prose avoid any suggestion of rime. Avoid also the use of poetic words, such as *morn, eve, oft, e'en, o'er, ere, methinks, forsooth, erstwhile.*

EXERCISES

I

Express accurately in your own words the thoughts in the following passages:

1. Fine art is that in which the hand, the head, and the heart go together.

2. Nothing great was ever achieved without enthusiasm.

3. He was like a cock who thought the sun had risen to hear him crow.

4. No man can produce great things who is not thoroughly sincere in dealing with himself.

5. It is much easier to be critical than to be correct.

6. He who has truth at his heart need never fear the want of persuasion of his tongue.

7. The greatest efforts of the race have always been traceable to the love of praise, as its greatest catastrophes to the love of pleasure.

8. Every great crisis of human history is a pass of Thermopylæ, and there are always a Leonidas and his three hundred to die in it if they cannot conquer.

9. The world is a comedy to those who think, a tragedy to those who feel.

10. What stamps a man as great is not freedom from faults, but abundance of powers.

11. In small proportions we just beauties see,
And in short measures life may perfect be.

12. Who to himself is law no law doth need,
Offends no law, and is a king indeed.

13. Words are like leaves ; and where they most abound,
Much fruit of sense beneath is rarely found.

14. There is a tide in the affairs of men,
Which, taken at the flood, leads on to fortune;
Omitted, all the voyage of their life
Is bound in shallows and in miseries.

15. So nigh is grandeur to our dust,
So near is God to man,
When Duty whispers low, *Thou must*,
The Youth replies, *I can*.

II

Retell in your own words the following passages :

1. I heard a true story, not long ago, of a lady, fond of dogs and accustomed to them, who went to visit a friend, the owner of a splendid but most formidable animal—a mastiff, if I remember rightly. The visitor did not happen to meet with the dog till she suddenly came upon him in a doorway she was about to pass through. It chanced somehow that she did not see him, and, stepping hastily, she unfortunately trod upon his foot or his tail. The huge fellow instantly laid hold of her; but before the dog's master, a short distance off, could hasten to the rescue, the lady had looked down, exclaiming quick as thought, "Oh, I beg your pardon!" whereupon the mastiff as quickly let go his grasp. It is plain that this lady had a proper respect for the feelings of dogs in general, prompting to an habitual kindly treatment of them, and instinct led her to apologize at once for the inadvert injury, as she would have done to a person.—*Atlantic Monthly*[1]

2. Conclusions, indeed, are not often reached by talk any more than by private thinking. That is not the profit. The profit is in the exercise [of talking], and above all in the experience; for when we reason at large on any subject, we review our state and history in life. From time to time, however, and specially, I think, in talking art, talk becomes effective, conquering like war, widening the boundaries of knowledge like an exploration. A point arises; the question takes a problematical, a baffling, yet a likely air; the talkers begin to feel lively presentiments of some conclusion near at hand; towards this they strive with emulous ardor, each by his own path, and struggling for first utterance; and then one leaps upon the summit of the matter with a shout, and almost at the same moment the other is beside him; and behold they are agreed. Like enough, the progress is illusory, a mere cat's cradle having been wound and unwound out of words. But the sense of joint discovery is none the less giddy and inspiriting. And in the life of the talker such triumphs, though imaginary, are neither few nor far apart; they are attained with speed and pleasure, in the hour of mirth; and by the nature of the process, they are always worthily shared.—STEVENSON[2]

III

Write a good prose reproduction of the following fable told in verse. Try in your own version to preserve the pleasing qualities of the original.

The Gossips tell the story of the Sparrow and the Cat,
The Feline thin and hungry and the Bird exceeding fat.
With eager, famished energy and claws of gripping steel,
Puss pounced upon the Sparrow and prepared to make a meal.

[1] Reprinted by permission of the Atlantic Monthly Press.
[2] From "The Essays of Robert Louis Stevenson," published by Charles Scribner's Sons. Used by permission.

The Sparrow never struggled when he found that he was caught
(If somewhat slow in action he was mighty quick of thought),
But chirped in simple dignity that seemed to fit the case,
"No Gentleman would ever eat before he'd washed his face!"

This hint about his Manners wounded Thomas like a knife
(For Cats are great observers of the Niceties of Life) ;
He paused to lick his paws, which seemed the Proper Thing to do,—
And, chirruping derisively, away the Sparrow flew!

In helpless, hopeless hunger at the Sparrow on the bough,
Poor Thomas glowered longingly, and vowed a Solemn Vow:
"Henceforth I'll eat my dinner first, *then* wash myself!"—
    And that's
The Universal Etiquette for Educated Cats.

ARTHUR GUITERMAN[1]

IV

Read the following description aloud several times until you
have a vivid picture of the scene described, then reproduce it in
your own words:

         In the field sloping down,
    Park-like, to where its willows showed the brook,
    Haymakers rested. The tosser lay forsook
    Out in the sun ; and the long wagon stood
    Without its team ; it seemed it never would
    Move from the shadow of that single yew.
    The team, as still, until their task was due,
    Beside the laborers enjoyed the shade
    That three squat oaks mid-field together made
    Upon a circle of grass and weed uncut,
    And on the hollow, once a chalk-pit, but
    Now brimmed with nut and elder-flower so clean.
    The men leaned on their rakes, about to begin,
    But still. And all were silent. . . .

EDWARD THOMAS[2]

V

After you have read the following poem several times aloud until you thoroughly understand it, reproduce it in prose in your own words:

BROOKLYN BRIDGE AT DAWN

Out of the cleansing night of stars and tides,
  Building itself anew in the slow dawn,
  The long sea-city rises : night is gone,
Day is not yet; still merciful, she hides
Her summoning brow, and still the night-car glides
  Empty of faces; the night watchmen yawn
  One to the other, and shiver and pass on,
Nor yet a soul over the great bridge rides.

Frail as a gossamer, a thing of air,
  A bow of shadow o'er the river flung,
    Its sleepy masts and lonely lapping flood;
Who, seeing thus the bridge a-slumber there,
  Would dream such softness, like a picture hung,
    Is wrought of human thunder, iron and blood?

RICHARD LE GALLIENNE[1]

ORAL EXERCISES

I

Retell closely either Franklin's or Stevenson's account of how he taught himself to write (see pages 39–41).

II

Read again the fable "Man's Threescore and Ten Years" (pages 19–20) and reproduce it in your own words.

III

Retell closely some topic that you have recently studied in history.

[1] Used by the author's permission.

IV

Reproduce in your own words some short poem or anecdote that you have lately read. Do not memorize the selection.

V

Retell in your own words the incident in "Robinson Crusoe" that is suggested by the picture facing page 26.

VI

Reproduce in your own words the incident in "Treasure Island" that is suggested by the picture facing page 54.

34. Translation a valuable means of retelling closely. Translation from a foreign language is one of the best exercises in reproducing closely the thought expressed by another. In order to translate a passage successfully, we must first understand the thought as it is expressed in the foreign language and then be able to reproduce this thought accurately in our own language.

It is sometimes desirable to translate *literally*, to give word by word, in the most exact manner, the English equivalent of each foreign construction. The chief value of such translation is that it enables us to understand the peculiarity, or *idiom*, of the foreign tongue. It is without value as a piece of English, however, unless the idiom is common to the two languages. "He went walking" is idiomatic in both German and English; but if we wish to say "I am better," and use the German idiom "It goes to me better," we are not speaking English at all.

We should never rest content, therefore, with merely translating words: we should notice the idiomatic expressions and translate them into idiomatic English. In many cases, too, even if a literally translated passage is grammatically correct, it will gain much in clearness and force by a free translation. Compare the following examples of foreign idioms and their English equivalents:

LITERAL TRANSLATION OF FOREIGN IDIOMS	IDIOMATIC ENGLISH EQUIVALENTS

LATIN

A book is to me.	I have a book.
Clad in armor as to his head.	His head covered by a helmet.
The army having been put to flight, Cæsar went into winter quarters.	After routing the army, Cæsar went into winter quarters.

FRENCH

At the house of you.	At your house.
What age has John?	How old is John?
How go you?	How are you?
I have sickness to the head.	I have a headache.

SPANISH

I have hunger.	I am hungry.
The boy serves for nothing.	The boy is good for nothing.
Your coffee puts itself cold.	Your coffee is getting cold.
How well to her falls that dress!	How well that dress fits her!

GERMAN

How goes it?	How are you?
To house.	At home.
Where cause you for yourself your clothes to be made?	Where do you have your clothes made?

EXERCISES

I

Below are a literal and an idiomatic translation of a Latin passage. Using the following questions as a guide, discover just what changes have been made which render the idiomatic version better than the literal: (1) Which translation has the greater number of sentences? (2) Which seems the better to you? Why? (3) Indicate all the awkward phrases and clauses in 1, and show how they have been avoided in 2.

1. LITERAL

Thither, about midnight, Cæsar, employing the same men as guides who had come as messengers from Iccius, sends for a relief to the townspeople Numidian and Cretan archers and Balearic slingers; at whose arrival zeal for fighting was inspired in the Remi, with the hope of a defense; and from the same cause the expectation of taking the town departed from the enemy. These, accordingly, delaying for a little while near the town and laying waste the fields of the Remi, all the villages and buildings to which they had been able to approach being set on fire, made toward Cæsar's camp with all their forces and pitched camp less than two miles off; which camp, as was shown by the smoke and fires, was extending more than eight miles in breadth.

2. IDIOMATIC

About midnight Cæsar, using as guides the messengers who had come from Iccius, sent Numidian and Cretan archers and Balearic slingers forward to relieve the town. Their arrival brought the Remi hope of defending themselves, and inspired them to fight; and for the same reason the enemy despaired of taking the town. And so, after delaying near the town a little while, to lay waste the fields of the Remi and to set fire to all the villages and buildings within reach, they hastened with all their forces toward Cæsar's camp and pitched their tents less than two miles off. Their camp, as was indicated by the smoke and fire, extended more than eight miles.

II

Select a passage in one of your foreign-language texts and make both a literal and an idiomatic English translation of it. Arrange the two versions of your translation in parallel columns on the page. Come to class prepared to point out and explain each detail in which the idiomatic English translation is superior to the literal.

35. Second method: retelling by condensing. The second method of reproducing another person's thought is to condense it. This method we naturally employ in retelling a lecture or a story, in reciting a lesson, and in writing an examination paper.

The first requirement in retelling by condensing is to understand the subject thoroughly. The second requirement is to pick out the main points. This we often find difficult, for we are likely to be led astray by something which is not important. To avoid this difficulty, we should follow the main thought only, condensing each important topic into one or two concise sentences. We should then arrange these in their proper order in the form of an outline, which should show clearly the subject and the principal topics.

The value of retelling by condensing is that it teaches us to select the really important ideas from what we are hearing or reading. Such ability is especially helpful in taking notes and in writing examination papers. Condensing also shows us how to avoid using too many words in expressing an idea.

36. General directions for retelling by condensing. 1. Read and re-read the passage to be condensed until you fully understand it. Notice the order of topics and the relation of one idea to another, so that in condensing the material you will not leave out necessary points or put in others that are superfluous.

2. Try to discover what points are most important. Unless you study the original closely, there is danger that you will write too fully about some topics and not fully enough about others.

3. Write down the principal topics. Express them as concisely as possible and arrange them in their proper order by means of an outline.

4. With your outline before you, write clearly and briefly what you wish to say about each topic. If you are condensing poetry, avoid any effect of rime or any borrowing of the poet's language.

EXERCISE

Acccording to the directions given above write a condensed reproduction of a topic discussed in your text in history, civics, or history of literature.

37. Taking notes as a means of retelling by condensing. One of the most valuable ways of retelling by condensing is taking notes on what we hear or read. We shall have frequent occasion to make reports on many subjects, and the sooner we begin to take good notes, the easier the work will be.

38. Taking notes on what we read. When taking notes on what we read, we should jot down only the main points. We should learn, moreover, to abbreviate wherever it is possible by omitting all unnecessary words and connectives and by using letters for proper names when these occur more than once. Below is a set of notes made on the first story in Rudyard Kipling's "Jungle Book." Observe how briefly the topics are worded and yet how easily the story can be constructed from them.

PUPIL'S NOTES ON THE STORY

"Mowgli's Brothers," Kipling's "Jungle Book," pp. 1–43.

1. Shere Khan (tiger) attacks woodcutter's fire.
2. Cutter's child strays—wolf carries him to den—child fearless among cubs.
3. Tiger demands child—wolf mother defends him—names child Mowgli.
4. M. accepted by wolf pack—taught wolf lore by Baloo (bear) and Bagheera (panther).
5. 10 yrs. later tiger demands M.—wolf leader old—dares not refuse.
6. M. steals fire from woodcutter's village—beats tiger into submission with blazing torch.

In taking notes on other forms of writing than narration we can often make even more condensed notes. In all cases, however, we should write the name of the author and title of the selection as well as the title of the book and the numbers of the pages on which the selection is printed. Below is a passage from a history, with greatly condensed notes.

THE HUNDRED YEARS' WAR (1338–1453)

Causes of the war. The long and wasteful war between England and France known in history as the Hundred Years' War was a most eventful one, and its effect upon both England and France so important and lasting as to give it a prominent place in the records of the closing events of the Middle Ages.

The war with Scotland was one of the things that led up to this war. All through that struggle France, as the old and jealous rival of England, was ever giving aid and encouragement to the Scots. Then the English possessions in France, for which the English king owed homage to the French sovereign as overlord, were a source of constant dispute between the two countries. Trade jealousies also contributed to the causes of mutual hostility.

Furthermore, upon the death of Charles IV of France, the last of the direct Capetian line, Edward III laid claim to the French crown in much the same way that William of Normandy centuries before had laid claim to the crown of England.

PUPIL'S NOTES ON THE PASSAGE

Causes of 100 yrs.' War (1338–1453), Myers, "Med. and Mod. Hist.," Revised Edition, pp. 186–187.

1. War important in effect on Eng. and Fr.
2. Causes:
    a. War with Scotland.
    b. Eng. poss. in Fr.
    c. Trade jealousies.
    d. Edward III (Eng.) claimed Fr. crown.

39. General directions for taking notes on what we read.
1. Read the selection through rapidly, but attentively, to get a clear idea of its contents.

2. Read it again more carefully for the details. Make your notes as you go along, remembering that *notes should be neither so numerous as to be confusing nor so few as to be misleading.* It is not necessary to make complete statements or to give all

THE FIGHT IN THE RIGGING

the details. A few well-chosen catchwords will bring the selection back when you come to rewrite it. These catchwords not only save time but also do away with copying the author's own words. Merely copying from what you read results in a habit of dependence and will make your work uninteresting.

3. Number the notes on each topic. Arrange them in such a way as to show clearly what are the main topics and what are the details that help to develop each topic. You will notice that most selections on which your notes are based are arranged in groups of sentences, called *paragraphs*, and that, as a rule, each of these groups deals with a single topic. This arrangement of the sentences by paragraphs will be of great use to you when you come to select the essential ideas.

4. When you have completed your notes, correct them by comparison with the original text.

40. Taking notes on what we hear. In taking notes on what we hear we should give the closest attention both to the separate statements and to their connection, that we may understand them before the speaker passes to something else. If a statement is not understood at first, we lose its meaning, since there is no chance to hear it a second time as there would be to read it a second time.

41. General directions for taking notes on what we hear.
1. Do not become so much absorbed in writing that you lose half of what is being said.

2. Get a clear idea of the general meaning without trying to remember exact words.

3. Make the first draft of your notes while the speech is being delivered, but do this in as few words as will give the meaning.

4. Use abbreviations and catchwords when you are sure that you can remember what they mean.

5. As soon as possible after the lecture make a second, more complete draft of your notes.

I

Read and take notes on two of the following narrative poems:

1. "In School-Days" or "Skipper Ireson's Ride," by Whittier.
2. "The Three Fishers," by Charles Kingsley.
3. "The Deacon's Masterpiece" or "The Last Leaf," by Holmes.
4. "An Incident of the French Camp" or "How they Brought the Good News from Ghent to Aix," by Browning.
5. Two other narrative poems that you have recently read.

II

Read a magazine story and make brief notes on it that will guide you in retelling it in condensed form.

III

Attend a lecture given in your school or for the general public, and take notes on what the speaker says. Follow the directions given in section 41.

42. Importance of an outline in retelling by condensing. In the selections that we have read and in the lectures that we have heard, we have noticed that each writer and speaker has dealt with his topics in some natural order of time or space or has arranged them in what seemed to him their logical relation one to another. In arranging his topics each used some kind of simple outline similar to the outlines that we made in the preparation of our oral compositions (see section 14).

Before we attempt to give a condensed version of any selection or lecture we should reconstruct the outline that the writer or speaker used in composing the original. This we can do if we have understood the original and have taken good notes. Each paragraph or each stanza in a selection that we have read should be represented in our outline by a topic. Likewise, each main point in a lecture should be indicated by a topic. If the writer or speaker has made use of a brief introduction and conclusion, each of these should be indicated in the outline by an appropriate topic.

EXERCISES

I

Carefully arrange in outline form the notes that you took on the two narrative poems in Exercise I of section 41.

II

Carefully arrange in outline form the notes that you took on the lecture indicated in Exercise III of section 41.

III

According to the directions given in section 39 take notes on the following selections. Number the paragraphs in each consecutively and group your notes to correspond to their respective paragraphs. By means of your notes and a careful re-reading of each paragraph discover the main topic of each and arrange these topics in the form of an outline.

HOW AN ALIEN BECOMES A CITIZEN OF THE UNITED STATES

At the present time who are citizens? Who may become citizens? What does citizenship mean? The Constitution answers the first of these questions thus: "All persons born or naturalized in the United States, and subject to the jurisdiction thereof, are citizens of the United States and of the state wherein they reside." But what is naturalization? How can one become naturalized? And what are the advantages of naturalization?

Briefly stated, naturalization is the process by which a foreigner becomes a citizen of another country. In the United States two acts are necessary to bring about this change: first, a formal renunciation, or giving up, of allegiance or loyalty to one's former country or ruler;

and second, a solemn declaration of allegiance, or loyalty, to the United States. That is, on becoming naturalized one must deny from henceforth all obedience to his native land and its rulers and become a loyal citizen of America. By the process of naturalization he becomes, for all practical purposes, as much a citizen or member of our country as if he had been born under the shadow of the Stars and Stripes.

A foreigner can be naturalized only by a Federal, state, or territorial court of record. At the time of his application he must be at least eighteen years of age. He may then take out his "first papers." To do so he must declare before the court his intention of becoming a citizen of the United States and of renouncing his allegiance to any foreign country or ruler. Not less than two nor more than seven years later he may appear in court and, on condition that he has reached the age of twenty-one and has been for five years a resident of the United States, may submit a petition in which he gives his full name, place of residence, occupation, date and place of birth, place from which he emigrated, and certain other information. This petition must be signed by himself and by two reliable witnesses who are American citizens and who must testify that they have known him for five years and that he is of good moral character. He must also declare that he is not opposed to organized government, that he does not believe in polygamy, that he renounces forever any hereditary title he may possess, and that he intends to become a citizen of the United States. The court cannot grant a certificate of naturalization, or "second papers," until ninety days after the petition has been filed nor within thirty days before a general election.

Aliens must be able to read and write English before they can be naturalized, and they must pass an examination in such subjects as American history, civics, and geography. There are some exceptions to the requirements just given, but owing to their rare occurrence or unimportance they do not need to be discussed here.—HOWARD COPELAND HILL, "Community Life and Civic Problems"

IGNORANCE IN ANIMALS

The animals unite such ignorance with such apparent knowledge, such stupidity with such cleverness, that in our estimate of them we are likely to rate their wit either too high or too low. With them, knowledge does not fade into ignorance, as it does in man; the contrast is like that between night and day, with no twilight between. So keen one moment, so blind the next!

Think of the ignorance of the horse after all his long association with man; of the trifling things along the street at which he will take fright, till he rushes off in a wild panic of fear, endangering his own neck and the neck of his driver. One would think that if he had a particle of sense he would know that an old hat or a bit of paper was harmless. But fear is deeply implanted in his nature; it has saved the lives of his ancestors countless times, and it is still one of his ruling passions.

I have known a cow to put her head between two trees in the woods —a kind of natural stanchion—and not have wit enough to get it out again, though she could have done so at once by lifting her head to a horizontal position. But the best instance I know of the grotesque ignorance of a cow is given by Hamerton in his "Chapters on Animals." The cow would not "give down" her milk unless she had her calf before her. But her calf had died, so the herdsman took the skin of the calf, stuffed it with hay, and stood it up before the inconsolable mother. Instantly she proceeded to lick it and to yield her milk. One day, in licking it, she ripped open the seams, and out rolled the hay. This the mother at once proceeded to eat, without any look of surprise or alarm. She liked hay herself, her acquaintance with it was of long standing, and what more natural to her than that her calf should turn out to be made of hay! Yet this very cow that did not know her calf from a bale of hay would have defended her young against the attack of a bear or a wolf in the most skillful and heroic manner; and the horse that was nearly frightened out of its skin by a white stone, or by the flutter of a piece of newspaper by the roadside, would find its way back home over a long stretch of country, or find its way to water in the desert, with a certainty you or I could not approach.

The hen hawk that the farm boy finds so difficult to approach with his gun will yet alight upon his steel trap fastened to the top of a pole in the fields. The rabbit that can be so easily caught in a snare or in a box trap will yet conceal its nest and young in the most ingenious manner. Where instinct or inherited knowledge can come into play, the animals are very wise, but new conditions, new problems, bring out their ignorance.

A college girl told me an incident of a red squirrel she had observed at her home in Iowa, that illustrates how shallow the wit of a squirrel is when confronted by new conditions. This squirrel carried nuts all day and stored them in the end of a drain pipe that discharged the rain water upon the pavement below. The nuts obeyed the same law that the rain water did, and all rolled through the pipe and fell upon the sidewalk. In the squirrel's experience, and in that of his forbears, all holes upon the ground were stopped at the far end, or they were like pockets, and if nuts were put in them they stayed there. A hollow tube open at both ends, that would not hold nuts — this was too much for the wit of the squirrel. But how wise he is about the nuts themselves!

Among the lower animals the ignorance of one is the ignorance of all, and the knowledge of one is the knowledge of all, in a sense in which the same is not true among men. Of course some are more stupid than others of the same species, but probably, on the one hand, there are no idiots among them, and, on the other, none is preëminent in wit. — JOHN BURROUGHS, "Ways of Nature"[1]

43. Examination another means of retelling by condensing. Nowhere is there greater need of careful writing than in answering examination questions. Throughout our whole school life we are apt to waste valuable time and fail to do ourselves justice unless we train ourselves in this special form of composition. We should take pains, therefore, to acquire skill in this form of writing early in our school career.

44. General directions for writing examination papers. Examination questions vary greatly, and individual teachers differ in their personal preferences as to the form of the work. For this reason, only the most general principles are stated here. Detailed instructions will be given by your teacher.

1. After reading a question think over your facts before you begin to write. If you have five minutes in which to answer each question, use two minutes of the time in thinking. *By thinking is meant, in this case, collecting your ideas on a given point, discarding the unimportant ideas, and properly connecting the others.* These three steps can be taken rapidly if the questions are definitely stated and you are familiar with the subject.

2. Arrange your statements in logical order.

[1] Used by permission of Houghton Mifflin Company, publishers.

a. Sometimes the answer to an examination question is best given in the form of a *condensed* statement. For example:

QUESTION. What are the qualities necessary for good notes?
ANSWER. Good notes should be brief, clear, and orderly in their arrangement.

b. If the question requires for its answer a fuller statement, make a list of the principal topics that you are to write about and arrange them in order. For example:

QUESTION. Write an account of your favorite character in a novel you have recently read.

In answering this question you should write on the following topics, making from each a separate group of sentences, or a paragraph: (1) the name of my favorite character and the part he plays in the story; (2) his chief characteristics; (3) one or two important incidents in the story that illustrate these characteristics.

3. Make your sentences brief and to the point. Long sentences are apt to become involved. Stringing words together for the sake of filling up space results in poor work and seldom deceives the teacher. Choose your words so carefully that every one counts. In your effort to secure brevity do not sacrifice accuracy or clearness of thought or expression.

4. It ought to be unnecessary to add that in *every* examination paper, whether in English or in any other subject, the writing, the grammar, the spelling, the capitalization, and the punctuation should be as nearly perfect as possible.

EXERCISE

Answer the following examination questions, observing the directions given in section 44:

1. Comment on the character of the hero in a story you have recently read.

2. Give a brief account of the best incident in that story.

3. Mention instances where the characters show any of the following qualities:

a. Courage.	d. Miserliness.	g. Cruelty.
b. Cowardice.	e. Cleverness.	h. Generosity.
c. Slyness.	f. Patriotism.	i. Nobility.

4. What kind of story do you like to read?

45. Third method: retelling by expanding. The third method of retelling another person's thought is to expand it. By this process the thought of another is amplified, his story or description elaborated and made more vivid, by means of details originally omitted or merely suggested. Here we are called upon to make liberal use of our own knowledge and to give free play to our imagination, but the additional matter should not be inconsistent or improbable with respect to the original.

Proverbs, epigrams, and similar concise statements of practical wisdom usually require no elaboration. In fables, allegories, and parables, however, we frequently find such a maxim as "Honesty is the best policy" or "Virtue is its own reward" amplified by means of concrete details which show the application of this principle to everyday life. Poetry, which in general is more concise than prose, is often better understood if it is liberally paraphrased and expanded.

Perhaps the most common example of retelling by expanding is to be found in the daily newspaper. News stories dealing with other than local events are based on brief telegraphic dispatches which contain nothing but a few bare facts. Until a writer on the newspaper staff expands these facts by adding amplifying details that will give them life and reality, they are colorless and uninteresting to the reading public. A comparison of the brief news dispatches on the bulletin board of a newspaper office and the complete news stories printed in the issue of the paper that follows will show how much has been added in the expanding process.

46. Value of retelling by expanding. Retelling by expanding is of great value, because it constitutes an important step toward original composition. We develop in our own way the ideas suggested by another. It is like taking a pencil sketch which somebody else has made and producing from it a finished picture, using our own taste as to colors and tones, lights and shades.

47. General directions for retelling by expanding. 1. Read carefully several times the sentence, the brief notes, or the passage to be expanded, to discover exactly what the writer has said. First of all, get the author's meaning.

2. Make an orderly list of all the points that the author has included.

3. Make a list of the interesting points and details that he has omitted. Try to supply whatever of importance the original passage leaves to the imagination of the reader.

4. From the two lists make the outline from which you intend to write.

5. Expand each main topic into a paragraph. Use the best words at your command, carefully avoiding the exact forms of expression used in the original passage.

6. Read over what you have written, to see whether you have said too much about one topic or not enough about another. Improve any paragraphs that need revising.

EXERCISES

I

Bring to class a list of news briefs copied from the bulletin board of a local newspaper, and with it bring a printed news story in which one of these briefs has been expanded. Be prepared to point out just how much was added by the newspaper writer.

II

Read one of the parables in the New Testament, and be prepared to state in a sentence the principal thought that was expanded and illustrated concretely by the details of the parable.

III

Read a fable and point out the central thought illustrated by it. Show how this thought was made more emphatic and interesting by being expanded.

IV

Suppose that you are a newspaper writer. Using the scant details given in one of the following groups, expand them into a news article of two hundred words or more:

1. Our team won meet by seven points. Allston Academy second place. Brighton High School third. Hanson won eleven points. Carder broke two-twenty record. Our boys lords of the town. Home Sunday evening.

2. Train hits automobile at Lewiston crossing. Hiram Dodge, wife, and nephew killed. Mrs. Dodge's sister fatally injured. Baby and dog unhurt. Family on the way to county high-school meet. Nephew a contestant.

3. Couple eloping in stolen car caught by girl's father and her jilted suitor. Girl refuses to return home with her father. Begs officers to give her cell in jail, as they had given her lover. Car being held for owner.

4. Cyclone hits Amesbury. Ten known dead. Thirteen missing. More than a hundred injured. Many families homeless. Property loss over five million. River reached maximum at six this morning. Dam safe if no more rain falls. City without lights and water. Mayor calls for aid.

5. Miss Isabel Hightower dead at age of eighty-seven. Leaves house to historical society. Large collection of interesting family relics. House built in 1760. Lover killed in Civil War. Miss Hightower active in Red Cross work during World War. Leaves Gordon Bryce, nephew, senior in medical college, all her money.

V

Expand one of the following sentences into a composition of one page:

1. It seemed that luck was against our team from the very start.

2. Never in all my life had I dreamed that such an opportunity would ever be mine.

3. If I win the hundred-dollar prize in the title contest, I know exactly how I shall spend it.

4. The view from my front window is more beautiful in autumn than in spring.

5. None of us had ever thought of Uncle John's taking such a step at his age.

48. Summary. The ability to express ourselves accurately and effectively in writing, as well as in speech, is fundamental to our success in life. By welcoming every opportunity for writing we may increase our skill in written expression.

Written composition differs from oral composition in two principal respects: it is more deliberately composed and it is slightly more formal. In subject matter the two types are closely akin.

Good form is highly important in written composition. Close attention should be given to grammar, spelling, capitalization, punctuation, margins, and indentations. All written work should be neat and legible.

There are three essentials of effective composition: (1) We must have something to say. (2) We must have some idea of how we wish to say it. (3) We must practice the different forms of expression until we can say it well. Familiar subjects are always the best. Mental alertness is a necessary characteristic of every person who wishes to find interesting subjects.

Reading the work of reputable writers will increase our knowledge. By means of wide reading in good literature we may unconsciously improve our own manner of expressing our thoughts.

Conscious imitation and emulation of experienced speakers and writers will render our approach to original composition-writing natural and easy. By such a process Lincoln, Franklin, and Stevenson taught themselves to think and to write more clearly. Reproducing the thoughts of others affords valuable self-cultivation in English. Retelling the thoughts expressed by another cultivates in us accuracy in hearing and in reading.

Retelling closely teaches us exactness in thinking and in writing, helps us to appreciate the merits of the best speakers and writers, and enlarges our vocabulary. Translation is most useful in increasing our ability to use the English language correctly.

Retelling by condensing helps us to select essential ideas, to connect them properly, and to express them concisely and forcefully. We find this form of writing especially useful in taking notes, in making outlines, and in writing examination papers.

Expanding another person's thought allows us to supply the omitted details. In this process we are taking a long and important final step in our approach to original composition-writing.

In expressing our own thoughts we should apply the principles that we have learned from retelling the thoughts of others. We can obtain ideas through reading, observation, and thinking. We can acquire accuracy and ease of expression by practice in writing.

CHAPTER IV

PLANNING AN ORIGINAL COMPOSITION

49. Approach to original composition. The study of oral composition has prepared us in three ways for writing original compositions. First, we have learned something about choosing a subject that we are capable of making clear and interesting to others. Secondly, we have had practice in selecting necessary material and in arranging it by means of a simple outline. Lastly, we have acquired some skill in presenting our subjects effectively in talks before our classmates.

From our practice in reproducing another person's thought we have learned that any piece of writing, to be of value, must contain a carefully developed thought. In retelling closely and in condensing what others have said and written we have depended wholly upon them for the thoughts for our compositions. Likewise we have followed their arrangement of topics, so that in each case we have had only to discover their outline, instead of constructing one of our own. Both of these methods of retelling have demanded chiefly that we first understand the author's thought and then find words of our own to express it accurately. Incidentally, however, we have had the opportunity to observe how more experienced speakers and writers arrange their topics and express their thoughts. We have also had occasion to increase our vocabularies to some extent, to improve ourselves in written expression, and to learn the proper arrangement of our composition on paper.

In expanding another person's thought we have taken the final step in our approach to original composition. Already we have found it necessary to employ a number of our individual ideas. In many instances we have had to construct our own outlines from the scant material that has been provided us. More and more we have been learning to depend on ourselves. If we have thus far made good use of our opportunities for practice in oral and written expression, we shall find the planning and writing of original compositions comparatively easy and natural.

50. Requirements of a good composition. When we write letters or more formal compositions, we do not write them chiefly to amuse ourselves but to let others know what we have experienced and what we are thinking about. It is true, if we have spent a happy vacation, heard some interesting bit of news, or read an entertaining new book, we find real pleasure in writing to our friends about it; but our main purpose is to make others understand and feel interested in what we say. How may we make sure that our friends will understand and feel an interest in our writing? If they are to understand, we must express ourselves clearly. If they are to feel interested, we must put spirit, liveliness, and vigor into what we say. How to be clear, then, and how to be forceful—these are the things we must learn first of all.

51. Steps in planning a composition. In planning a composition that shall be both clear and forceful three steps are essential: (1) the choice and limitation of the subject; (2) the selection of necessary material; (3) the careful arrangement of this material by means of an outline.

52. Choice and limitation of the subject. If the writing of compositions is to prove profitable and enjoyable, we must at all times exercise care in choosing our subjects. Otherwise we shall find ourselves handicapped from the very outset, and writing will become a burdensome task.

The first requirement of a good subject is that it shall be one in which we are personally interested. Naturally we must already have a considerable knowledge of such a subject and be able to learn something more about it if necessary.

The second requirement is that it shall not be too broad or general a subject, such as "Automobiles," "Newspapers," "Education," or "Outdoor Sports." We shall find it impossible to write clearly and forcefully about such large subjects as these, for we lack both the necessary information and the space for their adequate treatment. It is possible, however, for us to derive a properly limited subject from each of these. For example, we may have little difficulty in writing successfully on one or more of the following more definite subjects: "How we Earned our Car," "The Making of a School Paper," "Why I Desire a College Education," or "My Favorite Outdoor Sport." By selecting a properly limited subject and presenting the details of it in specific language we shall usually be able to interest our readers, whereas we shall fail utterly in our attempt if we carelessly choose a large subject and make only a few vague, general statements about it. A good subject should, of course, also have enough value in itself to justify the time spent in thinking and writing about it. (Read again what is said in section 12 about the choice of a subject.)

53. Choice of the title. Although the subject may be definite, the choice of a title, or the exact words in which the subject is to be expressed, is sometimes difficult. If the real subject is kept clearly in mind during the writing, it is often convenient and even desirable to reserve the final wording of the title until the composition is finished. As a rule, the title should be short. It may be so exact as to suggest in a single phrase the central idea of the writer. On the other hand, if the composition is humorous or highly imaginative, or for any reason is intended to keep the mind of the reader in suspense, the title may be such as to arouse the reader's curiosity. In the latter case the title must be one that will prove to be really appropriate and one that is not sensational. "Treasure Island" is a better title for Stevenson's story than "The Sea Cook," which he first chose, for it suggests the search for treasure and the voyage to the island. "Getting the Night News" is a better title than "The Work in a Newspaper Office at Night," for it suggests activity connected with an interesting process and it appeals to the reader's curiosity.

EXERCISES

I

From the following general subjects derive limited subjects that would be suitable for compositions of about six hundred words:

1. Transportation.
2. Inventions.
3. Climate.
4. Insects.
5. Vacations.
6. Physical Culture.
7. Domestic Science.
8. Athletics.
9. Famous Women.
10. Landscape Gardening.
11. Fashions.
12. Aëroplanes.

II

Make a list of five limited composition subjects from each of the following sources:

1. Your own experience.
2. Your observation of other people.
3. Your observation of nature.
4. Your knowledge of various kinds of business.
5. Your reading.

III

Bring to class a list of titles of books, stories, essays, poems, or magazine articles that you consider well chosen. Be prepared to defend your choice.

54. Point of view. When we have made a final selection of the subject on which we wish to write, we should next decide on our point of view. This may include (1) our position with respect to the object or scene described; (2) the time at which we view an object or scene, or the time at which an action that we are about to narrate occurred; or (3) our mental attitude and dominant interest, that is, our personal point of view. In addition, point of view usually includes the tense of the main verbs —most often the present, past, or past-perfect tense—and the person, whether first or third, in which we think best to write our composition. Having chosen our point of view, we should hold firmly to it throughout our composition; otherwise we shall fail to write clearly.

In description and in narration a definite point of view in space and time is always essential to clearness. Suppose that we have decided to write a composition entitled "The Concert on the River." Unless we have clearly in mind our point of view, we shall have difficulty in outlining the main headings; the beginning, as well as the entire composition, will more than likely be hazy and confusing. We might easily be guilty of such an absurd outline as the following:

THE CONCERT ON THE RIVER

1. Description of the canoes and the orchestra (from a position in one of the canoes).
2. The pleasure of canoeing and listening to music.
3. How the music sounded (from a position on the bluff).
4. The appearance of the canoes (from a position at the edge of the water).
5. The program played by the orchestra (heard from two different positions).
6. The end of the concert and the departure of the canoes (from a position in one of the canoes).

The absurdity of thus shifting the point of view is too manifest to need comment. A composition written by such an outline would simply confuse and disgust a reader. If, at the outset, we had decided to write from one point of view—a position either in one of the canoes or on the bluff—and had kept this point of view throughout, our whole composition would easily have assumed an orderly, unified form. Or we might have changed from our first point of view to another, if we had been careful to inform our readers of the change. It is highly important, therefore, that we should at all times keep clearly in mind our point of view, whether stationary or changing, and that we should indicate it in such a way that it will be obvious to the reader.

In writing narration we should inform the reader of the time point of view at the beginning of our story. If the time changes later, we should indicate such change.

In writing exposition and argument we should adopt the first-person or third-person point of view, decide upon the appropriate tense,—present, past, or past perfect,—and avoid changing these.

55. Selection of material. Suppose that our family has recently purchased an automobile with money earned by all the members of the family for that purpose. We shall naturally be inclined to choose as the subject of our first original composition "How we Earned our Car." Our intimate knowledge of this subject affords us an abundance of material, and we are eager to begin writing at once. If we were writing a letter to a relative or a friend telling him how we earned our car, we might be able to give him a fairly clear account of the process without stopping to select our material or arrange it according to the best plan. But, since we are writing for a large group of general readers who do not know us or our family, we shall need to make a more careful selection of material and arrange it in proper order.

At the top of a sheet of paper let us write the title representing our subject, and below it jot down all the ideas about our

A MARBLE TOURNAMENT

subject that present themselves. These ideas we may indicate by means of catchwords, phrases, or sentences. Since they come thick and fast, we should write rapidly so that none may escape. Such a list of topics as the following may be the result:

HOW WE EARNED OUR CAR

1. Our New Year's plan.
2. Father unable to buy a car the year before.
3. Advantages of having a car. (x)
4. Mother's illness. (?)
5. New roof on the house. (?)
6. All our neighbors had cars.
7. Our disappointment Christmas before last.
8. Mother chosen treasurer.
9. Many family discussions as to best car to buy. (?)
10. Father's small increase in salary.
11. We paid mother a dollar a week as salary.
12. Uncle Frank sent me a pig.
13. Father quit smoking and walked home from work.
14. I tried selling papers.
15. Fattened my pig and sold him.
16. Hated to sell him. (x)
17. Mother's needlework prize.
18. Mary clerked for Miss Cartwright.
19. Father taught in night school.
20. Tom mowed lawns and spaded flower beds.
21. Mother hired Mary and me on a commission.
22. Mother sold preserves and jelly.
23. Tom worked for construction company.
24. He clerked on Saturdays for Mr. Morse.
25. Our weekly report to mother.
26. Mother put money in savings bank.
27. None of us knew how much the other had.
28. I picked fruit for the neighbors.
29. Mother sold home products.
30. She paid me for delivering them.
31. Mary sold jelly for mother at Miss Cartwright's.

32. Mother's report as treasurer.
33. Mother surprised us all.
34. Grandfather's unexpected check. (?)
35. All went with father to buy the car.
36. Money left over. (?)
37. Father's remark as we rode home.
38. Going to grandfather's last summer in the car. (x)
39. Tom arrested for speeding. (x)
40. When we thought the car was stolen. (x)

56. Arranging material by means of an outline. Though the list that we have made may contain all the ideas related to our subject that we shall need, it is for two important reasons not an outline. First of all, as we examine our list we shall discover several topics that are not closely connected with our subject. Secondly, our topics are arranged in no definite order, and all topics appear to be of the same importance. If we should write a composition from this list as it stands, our readers would get only a very confused idea of our subject. They would doubtless put our composition aside unread as soon as they found that we did not know how to select our material or how to group it effectively. Before we attempt to write, therefore, we should construct an outline. In choosing and in arranging our topics properly we should be guided by the three fundamental laws of composition-building; namely, the law of unity, the law of coherence, and the law of emphasis.

57. The law of unity. *The law of unity requires that all topics in a composition be directly related to the subject and that all topics necessary to a clear presentation of the subject be included.*

Let us now proceed to revise our list of topics according to the law of unity. At the very outset we should remind ourselves that our subject is "How we Earned our Car," not the more general subject "Our Family Car." Let us examine each topic in order to determine whether it is closely related to our subject. After each one that is not directly concerned with the subject let us place the symbol (x). After each one that seems somewhat distantly related to the subject let us place the symbol (?). When we look back over our list we discover that we have eliminated topics 3, 16, 38, 39, and 40. We have also indicated that we question the need of topics 4, 5, 9, 34, and 36, some of which we may later discard. If we examine the remaining thirty topics, we shall possibly discover that they include everything that will be required for a clear presentation of our subject, "How we Earned our Car."

Our revised list now possesses a fair degree of unity, but not yet does it constitute a good plan. Our readers would grow dizzy trying to understand our composition if we dealt with our topics in such a confused order as that in which they now stand. We must therefore arrange them in an order that is natural and easy for the reader to follow. Obviously, too, we should decide upon a relatively small number of principal topics and subordinate the remaining topics to these. In this process of orderly arrangement we shall find the second fundamental law of composition-building a valuable aid.

58. The law of coherence. *The law of coherence requires that all ideas that are connected in thought be grouped together and that the principal topics in a composition be arranged according to their natural or logical order.*

With our unified list of topics before us let us select the principal topics—those that seem to constitute the framework of our composition. What topics may we group together? How shall we phrase the principal topics under which we arrange each group? Let us take another sheet of paper and try to answer these questions. We shall first look for the principal topics.

HOW WE EARNED OUR CAR

1. Buying our car last Christmas.
2. Our New Year's plan to earn a car.
3. Why we had not bought a car earlier.
4. How I made my part.
5. How mother earned her part.
6. How father saved and made his share.
7. How Tom obtained his part.
8. How Mary earned her share.
9. Mother's report in December.

As we look over our original list we may decide that these nine main topics will include all that we plan to say about our subject. Each topic will be the subject of a paragraph in our composition. But have we arranged our main topics in their natural time order? Proper courtesy demands, too, that we arrange topics 4, 5, 6, 7, and 8 in a different order. Bearing these points in mind, let us now rearrange our outline.

HOW WE EARNED OUR CAR

1. Why we had not bought a car earlier.
2. Our New Year's plan to earn a car.
3. How mother earned her part.
4. How father saved and made his share.
5. How Mary earned her share.
6. How Tom obtained his part.
7. How I made my part.
8. Mother's report in December.
9. Buying our car last Christmas.

Now that we have correctly arranged the principal topics of our outline, we may ask ourselves, How shall we group the remaining topics in our revised list (pages 73 and 74) so that each may contribute to the development of its appropriate main topic? Let us try the following arrangement:

HOW WE EARNED OUR CAR

1. Why we had not bought a car earlier.
   a. Heavy family expenses.
   b. Father's small increase in salary.
   c. Our disappointment.
   d. Our reconciliation.
2. Our New Year's plan to earn a car.
   a. Mother's plan.
   b. Mother elected treasurer.
   c. Our weekly reports.
3. How mother earned her part.
   a. A dollar a week as treasurer.
   b. Selling home products.
   c. Knitting sweaters and mufflers.
   d. Her needlework prize.
4. How father saved and made his share.
   a. Tobacco money and carfare.
   b. Extra work at night.
5. How Mary earned her share.
   a. Clerking in vacation.
   b. Selling homemade candy and jelly.
   c. Knitting silk neckties.
6. How Tom obtained his part.
   a. Clerking on Saturdays.
   b. Mowing lawns and spading flower beds.
   c. Keeping time for a construction company.
7. How I made my part.
   a. Fattening my pig.
   b. Picking fruit and helping mother.
   c. Selling my pig.
8. Mother's report in December.
   a. Our total earnings and savings.
   b. Mother's success over the rest of us.
   c. Grandfather's unexpected check.
9. Buying our car last Christmas.
   a. The selection of the car by the entire family.
   b. More than enough money.
   c. Father's remark as we rode home.

By comparing our final outline with our previous attempts at the correct arrangement of our material we shall see that we now have an orderly plan to guide us in writing clearly on our subject. Thus far we have satisfied the demands of the law of unity and the law of coherence. Let us now consider the third law of composition-building.

59. The law of emphasis. *The law of emphasis requires that the important topics of a composition be given their correct proportion of space and that, whenever possible, the most important topic be placed so as to attract the attention of the reader.*

When we read an account of a baseball game or of a fire, we generally find special attention given to one idea, and that idea is, as a rule, the most important. Usually it has more space devoted to it than is given to any of the others. It may be a spectacular home run, or some accident or deed of heroism at the fire. The writer, recognizing that these topics are the most important, has awarded them the most space. The ideas which catch our eye at the beginning and at the end of the account remain longest in the mind. What was in the middle of the account made some impression, but we remember best the beginning and the end. It is clear, then, that the most important positions in a composition are the beginning and the end.

Frequently in applying the law of coherence in working out a clear and orderly plan we at the same time satisfy the demands of the law of emphasis. Let us examine the outline that we have been constructing for our composition on "How we Earned our Car." Naturally our first question is, Which idea should be developed most fully? From the very nature of our subject this idea is the actual earning of the car by the members of our family. If we consult our outline we discover that we have planned to devote paragraphs 3, 4, 5, 6, and 7—five out of the total of nine paragraphs—to this most important idea. Our second question is, Which idea should be reserved for an emphatic ending? Since our composition is to be an account of how we earned our car by carrying out our New Year's plan, our readers will be most interested to learn of the success of our plan and the purchase of the car. These two topics we have properly reserved for the last two paragraphs. In our outline, therefore, we have conformed to both of the requirements of the law of emphasis. We may now regard the outline as complete.

60. The form of an outline. In making an outline we should indicate principal and subordinate topics by a definite system of numbering them and arranging them on paper. In our outline on page 77 the figures designate main topics; the letters represent subordinate topics. Figures, letters, and topics should be punctuated according to the practice illustrated in our outline. Furthermore, the subordination of topics should be indicated by indenting them and placing them under their appropriate main topics. Each principal topic, with its subordinate topics, constitutes the material for a paragraph.

In the next place, it is advisable in all outlines, except those prepared for a formal argument, to express each topic in the form of a brief phrase instead of a sentence. We should never employ both sentences and phrases as topics in the same outline.

Again, though few of our short compositions will require a separate paragraph as an introduction and another, final paragraph as a conclusion, it is well to consider the beginning and the ending of our composition and provide for them in making the outline.

Lastly, we should form the habit of devising a good outline for every composition that we write. Before we can be sure that it is a good outline we must test it to see whether it satisfies the laws of unity, coherence, and emphasis.

EXERCISES

I

Read over each of the following lists carefully. Now proceed to construct a good outline for each subject. (1) Guided by the law of unity, eliminate or add any topics that the adequate treatment of the subject may demand. Have a definite reason for including each topic. (2) In accordance with the law of coherence, discover the main topics and the subordinate topics, and arrange these in their proper order. (3) Examine the outline that you have thus far made, in order to see whether it satisfies the law of emphasis. If it does not, make any revision that may be necessary. Come to class prepared to explain and to defend your completed outlines in every detail.

MY PREPARATION FOR THE HIGH SCHOOL

1. The schoolhouse.
2. Where I lived.
3. My essay at graduation.
4. The work of the ninth grade (last year).
5. Sickness.
6. My favorite study.
7. The spelling-match.
8. Arithmetic.
9. My quarrel with Johnny Green.
10. Geography.
11. American history.
12. Grammar.
13. The seventh grade.
14. The eighth grade.
15. The number of boys and girls in my class.
16. Nature study.
17. Singing.
18. Teachers.
19. The playground.
20. My favorite teacher.
21. What I expect in high school.

HOW WE CELEBRATED LAST CHRISTMAS

1. The Christmas tree.
2. The decorations.
3. My grandfather.
4. The family party.
5. The games we played.
6. Christmas Eve.
7. Description of our house.
8. Arrival of relatives.
9. My grandmother.
10. My cousins.
11. My presents.
12. How we decorated the tree.
13. When we went to bed.
14. My strange dream.
15. Our burglar.
16. Tales grandfather told.
17. The dinner.
18. The plum pudding.
19. Candles.
20. The turkey.
21. How mother surprised us.
22. Who Santa Claus was.
23. Lighting the tree.
24. The accident.
25. A present for our dog.
26. How I was waked up.
27. The arrival of Santa Claus.
28. The jokes we played.
29. Putting the house in order.
30. My uncle's telegram.

THE MAKING OF A SCHOOL PAPER [1]

1. The editor in chief.
2. Difficulties of publishing a school paper.
3. Members of the editorial department.
4. Faculty supervisor.
5. Reporters.
6. Editorial department.
7. Managerial department.
8. Literary editors.
9. The managing board.
10. Exchange editor.
11. Business manager.
12. Staff artist.
13. Staff poet.
14. Duties of the faculty supervisor.
15. Getting advertisements.
16. Lack of promptness in editors and managers.
17. Lack of student support.
18. Failure of students to patronize advertisers.
19. Humorous-column editor.
20. Assistant business managers.
21. Staff meetings.
22. Influence of the faculty supervisor.
23. Athletic editors.
24. Cadet editors.
25. Society editors.
26. The reader's opinion of the paper.
27. Getting subscriptions.
28. Other members of the editorial department.

[1] Preserve your outline on this subject for future reference.

II

Study the following outlines carefully. Do they satisfy the laws of unity, coherence, and emphasis? If not, point out violations of these principles and reconstruct the outlines so that they conform to all three laws. (Read again section 54.)

MY HOME

1. The front of the house.
   a. Old-fashioned.
   b. Style of architecture.
   c. Color.
   d. The new roof.
   e. The east side porch.
   f. The vine-covered back porch.
2. The front yard.
   a. The street.
   b. The gravel walk.
   c. Flower beds.
   d. The lawn.
   e. The ornamental fence.
   f. The trees.
   g. The tennis court in the rear.
3. The interior of the house.
   a. My room upstairs.
   b. The front hall.
   c. The pictures I like best.
   d. The living-room.
   e. The library.
   f. The kitchen and the dining-room.
   g. The view from my window.
   h. The attic.
   i. Grandmother's old trunk.
   j. Other rooms.
4. The garage.
   a. Built of concrete.
   b. Spanish style.
   c. Our car.

5. Other houses on our street.
   a. The old red brick house.
   b. The new bungalow.
   c. The school building.

MY FIRST VISIT TO MY UNCLE'S HOME

1. Introduction.
   a. My age.
   b. Companions.
   c. Circumstances of my visit.
2. Amusements.
   a. Horseback riding.
   b. Fishing.
   c. Indoor games.
   d. Tennis.
   e. Old-fashioned barn dance.
3. Our journey.
   a. Preparations.
   b. Means of conveyance.
   c. Late start.
   d. A blowout.
   e. Interesting sights.
   f. Our arrival.
4. My uncle's home.
   a. Fine stock.
   b. Stables.
   c. Grounds.
   d. Old-fashioned house.
   e. Servants' quarters.
   f. Tennis courts.
5. My uncle's family.
   a. Aunt Betty.
   b. Jack, his dog.
   c. My four cousins.
   d. Hired man and cook.
6. My return home.
   a. Our accident.
   b. The quaint old inn.

III

In accord with the directions given in section 12 and section 52 select a subject for an original composition of about three hundred words, and prepare an outline that satisfies the demands of unity, coherence, and emphasis.

61. Summary. Oral composition and the writing of compositions in which we retell another person's thought have gradually prepared us for the writing of original compositions.

In order to make our readers understand and feel an interest in what we write, we must express our thoughts clearly and forcefully.

There are three steps in planning a composition: (1) the choice and limitation of the subject; (2) the selection of necessary material; and (3) the careful arrangement of this material by means of an outline.

In choosing a limited subject we should try to select also an effective title. We should, furthermore, decide on the point of view, and then keep this point of view definitely in mind throughout the planning and the writing of our composition.

In selecting the necessary material for our composition we should jot down all topics that seem to be related to the subject.

In choosing the topics from our list and arranging them in the form of an outline we should be guided by the three fundamental principles of composition-building; namely, the law of unity, the law of coherence, and the law of emphasis.

The law of unity requires that all topics in a composition be directly related to the subject and that all topics necessary to a clear presentation of the subject be included.

The law of coherence requires that all ideas that are connected in thought be grouped together and that the principal topics in a composition be arranged according to their natural or logical order.

The law of emphasis requires that the important topics of a composition be given their correct proportion of space and that, whenever possible, the most important topic be placed so as to attract the attention of the reader.

An outline, by its form and by the proper use of figures and letters to designate the topics, should show at a glance the principal and the subordinate topics. Topics should be expressed in the form of phrases instead of sentences. If the composition requires an introduction and a conclusion, these should be provided for in the outline. Each topic and the figure or letter that stands before it should be correctly punctuated.

The making of an outline according to the laws of unity, coherence, and emphasis should precede any attempt to begin writing a composition.

CHAPTER V

WRITING AN ORIGINAL COMPOSITION

62. Developing the outline into a composition. A large as well as an important part of our composition-writing has been done when we have prepared our outline. In accord with the laws of unity, coherence, and emphasis we have decided what topics we shall include, how we shall arrange them, and how much space we shall allot to each. We are now ready to develop our outline into a composition.

The writing, like the planning, of a satisfactory composition consists of three distinct steps: (1) writing the first rough draft of the composition from the outline; (2) revising and rewriting the composition before it is submitted for correction; and (3) revising and rewriting the composition after it has been corrected.

Our aim in all writing should be the discovery and use of the most effective means of expressing our thoughts. We can accomplish this aim only through numerous experiments and through painstaking revision and rewriting. From the very outset we should understand what every successful student of writing knows by his own experience to be true: *Good compositions are not merely written; they are rewritten.*

An outline is nothing more than the framework of a composition. Obviously, therefore, the expansion of each topic into a complete sentence and the grouping of these sentences in their respective paragraphs can in no true sense be regarded as the full *development* of the outline. Though the subtopics represent the main ideas to be used in developing the principal topic under which they stand, they themselves often require additional ideas for their development. Furthermore, the relationship between these subtopics must be shown by means of carefully constructed sentences. The relationship between the principal topics, which are the subjects of their respective paragraphs, must likewise be made clear.

A comparison of the outline that we made in the previous chapter and the composition that was written from it will show us more clearly what is meant by the *development* of an outline. The pupil who wrote the composition printed below began by writing out the best first draft that he could compose. Next, he carefully revised what he had written and rewrote the paper. A day or two later he read over his composition and made several other corrections and improvements. He then rewrote it a second time and made a copy of his outline, which he placed before the first page of his composition when he submitted it. Lastly, he examined his finished composition to see that he had not overlooked any violations of good form. Here we have his composition and his outline.

HOW WE EARNED OUR CAR

Christmas before last we were all greatly disappointed when father could not buy us a car, as he had planned. Mother's long illness and the repairs on our house that the fire of the previous summer necessitated had left very little of the money that father had been saving. Besides, father got only a small increase in salary at the end of the year. For these reasons he and mother decided that we had better wait to buy a car until we could pay cash. Mother sympathized with Mary

1. Why we had not bought a car earlier.

   a. Heavy family expenses.

   b. Father's small increase in salary.

   c. Our disappointment.

and Tom and me in our disappointment. Mary could not keep from crying, for all our neighbors had cars. But when we thought how fortunate we were in having mother still with us, we became reconciled to doing without a car.

On New Year's morning mother proposed that we make a resolution to earn a car during the coming year. We were not to touch father's salary, but were to get the money by doing extra work and by saving all we could. We readily agreed. Tom, Mary, and I decided at once that we would try to find jobs on Saturdays, and that we would stay in town and work during vacation instead of going to grandfather's, out in the country, as we usually did in summer. We elected mother treasurer at a dollar a week. Every Saturday night we were to report to her and turn over our earnings, which she would deposit in the savings bank. No one but mother was to know until December how much we had.

When we agreed to pay mother a dollar a week as treasurer, we thought that would be all she could earn; but we did not know mother. She hired Mary and me on commission, and paid us half of all we helped her to make out of the garden, the orchard, the cow, and the chickens. She and Mary also made preserves, sweet

d. Our reconciliation.

2. Our New Year's plan to earn a car.

a. Mother's plan.

b. Mother elected treasurer.

c. Our weekly reports.

3. How mother earned her part.
   a. A dollar a week as treasurer.

b. Selling home products.

pickles, jelly, and candy to sell. At odd times mother knitted sweaters and mufflers, and Miss Cartwright sold them in her shop. In addition, mother had the good luck to win a needlework prize of twenty-five dollars.

In order to earn his part, in addition to his salary, father quit smoking and walked home from work every day. Three evenings a week he taught bookkeeping in the night school. On the other three evenings he audited accounts for some of the stores. He was always telling mother that he was afraid she would get ahead of him.

Of course Mary could not make as much as the rest of us. During vacation she clerked in Miss Cartwright's shop. Miss Cartwright let her sell homemade candy and jelly that she and mother had made. Mary sold some silk neckties too that she had knitted. But she spent part of her money for clothes.

Tom was sure that he was making more than any of the rest of us. On Saturdays he clerked for Mr. Morse, and in the evenings he spaded flower beds and mowed lawns for several old ladies. In the summer he struck it rich and got a job keeping time for a construction company at five dollars a day. How I envied him!

At first it seemed that all the money I could earn would be what mother paid me for helping

c. Knitting sweaters and mufflers.

d. Her needlework prize.

4. How father saved and made his share.
   a. Tobacco money and carfare.
   b. Extra work at night.

5. How Mary earned her share.

   a. Clerking in vacation.

   b. Selling homemade candy and jelly.

   c. Knitting silk neckties.

6. How Tom obtained his part.

   a. Clerking on Saturdays.

   b. Mowing lawns and spading flower beds.
   c. Keeping time for a construction company.

7. How I made my part.

her. But, in March, Uncle Frank surprised me by sending me a pig to fatten. How proud I was of that pig, and how I did feed him! I kept the garden weeded and the cabbage almost stripped of leaves getting green stuff for him. Two of the neighbors saved all their garbage for me to give him. In the summer I earned several dollars picking berries and peaches. Almost every day mother paid me something for delivering milk, butter, eggs, and vegetables to the neighbors. When I sold my pig in December, I received forty-six dollars and eighty cents for him. Mary was terribly jealous of me, and so was Tom, though he would not admit it.

At breakfast on the day after I had sold my pig, mother made her report. We held our breath in eager expectation. During the year we had earned and saved one thousand and forty dollars. Mother had made more than any of the rest of us, and Tom came second. I was fourth. But that was not our only surprise. Grandfather had written mother that he wanted a share in our car and had sent her a check for a hundred dollars. The shouts of joy that we gave as mother finished her report must have waked every neighbor within two blocks of us.

Three days before Christmas all of us accompanied father to pur-

a. Fattening my pig.

b. Picking fruit and helping mother.

c. Selling my pig.

8. Mother's report in December.

   a. Our total earnings and savings.
   b. Mother's success over the rest of us.

   c. Grandfather's unexpected check.

9. Buying our car last Christmas.

chase the car. Though we each had at first wanted a different make, mother finally persuaded us all to agree to her choice. After paying cash for the car we each had fifty dollars left as a savings account in the bank to begin the new year with. As Tom drove us home father remarked, "Well, ours is a real family car."

a. The selection of the car by the entire family.

b. More than enough money.

c. Father's remark as we rode home.

63. The beginning of a composition. No part of a composition furnishes more scope for originality or requires more skill than does the introduction. Though no set rules can be given for beginning a composition, we can learn many of the general principles by observing the practice of reputable writers.

The beginning of a composition has a twofold purpose. First, it should acquaint the reader with what we intend to write about and with our point of view. Secondly, it should interest him to find out what is to follow. Frequently we can accomplish this purpose in a sentence or two. Sometimes, however, we may require a simple introductory paragraph in which to give our point of view, suggest an appropriate setting for what we have to say, and thus provide a natural, effective approach to the treatment of our subject. Whatever the length of the beginning, it should be of such a nature as to gain the reader's attention and, while making clear our general purpose, leave a pleasing sense of expectancy as to the details of our composition.

The three essential qualities of a good beginning are *clearness*, *directness*, and *appropriateness*. By putting ourselves in the place of our readers we can usually discover whether or not the beginning of our composition is likely to serve its purpose of informing and interesting others. Simplicity is a valuable aid to clearness in introducing our treatment of a subject. In every composition it is desirable to get to the actual discussion of our subject as quickly as clearness will permit. For this reason we should try to make the beginning concise and direct. Obviously, a good beginning must be appropriate to the subject that it introduces; otherwise we violate clearness.

EXERCISES

I

Comment on the following beginnings. Does each perform the twofold purpose mentioned above? Does each possess the three essential qualities of a good beginning? Can you suggest any improvement?

MARK TWAIN'S DOUBLE

Not long ago I heard the following interesting anecdote about Mark Twain. The story was told by an old friend of his and illustrates well a prominent trait in the great American humorist's character.

THE PEACEFUL REIGN OF QUEEN VICTORIA

"Uneasy lies the head that wears a crown." The truth of this saying has been illustrated in the life of many a monarch, but it seemed almost to be disproved in the case of Queen Victoria, whose long reign was one of peace and prosperity.

II

Comment on the beginning of the following selections: (1) "Man's Threescore and Ten Years," pp. 19–20; (2) "How we earned our Car," pp. 87–91.

64. The ending of a composition. Unless we are careful in devising a good ending for our composition, we may detract in either of two ways from the effect of what we have written. If we merely stop abruptly when we have developed the last main topic of our outline, instead of briefly rounding off the whole composition by means of a concise, effective ending, we leave the composition unfinished and thus demand too much of our readers. If, on the other hand, we do not know when to stop, and loosely add an unnecessary paragraph, we destroy whatever emphasis we may have attained by developing the most important topic last, and we usually bore the reader.

In short compositions we shall often need only a sentence or two by way of an ending. Sometimes, however, we may need a brief concluding paragraph. In such a paragraph we may give a concise summary of what has preceded, or we may make inferences from it. The conclusion should strengthen what has already been discussed rather than develop a new thought. Although a good ending should not attract attention in itself, it should not be so commonplace and mechanical as to cause a sudden drop in the reader's interest.

EXERCISES

I

Comment on the following ending. Does it seem to you a good one? If so, why?

THE CHARACTER OF QUEEN ELIZABETH

We must distinguish, therefore, between the private and the public character of Elizabeth. As a sovereign she was energetic, wise, and clever. As a woman she varied from grave to gay, wise to foolish, kind to cruel, and faithful to faithless. Elizabeth the queen was a strong and trustworthy ruler. Elizabeth the woman was often the creature of the hour.

II

Comment on the ending of the following selections: (1) "Man's Threescore and Ten Years," pp. 19–20; (2) "How we earned our Car," pp. 87–91.

65. Transitions from paragraph to paragraph. Each principal topic of our outline, as we have noticed, is developed by means of a group of related sentences into a division of the whole composition. Each of these divisions we call a paragraph. In order to make it easy for our readers to follow our thought throughout the composition, we should be careful to show the relation of each paragraph to the one immediately preceding and the one immediately following it. The connecting link between two paragraphs we call the *transitional device*. There are many of these devices for making clear the connection between successive paragraphs, thus enabling the reader to pass easily and naturally from one topic to another.

In narrations, in which we usually adopt the natural coherent order either of time or of cause and effect in arranging the incidents, we may use as transitional devices such phrases as "The next morning," "Having satisfied myself that the door was locked," "Such an insult I could not forget," or "Knowing his irritable nature."

In descriptions we usually arrange the paragraph groups of details in the natural order of either space or time relationship. For the guidance of our readers we may begin our paragraphs with such transitional phrases as "Across the street from our house," "In the center of the excited group," "This same scene viewed at sunset," or "As the man came nearer."

In exposition and in argument, transitions are more difficult to manage and are for this reason all the more necessary for our readers. Some of the most useful means of transition between paragraphs in these two types of writing are the following: (1) beginning a new paragraph with a word or a group of words referring to something mentioned in the preceding paragraph; (2) ending a paragraph with a sentence referring forward to what is to be discussed in the paragraph that follows; (3) transitional words and phrases, such as *however, therefore,*

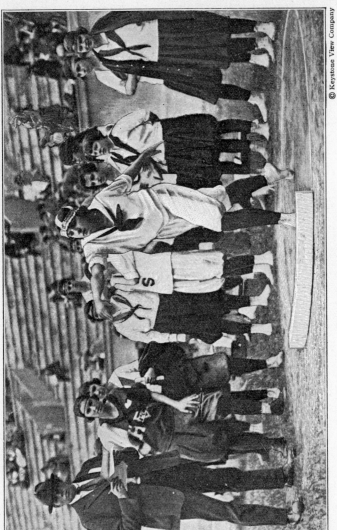

PUTTING THE SHOT

*moreover, furthermore, accordingly, notwithstanding, neverthe-
less, in addition to all this, in spite of this fact, for this reason,
in this way, by such a method, on the contrary*; (4) repetition of a word or a group of words used in the previous
paragraph; and (5) close connection of thought, so that no
formal transitional device is required.

In all our writing we should give attention to transition from
paragraph to paragraph; otherwise our compositions may seem
to the reader to violate the laws of unity and coherence.

EXERCISE

Point out and explain the transitional devices used in the following selections: (1) "Man's Threescore and Ten Years," pp. 19–20;
(2) "How we earned our Car," pp. 87–91.

66. Revising a composition before it is submitted. Our chief
aim in writing is, as we have noticed, to communicate our
thoughts, observations, and experiences clearly and interestingly to our readers. To do this we must make the reading of
what we have to say easy and entertaining. Because of the
complex nature of a composition and our lack of experience in
composing, we cannot expect to give our thought its best expression in the first, or even the second, writing. Only by carefully revising, polishing, and rewriting our compositions until
they honestly represent our best effort can we ultimately attain
real skill in writing.

Since we desire that our readers give their whole attention
to our thoughts, we should studiously avoid distracting their
attention by violations of the fundamental laws of structure
or the principles of good form. When we have written the
first rough draft of our composition, we have really taken only
the initial step in adequately presenting our subject to the
reader. If we have written this first copy in pencil and have

left wide margins and considerable space between the lines, we can do much in the way of revision by erasing, crossing out, and writing between the lines and in the margins. From the revised first draft we should make a neat second copy, which should be put aside for a day or two and then read over *aloud*, to discover in what ways we may improve it still further. Usually we shall find it necessary to rewrite the composition a second time.

In our work of revision we shall find the following questions and suggestions helpful:

1. Are there any topics not mentioned in my outline that really belong to the discussion of my subject? If so, where should they be brought in? Have I included any unnecessary topics? (The more we work with a subject, the better we come to understand it. We should not, therefore, consider the outline permanent and sacred if we find, in the process of writing, that we can improve it.)

2. Have I so arranged the topics of my composition that their relation one to another is natural and clear? If not, how can I improve the arrangement?

3. Have I indicated the more important topics of my composition by giving each its proper proportion of space? Have I placed the most important topic in the most emphatic position?

4. How can I improve the beginning of my composition? Does it serve the purpose of a good beginning? (See section 63.)

5. How can I improve the ending of my composition? Do I need a concluding paragraph? (See section 64.)

6. Have I made clear the relation of one paragraph to another by means of proper transitional devices? (See section 65.)

7. Have I one and only one paragraph for each principal topic?

8. Are any of the sentences that I have used too long? Are they clear? Do they sound natural and easy when I read them aloud?

9. Have I observed the rules of grammar?

10. Have I been careful in the choice of reputable and effective words? Have I permitted any slang expressions to creep in?

11. Are there any misspelled words that I have overlooked?

12. Have I punctuated all my sentences so as to make them readily intelligible to my readers?

13. Is my manuscript neat and correct in all details (see section 22)? If I were the reader, should I be likely to form a good opinion of the writer from the general appearance of the manuscript?

14. If I were the reader, should I really enjoy reading this composition? If so, why?

15. Does this piece of writing honestly represent my best knowledge of composition?

Remember that a good thought has little chance of impressing others favorably until it is well expressed. Readers must be won by our skill in making our compositions clear, interesting, and attractive.

67. Rewriting a corrected composition. Since our teachers in high school and in college are more experienced writers than we, they can usually give us valuable suggestions for the improvement of our compositions. Special corrections are indicated by means of symbols (see Appendix E) placed in the margin of each page, and general suggestions are often written on the outside of the paper. These corrections and suggestions are of little real value to us until we have revised and rewritten our composition in accordance with them. Within a week, therefore, after a corrected composition has been returned to us we should carefully revise it and rewrite it. This final version, together with the paper corrected by the teacher, should be submitted to show that we have understood and profited by the corrections and suggestions.

Failure to rewrite our compositions after we have been shown how to improve them results in a waste of our own and our teacher's time and effort. We should preserve all of our corrected compositions and read them over frequently throughout each course. Rereading them will show us to what extent we are becoming more skillful writers and will usually encourage us to take even greater interest in expressing ourselves well.

GENERAL EXERCISES

I

With the outline before you that you constructed from the topics on page 81, read the following selection:

THE MAKING OF A SCHOOL PAPER

A person picking up a copy of some school paper and reading it through from cover to cover in twenty or twenty-five minutes, lays it down with the feeling that after all it is a slight matter, hastily patched together and poorly printed. The truth, however, is that an immense amount of detail work is required to produce a good periodical. This work can be done more efficiently and more easily if it is distributed among the members of a publication board composed of two departments, the editorial and the managerial. Each of these departments is in turn composed of members among whom the work is still further divided.

The branch which seems to be the more important is the editorial department, at the head of which is the editor in chief. He is directly responsible for the efficient working of the whole system. If he knows his business, he distributes his work and his responsibility among the other members of the department and maintains personally only a general supervision. He must, however, plan the contents of the issues and see that every assistant knows what is required of him. He must also assign work outside of the regular routine of each subdepartment and must arrange the material when it is prepared. He has the important duty of writing at least the majority of the editorials; and since these may be a source of both good and evil to the school and to the paper, the editor in chief must be both a capable and a responsible person. Next in importance come the literary editors, the result of whose labors forms the first pages of the paper. By various means they get students to contribute stories and articles, which they examine and correct. In case of a shortage in supply of material they must themselves furnish it. To some readers the athletics editor seems most important, but he portrays, of course, only one side of school life. In his way, however, he can do much to make the paper popular. He reports athletic contests, discusses athletic possibilities and prophecies, and makes the paper interesting to athletically inclined readers. Since both boys and girls constitute the various athletic teams, a boy and a girl usually share the office of athletics editor. The activities of a cadet organization in both military and social affairs are reported by the cadet editor.

One feature of the paper appeals to everybody, and that is the collection of *bon mots* dropped in recitations and of good-natured criticisms of students' idiosyncrasies. This department is in charge of an editor, who has unofficial assistants in every class. A department which is proving itself of service to the board is the exchange column, also in charge of an editor. The latter's duties are to send out copies of the paper to other schools, to receive their copies, to criticize or commend the latter as he thinks proper, and to reproduce jokes from them. In large schools, where there are geniuses of all kinds, another member, who can write verse, is added to the department under the title of staff poet. His duty is, as his title implies, to write verses on timely topics, for the sake of giving variety to the paper. Where papers can afford the expense, another genius, a staff artist, is added to the board. His work is to embellish the covers with designs and the pages with cuts. Many times it is considered wise to have a body of substitutes, or understudies. This body is made up of reporters, who act as assistants to the editors, especially to the editor of the *bon mots*, and who are given the least important assignments.

The other department, the one that works behind the scenes, is the managerial. Its work of financing the paper is of great importance, since upon its efficiency depends the success of the finished product. The department is in charge of a business manager, who divides the work among his assistants. One or more of the latter obtain the advertisements and collect the money for them. The other assistants have charge of selling the paper.

Such is the mechanism required in publishing a good school paper. The board is a miniature government, with the editor in chief at its head. There is, however, someone higher in authority than the editor, and that person is the faculty supervisor. The latter might be called the managing editor, for his duties are similar to those of the editor. In some schools his participation is merely a matter of form, but in others he controls largely what enters into the paper, and can do much toward raising its standard.

Now, it would seem that publishing a paper is a simple thing. All one has to do is to set the clockwork in order and wind it up, and it goes by itself. But there are a number of difficulties which prevent the mechanism from running smoothly, and sometimes from running at all. We must not forget, while speaking in metaphors, that editors and managers are only human and therefore not perfect. They do not always accomplish the work they are supposed to and do not always prepare the manuscripts on time. This causes confusion in the system and trouble between the editor in chief and his assistants. Another difficulty experienced by the board is the lack of support by the student body. While not hesitating to criticize the contents of an issue, the students are seldom eager to contribute the kind of stories, news, and articles which they think the issue should contain. In not subscribing for the paper they deprive the treasury of an added source of income and lessen its value in the eyes of the advertisers. The latter condition is aggravated by the fact that students do not make it a rule to patronize the advertisers, who make possible the publishing of the periodical.

II

Now that you have read the composition printed above, expand the following outline by finding the subordinate topics that develop each main topic. Express all your subtopics as phrases.

THE MAKING OF A SCHOOL PAPER

1. The publication board.
2. The principal members of the editorial department.
3. Other members of the editorial department.
4. The managerial department.
5. The faculty supervisor.
6. The difficulties of publishing a school paper.

III

Come to class prepared to give a talk on one of the subjects outlined below (read again section 11):

HOW TO PLAN AND MAKE A DRESS

1. Introduction.
   a. Dressmaking an enviable accomplishment.
   b. Skill and judgment required.
2. Planning the dress.
   a. Purpose for which it is to be used.
   b. Finding suitable materials.
   c. Choosing an appropriate style.
   d. Selecting a satisfactory pattern.
3. Making the dress.
   a. Laying out the pattern on the material.
   b. Cutting.
   c. Basting.
   d. Fitting.
   e. Sewing.
   f. Finishing.
4. Pride in the completed dress.
   a. Economy.
   b. The joy of creating something.

HOW TO MAKE A TENNIS COURT

1. Preliminary considerations.
   a. Best time of the year.
   b. Choosing a suitable location.
2. Preparing the court.
   a. Clearing the ground.
   b. Leveling the ground.
   c. Rolling.
3. Completing the court.
   a. Laying off the court.
   b. Putting in the net posts.
   c. Constructing the backstops.
4. The finished court.

IV

Write a composition on the same subject on which you prepared your talk in Exercise III. Make any changes in the outline that you find necessary. Hand in the outline with your composition.

V

Make an outline for a composition of about three hundred words on one of the following subjects:

1. How to Install a Radio Telephone.
2. How to Prepare a Baseball Diamond.
3. My Visit to an Interesting Manufacturing Plant.
4. Why I Enjoy Keeping a Diary.
5. My Favorite Magazine.
6. Automobiles and Good Roads.
7. A Model Dairy.
8. How Plants Grow.

VI

Write out the first draft of your composition developing the outline that you made in Exercise V.

VII

According to the directions given in section 66, carefully revise and rewrite your composition. Before you submit it for correction be sure that it represents your best knowledge of composition.

VIII

From the list of subjects on page 30 select three subjects and write an appropriate beginning and ending for a composition on each.

IX

After you have made an outline of one of the subjects that you chose in Exercise VIII, write a composition of three hundred words or more developing your outline.

68. Summary. The writing of a satisfactory composition includes three distinct steps:

1. Writing the first rough draft from the outline.

2. Revising and rewriting the composition before it is submitted for correction.

3. Revising and rewriting the composition after it has been corrected.

Good compositions are not merely written; they are rewritten.

An outline is simply the framework of a composition. Each topic should be so developed that its relation to other topics will be clear.

The beginning of a composition should acquaint the reader with what we intend to write about and with our point of view. In addition, it should interest him to find out what is to follow. The three essential qualities of a good beginning are clearness, directness, and appropriateness.

A composition should end, not merely stop. A good ending should be concise, but it should be sufficient to round off and complete the whole composition. If a brief concluding paragraph is used, it may include a summary of what has preceded or contain inferences drawn from the previous discussion. The ending should strengthen what has already been discussed, rather than develop a new thought.

In order to make clear the relation of one paragraph to another, we should employ appropriate transitional devices.

In revising and rewriting our compositions we should be guided by the laws of unity, coherence, and emphasis and the demands of good form. No composition should ever be submitted until it represents our very best effort.

All compositions that have been corrected should be carefully revised and rewritten. Until this has been done we cannot consider our handling of a subject satisfactory or complete.

CHAPTER VI

LETTER–WRITING

69. Importance of letter-writing. For each of us the letter constitutes an important part of our writing. We make almost daily use of it in our social and business correspondence. More than any other form of written composition it affords us practice in the clear, natural, and entertaining expression of our thoughts and feelings. A letter expresses our individuality with great accuracy and vividness. By its contents, style, and form it impresses our reader favorably or unfavorably in respect to our personality and education. A correspondent whom we have never met has no other means of forming his estimate of us. The growth of a friendship begun through personal acquaintance often depends on our ability to write a good letter. So true an index of character is the letter that business men require persons seeking a responsible position to make application in writing. For these reasons letter-writing deserves special study.

Though the general principles of composition govern the writing of letters, there are certain particular rules relating to form and arrangement that we should follow. These rules are established by custom. Correct usage and courtesy to our correspondents demand conformity to them.

70. Kinds of letters. In spite of variations in length, subject matter, and general style, letters may be divided into two principal classes: (1) social letters, which include friendly letters, informal notes, and formal notes, and (2) business letters.

71. General form of letters. Good form and attractiveness in the appearance of letters require that the following details receive close attention:

1. *Paper*. Letters of all kinds should be written on unruled paper, preferably white, though slightly tinted stationery is permissible. Business letters are written on paper $8\frac{1}{2} \times 11$ inches. For social letters regular four-page sheets of correspondence paper should be used. Envelopes should match the paper, though in business correspondence government stamped envelopes are satisfactory.

2. *Ink*. The ink used should be black. If the letter is written on a typewriter, a black ribbon of good quality should be used.

3. *Legibility*. Select a pen adapted to your style of handwriting and write legibly. Avoid flourishes and shadings. Do not crowd lines too close together and do not run the letters of one line into those of the line above. Leave the proper amount of space between words and avoid running together the letters in the last word in a line. Punctuate distinctly. Business letters should, if possible, be typewritten. Social letters should be written with pen and ink.

4. *General appearance*. The entire letter should be neat and attractive in appearance. The writing should be correctly spaced and symmetrically arranged. An ample margin should be left on both sides, and at the top and bottom, of the page. Paragraphs should be properly indented. The various parts of the letter should be arranged according to the instructions contained in the following sections. See that the page is free from finger prints, blots, or unsightly erasures. Do all that you can in respect to the form and arrangement of your letter to make the reading of it easy and pleasurable for your correspondent.

5. *Pages*. In business letters write on only one side of the sheet. In social letters, where the folded four-page correspondence paper is used, it is proper to write on both sides of the sheet, and the pages should be written on in regular book order. If a social letter does not exceed two pages, it may be written on pages one and three.

6. *Folding*. If a business letter is to be inclosed in an official envelope (usually measuring about 4 × 10 inches), the sheet on which it is written should be folded twice horizontally so as to divide it into thirds. If a regular commercial-size envelope (usually measuring about $3\frac{1}{2}$ × $6\frac{1}{2}$ inches) is to be used, the sheet should be folded once horizontally in the center, and then the folded sheet should be folded twice at right angles to the central crease so as to divide it into thirds. The four-page sheet on which a social letter is written should be folded once horizontally across the center. In every case the folded letter should fit the envelope exactly and should be so placed that when it is removed from the envelope and unfolded it will be in the proper position for reading.

7. *Correctness*. Finally, and most important of all, a letter should be free from errors in grammar, sentence structure, spelling, and diction. In addition, it should be correctly divided into paragraphs and intelligently punctuated.

72. Parts of a letter. Although there are some slight differences of form, the essential parts of a letter are

I. The heading $\left\{\begin{array}{l}\text{1. Address of the writer.}\\ \text{2. Date.}\end{array}\right.$

II. The introduction $\left\{\begin{array}{l}\text{1. Name of the correspondent.}\\ \text{2. Address of the correspondent.}\\ \text{3. Salutation.}\end{array}\right.$

III. The letter proper.

IV. The conclusion $\left\{\begin{array}{l}\text{1. Complimentary close.}\\ \text{2. Signature.}\end{array}\right.$

V. The superscription $\left\{\begin{array}{l}\text{1. Name of the correspondent.}\\ \text{2. Address of the correspondent.}\end{array}\right.$

The heading. The heading of a letter is usually placed in the upper right-hand corner of the page, about an inch from the top. It should include the street (or rural route) and number, the town and state, and the date. In a letter to an intimate friend we may omit the address, although it is better to include it. The date should never be omitted.

The examples given below illustrate the proper arrangement and punctuation of the heading. It may be written in two, three, or even four lines, according to the length of the address, with either open or close punctuation. Furthermore, the lines of the address may be written in block form, or else each line after the first may be successively indented.

1. Block form with open punctuation:

137 East Tenth Street
Atlanta, Georgia
September 18, 1922

2. Successive indentation with open punctuation:

86 Brighton Road
Nashville
Tennessee
October 2, 1922

3. Block form with close punctuation:

3 Ellendale Place,
Los Angeles,
California,
November 21, 1922.

4. Successive indentation with close punctuation:

Rural Route 7,
Menardville, Ohio,
December 21, 1922.

The style of arrangement and punctuation adopted for the heading of the letter should be followed consistently in writing the inside address and the superscription.

The introduction. In a letter to any person who is not an intimate friend or relative there should be placed at the beginning of the letter his name and address, followed by an appropriate salutation. The name should begin about two line-spaces below the date, and at the left-hand side of the page, about an inch from the edge of the paper. This inch margin at the left should be observed on every page of the letter.

The name and address may consist of three or four lines, according to the length. In formal social letters the name and address are often placed at the close of the letter, at the left-hand side of the page and a little below the writer's name. In familiar letters it is permissible to omit them altogether. Like the heading, they may be written in block form or with successive indentation, and with open or close punctuation.

The salutation should begin even with the left-hand margin of the page and one line-space below the last line of the address. In familiar letters, where the name and address are omitted, or in formal social letters, where the name and address are placed at the end, the salutation should begin two line-spaces below the date. The form will vary according to our relations with our correspondent. In every form, however, the first word and the word which stands for the person's name should be capitalized; for example, *Dear Helen, My dear Uncle Robert. My dear Friend* is considered more formal than *Dear Friend*. In a formal social or business letter a colon usually follows the salutation. In a familiar letter a comma is sufficient. If the letter proper begins on the same line with the salutation, a dash may be placed after the colon or the comma. In this case the salutation is usually indented. The following examples illustrate salutations properly written and punctuated:

1. In a formal social or business letter:

My dear Mr. Crawford:
The book which you recently called to my attention, etc.

My dear Mr. Crawford:—The book which you recently called to my attention, etc.

2 In a familiar letter:

Dear Aunt Charlotte,
  The plan you propose for my vacation, etc.

Dear Aunt Charlotte,—The plan you propose for my vacation, etc.

The letter proper. The main part of the letter usually begins one or two line-spaces below the salutation, with the indentation of a paragraph. The subject matter should be paragraphed according to topics. Complete sentences should be employed throughout, and all pronouns and other words that are grammatically necessary should be expressed.

The beginning should be direct and original. There is no valid reason why the opening sentence should not begin with the pronoun *I*. No apology for not having written should be made unless the excuse is an extremely good one. Sudden illness, accident, or unexpected absence from home may need an explanation, but the less said about general negligence the better. No abbreviations, such as *mo.* for *month, Sat.* for *Saturday*, or the sign *&* for *and*, should be used, since they suggest haste and lack of consideration for our correspondent. Hackneyed expressions should be avoided, for a letter ought to express the individuality of the writer. A letter should not close too abruptly. On the other hand, such senseless remarks as "Since I can think of nothing more to write, I will now close" should never be used.

The conclusion. The conclusion is made up of two parts, the complimentary close and the signature. By the complimentary close we mean the concluding words of respect or affection, such as the following:

Sincerely yours,
Very truly yours,
Respectfully yours,
Your sincere friend,

Cordially yours,
Yours affectionately,
Yours with love,
Your loving daughter,

Only the first word should begin with a capital letter, and the last word should be followed by a comma. The place for the complimentary close is one line-space below the concluding words of the letter proper. The examples given below illustrate conclusions properly written.

1. My brother joins me in wishing you a happy vacation.

Your sincere friend,

Grant Moreland

2. Mother and I shall expect to see you in Denver next summer.

Sincerely yours,

Harriet Milman

3. I hope to have the pleasure of seeing you this summer.

Cordially yours,

Gordon Maverick

The signature is written one line-space below the complimentary close. In letters to intimate friends or to relatives we may sign merely our first name, but in other cases we should write our name in full. If the writer is a woman, it is customary for her to indicate whether or not she is married by inclosing her title in parenthesis at the left of her name or by prefixing her title to her husband's name, in parenthesis, immediately beneath her own. Below are given some examples of conclusions thus written.

1. An intimate friend:

Affectionately yours,

Marion

2. An unmarried woman:

Very truly yours,

(Miss) Eleanor Marsden

3. A married woman:

> Very truly yours,
>
> *Louise Medford*
>
> (*Mrs. Lawrence W. Medford*)

4. A widow who prefers to use her own name:

> Very truly yours,
>
> (*Mrs.*) *Louise Medford*

The superscription. The superscription is written on the envelope and includes the name and address of the person for whom the letter is intended. It may be arranged in three, four, or even five lines and should be placed symmetrically on the lower half of the envelope. Like the heading and the inside address, it may be written in block form or with successive indentation, and with open or close punctuation.

A man's name may be written in two ways: *Mr. Robert Kilmer*, or *Robert Kilmer, Esq.* The latter form is employed in writing to lawyers and other professional men and is most common in social correspondence. In the address of a letter to a married woman her husband's title should not appear. Hence such forms of address as *The Rev. Mrs. Spencer*, *Mrs. Dr. Trent*, and *Mrs. General Horton* are not in good taste.

In addition to the superscription, the name and address of the writer may be placed in the upper left-hand corner of the envelope. This insures the return of the letter if it is not delivered.

73. Qualities of the friendly letter. The principal charm of a friendly letter lies in its individuality and simple naturalness. The one who receives it should feel that it is written for him alone and with intelligent sympathy. The simple frankness thus implied must not be confounded with garrulity, egotism, or indiscretion. Directness and sincerity are perfectly consistent with dignity and even with a certain amount of reserve.

A good letter is definite in its purpose and in its statements. Exaggeration and misleading digressions are out of place if our intention is to give an accurate description, narration, or explanation. If our purpose is solely to amuse and excite to laughter, burlesque and nonsense are perfectly admissible. In any case the purpose of the letter should be apparent and should be suitably carried out.

The letter should also be suggestive in style. We should assume the intelligence, experience, and imagination of our correspondent and leave something to be supplied rather than exhaust everything ourselves. This is more courteous and more interesting than the encyclopedic method of writing.

Courtesy also requires care in the arrangement of the thought and in the form of the letter.

74. Subject matter of the friendly letter. Since a good letter will depend for its thought and form upon the personality of the writer, no absolute statement can be made as to what the letter should contain. Many people consider it essential to confine themselves to plain facts, or, as they call it, the "news." Undoubtedly our correspondent desires to hear what we are doing and planning to do; but it is possible that so-called "news" may degenerate into trivial gossip. Stevenson says: "I deny that letters should contain news (I mean mine; those of other people should). But mine should contain appropriate sentiments and humorous nonsense, or nonsense without the humor." This author's "humorous nonsense" was charming in itself, and bravely concealed, or rather ignored, the sad news of wasting sickness and personal suffering. If we have no humorous nonsense to express, we may confine ourselves to interesting description, narration, and explanation, based on our observation and experience and interpreted by our imagination.

Each of the letters printed below reveals the personality of the writer and his relation to his correspondent.

I

Robert Louis Stevenson to Annie H. Ide, daughter of the American Land Commissioner, to whom he had previously "given his birthday" and whom he had adopted as a "name-daughter" because, having been born on Christmas Day, she regarded herself as defrauded of her natural rights to a private anniversary

Valima, Samoa [November, 1891]

My dear Louisa,—Your picture of the church, the photograph of yourself and your sister, and your very witty and pleasing letter, came all in a bundle, and made me feel I had my money's worth for that birthday. I am now, I must be, one of your nearest relatives; exactly what we are to each other, I do not know; I doubt if the case has ever happened before—your papa ought to know, and I don't believe he does; but I think I ought to call you in the meanwhile, and until we get the advice of counsel learned in the law, my name-daughter. Well, I was extremely pleased to see by the church that my name-daughter could draw; by the letter, that she was no fool; and by the photograph, that she was a pretty girl, which hurts nothing. See how virtues are rewarded! My first idea of adopting you was entirely charitable; and here I find that I am quite proud of it, and of you, and that I chose just the kind of name-daughter I wanted. For I can draw, too, or rather I mean to say I could before I forgot how; and I am very far from being a fool myself, however much I may look it; and I am as beautiful as the day, or at least I once hoped that perhaps I might be going to be. And so I might. So that you see we are well met, and peers on these important points. I am very glad that you are older than your sister. So should I have been, if I had had one. So that the number of points and virtues which you have inherited from your name-father is already quite surprising.

. . . .

You are quite wrong as to the effect of the birthday on your age. From the moment the deed was registered (as it was in the public press with every solemnity), the 13th of November became your own *and only* birthday, and you ceased to have been born on Christmas Day. Ask your father: I am sure he will tell you this is sound law. You are thus become a month and twelve days younger [really, *older*] than you were, but will go on growing older for the future in the regular and human manner from one 13th of November to the next. The effect on me is more doubtful; I may, as you suggest, live forever; I might, on the other hand, come to pieces like the one-horse shay at a moment's notice; doubtless the step was risky, but I do not the least regret that which enables me to sign myself your revered and delighted name-father,

Robert Louis Stevenson[1]

II

Abraham Lincoln to Mrs. Bixby

Executive Mansion, Washington,
November 21, 1864.

Mrs. Bixby, Boston, Massachusetts.

Dear Madam: I have been shown in the files of the War Department a statement of the Adjutant-General of Massachusetts that you are the mother of five sons who have died gloriously on the field of battle. I feel how weak and fruitless must be any words of mine which should attempt to beguile you from the grief of a loss so overwhelming. But I cannot refrain from tendering you the consolation that may be found in the thanks of the Republic they died to save. I pray that our Heavenly Father may assuage the anguish of your bereavement, and leave you only the cherished memory of the loved and lost, and the solemn pride that must be yours to have laid so costly a sacrifice upon the altar of freedom.

Yours very sincerely and respectfully,
Abraham Lincoln

[1] From "Letters of Robert Louis Stevenson"; copyright, 1899, 1907, 1911, by Charles Scribner's Sons. By permission of the publishers.

III

Theodore Roosevelt to his son Kermit

Colorado Springs, Colo.,
April 14, 1905.

Blessed Kermit,

I hope you had as successful a trip in Florida as I have had in Texas and Oklahoma. The first six days were of the usual Presidential-tour type, but much more pleasant than ordinarily, because I did not have to do quite as much speaking, and there was a certain irresponsibility about it all, due, I suppose, in part to the fact that I am no longer a candidate and am free from the everlasting suspicion and ill-natured judgment which being a candidate entails. However, . . . in Kentucky, and especially in Texas, I was received with a warmth and heartiness that surprised me, while the Rough Riders' reunion at San Antonio was delightful in every way.

Then came the five days of wolf-hunting in Oklahoma, and this was unalloyed pleasure, except for my uneasiness about Auntie Bye and poor little Sheffield. General Young, Dr. Lambert, and Roly Fortescue were each in his own way just the nicest companions imaginable, [and] my Texas hosts were too kind and friendly and open-hearted for anything. I want to have the whole party up at Washington next winter. The party got seventeen wolves, three coons, and any number of rattlesnakes. I was in at the death of eleven wolves. The other six wolves were killed by members of the party who were off with bunches of dogs in some place where I was not. I never took part in a run which ended in the death of a wolf without getting through the run in time to see the death. It was tremendous galloping over cut banks, prairie-dog towns, flats, creek bottoms, everything. One run was nine miles long, and I was the only man in at the finish except the professional wolf-hunter Abernethy, who is a really wonderful fellow, catching the wolves alive by thrusting his gloved hands down between their jaws so that they cannot bite. He caught one wolf alive, tied up this wolf, and then held it on the saddle, followed his dogs in a seven-mile run, and helped kill another wolf. He has a pretty wife and five cunning children, of whom he is very proud, and introduced them to me, and

I liked him much. We were in the saddle eight or nine hours every day, and I am rather glad to have thirty-six hours' rest on the cars before starting on my Colorado bear hunt.

Your loving father,
Theodore Roosevelt[1]

IV

Theodore Roosevelt to his son Archie

White House,
May 10, 1908.

Dearest Archie,

Mother and I had great fun at Pine Knot. Mr. Burroughs, whom I call Oom John, was with us, and we greatly enjoyed having him. But one night he fell into great disgrace! The flying squirrels that were there last Christmas had raised a brood, having built a nest inside the room in which you used to sleep and in which John Burroughs slept. Of course they held high carnival at night-time. Mother and I do not mind them at all, and indeed rather like to hear them scrambling about, and then, as a sequel to a sudden frantic fight between two of them, hearing or seeing one little fellow come plump down to the floor and scuttle off again to the wall. But one night they waked up John Burroughs and he spent a misguided hour hunting for the nest, and when he found it he took it down and caught two of the young squirrels and put them in a basket. The next day under Mother's direction I took them out, getting my fingers somewhat bitten in the process, and loosed them in our room, where we had previously put back the nest. I do not think John Burroughs profited by his misconduct, because the squirrels were more active than ever that night both in his room and ours, the disturbance in their family affairs having evidently made them restless!

Your loving father,
Theodore Roosevelt[1]

75. Arrangement of the subject matter in paragraphs. In letters, as in all other forms of prose composition, each princi-

---

[1] From "Theodore Roosevelt's Letters to his Children," published by Charles Scribner's Sons. By permission of the publishers.

© Keystone View Company

CAMPING IN COLORADO

pal topic and the details belonging to it should be given a separate paragraph. The transition from paragraph to paragraph should be made as natural as possible by being based on the order of events or on some other relation by which one topic suggests another. Though it is rarely, if ever, necessary in writing friendly letters to construct a formal outline, we shall find that a little forethought as to the best arrangement of our main topics will enable us to make our letters more coherent and enjoyable to our readers. If the letter is short and concerns but one main topic, a single paragraph is adequate. You will notice that the two longer letters printed above are divided into paragraphs, whereas the two shorter letters consist of one paragraph each.

Observe the paragraphing and the transitions in the letters that follow. Note also the informal, conversational style in which each is written. Which reveals the greater amount of personality? What other desirable qualities of the friendly letter do you discover?

42 Ellsworth Road,
Wardwell, Mass.,
May 2, 19—.

Dear Bartlett,

You sounded rather disgusted with yourself in your last letter. How could you have helped having the mumps? It was not your fault that you had to take back the invitation for me to see the aëroplane meet. I laugh when I think of you squinting out over your puffed-up cheeks to see Wright go sailing past your house.

You needn't be sorry for me, even though I did miss the visit and the meet. Here's a moving-picture film of what I did Saturday. First scene: Tom Stowe and little sister Nan walking on rocks at Marblehead. Mother in the distance on a settee. Film jiggles when Tom steps on slippery seaweed. Second scene: All of a sudden around the cape comes a queer sort of motor boat with long flippers trailing after it in the water. Tom and Nan make motions of surprise. The motor boat begins to stick its nose out of the water higher and higher, until it stands right up on the ends of its flippers. Then it rises straight out of the water and sails off until it looks like a big dragon-fly. Audience applauds. Pen and Ink Film Co. Approved by Board of Censors.

You really can't think how surprised we were. It was the big hydroplane that the government had bought for a warship. Don't the things make a noise like a train of freight cars? I wanted to take a ride on one of the wings.

When you get over the mumps, I wish you'd see if you have an Ecuador postage stamp that you can spare. I'll trade you three Italian ones for it. I hope you'll be out before long.

Yours sincerely,

Tom Stowe

Greenacres Farm,
Glencoe, N. H.,
April 16, 19—.

Dear Marjorie,

Here I am at Glencoe for the whole summer. It really seems too wonderful to be true—visiting this old house of grandmother's. You know, it's a Revolutionary farmhouse. Indeed, it certainly does not hide that distinction, for I don't believe a paintbrush has touched it for ever so many years. The wall papers inside are almost covered with stains; but this does not trouble grandmother. She says she wants Greenacres to look just as it was when she first came here with grandfather. The rooms downstairs are large and airy, but those upstairs are small and delightfully cozy. Grandmother has given me the one she used to have, and she couldn't have suited me better. It's furnished in dark walnut—just the things she used so long ago. And, Marjorie, I just wish you could see the view from the windows. I know you would be sketching it in no time.

But the most interesting thing about Greenacres is the secret room. As I know your fondness for such things, let me tell you a little about it. First, where is it? Where do you suppose? Why, behind a large portrait of the man it sheltered long ago—my great-

great-great-grandfather. He seems a long way back, doesn't he? As it is behind a picture, it must naturally be high up on the wall. And so it is: you have to scale a stepladder before you can even see in.

It was in June, 1776, that, as my great-great-great-grandmother sat peeling apples by the kitchen window, a young soldier rushed up to the house. He said that some redcoats were on his trail, and that he must find a hiding-place. Grandmother jumped so that the apples rolled all over the floor; but the next minute she was over her surprise and had put the man in the secret room.

While he was in there he carved his initials on the wall, and as he was going that evening, he told grandmother—I can't write out all the *greats*—that sometime he would come back and thank her properly for sheltering him, and maybe sometime would add some initials to his own. He came back when the war was over and thanked her quite properly. Now, as you look into the room behind the picture, you can dimly see "B. M.," bracketed with "A. L." There is more to the story, but that must wait to be told.

And now, Marjorie, "the last the best of all the rest." I want you to come next week and see these sights with your very own eyes. Please, please come, Marjorie, and don't disappoint me.

Very lovingly your friend,

Estelle Wellwood

EXERCISE

Write letters suggested by two of the following topics. Try to make your letters natural and interesting.

1. Write to your father, supposing him to be away from home. Tell him all the home news.

2. Write a vacation letter describing the place where you are visiting and the persons whom you meet.

3. Write to a former teacher, describing your school life at the present time.

4. Write to a friend at home, describing some of the places you are visiting on an automobile trip and telling him of any accidents or interesting experiences you have had.

5. Write a letter giving an account of a recent athletic victory.

6. Write to a friend in another part of the country, telling him some of the things which he will probably not know about your own life.

7. Write to your mother, telling her of events that have happened during her absence from home.

8. Write to a friend who is ill in a hospital, making the letter as cheerful as possible. Tell him about the things that are happening (both in school and out of school) in which you think he will be interested.

9. Write to a friend an account of your trip as a contestant to the state meet of the Interscholastic League.

10. Write to your family your impressions after the first day in the home of a friend or relative whom you have never before visited.

76. Informal notes. Informal notes are brief friendly letters. Instead of being written in the third person like formal notes, they should be personal, simple, direct, and individual. They may be on any subject where brief friendly communication is desired. The arrangement of the informal note is similar to that of the friendly letter. The main difference between them is that in the informal note the writer's address is usually placed below the signature at the lower left side. Sometimes the street and number only are given, and usually the date is written out in words instead of in numbers. In some cases everything but the date is omitted.

The following are examples of informal notes:

I

AN INFORMAL INVITATION

Dear Mr. Whitney,

I hope that you will give us the pleasure of dining with us next Friday, October twenty-first, at seven o'clock. Our friend Mr. Cranston, who has spent the past year in South America, will be our guest over the *week-end, and I believe that you will enjoy meeting him and hearing an account of his travels.*

Yours sincerely,

Margaret Chandler

286 Prospect Street
October nineteenth

II

AN INFORMAL REPLY

Dear Mrs. Chandler,

It is kind of you to ask me to dinner. I shall be delighted to come, and shall enjoy hearing of Mr. Cranston's year in South America.

Yours sincerely,

James B. Whitney

17 Washington Street
October twentieth

III

Robert Louis Stevenson to John P——n, an English boy who had written a letter of appreciation to Stevenson

Valima, Samoa, December 3, 1893.

Dear Johnnie,—Well, I must say you seem to be a tremendous fellow! Before I was eight I used to write stories—or dictate them at least—and I had produced an excellent history of Moses, for which I got £1 from an uncle; but I had never gone the length of a play, so you have beaten me fairly on my own ground. I hope you may continue to do so, and thanking you heartily for your nice letter, I shall beg you to believe me yours truly,

Robert Louis Stevenson.[1]

[1] From "Letters of Robert Louis Stevenson"; copyright, 1899, 1907, 1911, by Charles Scribner's Sons. By permission of the publishers.

IV

To introduce the writer's daughter to Mr. Tennyson

My dear Mr. Tennyson,—I cannot let my daughter pass through London without asking your benevolence to give her the sight of your face. Her husband, Col. Wm. H. Forbes (himself a good soldier in the Massachusetts Volunteers in the War of the Rebellion), and Edith set forth tomorrow for England, France, and Italy, and I of course shall not think that they have seen England unless they see you. I pray you to gratify them and me so far. You shall not write a line the less and I shall add this grace to your genius. With kindest remembrance of my brief meeting with you,

Yours always,
R. W. Emerson

EXERCISE

Write four of the following informal notes, remembering that they should differ in length from letters of friendship:

1. A note accompanying a present to a friend.
2. A note of thanks to a relative or friend for a present just received.
3. A note to a school friend who has met with an accident or lost a friend. Express your sympathy and offer your help.
4. A reply to a note of sympathy.
5. Congratulations to a friend on his having won a prize at school.
6. A Christmas greeting to an absent friend.
7. An invitation to a friend in a distant town to make you a visit.
8. A note announcing some good news.
9. A note asking a school friend to join you on an excursion.
10. A reply to a note from a friend inviting you to a party.

77. Formal notes. Formal notes usually pertain to the etiquette of social life. Such notes should be written in the *third* person. The month, the day of the week, and the hour of the event for which the invitation is intended should be mentioned, though the year, except in wedding and commencement invitations and announcements, is usually omitted. The date and the hour should always be spelled out. The place and time of writing are written below the body of the note and at the left side. Everything in these two lines except the street number should be spelled out.

If the invitation and reply given on pages 120 and 121 were to be expressed in formal style, they would appear as follows:

I

A FORMAL INVITATION

Mr. and Mrs. Thomas Chandler request the pleasure of Mr. James B. Whitney's company at dinner on Friday evening, October the twenty-first, at seven o'clock.

286 Prospect Street
  October the nineteenth

II

A FORMAL REPLY, ACCEPTING

Mr. Whitney accepts with pleasure Mr. and Mrs. Chandler's kind invitation to dinner on Friday evening, October the twenty-first, at seven o'clock.

17 Washington Street
  October the twentieth

III

A FORMAL REPLY, DECLINING

Mr. Whitney regrets that he cannot accept Mr. and Mrs. Chandler's kind invitation to dinner on Friday evening, October the twenty-first.

17 Washington Street
  October the twentieth

EXERCISE

Write the following formal notes:

1. A note, in the name of your mother, inviting your teacher to take tea at your home. Name the day and hour.

2. A note, in the name of the class, inviting the principal of the high school to attend a class supper.

3. A note accepting an invitation to a dance.

4. A note declining an invitation to a birthday party.

5. A note accepting an invitation to the graduating-exercises of a school.

78. The business letter. In sections 71 and 72 the correct form for both social and business letters has been explained. In the present section, however, a few other details applying particularly to the business letter have been added.

The heading. If the paper used contains the printed business letterhead, which includes the address, the date only should be written where the full heading would otherwise be placed. The example given below illustrates the correct form.

GEORGE B. POWELL COMPANY

49 COURT STREET

AUSTIN, TEXAS

November 25, 1922

The salutation. In the business letter there are various forms of salutation.

1. *To one man:* Dear Sir *or* My dear Sir.

2. *To a firm:* Gentlemen *or* Dear Sirs.

3. *To a woman:* Dear Madam *or* My dear Madam.

4. *To a man and a woman:* Dear Sir and Madam.

5. *To a friend (in a semi-business form):* My dear Mr. Bond.

6. *To a group or firm composed of women:* Mesdames *or* Ladies.

The salutation is followed by a colon. A colon and dash should be used if the letter proper begins on the line with the salutation. A semicolon should *never* be used after the salutation.

1. Mr. Albert Radford
168 River Avenue
Palo Alto, California

Dear Sir:
We believe, etc.

2. James P. Quarles & Co.,
432 Fourth Street East,
Minneapolis, Minn.

Gentlemen:—Since you have not, etc.

The letter proper. If a business letter is written in answer to another, definite reference should be made to this fact. The following forms were once proper for such reference: *instant*, abbreviated to *inst.*, meaning the *present month*; *ultimo*, abbreviated to *ult.*, meaning the *past month*; and *proximo*, abbreviated to *prox.*, meaning the *next month*. For instance, *your letter of the 7th ult.* means *your letter of the 7th of last month*. Reputable business houses, however, now avoid even the full forms and prefer to insert the exact date in some such way as the following: *In reply to your letter of November 20.* Complete sentences should be written throughout the letter. Such forms as "*Yours of recent date received and contents noted*," "*Replying to your favor of the 5th, beg to say*," are considered discourteous and therefore poor business form.

The complimentary close. The complimentary close, which is placed one line-space below the body, is usually one of the following forms:

1. Yours truly,
2. Yours very truly,
3. Very truly yours,

4. Yours respectfully,
5. Respectfully yours,
6. Very respectfully yours,

Only the first word begins with a capital, and the whole is set off from the signature by a comma.

The signature. In a business letter the writer's name should be signed in full. If the writer is a woman, she should take care to give the initials or name by which she may be addressed (see section 72). If the letter is written by an individual for a company, the company's name should be signed, with the writer's name preceded by the word *per* or *by* signed under it.

1. Yours respectfully,

    James L. Osgood

2. Yours very truly,

    (*Miss*) *Alice M. Sherman*

3. Very truly yours,

    Henderson, McClure & Co.

    By J. F. Atwood

79. Qualities of the business letter. A business letter should possess four qualities:

First, a business letter should be clear, stating its purpose so distinctly that there is no possibility of its being misunderstood.

Secondly, a business letter should be complete, containing every detail which is necessary for transacting the business in hand. If any questions have been asked, they should be answered, and no necessary detail should be overlooked. For instance, if we order a watch by mail, we must be sure to give our full address, specify the style and price of the watch, and indicate the method by which we shall pay for it. If our letter is incomplete in any of these details, our order cannot be filled without delay and trouble to ourselves as well as to the watch company.

Thirdly, a business letter should be concise. Only those particulars should be given which the receiver of the letter needs to know, and they should be arranged in the briefest, most convenient form.

Fourthly, a business letter should be courteous. Even in cases where it is necessary to lodge a complaint or urge the payment of a debt, care should be used to word the letter with all possible politeness.

In a business letter we should be particularly careful as to arrangement, punctuation, spelling, and grammar. Neglect of these matters, which seem in themselves unimportant, is usually interpreted as an indication of ignorance or lack of business courtesy.

The following example illustrates the brief business letter containing an order for goods:

1420 Sequoia Road
Los Angeles, California
October 31, 1922

Home Magazine
64 Arcade Street
Chicago, Illinois

Dear Sirs:

You will find inclosed a post-office money order for $11.50, for which please send me the following books:

"Interior Decoration," by Harriet C. Ames.
"Landscape Gardening," by Myron Forbes.
"Attractive Bungalows," by H. C. Mason.

You may credit me with the remaining $3.00 by extending my subscription to the *Home Magazine* for one year.

Very truly yours,

Elizabeth Harcourt
(*Mrs. Myron G. Harcourt*)

The example printed below illustrates the letter of application for a position.

1938 Elmwood Avenue
Indianapolis, Indiana
May 7, 1922

Hanson, Fernald and Company
37 Commercial Avenue
Indianapolis, Indiana

Gentlemen:

Yesterday I was told by Mr. Hodgdon, who is in your sales department, that you are in need of a boy for office work. Since I am desirous of obtaining a position during vacation with a well-established firm where there will be chance for advancement, I should like to be considered an applicant for the position.

I have just graduated from the junior high school at the age of fourteen. My grades in all of my school subjects were good. I ranked fifth in a class of ninety-seven. During the last two summers I have been employed in the office of Boynton and Spencer. I have an opportunity to work for them again, but I prefer the training that I hope to get in your publishing-house. I believe that I am capable of doing the work required.

If you care for references regarding my character and my fitness for this position, you may write or telephone my high-school principal, Mr. Robert C. Dana, 146 Garfield Street, and Mr. J. H. Boynton, one of my former employers. I shall be glad to call at your office if you wish to see me.

Very respectfully yours,

Clinton H. Moseley

EXERCISE

Write four of the following business letters. Try to make them definite and courteous.

1. An answer to an advertisement for a clerk, stating your qualifications and experience and giving references.

2. A letter to a superintendent of schools, applying for a position as teacher. State education and experience and give references.

3. A letter to some person of influence, asking for a recommendation with a view to obtaining a position.

4. A letter renewing your subscription to some newspaper or magazine that comes to your home.

5. A letter to the proprietor of a summer hotel, inquiring about rooms and terms.

6. A letter to a clothing-house, calling attention to a mistake in filling an order.

7. A letter to an insurance company, stating that some property your father owns has been destroyed and asking that a representative of the company be sent to adjust the claim.

8. A letter to a manufacturer of athletic goods, ordering suits for a school team.

9. A letter applying for a position as stenographer in the office of a local firm.

10. A letter requesting immediate payment of a bill owed you and long overdue.

11. In reply to a letter of inquiry from some firm about your former stenographer write a letter highly recommending her for the position that she is seeking.

12. A letter advertising some article in a furnishing-store.

13. A letter to the customers of some store, notifying them of a change in the firm and asking them for their continued patronage.

14. A letter to a firm dealing in sporting-goods or millinery, asking them to send you a catalogue.

15. A letter to the manager of an athletic team in another town, proposing to play a game.

16. A letter to the postmaster of your town, notifying him of a change from your present address to another address in a different state.

17. A letter declining some office offered you in your school.

18. A letter to the registrar of a college or university, asking him to explain to you the entrance requirements.

80. Summary. The letter is a reliable index to the character and the education of the writer. For this reason letter-writing deserves special study.

Letters may be divided into two principal classes: social letters and business letters.

The parts of the letter are (1) the heading, (2) the introduction, (3) the letter proper, (4) the conclusion, and (5) the superscription.

Good form and correctness are essential in all letters.

Friendly letters should be natural and interesting, and attractive in form. They should contain something of description, narration, and exposition bearing on the personal experiences of the writer and his correspondent. Informal notes are short friendly letters. Formal notes should be brief and should be written in the third person.

Business letters should be clear, complete, concise, and courteous.

PART TWO

CHAPTER VII

THE PARAGRAPH

81. Value of detailed study of the paragraph. The paragraph, which is the unit of connected discourse, is a composition on a small scale. The detailed study of it, therefore, will give us a better understanding of composition-writing. Many writers insist, in fact, that constant practice in composing paragraphs is the surest way of gaining the ability to write well.

82. Definition of the paragraph. *A paragraph is a group of properly related sentences that develop a single topic effectively.* Clear and logical thought on any subject tends to resolve itself into groups of connected ideas. These ideas, when expressed in properly related sentences, constitute a paragraph. By means of the paragraph each topic that is included in the subject of the whole composition is developed and made to stand out with definiteness in relation to the other topics of the composition. Frequently a composition, such as a short editorial or a brief anecdote, demands only one paragraph. More often, however, it requires several paragraphs for the adequate development of its subject.

A paragraph is indicated by beginning the first line slightly farther to the right than the remaining lines. The space thus left is called the *indentation*. Though the paragraph is primarily much more than a device for pleasing the reader's eye and momentarily resting his attention, it serves both of these important purposes.

83. Length of the paragraph. The length of the paragraph is determined largely by two considerations: *the importance and the complexity of the topic* and *the length of the whole composition.*

In general, each principal topic requires a paragraph to itself, the length of which depends on the importance of the topic. When the subject is complex, the group of related ideas to be combined in one paragraph may be large; in this case special care must be taken to keep the paragraph from becoming involved.

Although the length of the paragraph depends chiefly on the topic, we must take into account also the length of the whole composition. For instance, in a sketch of the life of Robert Louis Stevenson the topics discussed may be (1) Boyhood, (2) Education, (3) Early Writings, (4) Search for Health, (5) Later Writings. If the composition is to be but one hundred and fifty words in length, all the material may properly be put into one paragraph. If, however, the composition is to be eight hundred words long, five paragraphs of varying length will be necessary.

No hard-and-fast rule can be laid down as to the length of the paragraph. We are the creators of our compositions, and we must decide the length of our paragraphs in accordance with our own development of the thought. Well-constructed long paragraphs tend to give weight and dignity to a piece of writing, whereas brief paragraphs are usually felt to be less formal. Short paragraphs contribute vigor and movement to narration.

A special rule should be observed in paragraphing conversation. Each separate speech, together with the author's comment (if any is included), should be written as a separate paragraph.

84. Requirements of the paragraph. A paragraph should be constructed according to three principles: (1) unity, which has to do with the choice of material with a view to completeness; (2) coherence, which has to do with the arrangement of material with a view to clearness; and (3) emphasis, which has to do with the arrangement of material with a view to force.

85. Unity in the paragraph. Unity requires that all the sentences composing a paragraph shall bear directly on the central thought. If the group of sentences contains a single sentence that does not contribute its share of meaning toward the development of the subject of the paragraph, unity is violated, and therefore the group of sentences is not really a paragraph.

86. Means of securing unity in the paragraph. The chief means of securing unity in the paragraph are two in number: (1) the adequate development of a single topic and (2) the avoidance of digressions.

87. The topic sentence. Since a paragraph is the development of a single topic, it must have a clearly defined central idea upon which every one of its sentences directly bears. This central idea is usually expressed definitely in one of the sentences of the paragraph, called the *topic sentence*. The topic sentence is most effective when short and striking. If the central idea is not formally stated, it must be clearly implied.

88. Position of the topic sentence. The topic sentence is often placed *first* in the paragraph, especially when a principle is to be illustrated, a general idea is to be made clear by argument, or a formal proposition is to be amplified. It is so placed in the following illustrations:

1. [Topic sentence] *The purpose of literary work, like its mood or spirit, may be various.* In a measure it varies with the department of literature to which the work belongs. The purpose of history, which brings before us the achievements of the past, is chiefly instruction. The oratory of the pulpit and the forum aims at persuasion. Fiction aims primarily at entertainment, though it may also be made the vehicle for religious, sociological, or moral teach-

ings. Poetry aims at pleasure by means of melody, felicity of expression, the picturing of moods and scenes, and the narration of interesting incidents or important events. When the purpose of a production is clearly apprehended we are prepared to judge of the wisdom of the author in his choice and adaptation of means.— F. V. N. PAINTER, "Elementary Guide to Literary Criticism"

2. [Topic sentence] *The forest is a sanitary agent.* It is constantly eliminating impurities from the earth and the air. Trees check, sweep, and filter from the air quantities of filthy, germ-laden dust. Their leaves absorb poisonous gases from the air. Roots assist in drainage, and absorb impurities from the soil. Roots give off acids, and these acids, together with the acids released by the fallen, decaying leaves, have a sterilizing effect upon the soil. Trees help to keep the earth sweet and clean, and water which comes from a forested watershed is likely to be pure. Many unsanitary areas have been redeemed and rendered healthy by tree-planting. —ENOS A. MILLS, "The Spell of the Rockies"[1]

Sometimes it is desirable to place the topic sentence *last* instead of first, especially to secure climax, or to state the central idea after the mind has been prepared for it by explanatory details. Such a placing of the topic sentence usually results in an increase of emphasis. The topic sentence in the following paragraph is stated at the end.

The judge, who was a shrewd fellow, winked at the manifest iniquity of the decision, and, when the court was dismissed, went privily and bought up all the pigs that could be had for love or money. In a few days his lordship's town-house was observed to be on fire. The thing took wing, and now there was nothing to be seen but fire in every direction. Fuel and pigs grew enormously dear all over the district. The insurance officers, one and all, shut up shop. People built slighter and slighter every day, until it was feared that the very science of architecture would in no long time be lost to the world. Thus this custom of firing houses continued, till in process of time, says my manuscript, a sage arose, like our

---

[1] Used by permission of Houghton Mifflin Company, publishers.

Locke, who made a discovery that the flesh of swine, or indeed of any other animal, might be cooked (*burnt*, as they called it) without the necessity of consuming a whole house to dress it. Then first began the rude form of a gridiron. Roasting by the string or spit came in a century or two later, I forget in whose dynasty. [Topic sentence] *By such slow degrees, concludes the manuscript, do the most useful and seemingly the most obvious arts make their way among mankind.*—CHARLES LAMB, "A Dissertation upon Roast Pig"

Now and then the topic sentence is stated at the *first* of the paragraph and *again*, in different words, at the *last*. This repetition tends to give clearness to the entire paragraph thought, as will be seen in the following illustration:

[Topic sentence] *The expression of our thoughts by means of language is a practice of so long standing that we accept it almost as an instinctive performance.* Nobody can remember when or how he learned to talk. Indeed, it is seldom possible to recall even those moments in later life when, after the art of speech had been acquired, we became familiar with particular words which, as we know well enough, must have been from time to time added to our personal vocabulary. We can, to be sure, remember when we were first introduced to the technical language of some particular science, as mathematics or medicine or political economy. We may even recollect the person from whom we first heard a new phrase which has since become a part of our habitual stock. And all of us are aware of specific additions to our vocabulary from that ephemeral element in everyday speech known as "slang," which is constantly providing us with strange terms that force themselves upon our attention because everybody employs them, and that rapidly die out only to be replaced by equally grotesque novelties. But the sum total of our retrospect accounts for only the minutest fraction of our whole outfit of words and phrases. [Topic sentence repeated in other words] *And were it not for our observation of infants, who cannot speak at all, and of young children, who are painfully learning the art of speech, we should inevitably believe that the expression of our thoughts in language was spontaneous action, quite independent of our own will and exertions, like breathing or the circulation of the blood.*—GREENOUGH and KITTREDGE, "Words and their Ways in English Speech"[1]

In many cases, especially in paragraphs of description or narration, the topic is *not actually stated in any part of the paragraph.* But if we have had a single topic clearly in mind throughout the writing, the reader can find it without trouble. A descriptive paragraph may be unified by means of a well-defined single impression. Though this central idea may nowhere be stated as a topic sentence, it nevertheless forms the subject of the paragraph. In the following paragraph the central idea that is clearly implied is "the gorgeousness of a sunset on the plains of the Southwest."

When supper was over the sun was almost down and it was seven o'clock, yet there was still no decay in the brilliance of the light. She went to the window and looked out, and the sight drew her, in spite of herself, into the open. She was in the emerald heart of a world of coral-pink. Softer than scarlet, more glowing than pink, the earth lay suffused, tinted like the embers of a dying fire. Gradually the plains became one rose; deep purple lowered in the sky, orange and gold and pearl; yet still the marvel and the richness of the rose claimed them and won them all, won them into its heart. Dorothy watched it; and for long minutes there was no change, no diminution of its irresistible splendor; the beauty was flaunted unendurably, as if God would forgive the world no jot of abasement before his terrible glory. Then slowly a gray veil began to film the heavens; for a moment, as the rose faded, the bright colors gleamed and displayed themselves again in bands and streaks and burning, prismatic spots; then, suddenly, as if the fire were dead, the wind blew the embers black, and night fell.—JAMES WEBER LINN, "The Girl at Duke's"[2]

[1] Used by permission of The Macmillan Company, publishers.
[2] Used by permission of *McClure's Magazine.*

EXERCISES

I

Read carefully the following paragraphs and point out in each the topic sentence:

1. Dogs have the same sensitiveness that we associate with well-bred men and women. Their politeness is remarkable. Offer a dog water when he is not thirsty, and he will almost always take a lap or two, just out of civility, and to show his gratitude. I know a group of dogs that never forget to come and tell their mistress when they have had their dinner, feeling sure that she will sympathize with them ; and if they have failed to get it, they will notify her immediately of the omission. If you happen to step on a dog's tail or paw, how eagerly — after one irrepressible yelp of pain — will he tell you by his caresses that he knows you did not mean to hurt him and forgives you ! — HENRY C. MERWIN, "Dogs and Men"[1]

2. Nature is filled with poetry. The great poet is God, and he has filled the universe with rhythm, harmony, beauty. Human poems are but faulty shells gathered on the shore of the divine ocean of poetry. The stars are the poetry of the skies. The planets and the stellar systems that circle in their glorious orbits preserve a sublime harmony of movement. The light that reaches us from distant worlds comes to us in rhythmical wavelets. Every human life is a poem — often an amusing comedy, but still oftener a moving tragedy. The tender friendships, the innocent joys, the noble aspirations, the high achievements of men, form the lyric poetry of human existence. The rippling of the forest stream with its shady banks of fern, the rhythmical roll and heavy roar of the ocean surges, are the poetry of the sparkling waters. The audible silence and mysterious whisperings of the dark and majestic forests, the modest hiding of the little violet that gives charm to some neglected spot, — this is the poetry of the woods and fields. Whether we look upon earth, or air, or sky, we may be sure that the unwritten poetry of God is there. In our best moments we feel its presence, — its mute yet eloquent appeal to our higher natures. It lifts us up into fellowship with him who thus speaks to us. — F. V. N. PAINTER, "Elementary Guide to Literary Criticism"

[1] Used by permission of the Atlantic Monthly Press, publishers.

3. The inn at Précy is the worst inn in France. Not even in Scotland have I found worse fare. It was kept by a brother and sister, neither of whom was out of their teens. The sister, so to speak, prepared a meal for us; the brother, who had been tippling, came in and brought with him a tipsy butcher, to entertain us as we ate. We found pieces of loo-warm pork among the salad, and pieces of unknown yielding substance in the *ragoût*. The butcher entertained us with pictures of Parisian life, with which he professed himself well acquainted; the brother sitting the while on the edge of the billiard table, toppling precariously, and sucking the stump of a cigar. In the midst of these diversions bang went a drum past the house, and a hoarse voice began issuing a proclamation. It was a man with marionettes announcing a performance for that afternoon.—ROBERT LOUIS STEVENSON, "An Inland Voyage"[1]

II

Write a paragraph of from six to twenty sentences developing one of the following topic sentences:

1. The training of a Boy Scout is good preparation for citizenship.
2. I enjoy reading modern poetry.
3. The view from my study window is entertaining.
4. Wide reading is a great help in learning to write.
5. Modern inventions have revolutionized home life.
6. Our car is always giving us a surprise.
7. I have discovered a substitute for going to the movies as a form of entertainment.
8. We have planned a balanced diet of home reading.
9. I have recently become interested in studying our native birds.
10. I have thought of a plan for increasing my vocabulary.

89. The avoidance of digressions. We must not yield to the temptation to run away from the main idea of the paragraph, however interesting to us may be some of the distantly connected thoughts which arise in our mind. We may be well informed about these associated facts and may wish to show our

[1] Used by permission of Charles Scribner's Sons, publishers.

knowledge, but we must remember that digression violates unity. In the following paragraph, note the digressions and observe the way in which the writer was led on farther and farther from his topic.

Probably one of the most interesting discoveries of modern times is that of an island in the Pacific Ocean. This island is sometimes known under the name of "Dawson's Island." It is on no map, but is located about twenty-three hundred miles from the coast of South America, and it is almost directly south of Lower California. The discovery is considered by many to be next in interest to that of the revealing of the walls of ancient Troy. The massive ruins of Troy in all stages of decay hide untold mysteries of an aboriginal race, which is supposed to have been highly civilized. This fact is shown from its statuary and architectural remains. The story of the famous siege of Troy told by Homer in the Iliad is therefore based on historic facts. The story of Troy, it should be said, is not the only story of the ancient Greeks which is based on fact, for we now know that the account of the labyrinth and the Minotaur has historic foundation. A German geographer has visited this Pacific island, and tells of its wonderful features of interest. The island is of volcanic origin, and is about ten miles long by five miles wide. On one side the shore is banked with volcanoes, and in the middle of a vast plain which lies beyond is a volcano so perfectly shaped that it might have been modeled by the hand of man. These immense volcanoes have been extinct for many years.

EXERCISES

I

Select from your reading and bring to class three or more paragraphs in which the principle of unity is well illustrated. Point out the topic sentence, if it is expressed, or formulate a statement of the topic in your own words. Be prepared to show that in each paragraph the writer keeps strictly to the central thought and avoids digressions.

II

Write a paragraph on one of the following subjects, observing carefully the means of securing unity :

1. An Amusing Incident I Recently Observed.
2. The Five-O'clock Subway Crowd.
3. Our Last Assignment in Domestic Science.
4. Our Last Assignment in Manual Training.
5. An Interesting Animal Trait.
6. Why a Writer Should Avoid the Use of Slang.
7. Waste on the Farm.
8. What is Pasteurized Milk ?
9. Our Best Bird Friend.
10. The Process of a Telephone Call.

90. Means of securing coherence in the paragraph. Coherence in the paragraph requires that the material shall be so arranged as to make the relation of the sentences and the meaning of the paragraph as a whole unmistakably clear. The chief means of securing coherence are two in number: (1) correct arrangement of material for the logical development of the topic sentence and (2) the use of connecting words and phrases to show the relation of the parts.

91. Logical development of the topic sentence. Since order is the fundamental means of securing coherence, we should try to develop our paragraphs in a natural and logical way. The chief means of developing the topic sentence are (1) by *repetition*, (2) by *details*, (3) by *definition*, (4) by *specific examples*, (5) by *comparison and contrast*, and (6) by *supporting the statement with reasons*. In many paragraphs the topic sentence is best developed by a combination of two or more of these methods.

92. Repetition. When the subject treated in the paragraph is somewhat obscure, or for any reason needs emphasis, it may be repeated in other words immediately after the topic sentence, or sometimes later in the paragraph. In writing we should avoid overworking this method. The following paragraph illustrates the use of repetition:

The Chinaman is probably the most frugal and least wasteful man on earth. He has to be. There are believed to be some four hundred million Chinamen in his corner of the earth, and they lack capital, machinery, and the means of communication and of international interchange of produce; so that their communities are too much self-contained and cannot earn largely. They must save or starve, and even with all their prudence and thrift they sometimes starve. At the hour of writing this paper, a fearful famine is going on in China and many people are dying of starvation. One never sees a Chinaman lose anything. China that he handles is never chipped or broken. When he supplies food, he has exactly enough, not too much or too little. With him thrift is an exact science.— W. CAMERON FORBES, "The Romance of Business"[1]

93. Details. One of the most common methods of paragraph development, especially in exposition and description, consists in giving the details of which the topic sentence is the general statement. This method is employed in the following expository paragraph:

[Topic sentence] *Shakespeare lived in a period of change.* In religion, politics, literature, and commerce, in the habits of daily living, in the world of ideas, his lifetime witnessed continual change and movement. When Elizabeth came to the throne, six years before he was born, England was still largely Catholic, as it had been for nine centuries; when she died England was Protestant, and by the date of Shakespeare's death it was well on the way to becoming Puritan. The Protestant Reformation had worked nearly its full course of revolution in ideas, habits, and beliefs. The authority of the Church had been replaced by that of the Bible, of the English Bible, superbly translated by Shakespeare's contemporaries. Within his lifetime, again, England had attained a national unity

[1] Used by permission of Houghton Mifflin Company, publishers.

and international importance heretofore unknown. The Spanish Armada had been defeated, the kingdoms of England and Scotland united, and the first colony established in America. Even more revolutionary had been the assertion of national greatness in literature and thought. The Italian Renaissance, following the rediscovery of Greek and Roman literature, had extended its influence to England early in the century, but only after the accession of Elizabeth did it bring full harvest. The names that crowd the next fifty years represent fine native endowments, boundless aspiration, and also novelty,—as Spenser in poetry, Bacon in philosophy, Hooker in theology. In commerce as well as in letters there was this same activity and innovation. It was a time of commercial prosperity, of increase in comfort and luxury, of the growth of a powerful commercial class, of large fortunes and large benefactions. Whatever your status, your birth, trade, profession, residence, religion, education, or property, in the year 1564 you had a better chance to change these than any of your ancestors had; and there was more chance than there had ever been that your son would improve his inheritance. The individual man had long been boxed up in guild, church, or feudal system; now the covers were opened, and the new opportunity bred daring, initiative, and ambition. The exploits of the Elizabethan sea rovers still stir us with the thrill of adventure; but adventure and vicissitude were hardly less the share of the merchant, priest, poet, or politician. The individual has had no such opportunity for fame in England before or since. The nineteenth century, which saw the Industrial Revolution, the triumphs of steam and electricity, and the discoveries of natural science, is the only period that has equaled the Elizabethan in the rapidity of its changes in ideas and in the conditions of living; and even that era of change offered relatively fewer new impulses to individual greatness than the fifty years of Shakespeare's life.—NEILSON and THORNDIKE, "The Facts about Shakespeare"[1]

In the following descriptive paragraph, details have been used to develop the topic sentence:

[1] Used by permission of The Macmillan Company, publishers.

[Topic sentence] *The appearance of the island when I came on deck next morning was altogether changed.* Although the breeze had now utterly failed, we had made a great deal of way during the night, and were now lying becalmed about half a mile to the southeast of the low eastern coast. Gray-colored woods covered a large part of the surface. This even tint was indeed broken up by streaks of yellow sand-bank in the lower lands, and by many tall trees of the pine family, outtopping the others—some singly, some in clumps; but the general coloring was uniform and sad. The hills ran up clear above the vegetation in spires of naked rock. All were strangely shaped, and the Spyglass, which was by three or four hundred feet the tallest on the island, was likewise the strangest in configuration, running up sheer from almost every side, and then suddenly cut off at the top like a pedestal to put a statue on.—ROBERT LOUIS STEVENSON, "Treasure Island"[1]

94. Definition. The topic sentence is often too concise to express exactly the idea about which the author wishes to write. Whenever this is true, it is necessary to define by restriction or illustrate by enlargement the meaning of the topic sentence. This method of paragraph development is most often used in formal exposition, such as the following passage:

[Topic sentence] *Criticism, as its etymology indicates, is the act of judging.* Literary criticism endeavors to form a correct estimate of literary productions. Its endeavor is to see a piece of writing as it is. It brings literary productions into comparison with recognized principles and ideal standards; it investigates them in their matter, form, and spirit; and, as a result of this process, it determines their merits and their defects. The end of literary criticism is not fault-finding but truth. The critic should be more than a censor or caviler. He should discover and make known whatever is commendable or excellent. At its best, criticism is not a mere record of general impressions but the statement of an intelligent judgment. It is not biased or vitiated by prejudice, ignorance, or self-interest; but, proceeding according to well-defined

[1] Used by permission of Charles Scribner's Sons, publishers.

principles, it is able to trace the steps by which it reaches its ulti-mate conclusions.—F. V. N. PAINTER, "Elementary Guide to Literary Criticism"

Frequently, as in the paragraph just given, the writer is care-ful to explain what the idea or topic does *not* include as well as what it *does* include.

95. Specific examples. Often the topic sentence is the state-ment of a general fact which requires for its clear development one or more specific examples. Notice how the author of the following paragraph has employed this method:

[Topic sentence] *All through life a person may find that what he wants brings him into conflict with others.* When he is a small child his appetite for candy conflicts with the ideas of health held by his parents. When he is a boy in school his effort to boss all sports causes trouble with his playmates. In manhood his attempt to have his own way brings conflicts with his family and associates. If in the effort to catch a train he drives his automobile at high speed through the city streets, he has trouble with the police. If he tries to avoid heavy financial loss by offering for sale spoiled food, the disagreeable taste of which he has concealed by a liberal mixture of chemicals, he is likely to be fined and imprisoned. Not-withstanding his opposition to free education, the government takes his property in the form of taxes for the support of the public schools. Prosperous in business and happy at home, he is com-pelled by society to leave wealth, family, and happiness to fight for a cause to which, perhaps, he is indifferent or even hostile.— HILL, "Community Life and Civic Problems"

96. Comparison and contrast. Occasionally the idea of a paragraph may be made clearer by means of comparison and contrast in developing the topic sentence. Not always are the two used in the same paragraph, but often they are combined. In the following paragraph, comparison has been used alone:

[Topic sentence] *The body of an animal may well be com-pared with some machine like a locomotive engine.* Indeed, the animal body is a machine. It is a machine composed of many parts, each part doing some particular kind of work for which a particular kind of structure fits it; and all the parts are dependent on each other and work together for the accomplishment of the total business of the machine. The locomotive must be provided with fuel, such as coal or wood or other combustible substance, the consumption of which furnishes the force or energy of the machine. The animal body must be provided with fuel, which is called food, which furnishes similarly the energy of the animal. Oxygen must be provided for the combustion of the fuel in the locomotive and of the food in the body. The locomotive is composed of special parts: the fire box for the reception and combustion of fuel; the steam pipes for the carriage of steam; the wheels for locomotion; the smokestack for throwing off waste. The animal body is similarly composed of parts: the alimentary canal for the reception and assimilation of food; the excretory organs for the throwing off of waste matter; the arteries and veins for the carriage of oxygen and food-holding blood; the legs or wings for locomotion.—JORDAN and KELLOGG, "Animal Life"[1]

Note in the following paragraph the use of contrast as a means of developing the topic sentence, which is here placed last:

In the old days the home was the center of merrymaking and amusement. Parties, dances, and social gatherings were usually held at the residences of the young people. The influence of the family circle was always present. In the city, at least, this is uncommon at the present time. Nowadays when the members of the family meet at the end of the day's work, if they are not so tired that they go to bed shortly after the evening meal, they generally seek amusement at the motion pictures, the club, the bowling-alley, the Y. M. C. A., the theater, or the concert hall. Thus the home not only loses a valuable opportunity to become the center of happiness, but recreation itself may become a danger. [Topic sentence] *Here, too, there is need for the school and the church to do work formerly done by the family.*—HILL, "Community Life and Civic Problems"

[1] Used by permission of D. Appleton and Company, publishers.

97. Statement supported with reasons. Frequently a topic sentence may be developed by setting forth the reasons upon which the general statement is based. If the topic sentence raises a question in the reader's mind, or leaves room for difference of opinion, it demands the statement of the supporting reasons for its development. The following paragraph is an illustration of the use of this method:

[Topic sentence] *Devote some of your leisure, I repeat, to cultivating a love of reading good books.* Fortunate indeed are those who contrive to make themselves genuine book-lovers. For book-lovers have some noteworthy advantages over other people. They need never know lonely hours so long as they have books around them, and the better the books the more delightful the company. From good books, moreover, they draw much besides entertainment. They gain mental food such as few companions can supply. Even while resting from their labors they are, through the books they read, equipping themselves to perform those labors more efficiently. This albeit they may not be deliberately reading to improve their mind. All unconsciously the ideas they derive from the printed page are stored up, to be worked over by the imagination for their future profit.—H. ADDINGTON BRUCE, "Self-Development"[1]

EXERCISES

I

Study the following paragraphs, pointing out the topic sentences and explaining the means by which they have been developed:

1. "Bad weather" is mainly the fear of spoiling one's clothes. Fancy clothing is one of the greatest obstacles to a knowledge of nature : in this regard, the farm boy has an immense advantage. It is a misfortune not to have gone barefoot in one's youth. A man cannot be a naturalist in patent-leather shoes. The perfecting of the manufacture of elaborate and fragile fabrics correlates well with our growing

---

[1] Used by permission of Funk and Wagnalls Company, publishers.

A CITY MARKET

habit of living indoors. Our clothing is made chiefly for fair weather; when it becomes worn we use it for stormy weather, although it may be in no respect stormy-weather clothing. I am always interested, when abroad with persons, in noting the various mental attitudes toward wind; and it is apparent that most of the displeasure from the wind arises from fear of disarranging the coiffure or from the difficulty of controlling a garment.—L. H. BAILEY, "The Outlook to Nature"[1]

2. Turn where you will, go where you will, today steel is always present, but it is not easy to realize how much steel has contributed to increasing the effectiveness of man's work. The part it has played, and still is playing, almost defies the imagination. Each steam shovel or steam hammer does the work of a small army. By moving levers a man whose greatest effort will not budge a weight of more than a few hundred pounds can put into motion and control absolutely mechanisms that handle with ease tons upon tons of stone or metal. There are cranes that handle masses of molten iron weighing as much as one hundred and fifty tons. There are hydraulic presses whose power is equivalent to seven thousand tons or more. In a power station of what was the Manhattan Street Railway Company there is a steam turbine of eight units, which produces *one hundred thousand horse power*. Skyscrapers, steamships, bridges—they all bear witness to the power that the mastery of steel has given to man.—W. CAMERON FORBES, "The Romance of Business"[2]

3. On the faces of the men the day's toil has written its record even as on the women, but in a much coarser hand. Fatigue has beaten down the soul of these men into brutish indifference, but in the women it has drawn fine the flesh only to make it more eloquent of the soul. Instead of listlessness, there is wistfulness. Instead of vacuity you read mystery. Innate grace rises above the vulgarity of the dress. Cheap, tawdry blouse and imitation willow-plume walk shoulder to shoulder with the shoddy coat of the male, copying Fifth Avenue as fifty cents may attain to five dollars. But the men's shoddy is merely a horror, whereas woman transfigures and subtilizes the cheap material. The spirit of grace which is the birthright of her sex cannot be killed— not even by the presence of her best young man in Sunday clothes. She is finer by the heritage of her sex, and America has accentuated

---

[1] Used by permission of The Macmillan Company, publishers.
[2] Used by permission of Houghton Mifflin Company, publishers.

her title. This America which drains her youthful vigor with over-work, which takes from her cheeks the color she has brought from her Slavic or Italian peasant home, makes restitution by remold-ing her in more delicate, more alluring lines, gives her the high privi-lege of charm—and neurosis.—SIMEON STRUNSKY, "The Street"[1]

4. Now, to be properly enjoyed, a walking tour should be gone upon alone. If you go in a company, or even in pairs, it is no longer a walking tour in anything but name; it is something else, and more in the nature of a picnic. A walking tour should be gone upon alone, because freedom is of the essence; because you should be able to stop and go on, and follow this way or that, as the freak takes you; and because you must have your own pace, and neither trot alongside a champion walker, nor mince in time with a girl. And then you must be open to all im-pressions and let your thoughts take color from what you see. You should be as a pipe for any wind to play upon. "I cannot see the wit," says Hazlitt, "of walking and talking at the same time. When I am in the country I wish to vegetate like the country,"—which is the gist of all that can be said upon the matter. There should be no cackle of voices at your elbow, to jar on the meditative silence of the morning. And so long as a man is reasoning he cannot surrender himself to that fine intoxication that comes of much motion in the open air, that begins in a sort of dazzle and sluggishness of the brain, and ends in a peace that passes comprehension.—STEVENSON, "Walking Tours"[2]

5. Regardless of personal danger, policemen often risk their lives for the safety of others. In New York City recently a patrolman at great hazard stopped three runaway horses attached to a fire engine; another bluecoat caught a mad dog which had already bitten five persons; two other officers almost perished in rescuing a number of people from a burning five-story tenement. Instances of similar heroism have occurred in every city in the United States.—HILL, "Community Life and Civic Problems"

6. The air is an invisible blotter that is constantly absorbing mois-ture. Its capacity to evaporate and absorb increases with rapidity of movement. Roughly, six times as much water is evaporated from a place that is swept by a twenty-five-mile wind as from a place in the dead calm of the forest. The quantity of water evaporated within a forest or in its shelter is many times less than is evaporated from the

---

[1] Used by permission of the Atlantic Monthly Press, publishers.
[2] Used by permission of Charles Scribner's Sons, publishers.

soil in an exposed situation. This shelter and the consequent decreased evaporation may save a crop in a dry season. During seasons of scanty rainfall the crops often fail, probably not because sufficient water has not fallen, but because the thirsty winds have drawn from the soil so much moisture that the water table in the soil is lowered below the reach of the roots of the growing plants.—Enos A. Mills, "The Spell of the Rockies"[1]

7. What are the great faults of conversation? Want of ideas, want of words, want of manners, are the principal ones, I suppose you think. I don't doubt it, but I will tell you what I have found spoil more good talks than anything else: long arguments on special points between people who differ on the fundamental principles on which these points depend. No men can have satisfactory relations with each other until they have agreed on certain *ultimata* of belief not to be disturbed in ordinary conversation, and unless they have sense enough to trace the secondary questions depending upon these ultimate beliefs to their source. In short, just as a written constitution is essential to the best social order, so a code of finalities is a necessary condition of profitable talk between two persons. Talking is like playing on a harp: there is as much in laying the hand on the strings to stop their vibrations as in twanging them to bring out their music.—Oliver Wendell Holmes, "The Autocrat of the Breakfast-Table"

8. Night is a dead and monotonous period under a roof; but in the open world it passes lightly, with its stars and dews and perfumes, and the hours are marked by changes in the face of Nature. What seems a kind of temporal death to people choked between walls and curtains is only a light and living slumber to the man who sleeps afield. All night long he can hear Nature breathing deeply and freely; even as she takes her rest she turns and smiles; and there is one stirring hour, unknown to those who dwell in houses, when a wakeful influence goes abroad over the sleeping hemisphere, and all the outdoor world are on their feet. It is then that the cock first crows, not this time to announce the dawn, but like a cheerful watchman speeding the course of night. Cattle awake on the meadows; sheep break their fast on dewy hill-sides, and change to a new lair among the ferns; and houseless men, who have lain down with the fowls, open their dim eyes and behold the beauty of the night.—Stevenson, "Travels with a Donkey"[2]

[1] Used by permission of Houghton Mifflin Company, publishers.
[2] Used by permission of Charles Scribner's Sons, publishers.

II

Bring to class paragraphs in which the topic sentence is developed by the following means, employed alone or in combination:

1. Details.
2. Definition.
3. Repetition.
4. Specific examples.
5. Comparison and contrast.

III

Develop by the use of details or specific examples each of the following topic sentences:

1. The house of my friend is ideally located.
2. The experiment was a very difficult one to perform.
3. Few students take advantage of the opportunities they have for self-cultivation in English.
4. Success is dangerous for many people.

98. Connecting words and phrases. Though we may secure adequate coherence in the paragraph by arranging our ideas in an orderly and logical manner, we may often gain added clearness by the use of reference words and connecting words and phrases to show the relation between our sentences and to indicate the direction in which our thought is moving. There are three ways of indicating this relationship: (1) by demonstrative words and phrases such as the personal and demonstrative pronouns and such demonstrative phrases as *on that occasion, in this case, under these circumstances, in this manner, for this reason*; (2) by repetition of the noun used in the preceding sentence or by the use of one of its synonyms; and (3) by conjunctional and adverbial words and phrases, such as *morever, hence, however, thereupon, finally, likewise, then, therefore, meanwhile, fortunately, in fact, near by, at length, of*

course, on the contrary, that is, after a short time, for instance.
Wherever such words and phrases are needed to make the
meaning of the paragraph more clear, they should be used; but
where the thought is eminently simple, we should, of course,
avoid using many words of reference.

In the following paragraphs notice the use of the words and
phrases in italics as a means of securing coherence:

1. Initiative is the ability to reason out a course of action and
to take that course decisively and energetically. *It* is one of the
basic elements in business success. Without *it* a business man need
never hope to travel far. However great *his* mental power, unless
he possesses the *quality of independent and energetic action he*
will always be among the laggards in the business world.—H. AD-
DINGTON BRUCE, "Self-Development" [1]

2. Mannerism is pardonable, and is sometimes even agreeable,
when the manner, though vicious, is natural. Few readers, *for
example*, would be willing to part with the *mannerism* of Milton
or of Burke. But a *mannerism* which does not sit easy on the man-
nerist, which has been adopted on principle, and which can be
sustained only by constant effort, is always offensive. *And such*
is the *mannerism* of Johnson.—MACAULAY, "Boswell's Life of
Johnson"

EXERCISES

I

Select from your reading and bring to class three paragraphs in
which coherence is obvious. Be prepared to show what methods
of development are followed and what reference words and connecting words and phrases are used.

II

Write a paragraph on a topic derived from one of the following
subjects. Give special attention to the methods of securing coherence. Underline reference words and connecting words and phrases.

[1] Used by permission of Funk and Wagnalls Company, publishers.

1. A Peculiar Pet.
2. Roadside Botany.
3. Christmas Shopping.
4. Our Milkman.
5. An Amusing Experience.
6. A Destructive Insect.
7. Making Concrete Blocks.
8. Our School's Greatest Need.
9. A Winter Sport.
10. The Red-Cross Sale of Christmas Seals.
11. An Interesting Subway Observation.
12. My Favorite Picture.
13. An Unusual Animal Trait.
14. The Pleasure of Word Study.

99. Emphasis in the paragraph. Emphasis requires that the different ideas in a paragraph be given space in proportion to their importance and that the most important ideas be placed at the beginning or the end of the paragraph.

100. Chief means of securing emphasis in the paragraph. We may secure emphasis in the paragraph in the following ways:

1. *Weigh carefully the relative values of ideas and give most space to the most important.* Details should be kept subordinate, and should be amplified only in proportion to their individual importance in relation to the main idea. Too much amplification and too great illustration of a simple statement will clearly result in violations of proportion.

2. *Develop the important idea expressed in the topic sentence so as to make the beginning and the ending of the paragraph emphatic.*

3. *Arrange ideas in the order of climax when the length and the nature of the paragraph warrant it.* That is, begin with the least important idea and arrange the other items in the order of their increasing importance.

The following paragraphs fulfill the requirements of emphasis:

1. He [Goldsmith] soon, however, grew tired and impatient of the duties and restraints of his profession; his practice was chiefly among his friends, and the fees were not sufficient for his maintenance; he was disgusted with attendance on sick-chambers and capricious patients, and looked back with longing to his tavern haunts and broad, convivial meetings, from which the dignity and duties of his medical calling restrained him. At length, on prescribing for a lady of his acquaintance, who, to use a hackneyed phrase, "rejoiced" in the aristocratical name of Sidebotham, a warm dispute arose between him and the apothecary as to the quantity of medicine to be administered. The Doctor stood up for the rights and dignities of his profession, and resented the interference of the compounder of drugs. His rights and dignities, however, were disregarded; his wig and cane and scarlet roquelaure were of no avail; Mrs. Sidebotham sided with the hero of the pestle and mortar; and Goldsmith flung out of the house in a passion. "I am determined henceforth," said he to Topham Beauclerc, "to leave off prescribing for friends." "Do so, my dear Doctor," was the reply; "whenever you undertake to kill, let it be only your enemies."—IRVING, "Life of Goldsmith"

2. Scarcely any passages in the poems of Milton are more generally known, or more frequently repeated, than those which are little more than muster rolls of names. They are not always more appropriate or more melodious than other names. But they are charmed names. Every one of them is the first link in a long chain of associated ideas. Like the dwelling-place of our infancy revisited in manhood, like the song of our country heard in a strange land, they produce upon us an effect wholly independent of their intrinsic value. One transports us back to a remote period of history. Another places us among the novel scenes and manners of a distant region. A third evokes all the dear classical recollections of childhood, the schoolroom, the dog-eared Virgil, the holiday, and the prize. A fourth brings before us the splendid phantoms of chivalrous romance, the trophied lists, the embroidered housings, the quaint devices, the haunted forests, the enchanted gardens, the achievement of enamored knights, and the smiles of rescued princesses.—MACAULAY, "Essay on Milton"

EXERCISES

I

Select from your reading and bring to class three paragraphs that embody the principle of emphasis. Be prepared to analyze them to prove the wisdom of your selection.

II

Study the following paragraph with reference to proportion, character of beginning and ending, and use of climax:

In so far as Americanism is merely patriotism, it is a very good thing. The man who does not think his own country the finest in the world is either a pretty poor sort of man or else he has a pretty poor sort of country. If any people have not patriotism enough to make them willing to die that the nation may live, then that people will soon be pushed aside in the struggle of life, and that nation will be trampled upon and crushed; probably it will be conquered and absorbed by some race of a stronger fiber and of a sterner stock. Perhaps it is difficult to declare precisely which is the more pernicious citizen of a republic when there is danger of war with another nation: the man who wants to fight, right or wrong, the hot-headed fellow who would plunge the country into a deadly struggle without first exhausting every possible chance to obtain an honorable peace, or the cold-blooded person who would willingly give up anything and everything, including honor itself, sooner than risk the loss of money which every war surely entails. "My country, right or wrong," is a good motto only when we add to it, "and if she is in the wrong, I'll help to put her in the right." To shrink absolutely from a fight where honor is really at stake, this is the act of a coward. To rush violently into a quarrel when war can be avoided without the sacrifice of things dearer than life, this is the act of a fool.— BRANDER MATTHEWS, "Parts of Speech"[1]

III

Write a paragraph on one of the following topic sentences, using one or more of the means for securing emphasis:

[1] Used by permission of Charles Scribner's Sons, publishers.

1. It is easy to understand why our team won the last game.

2. A successful dairy requires skillful management.

3. County demonstration agents should be better paid.

4. Motion pictures are proving useful in the teaching of history and literature.

5. Our kitchen is equipped with all modern labor-saving conveniences.

6. Stories of inventions fascinate me.

101. Transitional paragraphs. In longer and more formal compositions a short transitional paragraph may sometimes be used to make clear the logical connection between the main topics by linking the preceding paragraph with the one that follows. The example given below illustrates this use.

[Paragraph on the liberal attitude of England previously toward her colonies.]

[Transitional paragraph] *Adhering, Sir, as I do, to this policy, as well as for the reasons I have just given, I think this new project of hedging-in population to be neither prudent nor practicable.*

[Paragraph on the topic sentence "To impoverish the colonies in general, and in particular to arrest the noble course of their marine enterprises, would be a more easy task."]—BURKE, "Speech on Conciliation"

Occasionally a transitional paragraph is employed to connect an entire group of paragraphs with a group that follows. In addition, it sometimes includes a brief summary.[1]

GENERAL EXERCISES

I

Write paragraphs developing five of the following topics. Underscore your topic sentence and all transitional words and phrases. Immediately after each paragraph state what methods of securing coherence and emphasis you have used.

[1] Examine paragraph 13 in "Self-Cultivation in English."

1. The dog is man's best friend among the lower animals.

2. What stamps a man as great is not freedom from faults but abundance of powers.

3. The house was in the last stages of dilapidation.

4. The unexpected frequently happens.

5. Our guest was a queer old lady.

6. A boy has much better chances for success in the city than in the country.

7. Studying a foreign language greatly aids in the mastery of English.

8. Last summer I had a very narrow escape.

9. The best way to save time is to use it profitably.

10. My room was recently the scene of a tragedy.

II

Divide the following passage of conversation correctly into paragraphs. Place each speech, together with the author's comment about the speaker, in a separate paragraph. The first sentence belongs in a paragraph by itself.

The Sire de Malétroit raised his right hand and wagged it at Denis with the fore and little fingers extended. "My dear nephew," he said, "sit down." "Nephew!" retorted Denis, "you lie in your throat"; and he snapped his fingers in his face. "Sit down, you rogue!" cried the old gentleman, in a sudden, harsh voice, like the barking of a dog. "Do you fancy," he went on, "that when I had made my little contrivance for the door I had stopped short with that? If you prefer to be bound hand and foot till your bones ache, rise and try to go away. If you choose to remain a free young buck, agreeably conversing with an old gentleman—why, sit where you are in peace, and God be with you." "Do you mean I am a prisoner?" demanded Denis. "I state the facts," replied the other. "I would rather leave the conclusion to yourself."—ROBERT LOUIS STEVENSON, "The Sire de Malétroit's Door"[1]

III

Write a page or more of conversation. You may reproduce a conversation that you have recently overheard or in which you have taken part, or you may write an imaginary conversation on

[1] Used by permission of Charles Scribner's Sons, publishers.

one of the topics given below. Be sure that you divide your conversation correctly into paragraphs. In each speech indicate clearly which person is speaking. Avoid overworking the words *said*, *asked*, and *replied*.

1. Two boys discussing the approaching athletic meet.
2. Two girls discussing additions to their wardrobes.
3. A boy and a girl exchanging Christmas or vacation experiences.
4. Your mother and father talking about you.
5. A party-line telephone conversation that you overheard.
6. Your small brother or sister entertaining a visitor during your mother's absence from the room.
7. A modern high-school girl talking with her prim old-maid aunt about "flappers."

IV

Read again Palmer's "Self-Cultivation in English" and point out the topic sentence of each paragraph.

V

Analyze five of the paragraphs that your teacher will assign you in "Self-Cultivation in English." Point out the topic sentence, explain the method of coherent development, and indicate all transitional devices used in each paragraph.

VI

Following the directions given in Exercise V, analyze five paragraphs that your teacher will assign you in one of your texts in literature or history.

102. Summary. A paragraph is a group of related sentences that develop a single topic. It is a unit of writing, whether it is a separate paragraph that is a composition in miniature or one of the related paragraphs in a whole composition.

The length of the paragraph depends on two things: the importance and the complexity of the topic to be discussed and the length of the whole composition.

The paragraph should possess unity, coherence, and emphasis. Unity has to do with the choice of material and requires that the thought be focused on the central idea or topic. The means of securing unity in the paragraph are the adequate development of a single topic and the avoidance of digressions.

The topic sentence is often placed first in the paragraph, especially when a principle is to be illustrated, a general idea is to be made clear by argument, or a formal proposition is to be defended; it is sometimes placed last to secure climax, or to emphasize the central idea after the mind has been prepared for it by the use of explanatory details; it is sometimes placed first and then repeated at the end for emphasis or to give finish to a carefully elaborated thought; or it may be implied only, but in so clear a manner that the reader will not have difficulty in discovering what the central thought is.

Coherence in the paragraph has to do with the arrangement of the material with a view to clearness. The chief means of securing clearness are to seek definitely a natural and logical order of developing the central idea expressed in the topic sentence and to use connective words and phrases.

Emphasis in the paragraph has to do with the arrangement of the material with a view to force. The chief means of obtaining emphasis are to weigh carefully the relative values of ideas and give them space according to their importance; to place the most important idea either first or last in the paragraph; and to arrange the ideas in a climax of thought, if this will prove more effective than either of the other means.

A short transitional paragraph is often valuable in showing the logical connection between groups of paragraphs.

CHAPTER VIII

THE SENTENCE GRAMMATICALLY CONSIDERED

103. Nature and purpose of the sentence. *A sentence is the expression of a complete thought in words.* It is the unit of study in grammar, inasmuch as words have constructions only because of their relation one to another in the sentence. It is also the unit of expression in all kinds of writing. If we cannot express ourselves clearly and well in single sentences, we cannot express ourselves clearly and well in paragraphs or whole compositions. For this reason the sentence deserves detailed study.

Since punctuation is closely related to sentence composition, we can best study the rules of punctuation at the same time that we study sentences. In this chapter, therefore, numerous exercises in punctuation have been included. By means of these, and by frequent reference to Chapter X, we should learn to punctuate our own sentences correctly.

In conjunction with our study of the present chapter we shall find in Chapters XI and XXI much additional information that will prove helpful.

104. Kinds of sentences according to form. According to their form, sentences are *simple, compound, complex,* and *compound-complex.*

105. The simple sentence. A simple sentence is a sentence that contains but one subject and one predicate.

> 1. John drove the car.
> 2. This book was printed in England.

A simple sentence may contain, instead of a simple subject and a simple predicate, (1) a compound subject, (2) a compound predicate, or (3) a compound subject and a compound predicate, as the following illustrations show:

1. *Mrs. Houghton and her sister* live in New York. (Compound subject)
2. Helen *missed the step and sprained her ankle.* (Compound predicate)
3. *Friends and relatives called and expressed their deep sympathy.* (Compound subject and compound predicate)

Each of these three sentences is a simple sentence, for it consists of one, and only one, independent proposition.

106. Phrases. *A phrase is a group of closely related words that does not contain a subject and a predicate.* A simple sentence may include any number of phrases. In the following sentences each italicized group of words is a phrase:

1. The children *in the park* play *with the squirrels.*
2. *On my table* I found a letter *from my mother.*
3. My friend, *seeing his sister*, ran to meet her.
4. It is a pleasure *to read good books.*
5. *Two days having elapsed*, we gave up hope *of finding the children.*
6. The entire journey was, *in fact*, a dangerous one.

According to their form, phrases are classified as *prepositional phrases, participial phrases, infinitive phrases*, and *gerund* (or *verbal-noun*) *phrases.* Note an example of each in the following italicized phrases:

1. A friend *from the city* returned *with us.* (Prepositional phrases)
2. A man *reading a newspaper* was the only other passenger. (A participial phrase)
3. *To revisit my old home* would give me great pleasure. (An infinitive phrase)
4. I remember *seeing him leave the room.* (A gerund phrase)

Phrases may perform any one of five different functions in the sentence. The work that a phrase does in the sentence is the only means of determining its function. According to their use, therefore, we may classify phrases as *noun phrases, adjective phrases, adverbial phrases, verb phrases,* and *independent phrases.*

Noun Phrases

A phrase that performs the function of a noun is called a noun phrase.

1. *To cross the bridge* was dangerous.
2. We decided *to take the risk.*
3. His decision *to climb the mountain* could not be changed.
4. I always dread *writing letters.*
5. *Criticizing the actions of others* is his delight.
6. His duty is *to advise clients.*

Adjective Phrases

A phrase that is used to modify a noun or a pronoun is called an adjective phrase.

1. Here is a picture *of my mother.*
2. A stranger *wearing a soft, black felt hat* entered the room.
3. The letter, *being now almost illegible,* was copied.
4. The furniture was *of an unusual design.*
5. There was her name, *scrawled carelessly below.*

Adverbial Phrases

A phrase that is used to modify a verb, an adjective, or an adverb is called an adverbial phrase.

1. He made the trip *in his private car.*
2. The story is too long *to be read at one sitting.*
3. She has gone *to visit her mother.*
4. He conducted himself *like a gentleman.*
5. The plumber was slow enough *to try one's patience.*
6. *The guests having departed,* the old house again became quiet.
7. *The telegram coming unexpectedly,* we feared that an accident had befallen them.
8. *Our finances permitting,* we shall go abroad next year.

NOTE. The italicized phrases in the sixth, the seventh, and the eighth sentence are called *absolute phrases*. In each phrase a noun is used absolutely with the participle that follows. Each phrase serves as an adverbial modifier of the predicate of the sentence in which it stands.

VERB PHRASES

A phrase that is used as verb is called a verb phrase.

1. The fortune-teller *may have guessed* correctly.
2. The trained nurse *has been dismissed*.
3. We *shall walk* home.
4. They *could see* his shadow distinctly.
5. The story *should* never *have been told*.

NOTE. For a more complete explanation of verb phrases see pages 474–475.

INDEPENDENT PHRASES

A prepositional, participial, or infinitive phrase that is loosely introduced into the sentence and that has no grammatical relation to any part of the sentence is called an independent phrase. An independent phrase is most frequently either a modifier of an entire sentence or merely a transitional device.

1. That woman, *by the way*, is making a name for herself as a scientist.
2. You will, *in the first place*, be surprised to hear their decision.
3. *To make a long story short*, they were married secretly over a month ago.
4. *Speaking of bores*, I have never met his equal.
5. We shall enjoy the trip, *at any rate*.

Though a simple sentence may include any number of phrases, it can have only one subject and one predicate, as explained above. It must be limited to the expression of one proposition.

EXERCISES

I

State the *use* of each phrase in the first two groups of illustrative sentences in section 106.

II

State the *form* of each phrase in the illustrative sentences under noun phrases, adjective phrases, adverbial phrases, and independent phrases in section 106.

III

In the following sentences state (1) the form and (2) the use of each phrase. Give the reason for your classification in every instance.

1. Toward evening we came to a quaint little village paved with broken shells.
2. A boy, splashed with acid and badly frightened by the explosion, rushed out of the laboratory.
3. Calling to his comrades, he led the way into the cave.
4. At the blowing of the whistle every man returned to his work.
5. Our plan to reach Los Angeles within three days had failed.
6. Growing tulips for his friends is his avocation.
7. He always has time to be courteous to everyone.
8. With a steady income at last assured, he now had leisure for writing.
9. In the summer I enjoy sleeping out of doors.
10. Angela, strange to say, likes to study geometry.
11. I regret being unable to accompany you on your trip.
12. First of all, a dog wearing a silver collar attracted the attention of my friend.
13. In a small canoe we paddled up the river by moonlight.
14. Having several long assignments to prepare, I remained at home to complete my work.
15. For two hours we skated, the blood tingling in our veins.

IV

From your reading, copy fifteen simple sentences and bring them to class. Underscore each phrase and be prepared to classify it according to form and according to use.

V

In Chapter X study carefully the rules for the use of the comma in separating, or setting off, words and phrases in the sentence. Explain the use of all commas found in the sentences studied in the four preceding exercises.

VI

From each of the following groups of simple sentences form one simple sentence. Determine which sentence of the group contains the main thought to be expressed. Convert the other sentences of the group into phrases. In your completed sentences underscore each phrase and be prepared to classify it according to form and according to use. Apply the rules of punctuation studied in Chapter X wherever commas are needed in your sentences.

1.
They were panic-stricken by the appearance of a troop of English soldiers.
These were rapidly advancing.
They fled in breathless terror.

2.
His coat was of dark-green cloth.
It was trimmed with silver buttons.
He wore this coat on state occasions.

3.
The wharf was at the end of the street.
It was within a stone's throw of the warehouse.
It was two doors away from the shipping company's office.

4.
On this occasion a banquet was given Judge Wentworth.
He was a brother of the commandant.
Judge Wentworth had recently retired from practice.

5.
They were returning home.
They had been away twelve years.
They looked in vain for the familiar landmarks.

6.
Opposite her stood a young man.
He had been her brother's college chum.
She recognized him from his picture.
She introduced herself.

7.
{ Last night we saw a good play.
{ It was written by Franz Molnar.
{ The title of the play is "Liliom."

8.
{ Yesterday I received a letter.
{ In it was a check.
{ The check was from my uncle.

9.
{ In the heart of London lies a small neighborhood.
{ It consists of a cluster of narrow streets and courts.
{ Tourists usually avoid this neighborhood.

10.
{ His father was dead.
{ For five generations his ancestors had inhabited this inn.
{ He had inherited with the inn a large stock of jokes and stories.

11.
{ It was midnight.
{ The night was bitterly cold.
{ There was a loud knock at the door downstairs.
{ The knock woke me out of a sound sleep.

12.
{ It was an all-absorbing bag.
{ It was made of pigskin.
{ It had leather trimmings of a different shade.
{ The top was fastened with an ingenious metal lock.

107. The compound sentence. A compound sentence consists of two or more simple sentences related to each other in thought. As a member of a compound sentence, each simple sentence is called an *independent clause*. The relation between these clauses may be indicated by appropriate conjunctions, or the conjunction may be omitted if the relation is clearly implied.

1. The house rang with laughter, and the air was filled with the fragrance of tropical fruits.
2. They uttered no cry; not a sound escaped them.

Skill in the construction of compound sentences demands (1) clear thinking to discover the correct relationship between the thoughts that are to be connected and (2) a knowledge of the right connective words to indicate this relationship accurately. There are six principal thought relationships that may exist between the independent clauses of a compound sentence. Most of these are indicated by appropriate connectives; but when the thought relationship is entirely clear without the connective, the omission of the latter sometimes improves the force and euphony of the sentence.

Below are given the six principal relationships between the clauses of the compound sentence. Study the illustrative sentences closely and notice the typical connectives in each list.

1. *Continuation or repetition of the thought.* Example: The doors were opened, and the audience came crowding in. Connectives: *and, besides, also, moreover, likewise, furthermore.*

NOTE. In many instances the connection between clauses in either of these relationships is so clearly implied that no connective is used. The following sentences are illustrations:

1. The book is attractive in appearance; it is printed on parchment paper in large, clear type and is illustrated with a number of superb etchings.
2. The house was dilapidated; the yard was overgrown with weeds and grass; the front gate hung by a single rusty hinge.
3. Last night was a wild night: the thunder roared; the wind blew a gale; the rain fell in torrents.

Observe that wherever a connective has been omitted a semicolon or a colon has been used (see section 129, rule 1, and section 130, rule 2).

2. *Contrast.* Example: The bridal party assembled, but no bridegroom appeared. Connectives: *but, however, whereas, yet, still, notwithstanding, on the other hand.*

3. *Alternation.* Example: This machine is not rightly adjusted, or else we do not know how to operate it. Connectives: *or, nor, else, otherwise.*

4. *Correlation.* Example: Not only did his friends desert him, but his family also disowned him. Connectives: *both . . . and, not only . . . but also, either . . . or, neither . . . nor.*

5. *Consequence or inference.* Example : He has wealth and the ablest lawyers ; therefore his chance of acquittal is good. Connectives : *hence, therefore, thus, consequently, accordingly, so.*

6. *Reason.* Example : The temperature must have fallen considerably during the night, for I see icicles on the trees. Connective : *for.*

NOTE. The second clause in the sentence above does not state the reason for the truth of the first clause, but rather acquaints us with the reason for the *speaker's or writer's knowledge* of the truth of the first clause. An independent clause of reason should not be confused with a dependent clause of cause or reason. The italicized dependent clauses in the following complex sentences state the reason for the truth of the independent clauses : Ice floats *because it is lighter than water. Since a heavy frost came late in the season,* the fruit crop was seriously injured. (See the fifth relationship expressed by adverbial clauses, p. 175.)

Two cautions should be observed in the use of the compound sentence. First, we should avoid overworking the compound sentence in our writing. This we can do by judiciously employing simple and complex sentences, each of which is more flexible than the compound sentence. Secondly, we should not allow ourselves to adopt the careless habit of connecting the members of every compound sentence with either *and* or *but.* To break ourselves of this habit, or to avoid falling into it, we should use other conjunctions that indicate the same respective relationships as *and* and *but.* Better still, we should try to express by means of a simple or a complex sentence the thought that we have expressed in a compound sentence.

For a discussion of the improper use of a compound sentence for a complex sentence see section 172, rule 2. For a discussion of the wrong punctuation of a compound sentence see section 128, rule 7, *Caution,* and section 171.

EXERCISES

I

Write compound sentences in which you use properly each of the connectives listed under the six relationships between the clauses of the compound sentence. Think clearly and choose your connectives with care. Write other compound sentences in which the relation between the clauses is clearly implied without the use of a connective. (Preserve this exercise for later use.)

II

In studying the following sentences observe these directions: (1) supply the proper connective; (2) substitute other connectives and notice the change in meaning; and (3) determine which connective most accurately shows the relationship between the clauses.

1. He is poor, —— he is honest.
2. The clouds had disappeared, —— the day was ideal.
3. We desired good seats; —— we made our reservations early.
4. I do not wish to be a candidate, —— I will serve if I am elected.
5. She must derive an enormous income from her investments,—— she pays a large income tax.
6. I have no suitable dress to wear; —— I shall remain at home.
7. We tried to persuade her, —— she refused to come.
8. He studied hard for the examination; —— he failed.
9. Shall I take the package, —— will you deliver it?
10. The lights went out at ten o'clock; —— I did not solve all my problems in algebra.

III

Add to each of the following statements an independent clause that will result in a well-constructed compound sentence. Be sure that each added clause expresses a closely-related thought.

1. The players were not conscious of any special regard for each other.
2. The mountain-climbers met with many narrow escapes.
3. Thomas A. Edison is a great inventor.
4. The table was the picture of abundance. (Give particulars.)

5. The street was picturesque. (Give details showing this.)

6. With the dawn of a new day Boynton quickly forgot his recent experience.

7. The memory of the whole transaction flashed before him.

8. It was a bitterly cold day in January.

9. We should learn to punctuate intelligently.

10. Judge Carlton's life was an active one.

IV

In the following exercise point out in each compound sentence the independent clauses and state the relationship between them. Indicate all coördinating conjunctions. Point out all phrases and classify each according to form and according to use.

1. The children had rarely ventured into the field, but now they crept stealthily across the old stone bridge.

2. Holmes was, like Lowell, a humorist; and, like Lowell, he knew how to be earnest, serious, and even pathetic.

3. The Langtons must have gone away for the summer, for we have seen no signs of life about their house for the past week.

4. My precise examination of the room had done me good, but I still found the remoter darkness of the place too stimulating for the imagination.

5. His eyes goggled with earnestness; his mouth dropped open to catch every syllable that might be uttered; he leaned his ear almost on the doctor's shoulder.

6. He observed others closely and tried to profit by their experience; hence he was spared many humiliating reprimands.

7. She will probably arrive in a few days, for a letter was left here for her today by the postman.

8. The number of employers diminished; the number of employees increased.

9. Some means of preventing war must be found, else the same great waste of life and property from which humanity has suffered in the past will continue to blight the world in the future.

10. The steamship companies have advertised the attractions of America in all parts of Europe; they have kept agents at work in many countries; they have been an important factor in promoting immigration.

V

In Chapter X make a careful study of the rules for the use of the comma, the semicolon, and the colon in separating independent clauses. Explain the punctuation of all compound sentences in Exercise II and Exercise IV. Examine your own sentences in Exercise I and Exercise III to see whether they are correctly punctuated. Explain your punctuation of each sentence.

VI

From your reading copy and bring to class ten compound sentences. Underscore the connective, if one is used. After each sentence state the relationship between the independent clauses. Find examples of all six types. Explain the punctuation used in each sentence.

108. The complex sentence. A complex sentence consists of one independent clause and of one or more dependent, or subordinate, clauses. The construction of the complex sentence demands considerable skill. Clear thinking is necessary to determine which part of the sentence-thought should be put in the independent clause as the main thought and which part or parts should be subordinated to it. In addition, we must use care in the choice of the right connective to denote accurately the relationship intended. Because of the larger number of thought relationships between independent and dependent clauses, and because of a correspondingly greater number of connective and introductory words, the complex sentence is superior to the compound in variety and flexibility.

A dependent clause, like a phrase, is used as a single part of speech; but, unlike a phrase, it contains a subject and a predicate.

1. {
What he had said.
Whom we met.
When the whistle sounded.
}

Note that, although each of these clauses contains a subject and a predicate, in no case does it express a complete thought. The mind waits for something to be added.

2. {
I told her what he had said.
The man whom we met was my uncle.
The game began when the whistle sounded.
}

By joining to the clauses in group 1 other clauses, as in group 2, we have made three assertions and have thus completed the statement of thoughts which the original clauses left incomplete. In other words, the clauses of group 1 are dependent on other clauses for their meaning and are called *dependent*, or *subordinate*, *clauses*. The clauses "I told her," "The man was my uncle," and "The game began" are independent, because they make assertions which are not dependent on the rest of the sentence. They could stand alone. The sentences in group 2, each of which contains an independent clause and a dependent clause, are *complex sentences*.

109. Uses of dependent clauses. According to their use in the complex or the compound-complex sentence, dependent clauses are classified as *noun clauses*, *adjective clauses*, and *adverbial clauses*. In general, they have the same constructions as the part of speech whose function they perform.

110. Noun clauses. A noun clause performs the office of a noun. It may be introduced by such words as the following: (1) relative and interrogative pronouns and relative and interrogative adjectives, as *who, which, what, whoever, whichever, whatever, whoso, whosoever, whichsoever, whatsoever*; (2) conjunctive adverbs, as *where, when, how, why*; (3) other conjunctional words, as *that, whether, if, but* or *but that* (= *that not*). Often the substantival conjunction *that* introducing a noun clause is omitted, especially in speech.

He said [that] he would write to me.

The sentences given below illustrate the seven principal constructions of noun clauses. In each sentence point out the noun clause and be sure that you understand its use.

1. Who the stranger is does not interest me. (Subject of a verb)

2. We could not believe that he was deceiving us. (Direct object of a verb)

3. He gave whomever he encountered a helping hand. (Indirect object of a verb)

4. We had an excellent view of the stage from where we sat. (Object of a preposition)

5. The fact that he had set out very early accounted for his escape. (In apposition)

6. The report was that he had drowned. (Predicate nominative)

7. Honesty, good judgment, and industry made them who they are in the financial world. (Predicate objective)

EXERCISES

I

Point out the noun clauses in the following sentences and tell how each is used:

1. That the world is round has been proved.

2. The fact that the forests are being cut down accounts for the scarcity of water.

3. Often we judge a person by how he dresses.

4. My fear is that we shall be late.

5. Mother asked me where I had been.

6. Who knows but that the river may overflow tonight?

7. The town promised to give whoever should capture the robbers a reward of one thousand dollars.

8. Wealth alone has made him who he is.

9. It is in dispute why he did this.

10. Did you learn whether he passed in his examination?

II

Write two original sentences to illustrate each of the seven constructions of noun clauses.

© Keystone View Company

THE SAGEBRUSH OF IDAHO

111. Adjective clauses. An adjective clause performs the function of an adjective.

The man *who knocked* is a plumber.

Note that the clause in italics modifies the noun *man* and tells which man is meant. If an adjective clause limits or restricts the meaning of a noun or pronoun in this way, it is called a *restrictive* clause. Such a clause cannot be omitted without changing the meaning of the entire sentence.

Aunt Mary, *who visits us each summer*, is mother's only sister.

In this sentence the clause in italics, though grammatically a modifier of a noun, is not an indispensable part of the sentence. It may be omitted without changing the meaning of the independent clause, though by its use we gain additional information. Such a parenthetical clause is called *nonrestrictive* or *unrestrictive*.

Observe that a restrictive clause requires no punctuation, whereas a nonrestrictive clause is separated by a comma or commas from the rest of the sentence (see section 128, rule 6).

Adjective clauses are introduced by (1) relative pronouns, *who, which, that, but* (= *that not*) and (2) conjunctive adverbs, *where, when, whence, whither, why, wherein, wherewith, whereon, whereat, whereupon, whereby*.

EXERCISES

I

In the following sentences point out all adjective clauses. Tell what word each modifies and explain whether the clause is restrictive or nonrestrictive. Indicate the introductory word in each case and explain the use of that word in its clause.

1. This is the house that Jack built.
2. The farmer whose horse was stolen consulted a lawyer.

3. The old chapel belfry, where generations of bats have lived, was struck by lightning.

4. Those whose names were called rose.

5. The house where he was born yet stands.

6. We who went with him fared royally.

7. My older brother, whose judgment I respect, advised me to go to college.

8. There is no one born but must die.

9. The ground whereon we stood trembled.

10. Our high-school building, which was erected in 1912, is a fireproof structure.

11. He lacks the means wherewith he may clothe his family.

12. It is difficult to teach a cat, which is naturally active, any kind of athletic tricks.

13. The day when he returns will be a holiday.

14. The reason why we fail is usually that we lack a definite intention to win.

15. The foreman, whom everyone trusted, was never suspected of the murder.

II

Find in your reading and bring to class ten restrictive and ten nonrestrictive adjective clauses.

III

Write ten original sentences containing restrictive adjective clauses.

IV

Write ten original sentences containing nonrestrictive adjective clauses. Punctuate each sentence correctly (see section 128, rule 6).

112. Adverbial clauses. An adverbial clause performs the function of an adverb. It is introduced by conjunctive adverbs and subordinating conjunctions. The nine adverbial relationships expressed by adverbial clauses are the following:

1. *Time.* Example: The audience rose and cheered when the celebrated speaker was presented by the chairman. Introduc-

tory words: *when, before, after, while, since, till, ere, as, whenever, now that, as soon as, as long as, so long as.*

2. *Place.* Example: He remained where I left him. Introductory words: *where, wherever, whence, whither, whencesoever, whithersoever.*

3. *Manner.* Example: She walked as if she were going to a bargain sale. Introductory words: *as, as if, as though.*

NOTE. *Like* should never be used for *as* or *as if* (see section 164).

4. *Condition.* Example: He would have passed in his examination if he had studied harder. Introductory words: *if, unless* (= *if not*), *except, provided, provided that, on condition that, in case that, but that* (= *if not*), *so that*, and such imperatives as *suppose, let, say.* Often the introductory word is omitted, as in the sentence "Had I another life to live, I could not wish for greater happiness."

5. *Cause.* Example: We walked home because the cars had stopped running. Introductory words: *because, since, for, as, that* ("He grieved *that* his friend should have failed him thus").

6. *Purpose.* Example: We left early in order that we might not miss the train. Introductory words: *in order that, that, so that* ("He lent me his key *so that* I might open the door").

7. *Result.* Example: During the night it snowed so hard that all traffic was suspended for two days. (Notice that, in addition to expressing result, the dependent clause expresses degree: in this sentence it tells *how* hard it snowed.) Introductory words: *that, so that, but, but that.* ("It never rains *but* it pours." In this sentence *but* is equivalent to *that not.* The sentence means "It never rains *that* it does *not* pour.")

8. *Degree or comparison.* Example: His mind is as sluggish as his body is indolent. Introductory words: *as . . . as, just as, than, so far as, by as much as . . . by so much, as far as, in proportion as.*

9. *Concessions.* Example: Though I regard him as honest, I think that he should not be trusted too far. Introductory words: *though, although, whether, however, no matter, while, notwithstanding, notwithstanding that, whatever, whichever, even if* ("*Even if* you disagree with his beliefs, you will surely like him as a man").

EXERCISES

I

In the following sentences point out all adverbial clauses and tell what relation each expresses. Indicate the introductory words in the adverbial clauses.

1. I do as I must, but she does as she likes.
2. The apples froze because they were left out of doors.
3. Where thou goest, I will go.
4. Unless you speak distinctly, you will not be understood.
5. As we came out of the theater, father met us.
6. We study that we may learn.
7. Should you meet him, tell him that I have gone home.
8. One plays as well as the other.
9. No matter how late you may arrive, telephone me at once, for I am anxious to learn the result of your trip.
10. He slept so late that he missed his class.
11. We will deliver the package wherever you desire.
12. When at last she answered the telephone, she spoke as if she were angry.
13. Granted that I fail, the effort is worth while.
14. We can enjoy even unpleasant surroundings, provided we look for something interesting in them.
15. Since youth is precious, do not squander it.
16. She appeared much stronger than I had expected.
17. Suppose you had both wealth and fame, you would not be content.
18. As long as there is life, there is hope.
19. I should accompany him, but that I know that he would object.
20. We were amused that he should make such a mistake as that.

II

In Chapter X review all the rules for the use of the comma. Explain the punctuation employed in the sentences in Exercise I. Change the position of the adverbial clause in the sentence, wherever it is possible, and account for the use or the omission of commas.

EXERCISES ON THE COMPLEX SENTENCE

I

In studying the following exercise observe these directions: (1) Point out the independent and the dependent clause. (2) Tell how each dependent clause is used. (3) Mention the introductory word in each dependent clause.

1. I confess that I do not agree with you.
2. When I looked again I saw nothing.
3. They can wait until I am ready.
4. Then came the thought that I had left my native land.
5. The wireless telephone, which is now very expensive, may soon be within the reach of all.
6. He paced the deck as he talked.
7. Tell me where he has gone.
8. I could not enjoy the meal that the steward brought me.
9. That you can do the task has been proved.
10. I am not so stupid as you think I am.
11. The elements were so mixed in him that Nature might say to all the world, "This is a man."
12. The book pleased me because it aroused cherished memories.
13. Do you not see why I cannot grant your request?
14. A plain marble slab marks the spot where he lies.
15. I placed the flowers where she would see them.
16. Take the good the gods provide thee.
17. Earnest purpose strives ahead while dull sloth lags behind.
18. I will ask whether he has left a message for you.
19. The stupid old engine would not budge, even if the fireman should get up steam with attar of roses.
20. The accident occurred at a time when we least expected it.

21. When he came does not concern me in the slightest.

22. I am interested in when he left.

23. Jason, who was devoted to his master, would not admit the reporters.

24. Whither I go you cannot follow.

25. The reason why he fled is not known.

26. Judge Clark is the man to whom they submitted the case.

27. His present address is what I wish to know.

28. He promised whoever should find his purse a liberal reward.

29. Mr. Arnold Bennett says that most people cannot live on twenty-four hours a day.

30. When the Flood came along, for an extra monsoon,
'Twas Noah constructed the first pontoon.

31. When they said, "The train's gone!"
He exclaimed, "How forlorn!"

32. He who steals my purse steals trash.

33. "We must strike quickly," said the master, "for as the Book teaches, 'we spend our years as a tale that is told.'"

34. "We live," says Stevenson, "the time that a match flickers."

35. The manager, who speaks Spanish, will interpret what he is saying.

36. The world is so full of a number of things,
I'm sure we should all be as happy as kings.

37. She proclaimed herself ignorant by what she asked.

38. They dined on mince and slices of quince,
Which they ate with a runcible spoon.

39. While reading "Comus" she fell asleep.

40. The service that Spenser rendered our literature by his exquisite sense of harmony is incalculable.

II

Expand the following statements into complex sentences, using as many phrases and dependent clauses as you can in each sentence without losing the meaning of the principal statement:

1. The coming week will be notable.

2. A reception was given for their daughter, Mary Bryce.

3. The hum of an aëroplane attracted our attention.

4. They had come to the edge of the cliff.

5. The stranger sat by the kitchen fire.
6. They beheld a scene of disorder.
7. He would not listen to reason.
8. The guide lived in a secluded spot.
9. His father gave him excellent opportunities.
10. The officers approached the house cautiously.

III

Combine into complex sentences the following groups of words. Decide first upon the most important statement and make this the independent clause. The other statements may be converted into dependent clauses and phrases, according to their importance. In your completed sentences tell how each dependent clause is used, classify it, and name the introductory word.

1. { In the middle of the yard stood a man.
   { The yard had been empty a few minutes before.

2. { What he prides himself on is this.
   { Henry the Eighth broke the head of one of his ancestors.
   { He did it on one of his nocturnal rambles. (Phrase)
   { He did it with his walking stick. (Phrase)

3. { We had been camping out for a week.
   { We hailed a man in a car.
   { Our matches had given out.
   { He was able to supply us with a few.

4. { He lived a wanderer and a fugitive in his native land.
   { He had heroic qualities.
   { These would have graced a civilized warrior.
   { These would have rendered him the theme of the poet and the
   {   historian.

5. { My father failed in business.
   { My family came to America.
   { I was then six years old.

6. { There were two or three pretty faces among the women.
   { The keen air of a frosty morning had given them a bright-
   {   red tint.

7. {
The dog would look fondly up into his master's face.
The dog lay stretched at his feet.
He lazily shifted his position.
}

8. {
He found their attention gradually diverted to other talk and other subjects. (Phrase)
He concluded his remarks in an undertone to a fat-headed old gentleman.
The old gentleman sat next him.
}

9. {
Everybody had his tale of engine troubles.
We sat around the dull lamp in the cabin.
All hoped for better roads for the rest of the journey.
}

10. {
He was accompanied by the redoubtable Bantam.
He was a little rat of a pony. (Phrase)
He had a shaggy mane. (Phrase)
He stood dozing by the roadside.
He was unmindful of his approaching fate. (Phrase)
}

IV

In Chapter X review all the rules for the use of the comma, the semicolon, and the colon. Explain all the punctuation found in the sentences in Exercise I above. Examine your own sentences in Exercise II and Exercise III to see whether they are correctly punctuated. Explain your punctuation of each sentence.

113. The compound-complex sentence. A compound-complex sentence consists of two or more independent clauses and at least one dependent clause. With the increase of our ideas and the development of our powers of expression we may often find the compound-complex sentence useful. We should not form the habit, however, of using long and involved compound-complex sentences, for by so doing we are likely to write in a heavy, cumbersome style and fail to make our meaning altogether clear. The following is a typical compound-complex sentence:

Our friends, who had preceded us, promised that they would meet us; but when we arrived at the station, they were nowhere to be seen.

In our use of the compound-complex sentence we should not overload it with too many dependent clauses; otherwise the main statements may be obscured by the involved structure.

As a basis for the study of sentence variety select twelve fairly long paragraphs (not conversation) from four reputable modern writers. Choose three paragraphs from each author and count the number of simple, compound, complex, and compound-complex sentences in each paragraph. Next, find the total number of each kind of sentence used by each writer. Lastly, find the total number of each kind of sentence used by all four writers. Do you find as many compound and compound-complex sentences as simple and complex sentences? Do you find as many complex sentences as simple sentences? What does this exercise indicate as to the practice of these four writers?

114. Kinds of sentences according to use. According to their use, sentences are *declarative, interrogative, imperative,* and *exclamatory.*

A *declarative* sentence makes an assertion or statement.

> A person is known by the company he keeps.

An *interrogative* sentence asks a question.

> Are you interested in debating?

An *imperative* sentence states a command.

> Make as many persons happy as you can.

An *exclamatory* sentence is a declarative, interrogative, or imperative sentence uttered under the influence of strong feeling.

1. "Peace has been declared!" they shouted.
2. "How could you make such a mistake!" she cried.

Clauses beginning with *how* or *what* may be used in exclamations, the principal verb often being implied. Such clauses are followed by the exclamation point.

> 1. [See] What a blunder you have made!
> 2. How dearly you have paid for your ride!
> 3. What a beautiful rose that is!

115. Phrases and dependent clauses incorrectly used as sentences. A sentence, as we have learned, is the expression of a *complete* thought in words. Before any group of words can express a thought it must have both a subject and a predicate. A phrase does not contain both a subject and a predicate; therefore it cannot express a thought, and for this reason cannot be used as a sentence.

A dependent clause, though it has a subject and a predicate, cannot express a *complete* thought, for its meaning is dependent upon its relationship to the thought expressed by the independent clause with which it is used. Without its independent clause the dependent clause has no definite meaning. For this reason a dependent clause cannot be used as a sentence.

We should at all times avoid writing a phrase or a dependent clause as a sentence, for each is merely a fragment of a sentence (see section 170).

EXERCISE

In the following exercise classify each group of words as (1) a phrase, (2) a dependent clause, or (3) a sentence. Make a sentence in which you correctly use each phrase and each dependent clause.

1. That we had taken him by surprise was evident.
2. When we rose the next morning, having slept well.
3. Through no fault of his.
4. Leaving the old inn at sunrise and traveling in an easterly direction all day.
5. What a perfect day it was!

6. That being our only hope.

7. Whom he said he had met the year before.

8. Though the whole experience left no pleasant memory.

9. If that is true and if conditions are as favorable as you have been informed.

10. To relieve his suffering somewhat.

11. To make such a scene was not my intention.

12. While the gayety was at its height.

13. Not that he intended to act dishonestly.

14. The hare limped trembling through the frozen grass.

15. Wherever he happened to find anyone to listen to his story.

16. When Earth's last picture is painted.

17. Not failure, but low aim, is crime.

18. One impulse from a vernal wood.

19. That a wise man may be taught by a fool.

20. During his entire career of more than forty years of public service.

21. In the very heart of one of the most populous cities of the world.

22. Repeatedly the old guide had warned them of the danger.

23. Some of us call it autumn, and others call it God.

24. Gazing from the dizzy height as if entranced.

25. While through all the silent house she wandered.

26. Because I distinctly remember seeing such a man leave the bank as I entered.

27. Standing on tiptoe and reaching high with both hands as if longing to possess one of the bright stars.

28. In much less time than it takes to tell of the weird adventure.

29. Thus arriving on time in spite of the delay.

30. And much more interesting, I think.

31. In order to keep my appointment with him.

32. Unimpressed by all that he had witnessed and heedless of our counsel.

33. A book that I have greatly enjoyed reading and re-reading.

34. Whose place it will be difficult to fill.

116. Summary. A sentence is the expression of a complete thought in words.

Classified according to their form, sentences are simple, compound, complex, and compound-complex.

A simple sentence is a sentence that contains but one subject and one predicate. A simple sentence may, however, have a compound subject, a compound predicate, or a compound subject and a compound predicate; but it must not contain more than one independent proposition.

A simple sentence may contain any number of phrases. A phrase is a group of closely related words that does not contain a subject and a predicate.

According to form, phrases are classified as follows: (1) prepositional phrases, (2) participial phrases, (3) infinitive phrases, and (4) gerund (or verbal-noun) phrases.

According to use, phrases are classified as follows: (1) noun phrases, (2) adjective phrases, (3) adverbial phrases, (4) verb phrases, and (5) independent phrases.

A compound sentence consists of two or more simple sentences that are related to each other in thought. As a member of a compound sentence each simple sentence is called an independent clause.

The six principal relationships between the clauses of the compound sentence are as follows: (1) continuation or repetition of the thought, (2) contrast, (3) alternation, (4) correlation, (5) consequence or inference, and (6) reason.

We should avoid overworking the compound sentence, and should exercise care in the choice of the proper connective in each case (if a connective is needed).

A complex sentence consists of one independent clause and one or more dependent clauses.

A clause that has no definite meaning except when it is used in relation to some word or words in an independent clause is called a dependent clause.

According to their use in the sentence, dependent clauses may be classified as (1) noun clauses, (2) adjective clauses, and (3) adverbial clauses.

A noun clause performs the function of a noun. The principal constructions of noun clauses are the following: (1) subject of a verb, (2) direct object of a verb, (3) indirect object of a verb, (4) object of a preposition, (5) in apposition, (6) predicate nominative, and (7) predicate objective.

An adjective clause performs the function of an adjective. It may modify a noun or a pronoun in two ways: (1) restrictively and (2) nonrestrictively.

An adjective clause that is used restrictively requires no punctuation, but one that is used nonrestrictively should be set off from the rest of the sentence by a comma and a mark of end punctuation or by commas.

An adverbial clause performs the function of an adverb. It may stand in any one of the following relationships to the independent clause: (1) time, (2) place, (3) manner, (4) condition, (5) cause, (6) purpose, (7) result, (8) degree or comparison, and (9) concession.

A compound-complex sentence consists of two or more independent clauses and at least one dependent clause. We should practice using simple and complex sentences, and should use compound and compound-complex sentences sparingly.

Classified according to use, sentences are declarative, interrogative, imperative, and exclamatory.

Since a sentence is the expression of a complete thought in words, *a phrase or a dependent clause, which is nothing more than a fragment of a sentence, should never be written as a sentence.*

CHAPTER IX

THE SENTENCE RHETORICALLY CONSIDERED

117. Kinds of sentences. Rhetorically considered, sentences are classified as *loose, periodic,* and *balanced,* according to their construction.

A *loose* sentence is one that may be brought to a grammatical close before the end is reached.

He was sitting before the fire in a large armchair when we entered.

In this sentence the meaning is clear if we stop after *fire* or after *armchair*. Simple and complex sentences are loose or periodic, according to their order of arrangement. Every compound sentence, because of its form, is loose.

A *periodic* sentence is one that is not grammatically complete until the end is reached.

Having passed the house every day for two years, and knowing that the man was a cripple, I could not believe what the next-door neighbor told me.

This sentence is so constructed that it is not grammatically complete at any point before the period. Most simple and complex loose sentences may be made periodic by transposing adverbial phrases and clauses to the beginning of the sentence.

A *balanced* sentence is one in which the parts are alike, in that they are constructed according to the same pattern.

1. To err is human; to forgive, divine.
2. Helen is a girl from the country; Marian is a girl from the city.
3. It is the age that forms the man, not the man that forms the age.
4. On the one hand, the dangers are real; on the other hand, the benefits are great.

Here subject balances subject, and predicate balances predicate. In a balanced sentence the clauses are similar in form but are usually contrasted in meaning.

118. Effect of different kinds of sentences.   Our natural tendency is to write loose sentences, which in an easy, somewhat familiar style may be quite appropriate. The use of a large number of such sentences in formal writing, however, gives an impression of carelessness and lack of finish. Periodic sentences add strength and dignity to our writing, but if used exclusively they make the style stiff and formal. Balanced sentences are not usually suitable in narration or in description, but are well adapted to expository and argumentative writing in which persons, things, or ideas are contrasted. The following balanced sentences from Dr. Johnson's essay "The Life of Pope" illustrate this latter use:

The style of Dryden is capricious and varied; that of Pope is cautious and uniform. Dryden observes the motions of his own mind; Pope constrains his mind to his own rules of composition. Dryden is sometimes vehement and rapid; Pope is always smooth, uniform, and gentle. Dryden's page is a natural field, rising into inequalities, and diversified by the varied exuberance of abundant vegetation; Pope's is a velvet lawn, shaven by the scythe and leveled by the roller.

Short sentences give animation to the style, but a constant use of them becomes tiresome and detracts from smoothness of expression. The chief merit of the long sentence is that it brings a large number of related particulars into view and shows their relations more clearly or more economically than would several short sentences. The mind, however, tires of any one style of construction if it be carried to excess. Variety is obtained by the judicious use of loose and periodic, long and short, sentences.

EXERCISES

I

Classify the following sentences according to their grammatical and rhetorical construction, and, when possible, change the loose sentences to the periodic form:

1. The management thought best to dismiss the audience, although there was no immediate danger.

2. A tennis tournament will be held at the Beachcroft Country Club on May 28 and 29, under the auspices of the Allston Athletic Association.

3. The great burdens he had borne, the terrible anxieties and perplexities that had disturbed his life, and the peaceful scenes he had forever left behind swept across his memory.

4. The artist achieves excellent pictorial results in each of these groups, including from five to fifteen persons each.

5. He paced up and down the walk, forgetful of everything around him and intent only on some object that absorbed his mind, his hands behind him, his hat and coat off, and his tall form bent forward.

6. The leaves of the eucalyptus trees around the Plaza drooped motionless, limp and relaxed under the scorching, searching blaze.

7. He who has shared, with sympathy, the recounted experience of another man is thereby the more fitted to share in the actual lives of his fellows, and, knowing mankind better, is thereby more human.

8. If, in the future, an age of general well-being is to arrive, its children will turn, as all men who have the opportunity must, to what is best in human art — to the literature of Greece.

9. What his violins were to Stradivarius, and his frescoes to Leonardo, and his campaigns to Napoleon, that was his history to Macaulay.

10. My friends speak flattery; my enemies speak truth.

11. The other day, as I walked through the meadow, it seemed to me that the atmosphere had never been so full of fragrance before.

12. At long intervals, from out the sheltering branches of elm tree or of maple, rose the dull-red chimneys of a farmhouse, whose doorways and windows were half hidden by blossoming lilacs and syringa bushes; and again, on some green sea meadow or rocky headland, stood out the rough, gray stone walls of a rich man's summer home.

II

Express in a well-constructed periodic or loose sentence the thought contained in each of the following groups of sentences. Note whether you have made a simple, a complex, a compound, or a compound-complex sentence.

1. The farmer's life has been made easier of late years. The telephone keeps him in touch with his neighbors. The rural delivery brings him his daily paper. The gasoline engine does a great deal of his work. The automobile carries him quickly to town.

2. Nature is economical. No particle of matter is ever destroyed, though it undergoes numerous changes in form and in combination. Animals furnish plants carbon dioxide as food. Plants, in return, supply animals with vegetable food and with oxygen to breathe.

3. Mr. Edison and Mr. Burbank are two of the greatest benefactors of mankind. Consider the innumerable conveniences that we owe to Mr. Edison. Our gardens, our orchards, and our dining-tables give evidence of Mr. Burbank's wonderful work. In the Middle Ages each of these men might have been looked upon as a magician.

4. Fishing from a kite has two advantages. The fisherman may stand on shore while his bait is dropped far out at sea. There is no shadow to frighten timid fish.

5. Modern civilization is rapidly recognizing the equal rights of men and women. Both have the same educational advantages. They are rapidly becoming politically equal. Industrially women compete successfully with men.

III

Explain the punctuation of all sentences in Exercise I above.

IV

Explain the punctuation of the five sentences that you made in Exercise II above.

119. The essentials of a sentence.   The four essentials of a sentence are unity, coherence, emphasis, and euphony.

120. Unity. Since the sentence is the expression of a single complete thought, the first essential of the sentence is that it shall be a unit and show this oneness of thought.

1. A sentence violates the principle of unity if it contains too much. That is to say, if thoughts that are not closely enough related to form properly one sentence are crowded into a sentence and carelessly linked together by means of such conjunctions as *and* and *but*, unity is violated.

As we were driving out into the country yesterday, we met a young man wearing a golf suit, and we passed a car that was broken down, and on our way home we stopped at Mr. Beck's to get some flowers and fresh vegetables.

Although each clause has the same subject, the sentence as a whole is not a unit, because it combines ideas which are not closely related. The sentence in its present form contains three sentences:

As we were driving out into the country yesterday, we met a young man wearing a golf suit. Later we passed a car that was broken down. On our way home we stopped at Mr. Beck's to get some flowers and fresh vegetables.

To possess unity, then, a sentence must not contain unrelated ideas.

2. A sentence violates the principle of unity if it contains too little. Such violations occur whenever a simple, a complex, or a compound sentence is improperly written as two separate sentences. The three examples that follow illustrate this fault.

1. He walked home with me. Having met me at the door of the office. (Simple sentence)

2. We won the election. Though the opposition was strong. (Complex sentence)

3. I was late this morning. But I will be on time hereafter. (Compound sentence)

The phrase "having met me at the door of the office," and the dependent clause "though the opposition was strong," are fragments of sentences. They have no definite meaning except in relation to their respective independent clauses. The independent clause "but I will be on time hereafter" is related by contrast to the preceding independent clause and, combined with it, constitutes a single unified sentence. The three sentences should read:

> He walked home with me, having met me at the door of the office.
> We won the election, though the opposition was strong.
> I was late this morning, but I will be on time hereafter.

Avoid setting off as separate sentences such fragments of sentences as phrases and dependent clauses. Do not write as distinct simple sentences independent clauses that should be united to form one compound sentence. (See sections 115 and 170.)

3. A sentence violates unity if the relationship between its parts is not correctly indicated (see section 172).

Even when related ideas are grouped together in a sentence, care should be taken to show this relation clearly. This may often be accomplished by the proper use of connectives and by intelligent punctuation.

> I am not surprised that their team lost the game, they were poorly trained and were overconfident.

This sentence may be unified in two ways:

> I am not surprised that their team lost the game, for they were poorly trained and were overconfident.
> I am not surprised that their team lost the game; they were poorly trained and were overconfident.

In the original sentence a comma is used where we should expect a period or a semicolon. This misuse of the comma is called the *comma fault* or *comma splice*. It should be carefully avoided. (For a discussion of the comma fault see section 171.)

In a compound sentence, unity is often obscured through the careless choice of connectives.

Helen went to college, and Irene became a motion-picture actress.

Here the relation between the two independent clauses seems to be contrast, not mere addition. The sentence should therefore read:

Helen went to college, *but* Irene became a motion-picture actress.

Likewise, in a complex sentence, unity is frequently violated through lack of care in choosing connectives.

The patient's condition continued to grow worse, when he was given every attention.

Here the relation of the dependent to the independent clause appears to be concession, not time. The unified sentence should read:

The patient's condition continued to grow worse, *though* he was given every attention.

Often a compound sentence contains in one of its clauses a statement which should be made subordinate.

A well-dressed man admitted us to the house, and we afterward learned that he was the thief.

The unity of the sentence may be improved by converting it into a complex sentence, with the second member expressed as a subordinate clause.

A well-dressed man, who we afterward learned was the thief, admitted us to the house.

Sometimes a complex sentence contains in a subordinate clause a statement which should be made coördinate with the independent clause.

I employed a detective, by whose aid I recovered the ring.

A more unified sentence results if the compound form is used.

I employed a detective, and by his aid I recovered the ring.

4. Unity in the sentence is frequently violated by change of the point of view (see section 174).

The *vessel* made for the shore, and the *passengers* soon crowded into the boats, and the *beach* was reached in safety, and the *inhabitants* of the island received them with the utmost kindness.

Because of this frequent change of subject the mind travels in quick succession from the *vessel* to the *passengers*, and then to the *beach* and the *inhabitants*. A confusion of ideas results. This may be avoided by selecting one point of view, and by choosing one principal clause, to which the others may be subordinated as phrases and dependent clauses. The sentence then reads:

The vessel having made for the shore, the *passengers* soon crowded into the boats and safely reached the beach, where *they* were received with the utmost kindness by the inhabitants of the island.

Now there is one point of view, that of the passengers. The first independent clause in the original sentence has been subordinated as a phrase, and the final independent clause has been made dependent. The result is a well-unified complex sentence.

EXERCISE

Correct the following sentences to secure unity of thought and of form:

1. His little girl had been missing for two days, and the general belief was that the Indians had stolen her, and such proved to be the case.

2. Somebody had provided native fruits, and we had many other delicacies.

3. These birds fly swiftly and mostly by day, and their food consists of seeds and berries and small shellfish.

4. I asked him the direction to the park, and he could not tell me.

5. Everybody made a rush for the small cold-drink stand, and the proprietor soon sold out his entire stock.

6. His past life was investigated, and he was allowed to become a member of the order.

7. I could hear the sound of motors humming far up in the night sky, and they made me feel uncomfortable.

8. By doing this the bottle gets heated round the stopper, and if a thing is heated it expands.

9. He has no ambition, his father was indolent, he let the boy do as he pleased.

10. The shore of this island was rocky, and after a time we found a place suitable for landing and began preparations for our dinner.

11. The people of this island are lazy, and they steal all they can, and the state takes no care of them whatever.

12. Carving is an important acquisition in the routine of daily life, and all should try to acquire the ability to do it well.

13. While he is insane, he appears harmless.

14. The houses were mere shanties, and rags were stuffed in the cracks and holes.

15. In the winter we live in the city. While in the summer we go to the country.

16. They opened the doors for him to enter, and in a moment I heard them close again with a dull, vibrating sound, and then all became silent once more.

17. I read the book hurriedly, the latter part of which did not interest me at all.

18. The road was macadamized only two years ago, and now it is full of holes.

19. Grouped around him sat the fair maidens, and below in the arena all was ready for the sport.

20. There were aircraft of all descriptions round us, and I enjoyed watching them.

21. We reached home at nine o'clock. Saving three hours by making the trip in an automobile.

22. I strongly believe that domestic science should be taught in every high school, and the day is not far distant when every high school will offer courses in it.

23. My aunt enjoys playing with children, but she is very old.

24. He moved to this state when my father was a boy, and there were very few schools in the country then, so my brothers and I were sent to school in town, but conditions have now improved.

25. My uncle left home when I was three years old. But I do not remember him.

121. Coherence.   A second essential of the sentence requires that the grammatical construction and the proper relationship of words in the sentence be made unmistakably clear.

1. Coherence is violated when a word, a phrase, or a clause is so placed that it appears to modify the wrong word in the sentence.

Such words as *nearly, not,* and *only* should be carefully placed with respect to the word that each is intended to modify. Observe the changes in meaning that result from shifting the position of these words in the following sentences:

1. I caught *nearly* a hundred fish.
2. I *nearly* caught a hundred fish.
3. All men are *not* criminals.
4. *Not* all men are criminals.
5. *Only* I saw him speak to her.
6. I *only* saw him speak to her.
7. I saw *only* him speak to her.
8. I saw him *only* speak to her.
9. I saw him speak to her *only*.

Coherence is sometimes violated by the careless placing of the two members of correlative connectives, such as *both . . . and, either . . . or, neither . . . nor, not only . . . but also, on the one hand . . . on the other hand*. The correlatives should be placed immediately before the words that they connect. The words connected should always be in the same construction. The sentences that follow show the connectives properly placed:

1. I not only saw him but heard him also.
2. He came neither by train nor by automobile.

Modifying phrases should be placed next to the words that they modify.

> I sat watching the men play golf *on the front porch.*

Here the phrase is too far separated from the word it modifies. Transpose the phrase, and the sentence becomes coherent:

> I sat on the front porch watching the men play golf.

A relative clause should be placed as near as possible to the word that it modifies.

> He carried a bag of peanuts in his hat, *which he fed to the elephants.*

The sentence slightly rearranged is coherent:

> In his hat he carried a bag of peanuts, which he fed to the elephants.

Sometimes a phrase or a clause is, through carelessness, so placed in the sentence that it may be construed with what has preceded or with what follows. This arrangement is called the *squinting construction.*

> 1. He said *in spite of protest* he would go.
> 2. Tell my friend, *if she is at home*, I will call to see her.

To make the meaning clear, we may write these sentences in either of the following versions:

> 1. { In spite of protest he said he would go.
>   { He said he would go in spite of protest.
> 2. { If my friend is at home, tell her I will call to see her.
>   { Tell my friend I will call to see her if she is at home.

Coherence demands, therefore, that all words, phrases, and clauses be placed as near as possible to the word or words which they modify.

2. Coherence is often violated by the incorrect reference of participial phrases, verbal-noun phrases, infinitive phrases, and elliptical clauses (see page 477 and sections 159, 160, and 161).

A participial phrase, a verbal-noun phrase, an infinitive phrase, or an elliptical clause introducing a sentence must *logically* refer to the agent of the action expressed. As a rule, the word denoting the agent of the action is the subject of the principal verb. The reference of the italicized expression in each of the following sentences is therefore incorrect:

Listening intently, a noise was heard.
Upon entering the room, no one was seen.
To catch the ghost, a trap was devised.
While setting the trap, the door opened noiselessly.

Each sentence becomes coherent when the word denoting the agent of the action is made the subject of the principal verb.

Listening intently, my aunt heard a noise.
Upon entering the room, we saw no one.
To catch the ghost, she devised a trap.
While setting the trap, she saw the door open noiselessly.

Coherence requires, then, that each participial phrase, verbal-noun phrase, infinitive phrase, or elliptical clause be made to refer logically to a *particular* and *definitely expressed* antecedent contained in the sentence.

3. Coherence is frequently violated by the incorrect reference of pronouns (see section 150).

1. I may go to the lecture, for *he* is my chum's uncle.
2. We went trout-fishing, but caught only two of *them*.
3. He struck him as *he* passed *him*.
4. I saw a bird in a beautiful cage, *which* I bought.
5. Mrs. Ward told Mrs. Gray that *her* children were playing in *her* flower bed.

In the first two sentences the pronouns have no definite antecedents expressed. In the last three the pronouns may refer to two antecedents, and for this reason the reference is ambiguous. All five sentences may be made coherent by some such reconstruction as the following:

1. I may go to the lecture, for the speaker is my chum's uncle.
2. We went trout-fishing, but caught only two trout.
3. Mr. Hoyt struck the burglar as the latter passed him.
4. In a beautiful cage I saw a bird, which I bought.
5. Mrs. Ward said to Mrs. Gray, "Your children are playing in my flower bed."

Coherence demands, therefore, that every pronoun be given a *particular* and *definitely expressed* antecedent.

4. Coherence is violated when the grammatical construction is changed after a coördinate conjunction. To secure coherence, then, see that the construction that follows a coördinate conjunction is identical with the construction that precedes it.

1. This is a good book, *and which I advise you to read.*
2. He said that he would come if he could, *but not to look for him.*

In the first sentence *and* connects an independent clause and a dependent clause. In the second, *but* joins a dependent clause and an infinitive phrase. Corrected, the sentences read:

1. { This is a good book, and I advise you to read it.
   { This is a good book, which I advise you to read.
2. He said that he would come if he could, but that we should not look for him.

The coherence of a sentence is better if the same voice of the main verb is used throughout the sentence.

I *wrote* to him, but my letter *was* not *answered.*

The sentence may be improved in either of two ways:

1. I wrote to him, but he did not answer my letter.
2. I wrote to him, but I received no answer to my letter.

MAN'S CONQUEST OVER NATURE

From Caldwell and Eikenberry's "Elements of General Science"

The coherence of a sentence may often be improved by arranging phrases or clauses in a series in parallel construction (see section 173). In the balanced sentence the independent clauses are thus arranged. Phrases or dependent clauses may sometimes be advantageously placed in parallel construction. The following sentences are illustrations:

1. *On the land, on the sea, in the air,* and *under the water* there were engines of warfare.

2. A man *who provides well for his family, who maintains an honest public record,* and *who contributes freely to civic improvement* is an asset in any community.

Coherence requires, then, that the construction that follows a coördinate conjunction be the same as that which precedes it.

EXERCISES

I

Correct the following sentences so that they will have the same construction before and after coördinate conjunctions. Notice the voice of the verbs.

1. It was some time before he could get into the regular track of gossip, nor could the strange events be comprehended by him.

2. The children promised to be careful and that they would come home early.

3. We accepted Carter's promise in good faith and believing him to be honest.

4. Nora is a well-trained, industrious maid, and who rarely asks for an afternoon off.

5. There were never more mischievous twins than Betty and Billy; the former to think up pranks, and they both carry them out.

6. I got your letter Thursday, but the package you mentioned has not been received.

7. Fred is energetic, and who is very reliable.

8. We attended the game, but not expecting that our team would be defeated.

II

In the following exercise (1) point out the error in each sentence and (2) correct the sentence to secure coherence of thought and of form:

1. The engines became overheated, and after talking the matter over they decided to camp where they were.

2. We put on our bathing-suits, and Helen, which is my cousin's name, ran down to the water first.

3. We all decided that the race, at any rate, had served the purpose.

4. Having been gone for six days, he sent out a man to look for him, but he could not find him.

5. All books are not worth reading.

6. Grandfather is very active for his years, and is proud of it.

7. We had to walk back to the farmhouse, drenched with rain, which was nearly half a mile away.

8. Two persons were only saved by sliding down a conductor pipe.

9. Having shown him his bedroom, he retired.

10. And thus the son the fervent sire addressed.

11. Glancing out of the window of my study, an unusual sight attracted my attention.

12. Saturday all of us went nutting, but we found only about a peck of them.

13. Being the youngest child, mother hated to see me leave home.

14. My watch is either fast or your clock is slow.

15. You look as if you were frightened in that picture.

16. He told us to get his football suit, and that he should not be home till evening.

17. Uncle David telephoned Mr. Joyce that his sheep were in his pasture.

18. Passengers are warned not to alight from the car while moving.

19. When nine years old, my grandmother came to live with us.

20. Orville nearly made a hundred dollars last summer.

21. I promised her, when leaving, I would tell her.

22. He showed us pictures of the menagerie in the auditorium.

23. Being in a cage, I did not feel afraid of the lion.

24. Some women have a habit of powdering their noses, no matter where they are, and seeming to enjoy it.

122. Emphasis. Emphasis, the third essential of the sentence, requires an arrangement of words that brings into prominence the central idea and subordinates the minor details.

1. Ideas placed at the beginning or at the end of a sentence receive the greatest emphasis.

> Many a man has sacrificed his life for wealth, it is true.

As the sentence now stands, the end is weak. Rearrangement improves the emphasis:

> Many a man has sacrificed his life, it is true, for wealth.
> Many a man, it is true, has sacrificed his life for wealth.

By placing the unimportant clause "it is true" in an unemphatic position we may improve the force of the sentence.

Words placed out of their natural order in a sentence become more emphatic. Note the improvement effected, in the sentence given above, by transposing the phrase *for wealth* to the beginning of the sentence:

> For wealth many a man, it is true, has sacrificed his life.

The sentence now has proper emphasis.

The following sentences are examples of emphasis thus secured:

1. *Back* surged the crowd.
2. *By the fire* he sat all the morning.
3. *Last of all* marched the clown.
4. *"Fire!"* he shouted.
5. *Great* is the influence of money.
6. *To him* belongs the credit for my rescue.

Transposing words and phrases out of their natural order and inverting the entire sentence are both useful devices for obtaining emphasis.

A periodic sentence is, by its very nature, more emphatic than a loose sentence. Compare the two versions of the following sentence:

A mysterious silence reigned about the old ruin. (Loose)
About the old ruin a mysterious silence reigned. (Periodic)

Such a periodic sentence as this may frequently be rendered even more emphatic by inversion:

About the old ruin reigned a mysterious silence.

2. Ideas are often made emphatic by contrast or antithesis.

1. Worth makes the man, and want of it the fellow.
2. Man is finite; God is infinite.
3. Education may be acquired; culture is innate.
4. The spirit is willing, but the flesh is weak.
5. I judge by actions, not mere words.

In such expressions of contrast the balanced sentence is effective.

3. Emphasis may be gained by the use of climax. That is, coördinate words, phrases, and clauses are arranged in the order of their increasing importance.

Friends, life itself, reputation, social position, had no longer any attraction for him.

In this sentence the ideas are not arranged in the order of their importance. The sentence should read:

Social position, friends, reputation, life itself, had no longer any attraction for him.

4. Emphasis, as well as unity (see section 120, rule 3), may be secured by putting subordinate thoughts in dependent clauses. This leaves the independent clause for the main thought.

1. My train was late, and I missed my class.
2. When Watt observed the power of steam, he was helping his wife prepare breakfast.

Proper subordination renders both of these sentences emphatic:

1. Because my train was late, I missed my class.
2. While helping his wife prepare breakfast, Watt observed the power of steam.

5. Emphasis is enhanced by economy in words. If words do not add to the meaning of a sentence, they make it less effective and should be omitted.

1. All was darkness, and not a ray of light could be seen.
2. He had asked him once, and he refused to repeat the question again.

The first sentence is an example of *tautology*, or repetition of the thought; the second is an example of *redundancy*, or the use of words not necessary to the sense. The following sentences are more emphatic:

1. All was darkness.
2. He refused to repeat the question.

6. Sentences in the active voice are more emphatic than those in the passive.

Your invitation was received by me.

This sentence is much less forceful than the active version:

I received your invitation.

EXERCISE

In the following exercise show in what respect each sentence is lacking in emphasis, and improve the emphasis by reconstructing the sentence:

1. In this remote and secluded town she lived apart and unknown for some time.
2. A man was killed by an automobile while crossing the street yesterday.
3. He saw before him ruin, defeat, disaster, and broken health.

4. Summer is warm, but extremely pleasant; while winter brings dark, gloomy days and bitter cold.

5. While the storm was raging, a tree was struck by a flash of lightning, which was the only flash seen during the storm, and which looked like a ball of fire.

6. The book was expensive, so I could not buy it.

7. He seems to enjoy the universal esteem of all men.

8. King Arthur knew that he was dying and called his last true knight, Sir Bedivere, to him.

9. Modred, the treacherous knight, had been planning to capture King Arthur's kingdom for some time.

10. The next day King Arthur told how he had seen flames playing about the castle walls the previous evening.

11. On account of her great work among the poor, Guinevere was made abbess at the death of her predecessor.

12. It is a great privilege to assemble and meet together.

13. While the thief looted the house, the family slept.

14. The gate is wide and the way is broad that leads to destruction.

15. Insects, men, beasts, all are creatures of God's hand.

16. It was once believed that men reach their decisions by reasoning and that decisions are made by women through intuition.

17. We returned back home weary and exhausted.

18. Some people seem to think that civilization is a curse, which is not true at all.

19. He gazed longingly at the fruit.

20. Two of Mrs. Judson's friends arrived unexpectedly, and I knew she did not have room for all of us, so I made preparations to come home, but she would not let me.

21. Be that as it may, you should have refused to remain, since you knew what inconvenience you were causing.

22. A preposition is an unemphatic word to end a sentence with.

23. She is a poor widow woman without any money or property.

24. I was assured by the manager that the seats had been reserved.

123. Euphony. The fourth essential of the sentence is euphony. A sentence should be constructed with due regard to its pleasing effect on the ear, though care should be taken not to sacrifice sense to sound.

1. Euphony is secured by the rhythmical phrasing of the sentence. That is, words, phrases, and clauses should be so skillfully arranged that the harmonious flow of sounds adds to our enjoyment of the sentence. Oral reading in standard prose and observant practice in phrasing our own thoughts will help us to cultivate a sense of rhythm. The following passages illustrate harmonious phrasing:

1. During the whole of a dark, dull, and soundless day in the autumn of the year, when the clouds hung oppressively low in the heavens, I had been passing alone, on horseback, through a singularly dreary tract of country; and at length found myself, as the shades of the evening drew on, within view of the melancholy House of Usher.—POE, "The Fall of the House of Usher"

2. O toiling hands of mortals! O unwearied feet, traveling ye know not whither! Soon, soon, it seems to you, you must come forth on some conspicuous hilltop, and but a little way further, against the setting sun, descry the spires of El Dorado. Little do ye know your own blessedness; for to travel hopefully is a better thing than to arrive, and the true success is to labor.—STEVENSON, "El Dorado"[1]

2. The euphony of a sentence is improved by avoiding the careless repetition of a word at brief intervals. Compare the two sentences given below, and note the improvement in the second sentence:

1. He ordered the captain to order the soldiers to preserve good order.
2. He directed the captain to see that the soldiers preserved good order.

The study of reputable English authors shows, however, that skillful repetition may be employed to good effect.

The poet is a heroic figure, belonging to all ages; whom all ages possess, when once he is produced; whom the newest age as the oldest may produce, and will produce, always when Nature pleases.

[1] Used by permission of Charles Scribner's Sons, publishers.

3. The euphony of a sentence is enhanced by avoiding the repetition of like sounds.

I cannot understand how a man of his standing can take such a stand on this matter.

A little care in the choice of words overcomes this monotony.

I cannot understand how a person of his reputation can hold such views on this matter.

Rime in prose should always be avoided. Compare these two sentences:

1. He was suffering, he said, from a cold in his head.
2. He was suffering, he told me, from a cold in his head.

EXERCISE

In the following exercise (1) point out the error in each sentence and (2) correct the sentence to improve the euphony:

1. Did you ever see such a series of sibilant sounds!
2. In India innocent infants are thrown into the Ganges.
3. Billy ran away, but he could not stay.
4. One cannot imagine what a monotonous being one becomes if one is forced to associate constantly with oneself.
5. She said,—loudly enough for those near to hear, I fear,—"What a fright!"
6. Looking up, Tom Sawyer saw a stranger approaching of strange appearance. "Good morning," said the stranger.
7. It seemed to us that we had never seen such scenes before.
8. Next day, in walked John Ray to say he would pay us on the first of May.
9. I am glad the dog was not mad.
10. The annual agricultural exhibit will have special interest this year, especially for farmers.
11. The superfluity and profusion of his allusions is confusing.
12. To fly through the sky at night is my delight.

13. I will sign the petition on one condition.

14. The civilization of every nation depends on education.

15. The moment the movement is mastered, the fingers take care of the rest.

REVIEW EXERCISE

In the following exercise (1) point out all errors and (2) correct the sentences according to the rules and principles already stated in this chapter:

1. Hated and persecuted by the people of his time, we cannot help sympathizing with Shylock.

2. While waiting in the court, a noble maiden named Lynette entered and asked the king to give her Sir Lancelot.

3. Mr. Scott shot a burglar as he was entering his house.

4. You may either spend the summer at Colorado Springs or Los Angeles.

5. Although blessed with a loving wife, she was too ambitious for the advancement of her husband.

6. He was kind to his family where some fathers were not.

7. One day when camping it had been threatening rain.

8. We occasionally saw a straw hat here and there.

9. Addison was always remarkable for his wit and humor, but he never returned an insult.

10. The boat pushed off to the shore, but speedily returned with a dying man, who, they affirmed, had been mortally wounded from a blow which had been received from a piece of wood, which they had placed in the boat.

11. In spite of Dr. Johnson's rude, rough ways, and although he ate like a pig, he had many friends.

12. The old veteran was delighted by a visit from his two twin granddaughters.

13. Soon the sky grew dark and then darker; then the thunder began, and soon came the rain, and all nature was refreshed, but we were more than refreshed, as we could find no shelter.

14. He is a man of truth and veracity.

15. Brother and I feared that mother would never recover her health again.

16. Tell me whom you saw and the gossip you heard.

17. When we came along the road, we came to a field where a pleasant-faced peasant was making hay.

18. The leaves of plants radiate the heat which comes to them from the sun with great rapidity.

19. They urged me to go and that I should not worry about their safety.

20. We neither know him nor his family.

21. Do you suppose she would accept this rose?

22. Our team won the meet, but it was a great surprise to everybody.

23. When I found the fountain pen, I was walking along the street.

24. Snow was falling out of doors; within, warmth and cheer prevailed.

25. Being a stranger, the bank refused to pay him the money.

26. No one had heard from him since he left, which seemed strange.

27. Billy had a dollar in his bank and lost it.

28. It is true, I suppose, that he stole the money, anyway.

29. There were two brothers and their sister walking through a wood, and in some way the sister became separated from her brothers and met a man who offered to show her the way.

30. Drinking this, Comus can have no power over them.

31. One day Modred was in the garden, and there he saw Guinevere and Lancelot. However, Lancelot saw him and he soon beat a hasty retreat.

32. His estimate, then, is that the industrious and skilled in all trades are better off or in improved circumstances to an extent that should be admitted, as most decided and perceptible, over their condition and circumstances ten years ago.

33. When morning came, he felt the same.

34. I not only wasted a considerable amount of time, but money also.

35. Aunt Helen saw me coming home in the mirror.

36. Having landed in New York, Mrs. Nelson went to meet her husband.

37. Mr. Nelson is a lawyer, and who has been very successful in his practice.

38. We feared in the morning it would rain.

39. As a clerk, Sims was honest, accurate, prompt, and neat.

40. Mother wrote Aunt Eleanor that Marion was going to visit her.

41. The very things which I needed for the journey which I was going to make with my friends were not to be procured in the little village which was then my home.

42. They were advised to take a lunch with them, which they did.

43. A trout can catch a minnow while it is swimming.

44. I slept till eight o'clock and I tried to get some breakfast, and so I was late at class.

45. The physician came, relieving the patient as soon as he arrived.

46. Tom told Bob that his answer to the problem was wrong.

47. Many persons can only speak one language.

48. Our town is very progressive, and they keep the streets in good condition.

49. I will not promise, even if you insist.

50. Very bad roads were encountered, thus causing the tourists to be a day behind their schedule.

124. Summary. Rhetorically considered, sentences are loose, periodic, and balanced, according to their construction.

A loose sentence is one that may be brought to a grammatical close before the end is reached.

A periodic sentence is one that is not grammatically complete until the end is reached.

A balanced sentence is one in which the parts are alike, in that they are constructed according to the same pattern.

The essentials of a good sentence are unity, coherence, emphasis, and euphony.

Sentence unity is violated in the following ways:

1. By putting too much in the sentence.

2. By putting too little in the sentence.

3. By failure to indicate correctly the relationship between the parts of the sentence.

4. By change of the point of view.

Sentence coherence is violated in the following ways:

1. By placing a word, a phrase, or a clause so that it appears to modify the wrong word in the sentence.

2. By incorrect reference of verbal phrases.

3. By incorrect reference of pronouns.

4. By change in grammatical construction after a coördinate conjunction.

Sentence emphasis is secured in the following ways:

1. By placing at the beginning and at the end of the sentence the words that are to receive the greatest emphasis.

2. By the use of contrast.

3. By the use of climax.

4. By putting subordinate thoughts in dependent clauses.

5. By strict economy in words.

6. By the use of the active voice.

Sentence euphony is improved in the following ways:

1. By rhythmical phrasing.

2. By avoiding the careless repetition of words.

3. By avoiding the repetition of like sounds introduced at brief intervals.

CHAPTER X

PUNCTUATION

125. Value of punctuation. In all our speech we depend upon the modulation and inflection of the voice to help others in correctly interpreting our utterances. In writing we attempt, by means of certain arbitrary signs called *marks of punctuation*, to aid the reader in the accurate interpretation of our thoughts. The chief value of punctuation is to indicate the structure of a sentence and the manner in which it is to be read.

126. Requirements of accurate punctuation. For our guidance the usage of a majority of the best writers regarding punctuation may be stated as more or less definite rules. We should understand at the very beginning, however, that punctuation is a means, not an end in itself. We employ marks of punctuation to render the meaning of a sentence definite and clear; we do not write sentences (except in exercises in punctuation) to illustrate the use of these marks. Furthermore, neither the mere memorizing of the rules of punctuation nor the haphazard insertion of marks of punctuation at points in the sentence where we "feel" that they are needed will enable us to punctuate accurately. *Remember that punctuation incorrectly used misleads, rather than guides, the reader in the proper interpretation of a sentence.*

The intelligent punctuation of a sentence is based upon three fundamental requirements: (*1*) *an exact understanding of what we wish to say;* (*2*) *a thorough knowledge of the grammatical structure of the sentence; and* (*3*) *an accurate knowledge of the rules of punctuation.*

127. General directions for punctuation. 1. After you have studied the rules of punctuation and the illustrations of their use, memorize the rules accurately.

2. Observe the punctuation used by the best modern writers. Pause here and there in your reading to see if you can explain all the punctuation used in the sentences of a paragraph.

3. Punctuate each sentence as you write it.

4. In *all* your writing make accurate punctuation a habit.

5. Marks of punctuation should not be placed at the beginning of a line, but at the end of the line preceding. The only exceptions to this rule are the dash, the parenthesis, the bracket, and the quotation mark.

6. Do not punctuate unnecessarily. *Have a definite reason for every mark of punctuation that you use.*

128. The comma. In general, the comma shows a slight pause in the progress of a sentence, or the omission of words, or the addition of words, phrases, and clauses not absolutely necessary for the complete expression of the thought. The following rules governing the use of the comma should be intelligently applied:

1. *Direct address.* A comma or commas should be used to separate from the rest of the sentence words in direct address.

1. Helen, have you heard the latest news?
2. Please tell me one more story, Uncle John.
3. That one stamp, my friend, cost me a small fortune.

NOTE. The salutation introducing a formal address or preceding a formal letter should be followed by a colon (see section 130, rule 3).

2. *Appositive expressions.* A comma or commas should be used to separate appositive words and phrases from the rest of the sentence, unless the relation is restrictive.

1. Governor Warrington, the principal speaker, delivered a memorable address.

2. Salt, or sodium chloride, is an essential commodity.

3. My friend Mr. Walsh has resigned his position.

NOTE 1. An appositive recognized as a part of a name should not be separated from the rest of the name.

William the Conqueror defeated Harold the Saxon at the battle of Hastings in 1066.

NOTE 2. An appositive word, phrase, or clause that is referred to merely as a word, phrase, or clause should not be separated from the rest of the sentence by a comma or commas.

1. The word *salary* has an interesting history.

2. The phrase *far from the madding crowd* is the title of one of Thomas Hardy's novels.

3. The expression *take it from me* is ordinarily used as slang.

3. *Words, phrases, or clauses in a series.* If in a series of words, phrases, or clauses the conjunctions are omitted except between the last two, each member of the series except the last should be followed by a comma.

1. Robert Louis Stevenson wrote essays, novels, short stories, verses, and dramas.

2. Delegates to the convention are arriving by boat, by train, by automobile, and by aëroplane.

3. The whole town wondered why he had come, what he would do, and when he would return to Washington.

NOTE 1. In a series of adjectives modifying the same noun coördinately, each adjective except the last should be followed by a comma.

Grandmother gave me a quaint, old-fashioned, inlaid chest.

NOTE 2. A comma is used to separate pairs of words or phrases used in a series.

Winter or summer, day or night, cold or hot, wet or dry, he always carries his umbrella and overcoat.

4. *Introductory words, phrases, or clauses.* An introductory *participial* phrase or an introductory clause (unless very short and closely connected with the following clause) should be

separated from the rest of the sentence by a comma. An introductory word or a *prepositional* phrase may be followed by a
comma if clearness demands its use.

1. Having arrived ahead of time, we waited for our friends.
2. Wearied by his life in London, Soames went to live in Italy.
3. The game having ended, we returned home.
4. When the whistle sounded, the game began.
5. Though he has enjoyed exceptional opportunities, he has made
very little use of them.
6. What motive she could have had for acting in this way, no one
could guess.
7. Now, what does he know about chemical engineering?
8. In the presence of Claudia, Bryson always lost his power of speech.

NOTE. *Yes* and *no* and such words as *indeed*, *still*, *fortunately*, and
similar words, when used to introduce a sentence or a clause, should
always be followed by a comma.

1. Yes, the game Saturday will be a hard fight.
2. Indeed, he is an admirable old character.

5. *Parenthetical expressions.* Commas should be used to
set off words, phrases, or clauses that interrupt the thought or
the grammatical order of a sentence. Some of the more common parenthetical expressions are *moreover, however, furthermore, in fact, for example, for instance, of course, no doubt, in
short, it is true, I suppose, it is said.*

1. I am greatly surprised, moreover, that my letter did not reach you
before you left.
2. Consider, for instance, this aspect of the question.
3. Yours is a legitimate, though somewhat unusual, excuse.
4. The day, cold as it was, proved ideal for the game.
5. Old Jasper, you may be sure, knows where the key is kept.

6. *Nonrestrictive phrases and clauses.* A comma or commas
should be used to set off a nonrestrictive phrase or clause from
the rest of the sentence. A phrase or a clause which, though

loosely a modifier of some word, may be left out without affecting the meaning of the rest of the sentence is called *nonrestrictive*.

1. His father, wearied by the long journey, lay down to rest.
2. In a few words our principal introduced Dr. Allison, who rose and addressed the student body.
3. My chum lent me his copy of "The Life of Theodore Roosevelt," which I read during the holidays.

NOTE. A restrictive phrase or clause should *not* be set off by a comma or commas, for such a phrase or clause is essential to the meaning of the sentence and therefore cannot be omitted.

> 1. The house standing on the hill is my home.
> 2. He who will not work shall not eat.
> 3. The book that I am reading is a novel.

7. *Coördinate clauses connected by a simple conjunction.* A comma should be used to separate the clauses of a compound sentence, *provided the clauses are connected by one of the simple conjunctions (and, but, or, nor, for), are reasonably short, and are not internally punctuated with commas*; otherwise a semicolon should be used (see section 129, rule 1).

1. We inquired for Laider at the old inn, but no one had ever heard of a person by that name.
2. We had never before experienced such wonderful climate, and we were delighted by the unusual scenery.

NOTE 1. Coördinate dependent clauses connected by a simple conjunction, if they are not closely connected in thought, should also be separated by a comma.

Major Aldington, who distinguished himself in the World War, and who has been reëlected mayor of our city, has gone to Washington on business.

NOTE 2. If the coördinate clauses are very short and are closely related in thought, the comma is often omitted.

1. The lightning flashed and the thunder roared.
2. When I saw him again and when he smiled, I forgave him.

NOTE 3. Coördinate clauses joined by a conjunctive adverb should be separated by a semicolon (see section 129, rule 1, Note 1).

NOTE 4. A comma may be used to separate coördinate clauses that are not joined by a conjunction, *provided the clauses are short, are not internally punctuated with commas, and are closely related in thought*; otherwise a semicolon should be used (see section 129, rule 1).

1. He ate no flesh, he drank no wine, he never knew the use of tobacco.
2. I came, I saw, I conquered.
3. What she said, what she thought, what she wore, made a lasting impression on the little company.

NOTE 5. Rule 3, above, applies to the punctuation of coördinate clauses in a series in which the conjunction is expressed between the last two clauses only.

1. We found the key, I unlocked the chest, and together we opened it.
2. Tell me what you wore, whom you saw, and what each said.

Caution. Do not use a comma to separate the clauses of a compound sentence not connected by a conjunction unless the clauses are very short, are not internally punctuated with commas, and are closely related in thought. Usually the semicolon is the better punctuation between coördinate clauses not joined by a conjunction. The use of a comma for a semicolon or for a mark of end punctuation is called the comma fault. This is a serious error in sentence construction and should be carefully avoided. (See section 171.)

8. *Direct and indirect quotations.* A comma or commas should be used to separate a direct quotation from the rest of the sentence, unless some other mark of punctuation is required. Observe carefully the following models:

1. "I am glad to see you," she said.
2. She said, "I am glad to see you."
3. "I am glad," she said, "to see you."
4. "When did you come?" she asked.
5. She asked, "When did you come?"
6. "When," she asked, "did you come?"

NOTE 1. Notice in sentence 4 that no comma is used after the question mark.

NOTE 2. If the verb of saying and its subject precede a direct quotation of more than one sentence, a colon is used instead of a comma (see section 130, rule 1).

NOTE 3. No comma or commas should be used if the direct quotation is closely incorporated in the sentence and is not preceded or followed by a verb of saying.

The banquet hall rang with derisive cries of "Toss him in a blanket," "Throw him down the fire escape."

NOTE 4. No comma should be used before an indirect quotation.

> 1. She said that she was glad to see me.
> 2. She asked me when I had come.

9. *Omission of important words.* A comma should be used to indicate the omission of important words that are clearly implied.

1. The doctor came in his automobile; the policeman, in a motor boat.
2. Grandfather's boyhood was spent in the country; father's, in the city.

10. *Limiting or identifying words or figures.* A word or a group of figures used to limit or identify a preceding word or expression should be separated by a comma, or by commas, from other expressions. This rule includes the setting-off of (1) a second geographical name, (2) a title following a proper name, and (3) portions of dates, as illustrated in the examples below:

1. Portland, Maine, and Portland, Oregon, are both interesting cities.
2. Norman Faraday, Jr.
3. Thornton Wakefield, Esq.
4. Denby and Pearson, Architects.
5. November 11, 1918, is a memorable date.
6. We shall arrive Wednesday, October 17.
7. The letter was written New Year's Day, 1922.
8. At the top of the page was the date "23 August, 1921."

11. *Mild interjections.* After a mild interjection a comma is usually preferable to an exclamation point.

> 1. Oh, that makes no difference.
> 2. But alas, it does make a difference.
> 3. Why, when did you arrive?
> 4. Well, I wish you would listen!

12. *Punctuation for greater clearness.* In order to insure the immediate proper reading of a sentence, a comma is sometimes used where no mark of punctuation would otherwise be considered necessary.

1. Ever since, we have been coming to this place for the summer months.

2. What his reason for making such a will had been, had been explained by his lawyer.

3. Such an act as that at a time when every man who had an ounce of patriotism in him was bending every energy to win the war, was unpardonable.

EXERCISES

I

In the following exercise (1) classify each sentence grammatically and (2) punctuate the sentence correctly, giving the rule governing the use of each comma:

1. The man who proved to be an escaped convict had in his possession one of the missing papers.

2. Consequently if a person cannot be happy without remaining idle idle he should remain.

3. Extreme *busyness* whether at school or college kirk or market is a symptom of deficient vitality.

4. Hope they say deserts us at no period of our existence.

5. Considered not as verse but as speech a great part of his poetry is full of strange and admirable merits.

6. When they told Joan of Arc she should be at home minding women's work she answered that there were plenty to spin and wash.

7. "But mother" said Jean "they will all be expecting me."

8. Our fireside guest a retired sea captain loved the lights and beacons the mist and fogbells the sleet and surge of winter.

9. I rose softly slipped on my clothes opened the door quietly and beheld one of the most amusing scenes that I have ever gazed upon.

10. Like many other authors Whittier was attracted in the autumn of his life to the rich fields of oriental literature.

11. My father I assure you was a conscientious man and ever bore in mind the golden maxim "Spare the rod and spoil the child."

12. The civilization the manners and the morals of dogkind are to a great extent subordinate to those of his ancestral master man.

13. The cat an animal of franker appetites preserves his independence.

14. My dog is a little very alert well-bred intelligent Skye.

15. Miss Willoughby is a slight though very energetic woman.

16. Aunt Jane old and crippled as she was took an active part in our indoor amusements.

17. His old friends were not to be neglected but it seemed hardly decent to desert the new.

18. What do you suppose she asked me then my dear?

19. Irving was born in 1783; Longfellow in 1807; and Holmes in 1809.

20. Marjorie had bright mischievous laughing blue eyes and wavy light brown hair.

21. Their father by the way when he learned of their curious predicament merely laughed and said "Well boys you will have to get out of this affair the best way you can."

22. Ever since I have felt ill at ease in that old house.

23. David Lowney M.D. was born in Edinburgh Scotland June 7 1878.

24. Is that man who accompanied you home last night a friend or is he merely an acquaintance?

25. She was offended not because I had accepted the position but because I did not ask her advice beforehand.

26. Sink or swim live or die survive or perish I give my hand and my heart to this vote.

27. The cook having eloped with the butler we were compelled to prepare our own breakfast.

28. His voice survived in its full power and he took pride in using it.

29. Some of our party fished others rowed on the lake and others tramped over the hills.

30. Why this is not my luggage porter.

31. I yelled I waved my arms I blew a blast on the conch shell but I could not attract the attention of the sailors.

32. When he learned that I was a graduate of Harvard he immediately took greater interest in me.

33. Now when I am sad I like nature to charm me out of my sadness like David before Saul.

34. I was so lonely that I gladly talked with anyone wise or foolish drunk or sober.

35. Fortunately I had not worn my coral necklace which grandmother had given me as a graduation present.

36. "Do you believe in dreams?" asked my friend as he gave mother a knowing wink.

37. The guide believing that we had money to spend freely gave our party every attention.

38. Her flower garden not to mention her large family kept her constantly employed and interested in life.

39. Why he should suspect Venable who is the very soul of honor of doing such a thing I cannot understand.

40. The natives regarded him with awe nor would they permit him to touch the sick child.

41. From her position at the window she could see who each guest was what she wore and how she was received by the hostess.

42. Why do you expect me to believe such a doubtful if not utterly false statement as that?

43. Lanham jealous of Warner's popularity tried to secure his dismissal from the team.

44. He laughed he ran he leaped he sang for joy.

II

In Chapter VII study the sentences in the paragraphs on pages 148 and 149 and account for all commas used.

III

Bring to class two original sentences to illustrate each rule for the use of the comma.

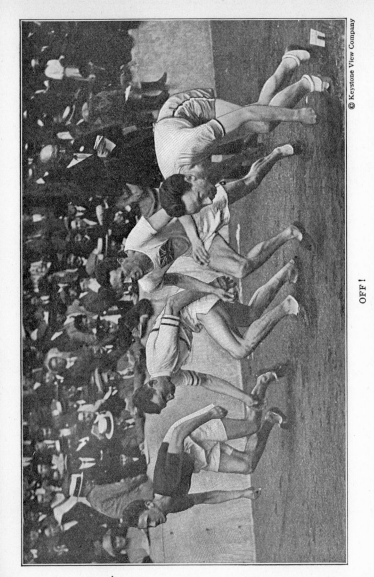

OFF!

The start of the 800-meter run

129. The semicolon. The semicolon marks a greater degree of separation than does the comma. It is properly used only when it separates coördinate independent clauses, coördinate dependent clauses, or coördinate phrases. It should never be placed, therefore, between an independent and a dependent clause, or between a clause and a phrase.

1. *Coördinate independent clauses.* A semicolon should be used between the clauses of a compound sentence when they are not joined by a conjunction. (For the exception to this rule see section 128, rule 7, Note 4. Read also the caution that follows the rule.)

1. Let them keep their past; we have our future.
2. The blue sky now turned more softly gray; the stars gradually disappeared; the east began to kindle.

NOTE 1. A semicolon should be used between the clauses of a compound sentence when they are joined by a conjunctive adverb, such as *however, moreover, hence, consequently, therefore, accordingly, likewise, furthermore, so, also, still, nevertheless, then, besides, otherwise.* A comma is sometimes placed after the conjunctive adverb.

1. I missed the eight-ten train; however, I arrived at the office before my client appeared.
2. The natives looked on Jukes with considerable suspicion; hence he found it impossible to secure the specimens that he desired for the museum.

NOTE 2. A semicolon should be used between the clauses of a compound sentence connected by a simple conjunction, provided the clauses are somewhat long or are internally punctuated with commas.

1. All sluggish and pacific pleasures are, to the same degree, solitary and selfish; and every durable bond between human beings is founded in or heightened by some element of competition.
2. He spoke to the dog, calling it to him; but in his voice was a strange note of fear that frightened the animal.

Even though the clauses joined by a simple conjunction are not internally punctuated with commas, they are sometimes separated by a semicolon, especially if the second clause explains the first or is sharply contrasted with it in thought.

1. Do not count too surely on success; for there is many a slip between the cup and the lip.

2. At times Scott's characters will speak with a true heroic note; but on the next page they will be wading wearily forward with an ungrammatical and undramatic rigmarole of words.

2. *Coördinate dependent clauses or coördinate phrases.* A semicolon should be used to separate coördinate dependent clauses and coördinate phrases, provided the clauses or phrases have a common dependence on a preceding or succeeding clause and are long or are internally punctuated with commas.

1. If only the others could be there also; if only there were no cold anywhere, and no nakedness, and no hunger; if only it were as well with all men as it was with him,—he could rest supremely happy.

2. Youth is the time to go flashing from one end of the world to the other in mind and body; to hear the chimes at midnight; to see the sunrise in town and country; to write halting verses; to run a mile to see a fire.

3. *Introductory expressions.* A semicolon often precedes such words, phrases, and abbreviations as *namely, as, that is, for example, for instance, e.g., i.e., viz.,* when they introduce an explanation or an illustration. In modern practice the introductory expression is often preceded by a comma, or a comma and a dash, instead of a semicolon, especially if the explanation or illustration following the introductory expression is a word or a phrase. A comma usually follows such introductory expressions, although it is sometimes omitted after the abbreviated forms.

1. While I was in college, my generous father proved to be my most serious handicap; that is, he furnished me too liberal an allowance.

2. The Greeks invented the three orders of architecture, namely, the Doric, the Ionic, and the Corinthian.

3. Both crimes, it was discovered, were committed by the same man, —namely, the interne.

4. Grammatically considered, according to their form, sentences are of four kinds, i. e. simple, compound, complex, and compound-complex.

EXERCISES

I

In the following exercise (1) classify each sentence grammatically and (2) give the rule for each comma and semicolon used:

1. One thing in life calls for another; there is a certain fitness in events and places.
2. The difficulty of literature is not to write, but to write what you mean; not to affect your reader, but to affect him precisely as you wish.
3. Literature in many of its branches is no other than the shadow of good talk; but the imitation falls far short of the original in life, freedom, and effect.
4. All natural talk is a festival of ostentation; and, by the laws of the game, each accepts and fans the vanity of the other.
5. Concord was the home of four men famous in American literature, namely, Thoreau, Alcott, Emerson, and Hawthorne.
6. Hadley was handicapped by entering college a month late; furthermore, he was compelled to earn a part of his expenses.

II

In the following exercise (1) classify each sentence grammatically and (2) supply all necessary commas and semicolons, giving the rule for your use of each mark of punctuation:

1. When literature holds before us the vision of the ideal it points us to the future when it gives us a more sympathetic insight into the men and women with whom our lot is cast it points us to the present when it restores to us the men and events long since vanished it points us to the past.
2. You have a pair of eyes how can you fail to observe what is going on about you?
3. Examinations are formidable even to the best prepared for the greatest fool may ask more than the wisest man can answer.
4. These hardy ancestors of ours were not simply fighters and freebooters they were men like ourselves their emotions awaken instant response in our souls.
5. That such doctors should differ will excite no great surprise but one point in which they seem to agree fills me I confess with wonder.

6. Fiction is to the grown man what play is to the child it is there that he changes the atmosphere and tenor of his life and when the game so chimes with his fancy that he can join in it with all his heart when it pleases him with every turn when he loves to recall it and dwells upon its recollection with entire delight fiction is called romance.

7. Pitiful is the case of the blind who cannot read the face pitiful that of the deaf who cannot follow the changes of the voice.

8. Forbes had previously told me that the old house was said to be haunted moreover I had for several days felt that I was not the only occupant.

9. Talk costs nothing in money it is all profit it completes our education it founds and fosters our friendships and it can be enjoyed at any age and in almost any state of health.

10. Three of the greatest periods of English literature coincide as Professor Palmer observes with the reigns of the three English queens namely the reigns of Elizabeth Anne and Victoria.

11. With George Eliot law is like fate it overwhelms personal freedom and inclination.

12. The water of Lethe has one excellent quality for a single draft of it makes people forget every care and sorrow.

III

Find in other textbooks, or in your reading, twelve or more sentences illustrating the various rules for the use of the semicolon.

IV

Bring to class two original sentences illustrating each of the rules for the use of the semicolon.

130. The colon. The colon marks a greater degree of separation than does the comma or the semicolon. In general, it is the mark of anticipation; that is, it stands before a group of words, phrases, clauses, or sentences which have been introduced by the expression which has preceded. Its use implies greater formality than does the comma.

1. *Formal statements, long quotations, and lists of items.* A colon should be used before formal statements, long formal quotations, or lists of items preceded by a general introductory expression. Frequently some such introductory phrase as *the following, as follows, in the following manner, for this reason,* or *in this way* precedes the colon. Often, however, such a phrase is merely implied.

1. The capital leading questions on which you must this day decide are these two: first, whether you ought to concede ; and secondly, what your concession ought to be.

2. At the annual dinner of the Pioneer Club, Dr. Blount spoke as follows: "As I look back over the years . . ."

3. As I left, my old friend quoted the following lines for my encouragement :

> Greatly begin ! though thou have time
> But for a single line, be that sublime;
> Not failure, but low aim, is crime.

4. Last summer I read three unusually interesting books : "Joseph Vance," "If Winter Comes," and "The Americanization of Edward Bok."

2. *An explanation or an illustration.* A colon should be used to separate the two parts of a sentence if the second part is an explanation or an illustration of the first part, provided the second part is not introduced by such an expression as *namely, that is,* etc. (see section 129, rule 3).

This, then, is the plastic part of literature : to embody character, thought, or emotion in some act or attitude that shall be remarkably striking to the mind's eye.

3. *Formal salutations.* A colon should be used after the salutation preceding a formal letter or a formal address.

1. My dear Sir :
    In reply to your letter, etc.

2. Ladies and Gentlemen :—On an occasion such as this, etc.

EXERCISES

I

In the following exercise (1) classify each sentence grammatically and (2) supply all necessary commas, semicolons, and colons:

1. Two qualities stand out supreme in Hugo's masterpiece "Les Misérables" flaming indignation and tender sympathy.

2. In his note to Lincoln written after the Gettysburg address Edward Everett said "I should be glad if I could flatter myself that I came as near to the central idea of the occasion in two hours as you did in two minutes."

3. Wherever a man is he will find something to please and pacify him in the town he will meet pleasant faces of men and women and for the country there is no country without some amenity.

4. We hold these truths to be self-evident that all men are created equal that they are endowed by their Creator with certain inalienable rights that among these are life liberty and the pursuit of happiness.

5. The English language is composed of two elements the Saxon which includes the Danish Swedish and other related languages and the classical which includes the Latin and the Greek.

6. Cambridge was the home of three noted literary men Holmes who is known as "The Autocrat" Lowell whose quaint Yankee humor sparkles in "The Biglow Papers" and Longfellow who is greatly loved by young readers as the author of "Evangeline."

7. Benjamin Franklin was a versatile man he was a printer an inventor a writer a statesman and a public benefactor.

II

Select from your reading or from other textbooks six sentences illustrating the various rules for the use of the colon.

III

Bring to class two original sentences illustrating each of the rules for the use of the colon.

131. The period. The following rules for the use of the period should be carefully observed:

1. *After declarative and imperative sentences.* A **period** should be placed at the end of a declarative or an **imperative** sentence.

    1. We arrived at four o'clock.
    2. Always speak distinctly.

NOTE. A period should *not* be used in the place of a **comma or a** semicolon to separate members of the same sentence. Such **a practice** results in the *period fault* (see section 170).

Incorrect : We missed the train. Just as mother had predicted.
Correct : We missed the train, just as mother had predicted.
Incorrect : I believe that the investment is a safe one. However, I do not urge you to put your money into it.
Correct : I believe that the investment is a safe one; however, I do not urge you to put your money into it.

2. *After an abbreviation.* A period should be used **after an** abbreviation.

    1. On the title-page was printed "Arnold Merriam, D. D., LL. D."
    2. Mrs. Howard C. Joyce organized the S. P. C. A. in our town.

NOTE. Abbreviations which represent chemical symbols are **properly** written without a period following. For example : NaCl, H_2O, H_2SO_4. A few other abbreviations, such as *MS* (*= manuscript*) and the **phrase** *per cent* (*= per centum*), may be written with or without the period.

3. *After letters and figures indicating divisions of an outline.* A period should be placed after a letter or a figure indicating a division of an outline. (See the outlines in Chapters II, IV, and V.)

A period is also used after figures preceding consecutively arranged items in a list or an exercise, as in the various exercises in this book.

NOTE 1. If a figure or a letter is inclosed in parentheses, it should not be followed by a period.
NOTE 2. A figure placed in the upper right corner of a page to designate the page number should *not* be followed by a period or any other mark of punctuation.

4. *After sideheadings.* A period should be used after words and phrases written as sideheadings of a paragraph or other division of a piece of writing. The punctuation of the title of each section of this book illustrates this rule.

NOTE. A title or heading centrally spaced on the page should *not* be followed by a period.

5. *After topics of an outline.* A period is generally used after each phrase topic of an outline. If the topic is a sentence, the period must be used. (See the outlines in Chapters II, IV, and V.)

EXERCISES

I

In the following exercise supply the correct punctuation:

1. History is one long illustration
2. Take time to think before you decide
3. Mrs G C Howe received the degree of M A last June
4. I hope to see you in San Francisco this summer. If we are there at the same time
5. We left our cards. There being nothing else that we could do

II

Write and punctuate correctly the proper abbreviations of the following words and phrases. Consult Appendix D and an unabridged dictionary if necessary.

1. Anonymous, manuscripts, Bachelor of Arts, Civil Engineer, Madame, Monsieur, Messieurs, Mademoiselle, Member of Congress, Fellow of the Royal Society, Doctor of Laws, Doctor of Dental Surgery.
2. Forenoon, noon, afternoon, in the year of our Lord, before Christ, east longitude, south latitude.
3. California, Illinois, Minnesota, North Dakota, Maine, Florida, South Carolina, Alabama, Colorado, New Jersey, Wyoming, West Indies.

132. The question mark. The following rules for the use of the question mark should be observed:

1. *Direct question.* A question mark should be placed after a direct question.

Mother, when do you expect Uncle John?

NOTE 1. A question mark should never be placed after an indirect question.

I asked mother when she expected Uncle John.

NOTE 2. Frequently the sentence is not expressed in the interrogative form, and only the question mark shows that it is meant to be a question.

You will go? You have not met him?

NOTE 3. Questions in a series usually have a question mark after each member of the series.

What will people not do for money? for fame? for social position?

2. *Doubtful statement.* A question mark inclosed in parentheses should be used to indicate doubt as to the accuracy of a statement.

In the year 1805 (?) Irving made his first voyage to Europe.

NOTE. The question mark should *not* be used, as in the following sentence, to indicate irony or humor:

Incorrect: What a beautiful (?) spring hat!

133. The exclamation mark. The following rules for the use of the exclamation mark should be observed:

1. *Words, phrases, or sentences.* An exclamation mark should be used after words, phrases, or sentences which express strong emotion, doubt, or irony.

1. O world, I cannot hold thee close enough!
2. That man a poet! The idea!
3. What an angelic disposition she has!

2. *Interjections*. An exclamation mark should generally be placed after an interjection or other exclamatory word (see section 128, rule 11).

> 1. Alas! What was I to do?
> 2. Hold! Hold! Give the man a chance.

NOTE. If an interjection is repeated, a comma may be used to separate the words, and the exclamation mark may be placed only at the end, especially where it is not the writer's intention to make each of the words emphatic.

> 1. Ha, ha, ha! That's the best joke I ever heard.
> 2. Aha! aha! I've caught you this time. (Emphasis)

EXERCISE

In the following exercise (1) classify each sentence grammatically and (2) supply questions marks and exclamation marks, as well as all other necessary punctuation, and give the rule for each mark of punctuation used:

1. And what is love but a rose that fades
2. "Brave Admiral speak what shall I say"
   "Why say 'Sail on sail on and on'"
3. Lord God of Hosts be with us yet
   Lest we forget—lest we forget
4. Wild little bird who chose thee for a sign
   To put upon the cover of this book
5. Alas why must you leave us alone
6. O ho listen to that What did I tell you
7. What pearls of wisdom O gigantic intellect
8. Wonderful Wonderful I never dreamed of such grandeur
9. What was the fate of Julius Cæsar of Hannibal of Napoleon
10. How good is man's life the mere living how fit to employ
    All the heart and the soul and the senses forever in joy

134. The dash. In general, the dash should be used to indicate an abrupt break in the structure of a sentence or a suspension in the thought. The rules for the use of the dash are as definite as those governing the use of other marks of punctuation. Careless writers frequently misuse the dash. They seem to have but one rule of punctuation: When in doubt use a dash. Such a slovenly practice should be avoided by accurately applying the following rules:

1. *Change in the construction of the sentence.* A dash should be used to indicate a change in the construction of a sentence.

She was reading—what is the title of that last novel by Page?

2. *Parenthetical expressions.* Dashes are frequently used instead of parentheses to set off parenthetical expressions that are not logically or structurally connected with the rest of the sentence (see section 128, rule 5; also section 135).

That dog—I know it is hard for you to believe it now—was once the winner of a first prize.

3. *Summarizing expressions.* A dash should be used to separate an informal enumeration from the expression that summarizes the thought contained in the enumeration.

1. These are not the elements that constitute a great nation—gold and merchandise, banks and railways, crowded ports and populous cities.
2. Gold and merchandise, banks and railways, crowded ports and populous cities—these are not the elements that constitute a great nation.

Note 1. A dash frequently precedes an expression following an apparently completed sentence but referring to the whole sentence or some part of it.

When the bells had ceased ringing, the woods, the clouds, the little village, and the very air itself seemed asleep—so silent was it everywhere.

Note 2. A dash is frequently used to set off an appositive word or phrase loosely introduced into the sentence. Such an appositive often emphasizes the word or phrase with which it agrees.

1. His father was a successful failure—a hero of defeat.
2. What memories that song awoke—memories I had supposed long since dead!

4. *For dramatic or rhetorical effect.* A dash may sometimes be used to mark a pause intended to heighten the dramatic or rhetorical effect of the sentence.

1. Young man, had I your youth and splendid opportunities, I should never think of failure—never, never, never!

2. The king of France, with twice ten thousand men,
Marched up the hill, and then—marched down again.

5. *Omission of letters or figures.* A dash should be used to indicate the omission of letters or figures.

My maternal grandfather, Judge H——n, was born at S——d, in the year 18—.

6. *In combination with other marks of punctuation.* A dash may be used after a colon following a formal salutation, provided the first sentence of the letter or speech begins on the same line with the salutation.

My dear Madam:—In reply to your letter, etc.

A dash is now rarely used with a comma, unless the comma would be required even if the dash were not used.

7. *Preceding references.* A dash should precede a reference following a prose quotation. (See the punctuation preceding each reference that is placed after the paragraphs quoted in Chapter VII.)

Many otherwise highly civilized Europeans are as timid in addressing a telephone as they would be in addressing a royal sovereign.—ARNOLD BENNETT, "Your United States"

EXERCISES

I

In the following exercise (1) classify each sentence grammatically and (2) supply dashes, as well as other necessary punctuation, and give the rule for each mark of punctuation used:

1. Statues paintings churches poems are but shadows of himself shadows in marble colors stone words.

2. I awoke from a horrible dream and found that I was grasping the bedpost.

3. At last I think it was the third night our party decided that the Wareham ghost was nothing but a myth.

4. Silver had two guns slung about him one before and one behind besides the great cutlass at his waist and a pistol in each pocket of his square-tailed coat.

5. Mrs. Paige allow me the pleasure of introducing my friend Mr. oh why can I never remember your name

6. The log house was made of unsquared trunks of pine roof walls and floor.

7. A Scotch collie a large black cat a raccoon and a garrulous parrot these were the members of Ward's queer household.

8. After an ominous pause the timid young man said to the girl beside him "I am going to propose that we go down town and get some ice cream the next time I come."

9. That was a most wonderful experience an experience I can never forget.

10. When you meet her let me caution you beforehand do not tell her anything about my college record.

11. The poem begins with a funeral and ends with a marriage a sort of "Divine Comedy" cheerful at the close.

12. Love growth honor sympathy idealism faith fortitude truth tolerance coöperation these are the fundamentals and it is on these that the masters put the stress.

II

From your reading find and bring to class ten sentences in which the dash is correctly used. Be prepared to give the rule for each mark of punctuation used in these sentences.

135. Parentheses. The following rules for the use of parentheses should be observed:

1. *Explanatory expressions.* Parentheses are often used to inclose explanatory words, phrases, or clauses having no gram-

matical dependence on the rest of the sentence. In this use parentheses are felt to be slightly more formal than are dashes.

1. Then Soames began to cross-question me (Marjorie had assured me that he would), and he asked me all about my income and my prospects of advancement.

2. At the end of our interview Soames gave his entire consent to our marriage (as Marjorie had predicted he would do).

NOTE 1. No other mark of punctuation should be used with parentheses, unless (as in the sentences above) such a mark would be required if the parenthetic matter were omitted.

NOTE 2. Parentheses may also be used to inclose a phrase or a clause that forms an integral part of the syntax of the sentence.

> What changes (if any) would you suggest?

2. *Figures and letters marking divisions.* Parentheses should be used to inclose figures and letters included in the text of a piece of writing to indicate division or order of enumeration.

The four forms of discourse are (1) narration, (2) description, (3) exposition, and (4) argument.

136. Brackets. Brackets should be used to inclose explanations, comments, queries, corrections, criticisms, or directions inserted in the text by some other person than the original speaker or writer.

1. I remember seeing him [Stevenson] for the last time in 1888.

2. I have always maintained, as I always shall [maintain], that the sentence was unjust.

3. My uncle's home, like most of the historic old houses of New England, had much more atmosphere than fresh air. [Laughter]

EXERCISE

In the following exercise classify each sentence grammatically, and supply parentheses and brackets, as well as all other necessary punctuation, and give the rule for each mark of punctuation used:

1. I brought my old friend home with me to spend the night never suspecting that he would remain my guest for a whole month.

2. My acquaintance began with her Mrs. Eastman when I was in the hospital.

3. The genial old fellow we never dreamed that he was a private detective was a great favorite with all the hotel guests.

4. In one of the queerest corners of the town Marblehead there stands a house as modest as the Ames house is magnificent.

5. My friends this speech of mine I may as well admit it at the outset was written by my wife. Laughter and applause.

137. Quotation marks. The following rules for the use of quotation marks should be observed:

1. *Direct quotations.* Quotation marks should be used to inclose a direct quotation.

1. "What a wonderful view this is!" exclaimed my friend.

2. "Were you," she asked, "in college with my son?"

3. "Yes," I replied, "I knew Harry well. We played on the basket-ball team together."

NOTE 1. If the quotation is interrupted by a parenthetical expression (such as *she asked* and *I replied* in the second and third sentences above), the quotation is closed before the expression and opened again after it (see section 128, rule 8).

NOTE 2. Indirect quotations should not be inclosed in quotation marks.

> She asked me whether I had been in college with her son.

NOTE 3. Proverbs and well-known quotations from such sources as the Bible or the writings of Shakespeare may be written without quotation marks.

1. This is the central idea of the story: a little child shall lead them.

2. The life of that family for the last three generations proves true this familiar saying: the evil that men do lives after them.

2. *Long quotations.* In an uninterrupted quotation consisting of several paragraphs or stanzas, quotation marks should

be used at the beginning of each paragraph or stanza, but at the end of the last one only.

3. *Quotation within a quotation.* Single quotation marks should be used to inclose a quotation within a quotation.

"In spite of all my attempts to restrain him," sobbed Vivian, "he leaped to his feet and shouted, 'That's a lie.'"

4. *Titles.* According to the best usage, quotation marks are used to inclose the *quoted* title of (1) a poem, a story, an essay, an article, a chapter, or any other division of a book or other publication; (2) a single musical composition; (3) a picture; or (4) a statue. The *quoted* title of a book may likewise be inclosed in quotation marks, or, like the *quoted* title of a magazine or a newspaper, it may be indicated by the use of italics (see section 142, rule 1).

1. I read "The Floor of Heaven" in the *Atlantic Monthly*.
2. At the recital, Helen played Mendelssohn's "Spring Song."
3. "The Song of the Lark" was painted by Jules Breton.
4. On the lawyer's desk was a copy of Rodin's "The Thinker."
5. Have you read George Eliot's "Adam Bede"?

Note. A title that stands at the head of a composition should not be inclosed in quotation marks unless the title is itself a quotation.

5. *Quotation mark used with another mark of punctuation.* When a quotation mark and some other mark of punctuation both follow a word, they should be arranged in the order illustrated in the following sentences:

1. He shouted, "Can you hear me?"
2. Did she say, "I refuse"?
3. "How shall I explain your absence?" I asked.
4. Hamblen considers that, I suppose, another of his "inalienable rights"; the judge, however, may think differently.
5. "Never," he declared, "have I read a better book."

6. *Miscellaneous uses.* Quotation marks may be used to inclose (1) slang words, (2) nicknames, (3) unusual or coined words, or (4) words used humorously or ironically.

1. I never saw Dean Blake more "dolled up" than he was at the faculty reception for the seniors.

2. "Diogenes" Brodie was a terror to all freshmen.

3. It was an amusing sight watching that tall Wilson boy "pogoing" along with tiny May Bryce.

4. At the end of the first semester a number of students suddenly decide to leave college "to help father in his business" or "to rest their eyes."

Note. Slang, nicknames, or words used humorously or ironically need not be apologized for by placing them in quotation marks when they are used in colloquial or humorous writing.

EXERCISES

I

In the following exercise (1) classify each sentence grammatically and (2) supply quotation marks, as well as all other punctuation, and give the rule for each mark of punctuation:

1. Genius said Professor James Frederick Ferrier is nothing else than the power of seeing wonders in common things

2. Have you read Good Company a poem by Karle Wilson Baker

3. On rising the lecturer held up a sheet of paper and said You see before you referring to the paper all that you have to fear or hope

4. Come to Concord wrote Ellery Channing to Hawthorne once upon a time Emerson is away and nobody is here to bore you

5. Bryant's biographer says The aged poet wrote to a friend Is there a penny-post do you think in the world to come Do people there write for autographs to those who have gained a little notoriety Do women there send letters asking for money

6. Nonsense exclaimed Uncle John I don't believe a word of it

7. Having observed the baby hippopotamus Nell said Isn't he a dear

8. We presented Miss Blake with a framed copy of The Age of Innocence Mary announced

9. The wisest man I ever knew observed the cynic chose **as the** motto of his happy life this simple statement ignorance is bliss

10. When she met you at the door asked Barbara did she **exclaim** **as** usual Well of all things

II

From your reading find and bring to class ten sentences illustrating the rules for the use of quotation marks.

III

Write two sentences to illustrate each of the rules for the use of quotation marks.

138. The apostrophe. The following rules for the use of the apostrophe should be observed:

1. *Possessive case.* An apostrophe should be used to indicate the possessive case.

1. He enjoyed children's games.
2. Peter's wife's mother lay sick of a fever.
3. Have you read Burns's poems and Dickens's novels?
4. Miss Ames is in either the boys' or the girls' study hall.

NOTE. The pronouns *ours, yours, hers, its, theirs,* and *whose* should never be written with an apostrophe (see section 147, rule 10).

2. *Plural of letters and figures.* An apostrophe should be used to form the plural of letters and figures.

1. Your *u's* and *n's* are too much alike.
2. Your *3's* resemble your *5's*.
3. The B.P.O.E.'s gave a dance at their hall last night.

3. *Contractions.* An apostrophe should stand in the place of the letter or letters omitted in a contraction.

1. We didn't retire until twelve o'clock.
2. I can't vouch for the truth of the statement, but I've heard that they're wealthy.

NOTE. The apostrophe should always be carefully placed between the letters where the omission occurs. An apostrophe frequently marks the omission of the first two figures in a year date.

He is a member of the famous class of '95.

139. The hyphen. A hyphen is used (1) to separate the parts of many compound words and (2) to mark the division of a word into syllables.

self-government, well-known; al-le-vi-ate, zo-ol-o-gy

140. The caret. A caret (∧) should be used to indicate the unintentional omission of a word or a group of words in a line of manuscript. The omitted word or group of words is written above the line, and the caret indicates the point at which the omission occurs.

pay me

He has not paid me a cent, and he will never ∧ until I bring suit against him.

141. Points and asterisks. Points (. . .) or asterisks (* * *) should be used to indicate that portions of material have been omitted from a quotation.

1. Whitman's "Leaves of Grass" . . . should be in the hands of all parents and guardians as a specific for the distressing malady of being seventeen years old.

2. Of all the rides since the birth of time,

. . . .

The strangest ride that ever was sped
Was Ireson's out from Marblehead!

142. Italics. Italics should be indicated in manuscript by underscoring with one straight line the letter, word, phrase, or other unit of expression that would be printed in italic type. The following rules for the use of italics should be observed:

1. *Titles.* Titles of newspapers, magazines, and manuscripts, if quoted, are usually printed in italics. Quoted titles of books, if not inclosed in quotation marks, should be italicized (see section 137, rule 4).

1. I have read two stories in *Scribner's Magazine.*
2. I enjoy reading *Life.*

NOTE. If the title of a book, poem, story, or essay begins with the article *the*, the article should be included in the title. In writing the title of newspapers and magazines *the* is usually not capitalized or italicized.

1. Have you read "The Ordeal of Richard Feverel"?
2. I have read "The Enemy" in the *Century Magazine.*
3. The account of her marriage appeared in the New York *Evening Post.*

2. *Emphasis.* Italics may be used to give special emphasis to a word or group of words. Such use is illustrated in section 126. Italics should not be overworked, however, for they are at best merely a mechanical means of securing emphasis.

3. *Sideheadings.* Italics may be used as a device for making sideheadings stand out in contrast with the Roman type. Such use is illustrated at the beginning of most of the rules in this chapter.

4. *Foreign words.* Foreign words and phrases not yet incorporated into the English language should be italicized when used in connection with English words.

1. In spite of all her wretchedness there remained a certain *joie de vivre* in the expression of her eyes.
2. Many of his statements I accept *cum grano salis.*

NOTE 1. Foreign words that have been Anglicized should not be printed in italics.

encore, dramatis personæ, vice versa, facsimile, garage

NOTE 2. Usually the following abbreviations of foreign words are not italicized:

etc., cf., e.g., i.e., vs., viz.

5. *Words, letters, and figures.* Words, letters, and figures referred to merely as such (without particular reference to the meaning) should be italicized.

1. *And, but,* and *so* were the only connectives that he used.
2. Your *o's* and *a's* are indistinguishable.
3. Make your *1's* and *7's* more carefully.

6. *Names of ships.* Names of ships should be italicized.

My aunt went to Europe on the *Olympic*, but returned on the *Homeric*.

EXERCISES

I

Punctuate and italicize the following sentences correctly and state in each case the rules involved:

1. Why Mrs Ames I read the Herald every week said my aunt.
2. My escort said bon jour whereas he meant au revoir.
3. The sinking of the Titanic in April 1912 was a great disaster.
4. How many persons in the class have read Mrs Comers story The Preliminaries in the Atlantic Monthly asked our instructor.
5. I prefer Henry Esmond to Vanity Fair.
6. The Americanization of Edward Bok which is the autobiography of the former editor of the Ladies Home Journal is a book that you will enjoy reading wrote my grandfather.
7. Our home was built in the early 70s.
8. She has acquired the provoking habit of beginning each sentence with and so and ending it with you know.

II

Write two original sentences illustrating each use of italics. Be sure that your sentences are correctly punctuated throughout.

143. Capital letters. The following rules for the use of capital letters should be observed:

1. *First word of every sentence and every line of poetry.* The first word of every sentence and the first word of every line of poetry should begin with a capital letter.

1. The old house was shrouded in mystery.
2. Under the wide and starry sky
   Dig the grave and let me lie:
   Glad did I live and gladly die,
   And I laid me down with a will.—STEVENSON

2. *First word of every direct question.* The first word of every direct question should begin with a capital letter.

1. Then came the sobering reflection, Should I have acted differently under similar circumstances?
2. The momentous question What shall I wear to the dance? has given me no peace since I received the invitation.

3. *First word of every direct quotation.* The first word of every direct quotation should begin with a capital letter.

She asked, "Why did you return?"

NOTE 1. Do not begin the first word of an indirect quotation with a capital letter.

She asked me why I had returned.

NOTE 2. If a sentence quotation is broken by a parenthetical expression such as *he said, she asked, I replied*, the second part of the quotation should not begin with a capital letter.

"Why," she asked, "did you return?"

NOTE 3. A quoted phrase incorporated in the writer's own sentence should not begin with a capital letter.

Catherine was fond of "beginning doubtfully and far away" when she had an unusual piece of gossip to tell.

4. *Proper nouns and proper adjectives.* All nouns used as names of persons, races, languages, towns, cities, counties,

states, countries, oceans, bays, lakes, rivers, streets, avenues, parks, squares, events in history, epochs of time, political parties, religious, social, and educational institutions, religious sects, etc., and the adjectives derived from such nouns, should begin with a capital letter.

Thomas Hardy, Caucasian, the French language, Springfield, Los Angeles, Middlesex County, Wisconsin, Alaska, Pacific Ocean, Galveston Bay, Lake Ontario, St. Lawrence River, Commerce Street, Fifth Avenue, Brackenridge Park, Alamo Plaza, Norman Conquest, the Middle Ages, Republican, Presbyterian, Carlton College, Young Men's Christian Association, American Indians, English literature.

NOTE 1. The words *negro*, *gypsy*, and *italic* or *italics* are properly written without capital letters.
NOTE 2. Many words derived from proper nouns are no longer written with capital letters, because long usage has caused them to lose all association with the words from which they are derived.

dahlia (from *Dahl*); bedlam (from *Bethlehem*); macadamize (from *McAdam*); boycott (from *Boycott*).

5. *Names of days and months.* Names of the days of the week and names of the months, but *not* the names of the seasons, should begin with a capital letter.

Wednesday, February, autumn

6. *Sections of a country.* Names of the points of the compass, when they designate parts of a country, should begin with a capital letter, but *not* when they indicate merely direction.

1. Father owns a large ranch in the Southwest.
2. Our house faces east.

7. *Common nouns used in proper names.* When such common nouns as *river, lake, street, avenue, park, county, college, university, high school, company, society, railway*, etc. are used as a part of a proper name, they should begin with a capital

letter, but *not* otherwise. Observe closely the capitalization in the following models:

1. Have you ever seen Yellowstone Park?
2. I met many people strolling in the park.
3. I am a student of the Richmond High School.
4. I entered high school at the age of twelve.
5. The factory of the Grayson Electric Company was on Garfield Street.
6. The company failed in business.

8. *Titles of honor or office.* Titles of honor or office should begin with a capital letter when used formally or in connection with a proper name, but *not* otherwise.

1. The Secretary of State conferred with the President.
2. We asked the advice of Judge Malcolm Wade and Dr. Philip Loring.
3. The judge and the doctor gave us the same advice.

9. *Titles of family relationship.* Words denoting family relationship, such as *uncle, aunt, cousin, grandfather, grandmother*, should begin with capitals *only when they are used with the name of the person*. Observe carefully the following sentences:

1. I have been visiting Uncle John and Aunt Clara.
2. My cousin has returned to her grandmother's home.
3. Tell me, mother, of the first time you met father.

10. *Literary titles.* In literary titles the first word and all other important words should begin with a capital letter.

1. Have you read "The Rime of the Ancient Mariner"?
2. We enjoyed reading "Mammon and the Archer."
3. His text was taken from the Epistle to the Romans.
4. The passage is found in the Old Testament.

11. *Words naming or referring to the Deity.* All names of God, as well as expressions used as titles of the Deity, should

begin with a capital letter. Pronouns referring to the Deity are usually capitalized only in case of possible ambiguity as to the noun to which they refer.

> **1.** May the Lord prosper your undertaking.
> **2.** In all things let His will be done.

12. *Names of school classes.* The words *freshman, sophomore, junior,* and *senior* may begin with either a capital or a small letter when they are used with the word *class*; otherwise they should be written with a small letter.

> **1.** She is a member of the Senior Class (*or* senior class).
> **2.** The freshmen and the sophomores have an annual push-ball contest.

13. *I and O.* The words *I* and *O* should always be capitalized. The word *oh* is capitalized only at the beginning of a sentence.

14. *Personification.* Words representing personification are usually capitalized.

> Behold where Night clutches the cup of heaven
> And quaffs the beauty of the world away!

GENERAL EXERCISES

I

Copy the following passage, dividing it correctly into sentences and supplying all necessary punctuation, capital letters, and italics:

after a sojourn at a deserted mining station in the california coast range the story of which is told in the silverado squatters stevenson with his wife and stepson lloyd osbourne returned to scotland chronic lung disease had now settled upon him and he was subject to cough hemorrhage and fever for the next few years he spent the summers in scotland the winters in switzerland or southern france and then he tried to live in england it was during one of his visits to the scotch highlands 1881 that he wrote the merry men a story of the terrors of the sea and that he began his best known book treasure island the interesting facts connected with the origin and development of this story are told in the next section of this introduction the success of this book in 1883 was but the prelude to other successes in 1886 came kidnapped and the strange case of dr jekyll and mr hyde the former which stevenson regarded as his best is a story of adventure in the highlands soon after the jacobite rebellion of 1745 its chief character alan breck stewart is drawn with greater subtlety and truth than john silver in treasure island the earlier triumph of stevensons art so close is kidnapped to the soil that in the long flight of alan and david the wind seems to turn the pages of that swift record and the smell of the heather comes with it dr jekyll and mr hyde is an allegory of the struggle between good and evil in human nature

II

Account for all the punctuation used in three or more paragraphs that your teacher may assign you in "Self-Cultivation in English" or in one of your texts in literature or history.

III

Copy the following passage, dividing it properly into paragraphs and sentences and supplying all necessary punctuation, capital letters, and italics:

novelists it seems are no heroes to their barbers mr thomas hardys barber recently confided to mr f hadland davis that in his opinion the novelist is a sadly overrated man the barbers comments as reported by mr davis to the bookman were these he is such a quiet little man youd never know it was thomas hardy he wears an old overcoat and carries a baggy umbrella he used to talk to me about london as it was years ago when cockfighting was all the rage ive never read any of his books nor do i care to read them americans seem to think a lot of him one of them came in here the other day have you seen thomas hardy he asked me oh yes i said he sat in the chair youre sitting in in this chair shouted the american much excited yes i replied i cut mr hardys hair did you keep the hair you cut off asked my customer putting his hand into his pocket no said i i didnt well thats a pity replied the yankee because if you had id have bought it *Youth's Companion*

IV

Write a page or two of dialogue on any subject that you may select. Be sure that it is correctly divided into paragraphs and properly punctuated.

V

In your study of punctuation and in your application of the rules of punctuation in your own writing, are you following the six directions given in section 127? Read these directions again and answer this question frankly.

CHAPTER XI

SPECIAL CAUTIONS IN GRAMMAR AND SENTENCE STRUCTURE

144. Purpose of this chapter. Before we can speak and write correctly we must not only understand the rules and principles of composition but must also overcome any bad habits of expression into which we have ignorantly or carelessly fallen. By closely watching our speech we may break ourselves of such bad habits and establish in their stead habits of correct expression. Solecisms, or violations of the rules of grammar, we must learn to avoid first of all. (For the definition of *solecism* see section 181. The list of errors in diction in section 186 includes many examples of solecisms.) In the present chapter a number of details of grammar and sentence structure that are often overlooked or imperfectly understood are explained and illustrated. By studying these explanations closely and by correcting the sentences given in the various exercises we shall be able to improve the correctness of our speech and writing. *We should remember that only through self-cultivation can we learn to avoid mistakes in the expression of our thoughts. Errors in grammar and sentence structure constitute the most serious violations of good form in composition.*

In addition to studying this chapter closely when it is assigned by the teacher, we should make regular use of it for reference throughout our study of composition. Likewise, the other chapters dealing with sentence structure, as well as those chapters devoted to punctuation, diction, grammar, and spelling, we should use for frequent reference.

I. Special Cautions in Grammar

A. *Agreement of Subject and Predicate*

145. General rule of agreement. A verb should agree in number and person with its subject, *not* with its predicate nominative.

1. They are the committee appointed.
2. His chief interest in life was good books.

146. Special rules of agreement. The following rules of agreement between subject and predicate should be carefully observed:

*1. Compound subject joined by **and**.* A compound subject joined by *and* usually requires a plural verb.

1. Tennis and rowing are my favorite forms of exercise.
2. Constance and I are cousins.

Note. If the parts of a compound subject joined by *and* are nearly synonymous, or together constitute a single idea or unit, a singular verb is required.

1. In youth his end and aim was a college education.
2. The St. Paul and Milwaukee has recently declared a dividend.

*2. Compound subject joined by **or** or **nor**.* A compound subject joined by *or* or *nor* requires a singular verb if each portion of the subject is singular.

1. Either your clock or my watch is wrong.
2. Neither Tom nor Fred has returned.

Note. If the members of a compound subject joined by *or* or *nor* differ in person or number, the verb should generally be of the person and number required by the part of the subject nearer the verb.

1. Neither you nor he has my permission.
2. Has he or I the better claim to the property?
3. Do you or Ann know who the visitor is?
4. It seems that either they or I am mistaken.

Careful writers usually avoid such sentences as these by resorting to the following arrangement:

1. Neither of you has my permission.
2. Has he a better claim to the property than I?
3. Do you know who the visitor is, or does Ann know?
4. It seems that they are mistaken, or that I am.

3. *Nouns plural in form but singular in meaning.* Such nouns as *news, measles, mumps, molasses, gallows, physics, economics, mathematics, trumps,* though plural in form, are singular in meaning and require a singular verb.

1. Measles is often injurious to one's eyes.
2. Economics is his favorite study.

NOTE. Such words as *athletics, politics, means,* and *pains* (meaning *care*) may be considered either singular or plural.

1. Athletics forms (*or* form) an important part of school activities.
2. Great pains was (*or* were) taken to provide for their comfort.

4. *Collective nouns.* Collective nouns, such as *school, class, team, company, audience, committee, jury, family, flock, herd, squad, regiment, nation,* may take either a singular or a plural verb, according to their meaning.

1. Our team was victorious.
2. The family has recently moved away.
3. The jury have not yet agreed on the evidence.
4. The audience were of different opinions regarding the speaker's meaning.

NOTE I. Nouns denoting quantity and amount, such as *half, part, portion, number,* may take either a singular or a plural verb, according to their meaning.

1. Half of the street has been paved.
2. Half of the audience were foreigners.
3. The number of automobile accidents in this city is alarming.
4. A number of accidents occur every day.

NOTE 2. Expressions indicating sums or multiples of numbers properly require a singular verb, though usage tolerates a plural verb.

> 1. Twelve and five is seventeen.
> 2. Nine times six is fifty-four.

5. *Intervening expressions.* The number of the subject is not affected by other words connected with it by such expressions as *with, along with, together with, in company with, accompanied by, as well as, including, no less than, in addition to.*

1. The estate, including a large number of rare books and paintings, was sold.

2. Mrs. Felton, with her three daughters, is spending the summer in Colorado.

6. *Relative pronoun used as subject.* A relative pronoun is of the same person and number as its antecedent. When a relative pronoun is used as the subject of a verb, care must be exercised in choosing the right person and number of the verb.

1. I, who am your friend, advise you to refuse his offer.

2. She is one of the noblest women who have ever lived.

3. The recent fire was among the most disastrous that have occurred in the history of our town. (In this sentence *that* is plural to agree with the implied antecedent *fires.*)

7. *Indefinite pronouns, adjectives, and nouns.* Such indefinite words as *each, every, either, neither, anyone, everyone, someone, no one, one, anybody, everybody, a person,* are singular and therefore require singular verbs and singular pronouns.

1. Each has his faults.

2. A person is judged by his associates.

3. Everybody learns by experience to know himself.

NOTE 1. *All, none,* and *some* may take either a singular or a plural verb, according to their meaning.

> 1. All has been lost.
> 2. All were present.

3. None has (*or* have) been found to solve the mystery.
4. Some of the fruit has rotted.
5. Some were late in arriving.

NOTE 2. *Both, few, many,* and *several* take a plural verb.

1. Many are called, but few are chosen.
2. Several have asked for an explanation.

8. *Ungrammatical use of* **don't** *and* **was**. *Don't* (the contraction of *do not*) should never be used with a third-person *singular* subject. Such expressions as *he don't, it don't, that don't, don't he? don't it? don't that?* should be avoided.

Correct: He doesn't enjoy reading poetry.
Correct: Doesn't that surprise you?

Was should never be used with a second-person subject. Such expressions *you was* and *was you?* should be avoided.

Correct: You were mistaken in your guess.
Correct: Were you at the dance last night?

EXERCISES

I

In the following sentences point out, explain, and correct all errors in agreement of subject and predicate:

1. Neither his son nor his wife know where he is.
2. There was twelve people injured in the wreck.
3. Everybody in the crowd were ready for their breakfast.
4. A number of books is missing from the library.
5. Our class elect officers each year on the first Monday in October.
6. Mumps are sometimes a dangerous disease.
7. Wasn't you proud of our team yesterday?
8. He is a man who don't take any interest in politics.
9. Have either of you solved the last problem?
10. Each of them have been absent twice.

II

In the following sentences supply the proper person-and-number form of the verb and explain why the form supplied is correct:

1. The mob —— dispersed with tear bombs.
2. Relaxation, in addition to good food, —— improved her health.
3. Mother belonged to that large class of women who —— continually sharing other people's troubles.
4. A part of his crop —— destroyed by rain.
5. One of the oldest houses in the village —— being repaired.
6. The sum and substance of the company's decision —— that no indemnity would be paid.
7. There —— only a small congregation at church Sunday.
8. —— you present at the class reunion?
9. The molasses —— too thick to run freely.
10. Either you or he —— been deceived.

B. *Nouns and Pronouns*

147. Case. 1. *Subject of a finite verb.* A noun or a pronoun used as the subject of a finite verb is in the nominative case.

1. We and they spent last vacation at the same camp.
2. She and I have many friends in common.

2. *Predicate nominative.* A noun or a pronoun used as a subjective complement after a finite verb is in the nominative case.

1. He remained a private throughout the war.
2. Helen's guests for the week-end were Clara and I.
3. It was I who saw him fall.

NOTE 1. A noun or a pronoun that stands in the predicate and, in addition to completing the meaning of the verb, defines or describes the subject is called a *subjective complement* (see section 325, 2).

NOTE 2. Do not attempt to use a pronoun in the objective case as a predicate nominative.

> *Incorrect:* It is me. That was her. These are them.
> *Correct:* It is I. That was she. These are they.

3. *After than and as.* A noun or a pronoun following *than* or *as* is in the nominative or the objective case, according to its construction in the elliptical clause of which it is a part.

1. John is more courteous than Frank [is courteous].
2. I like him better than [I like] her.

4. *Object of a verb or of a preposition.* A noun or a pronoun used as the object of a verb or of a preposition is in the objective case.

1. Whom did you meet?
2. Between you and me, I think he is wrong.

5. *Subject and complement of an infinitive.* A noun or a pronoun used as the subject or as the predicate complement of an infinitive is in the objective case.

1. They believed me to be him.
2. The woman whom they thought to be her proved her innocence.

NOTE. In sentences in which the infinitive *to be* is used without a subject, the predicate complement is in the nominative case.

1. Margaret intends to be a nurse.
2. Who am I supposed to be?

6. *Appositives.* Appositive nouns and pronouns are in the same case as the word with which they are in apposition.

1. She gave her guests, Doris and me, a week-end party.
2. They, he and his sister, have returned to college.

7. *Possessive wrongly applied to inanimate objects.* In general, the possessive case should not be used of any nouns except those denoting persons or animals. An *of*-phrase should be used of inanimate objects.

1. My friend's hair is brown.
2. The dog's collar is too small.
3. The cover of the book (*not* the book's cover) is green.

NOTE. There are a few recognized exceptions to this rule, such as *a day's outing, a hair's breadth, for conscience' sake, the law's delay.*

8. *Possessive wrongly used to denote the object of an action.* The possessive of a noun denoting the object of an action should be avoided. An *of*-phrase should be used instead.

Incorrect: The president's inauguration occurs tomorrow.
Correct: The inauguration of the president occurs tomorrow.

9. *Possessive with verbal nouns.* A noun or a pronoun used to modify a verbal noun should be in the possessive case.

1. Philip's hearing is not acute.
2. I remember his asking me for my autograph.
3. Do you object to my leaving early?

10. *Possessive sign wrongly used.* Unlike nouns, personal and relative pronouns require no possessive sign to indicate the possessive case: *ours, yours, his, hers, its, theirs,* and *whose*. Remember that *it's* is a contraction of *it is*, and that *who's* is a contraction of *who is*.

Like the possessive form of nouns, the possessives *one's, no one's, one another's, each other's,* and *others'* are correctly written with the possessive sign.

NOTE. The possessive *whose* is usually restricted to objects that have life. *Of which* is used of things without life, though *whose* is sometimes employed for the sake of euphony.

1. Mrs. Ames is the woman whose niece you met.
2. My dog, whose name is Toby, is a Scotch terrier.
3. The house, the gloom of which oppressed me, had been the family residence for three centuries.

148. Number. Avoid making the singular form of a noun serve at the same time as both singular and plural.

Incorrect: She is one of the most beautiful, if not the most beautiful, woman I have ever seen.
Correct: She is one of the most beautiful women I have ever seen, if not the most beautiful woman.

149. General rule of agreement for relative pronouns. A relative pronoun agrees with its antecedent in gender, number, and person, but its case is dependent upon its construction in its own clause.

As to the genders of relative pronouns, bear in mind the following: *who* is either masculine or feminine and should be used to refer to persons and personified objects; *which* is either masculine or feminine when used to refer to animals, but neuter when otherwise used; *what* is neuter; and *that, as,* and *but* (= *that not*) are of all three genders.

Since relative pronouns have the same person-and-number form for all three persons and for both numbers, their person and number must be determined in each case by noting the person and number of the antecedent.

1. It is I who am suspected, not she.
2. We have sold the dogs which we trained.
3. Did she hear what I said?
4. There is no one here but knows of his failure.
5. She set before us such food as she had.

The case of *who* and *whoever* requires close attention. The construction of each relative pronoun in its own clause is the only means of determining the correct inflectional form to be used.

1. Nora was a maid who we thought was honest.
2. Marie is a maid whom he says we can trust.
3. The question of who was guilty puzzled us.
4. She helped whoever was in distress.
5. Be courteous to whomever you meet.

150. Reference of pronouns. A pronoun should have as its antecedent a *particular* person, animal, or thing, and this antecedent should be a *definitely expressed* noun or pronoun. The reference of a pronoun to its antecedent should in every instance be unmistakably clear.

Incorrect: Helen told Julia that she was mistaken.
Correct: Helen said, "Julia, you are mistaken."
Also correct: Helen said, "Julia, I am mistaken."
Incorrect: I tried to assist him, but he refused it.
Correct: I offered him my assistance, but he refused it.
Also correct: I tried to assist him, but he refused my assistance.

1. *Incorrect reference of* **which.** Usually the relative pronoun *which* should not be made to refer to an entire clause or sentence. It should have a single noun (such as *fact, conclusion, decision, act, condition,* etc.) as its antecedent. Frequently it is advisable to avoid the use of *which* by employing some other construction.

Incorrect: He made up his mind to return to college, which surprised me.
Correct: He made up his mind to return to college—a decision which surprised me.
Better: His decision to return to college surprised me.

2. *Reference to an unexpressed antecedent.* Avoid the use of a pronoun or a pronominal expression seeming to refer to an unexpressed antecedent. Use the implied antecedent instead of the pronoun.

Incorrect: He is a bee-keeper and has lately acquired several large swarms of them.
Correct: He is a bee-keeper and has lately acquired several large swarms of bees.
Incorrect: Cane sugar is scarce, because that crop was almost a failure last year.
Correct: Cane sugar is scarce, because the sugar-cane crop was almost a failure last year.

3. *Indefinite use of* **it** *and* **they.** Except in such impersonal expressions as *it rains, it is cold, it seems,* the use of *it* without an antecedent should be avoided.

Incorrect: In this guidebook it says that the castle was built in 1370.
Correct: This guidebook says that the castle was built in 1370.

Except in such colloquial expressions as *they say*, the use of *they* without an antecedent should be avoided.

Incorrect: They have many interesting customs in Japan.
Correct: The Japanese have many interesting customs.

4. *Indefinite use of **this, that, these**, and **those**.* Avoid the indefinite use of *this, that, these,* and *those* as demonstrative adjectives.

Incorrect: My aunt is one of those prim old maids.
Correct: My aunt is a prim old maid.

NOTE. When *this, that, these,* or *those* modifies a noun that is the antecedent of a relative pronoun, the demonstrative adjective is no longer used indefinitely.

Correct: My aunt is one of those prim old maids who cannot endure the slightest disorder.

EXERCISE

In the following sentences point out, explain, and correct all errors in the person, number, gender, case, or reference of nouns and pronouns:

1. The contractor employed whomever wanted to work.
2. She is younger than me.
3. I discovered the forgetful person who mislaid my book to be I.
4. Do you object to me attending the dance?
5. America's discovery occurred in 1492.
6. To her nieces, Alta and I, Aunt Jane gave her rings.
7. Everyone awaited their turn at the cashier's window.
8. Who, may I ask, do you wish to see?
9. That is him standing in the doorway.
10. I was tardy yesterday, which embarrassed me greatly.
11. I am tired of reading these modern plays.
12. Mother told sister she was going to be late.
13. They have too many rules in college restraining freshmen.
14. The missionary whom we thought had died came to visit us.
15. There was a story written by Jack London in the book which I read.

HARVESTING ICE

16. We went berrying and picked nine quarts of them.

17. During her illness the doctor allowed none but he to see her.

18. Many people live only for the future, which is a great mistake.

19. Father advised me to go to school, but I disregarded it.

20. This is one of the warmest, if not the warmest, day that we have had this summer.

21. Thomas A. Edison is one of the greatest inventors who has ever lived.

22. Each of us took our places in the line.

23. Do you approve of Julia receiving company at her age?

24. Each of the children resemble their mother.

25. Hatching chickens by artificial incubation is very satisfactory, for they are simple and inexpensive in operation.

C. *Adjectives and Adverbs*

151. Expressions of comparison. 1. *Comparative degree used in speaking of two persons or things.* In speaking of two persons or things, avoid using the superlative degree of **an** adjective or an adverb. Use the comparative.

Incorrect: Sue is the prettiest of the twins.
Correct: Sue is the prettier of the twins.
Incorrect: Of the two captives, Morse was treated most cruelly.
Correct: Of the two captives, Morse was treated more cruelly.

2. *Use of **other or else** to exclude the person or thing compared.* In comparing a person or thing with the rest of its class, use *other* or *else*, as the meaning requires, with the comparative degree of the adjective or of the adverb to exclude the person or thing compared.

Incorrect: She is prettier than any girl in school.
Correct: She is prettier than any other girl in school.
Incorrect: He studies harder than anyone in the class.
Correct: He studies harder than anyone else in the class.
Incorrect: She dresses more extravagantly than any girl in school.
Correct: She dresses more extravagantly than any other girl in school.

3. *Use of* **all** *with the superlative degree*. With the superlative degree of an adjective or an adverb comparing a person or thing with the rest of its class, *all*, not *any*, should be regularly used to indicate the entire class with which the person or thing is compared.

Incorrect: She is the prettiest of any of the girls in school.
Correct: She is the prettiest of all the girls in school.
Better: She is the prettiest girl in school.
Incorrect: He spoke most distinctly of any of the boys on the debating team.
Correct: He spoke most distinctly of all the boys on the debating team.

4. *As and* **than** *in comparisons*. In expressions of comparison *as* and *than* should not be confused.

Incorrect: Today is as warm if not warmer than yesterday.
Correct: Today is as warm as yesterday, if not warmer [than yesterday].
Incorrect: He is older but not so gray as his brother.
Correct: He is older than his brother, but not so gray.

A comparison should be fully stated before a qualifying expression is added to the sentence.

5. *Adjectives and adverbs having only an absolute meaning*. A few adjectives and adverbs, such as *level, round, square, perfect, faultless, immaculate, absolute, unique, perfectly, absolutely, uniquely*, have only an absolute meaning and are therefore incapable of comparison.

Incorrect: That was a most unique experience.
Correct: That was a unique experience.

NOTE. Fairly reputable usage permits such expressions as *more perfect, most perfect, more conclusive, most conclusive*, and a few other similarly illogical comparative and superlative forms.

152. Adjectives and adverbs not to be confused in use. Great care should be exercised in the proper choice of an adjective or an adverb to be used in the constructions explained below.

1. *Use of an adverb or a predicate adjective after certain verbs.* After such verbs as *stand, look, sound,* an adjective denotes a condition or a quality of the subject, whereas an adverb denotes the manner of the action expressed by the verb.

> 1. The boy looked shy.
> 2. The boy looked shyly at her.
> 3. His voice sounded harsh.
> 4. His voice sounded harshly on the still air.

NOTE. Such verbs as *be, seem, appear, smell, taste, feel, sound, prove, grow, turn,* and *remain* are usually, if not always, followed by an adjective.

> 1. He looks well.
> 2. I feel ill.
> 3. She seems better.
> 4. The fruit tastes sour.

2. *Use of an adverb or a predicate objective after certain verbs.* After several verbs, such as *fasten, keep,* and *hold,* an adjective completes the predicate and denotes a condition or a quality of the object resulting from the action of the verb, whereas an adverb denotes the manner of the action expressed by the verb.

> 1. He fastened the door secure.
> 2. He fastened the door securely.
> 3. She swept the floor clean.
> 4. She swept the floor briskly.

3. *An adjective not to be used as an adverb.* Avoid using an adjective to perform the function of an adverb. Do not form the habit of using *real* for *very,* or *some* for *somewhat.*

> *Incorrect:* She came too frequent.
> *Correct:* She came too frequently.
> *Incorrect:* The guide woke me real early.
> *Correct:* The guide woke me very early.
> *Incorrect:* The patient feels some better.
> *Correct:* The patient feels somewhat better.

153. Number agreement of *this* and *that*. Avoid the use of the plural demonstrative adjectives *these* and *those* with such singular nouns as *kind, sort,* and *species*. Use *this* and *that*.

> *Correct:* I am tired of this kind of menu.
> *Correct:* Do you like that sort of fish?

NOTE 1. Do not use the article *a* or *an* after *kind of* or *sort of* (see section 186).

NOTE 2. With the plural forms *kinds* and *sorts* the plural adjectives *these* and *those* are correctly used, as in the following sentences:

> 1. These kinds of foods are wholesome.
> 2. Those sorts of books should be suppressed.

EXERCISES

I

In the following sentences point out, explain, and correct all errors in the use of adjectives and adverbs:

1. Frank is the tallest of any of my brothers.
2. Of the two hats I bought the least expensive.
3. She writes more rapidly but not so accurately as her sister.
4. Texas is larger than any state in the United States.
5. Today is some cooler than yesterday was.
6. Do you hear from Grace real often?
7. I predict that you will fail most absolutely.
8. Morley's second novel is as good, if not better than, his first one.
9. Please try to write more legible.
10. I have always disliked flatterers and those kind of people.

II

Write sentences in which you use appropriate predicate adjectives after the following verbs: *seem, appear, smell, taste, sound, feel, prove, grow, turn, remain.* In each sentence explain why an adjective, not an adverb, should be used.

III

Write sentences in which you use appropriate adjectives as objective complements after the following verbs: *wrap, raise, nail, shoot, paint, bind, fill*. Write sentences in which you use these same verbs followed by appropriate adverbs of manner.

D. *Verbs*

154. Principal parts of difficult verbs. The principal parts of a verb are (1) the first person singular of the present tense, (2) the first person singular of the past tense, and (3) the past participle. The principal parts of the following difficult verbs should be memorized, and should be used in short model sentences in order to fix them in mind.

PRESENT TENSE	PAST TENSE	PAST PARTICIPLE	PRESENT TENSE	PAST TENSE	PAST PARTICIPLE
am (be)	was	been	choose	chose	chosen
awake	awoke	awaked	come	came	come
	awaked		deal	dealt	dealt
bear	bore	borne	dive	dived	dived
		born	do	did	done
begin	began	begun	drag	dragged	dragged
bend	bent	bent	draw	drew	drawn
bid	bade	bidden	dream	dreamed	dreamed
	bid	bid		dreamt	dreamt
bite	bit	bit	drink	drank	drunk
		bitten	drive	drove	driven
bleed	bled	bled	drown	drowned	drowned
blow	blew	blown	dwell	dwelt	dwelt
break	broke	broken		dwelled	dwelled
bring	brought	brought	eat	ate	eaten
burn	burned	burned	fall	fell	fallen
	burnt	burnt	fight	fought	fought
burst	burst	burst	flee	fled	fled
catch	caught	caught	flow	flowed	flowed

fly	flew	flown	set	set	set
forget	forgot	forgotten	shake	shook	shaken
		forgot	shed	shed	shed
freeze	froze	frozen	shine	shone	shone
get	got	got	show	showed	shown
go	went	gone			showed
grow	grew	grown	shrink	shrank	shrunk
hang	hung	hung	sing	sang	sung
hang	hanged	hanged	sit	sat	sat
heat	heated	heated	slay	slew	slain
hold	held	held	slide	slid	slid
kneel	knelt	knelt			slidden
know	knew	known	slink	slunk	slunk
lay	laid	laid	speak	spoke	spoken
lead	led	led	spend	spent	spent
lend	lent	lent	spit	spit	spit
lie	lay	lain		spat	spat
lie	lied	lied	steal	stole	stolen
light	lighted	lighted	strive	strove	striven
	lit	lit	swear	swore	sworn
loose	loosed	loosed	sweep	swept	swept
lose	lost	lost	swim	swam	swum
mean	meant	meant	take	took	taken
pay	paid	paid	tear	tore	torn
prove	proved	proved	throw	threw	thrown
raise	raised	raised	thrust	thrust	thrust
read	read	read	tread	trod	trod
rid	rid	rid			trodden
ride	rode	ridden	wake	waked	waked
ring	rang	rung		woke	
rise	rose	risen	wear	wore	worn
run	ran	run	weave	wove	woven
say	said	said	weep	wept	wept
see	saw	seen	write	wrote	written

155. Six troublesome verbs. Avoid confusing the forms of the transitive verbs *lay, set,* and *raise* with the forms of the intransitive verbs *lie, sit,* and *rise*. The principal parts of these six verbs should be accurately memorized.

Transitive Verbs			Intransitive Verbs		
lay	laid	laid	lie	lay	lain
set	set	set	sit	sat	sat
raise	raised	raised	rise	rose	risen

A clear understanding of the meanings of these six verbs is the only reliable guide to their correct use.

lay, to put or deposit something in place; to cause a person or a thing to lie.

lie, to recline; to occupy a position, or be in a state of rest.

set, to place or put something in position; to cause a person or a thing to sit.

sit, to assume a sitting-posture; to occupy a position, or be in a state of rest.

raise, to lift something, or cause it to rise.

rise, to ascend, or go up; to become erect, or assume an upright posture.

EXERCISES

I

In the blanks left in the following sentences supply the proper forms of *lay* and *lie* and give the reason for the forms used:

1. She has —— in that position for two days.

2. Mother —— the baby on the bed, and there she was —— when I reëntered the room.

3. His uncle was —— in the room where he had —— for three years.

4. The rain has —— the dust, which for weeks has —— on trees and houses.

5. Tom and Jerry were —— the new water pipe while the rest of us were —— in the shade.

6. Let sleeping dogs ——.

7. When we had —— our plans before him, we left.

8. Covers had been —— for thirty guests.

9. Where have you —— my book?

10. All night my book had —— on the front step, where I had —— it when I went to play ball.

II

In the blanks left in the following sentences supply the proper forms of *set* and *sit* and give reasons for the forms used:

1. Last week father —— the old blue hen on fifteen eggs out in the woodshed, and there she has been —— ever since.
2. I have —— still so long that I need exercise.
3. In the midst of a spacious lawn was —— a large white house.
4. The house —— back from the road.
5. As soon as we had —— the house in order, we —— down to rest.
6. I enjoy —— down again after —— out plants all the afternoon.
7. Do you think that this coat —— well?
8. Often I have —— for hours listening to Uncle Caleb's stories.

III

In the blanks left in the following sentences supply the proper forms of *raise* and *rise* and give reasons for the forms used:

1. When I had ——, I —— the shades of both windows.
2. We shall —— the flag when the sun ——.
3. When we ——, we discovered that the river was ——.
4. In spite of an abundant supply of food, prices continue to ——.
5. The fermentation of the yeast —— the sponge.
6. The dough has —— to the top of the pan.
7. The man across the aisle ——, —— his hat, and offered to —— the window for me.
8. Do you think that the wheat will —— after such a beating rain as this?

156. Uses of *shall* and *will*, *should* and *would*. Observe the following rules for the correct use of the auxiliaries *shall* and *will*, *should* and *would*:

1. *In statements of simple futurity.* To represent simple futurity, use *shall* or *should* in the first person and *will* or *would* in the second and third persons, both singular and plural. The following scheme should be memorized and the illustrative sentences carefully studied:

I shall (should)   we shall (should)
you will (would)   you will (would)
he will (would)   they will (would)

1. I shall be seventeen years old in November.
2. We shall return home Thursday.
3. If I had been invited, I should have gone.
4. You will reach your destination Friday, I suppose.
5. I have recently read a novel that you would enjoy reading.
6. He will be surprised to see you.
7. They will call for us at eight o'clock.

NOTE. *Will* is used in the second and third persons to express polite commands.

1. You will report to me as soon as you have returned.
2. He will deliver this letter to the general at once.

2. *In statements of determination, resolution, desire, or promise.* To express determination, resolution, desire, or promise on the part of the speaker, use *will* or *would* in the first person and *shall* or *should* in the second and third persons, both singular and plural. The following scheme should be memorized and the illustrative sentences carefully studied:

I will (would)   we will (would)
you shall (should)   you shall (should)
he shall (should)   they shall (should)

1. I will refuse every offer of compromise.
2. We will accompany you to the boat if you wish.
3. You shall not leave this house tonight.
4. Were you my child, you should obey me.
5. He shall pay me every cent he owes.
6. They shall do as you say.

NOTE. *Shall* is used in the second and third persons to express prophecy.

1. Thou shalt lower to his level day by day.
2. Your young men shall see visions, and your old men shall dream dreams.

3. *In questions.* (1) If the subject is in the first person, use *shall* and *should*, except in repeating a question addressed to the speaker.

1. Shall I see you at the reception? (*Answer:* Yes, you will see me.)
2. Shall we walk or ride? (*Answer:* We shall walk.)
3. Will you lend me the book? (*Answer:* Will I lend you the book? Indeed, I will.)

(2) If the subject is in the second or third person, use the auxiliary that you anticipate in the answer. The auxiliary used in the answer should be chosen according to the rules already given for statements.

1. Shall you attend the reception? (*Answer:* I shall . . .)
2. Will you meet me promptly at seven? (*Answer:* I will . . .)
3. Should you attend college if you had the money? (*Answer:* I should . . .)
4. Would you go if you were in my place? (*Answer:* I would . . .)
5. Will she recover ? (*Answer:* She will . . .)
6. Would she care to see me? (*Answer:* She would . . .)
7. Shall he be punished? (*Answer:* He shall . . .)

4. *In indirect statements and indirect questions.* (1) In indirect statements *shall* and *will*, *should* and *would*, should agree with the forms used in the corresponding direct statement, except that when the first person with *shall* or *should* in the direct statement becomes the second or third person in the indirect statement, *shall* or *should* is retained, and that when the second person with *will* and *would* in the direct statement becomes the first person in the indirect statement, *will* and *would* are changed to *shall* and *should*.

1. My friend said, "I will go." (Direct statement)
2. My friend said he would go. (Indirect statement)
3. My friend says, "I shall go." (Direct statement)
4. My friend says he shall go. (Indirect statement)

5. My friend says, "You will be late." (Direct statement)
6. My friend says I shall be late. (Indirect statement)
7. My friend said, "You will be late." (Direct statement)
8. My friend said I should be late. (Indirect statement)

(2) In indirect questions retain the auxiliary used in the direct question, unless a change of tense (*shall* to *should*, *will* to *would*) be necessary.

1. What shall I tell her? (Direct question)
2. You ask me what you shall tell her. (Indirect question)
3. He asked me what he should tell her. (Indirect question)
4. Will you tell me? (Direct question)
5. You ask me whether I will tell you. (Indirect question)
6. He asked me whether I would tell him. (Indirect question)

5. *Use of **would** to express a wish.* *Would* is often used to express a wish.

1. Would that I were there!
2. Would that he had told us earlier!

6. *Use of **would** to express customary or habitual action.* *Would* is frequently used in all three persons to indicate customary or habitual action.

1. Every day we would go swimming.
2. About six o'clock each evening you would see a long line of hungry tourists waiting for the first stroke of the gong.
3. He would often read a new novel through at one sitting.

7. *Use of **should** for **ought**.* *Should* is very frequently used in all three persons as a synonym of *ought* to express duty, obligation, propriety, or expectation.

1. I should write her a letter of condolence.
2. You should be more considerate.
3. He should have written us that he was coming.
4. We should arrive at camp before sunset.

NOTE. Avoid such vulgarisms as *should ought* and *had ought*.

8. *Use of* **shall** *and* **should** *in provisional statements.* **Shall** and *should* are used in all three persons in dependent clauses that make provisional statements.

1. If I should change my mind, I would notify you.
2. Should you meet her, would you speak to her?
3. An official who should betray such a trust would be removed from office.

EXERCISES

I

In the blanks left in the following sentences supply either *shall* or *will*, according to the rules given above, and state your reason for the use of each auxiliary:

1. They —— not impose on my generosity any longer.
2. —— I tell the doctor that you are waiting?
3. —— you inform the postman of my change of address?
4. I —— drown; no one —— rescue me.
5. Miss Ames, you —— give the patient one capsule every hour.
6. Before you die you —— see that I am right.
7. —— I protect you? Why, certainly.
8. You —— not punish an innocent man.
9. —— I see you again before you sail?
10. When —— we three meet again?
11. Our friends —— be surprised to hear the news.
12. Generations as yet unborn —— cherish the spot where we are now standing.
13. We —— never have a truer friend than Cranston.
14. You —— now prepare to hand in your papers.
15. I —— not attempt to excuse myself.
16. Julia and I —— enter college in September.
17. —— you and your sister return to school this autumn?
18. —— she forgive me for my stupidity?
19. If you —— lend me your dictionary, I —— return it early in the morning.
20. My mother says that we —— be tardy, but I think that our teacher —— excuse us if you —— use your winning smile when you explain why we are late.

II

In the blanks left in the following sentences supply either *should* or *would*, according to the rules given above, and state your reason for the use of each auxiliary:

1. I —— ask for more time if I were you.
2. —— I tell him the whole wretched story?
3. Do you suppose that he —— believe me?
4. What —— you do if you were in my place?
5. If I had the book, you —— have it.
6. —— you be disappointed if I were not to come?
7. —— you accept a position as stenographer in our firm?
8. They —— willingly help us if they could.
9. They —— be thankful for their good health.
10. —— that I had never taken the risk!
11. If I —— tell you the truth, —— you believe me?
12. In the evening we —— sit on the lawn and watch the fireflies.
13. They —— not listen to our warning.
14. He promised his mother that he —— not go swimming.
15. She reminded him that he —— come home early.

III

Write twenty sentences illustrating the various proper uses of *shall*, *will*, *should*, and *would*. In each sentence be sure that the auxiliary used is the correct one.

157. Additional cautions regarding tense. 1. *Present tense used in the statement of a general truth.* A statement that is permanently true should be expressed in the present tense.

1. Though ancient peoples believed that the earth was flat, Magellan proved that it is round.
2. At a very early age I learned that honesty is the best policy.

2. *Past tense wrongly used for past-perfect tense.* Avoid using the past tense where the past-perfect tense is logically required.

Incorrect: I attended college only two months when I was forced to withdraw to help father.

Correct: I had attended college only two months when I was forced to withdraw to help father.

3. *Perfect infinitive incorrectly used for present infinitive.* Avoid using a perfect infinitive unless it designates an action completed at the time indicated by the principal verb.

Incorrect: I should have liked to have met your mother.
Correct: I should have liked to meet your mother.
Incorrect: I intended to have written to you.
Correct: I intended to write to you.

NOTE. With *ought* the perfect infinitive is properly used.

Correct: I ought to have warned you of the danger.

4. *Present participle incorrectly used for perfect participle or past tense.* Avoid using a present participle unless it designates an action going on at the same time as the action indicated by the principal verb.

Incorrect: Leaving his home at an early age, Joyce had lived a life of hardship.

Correct: Having left his home at an early age, Joyce had lived a life of hardship.

Incorrect: I completed the grammar school at the age of eleven, entering high school the next year.

Correct: I completed the grammar school at the age of eleven and entered high school the next year.

5. *Past participle incorrectly used for the past tense.* Avoid the crude error of using the past participle for the past tense.

> *Incorrect:* Then Mary begun to cry.
> *Correct:* Then Mary began to cry.
> *Incorrect:* We sung our school song.
> *Correct:* We sang our school song.

6. *Confusion of the past tense and the past participle in the formation of the perfect tenses.* Avoid the crude error of using

the past-tense form of the verb instead of the past participle in the formation of the perfect tenses.

> *Incorrect:* It had began to rain before we left.
> *Correct:* It had begun to rain before we left.
> *Incorrect:* The bell has rang.
> *Correct:* The bell has rung.

158. Uses of the subjunctive mood. The special subjunctive forms *be* and *were* should be carefully distinguished from the corresponding indicative forms in the following uses of the subjunctive mood:

1. *To express a wish.* The subjunctive mood is used to express a wish.

> **1.** Peace be to his ashes!
> **2.** O that she were here!

2. *To indicate uncertainty, improbability, or a condition contrary to fact.* The subjunctive mood is used to indicate uncertainty, improbability, or a condition contrary to fact.

1. If he be an honest man, I am no judge of men.

2. If Thornton be elected captain, we shall have a strong team.

3. If I were you, I should not hesitate a moment in accepting the position.

4. I wish that mother were here.

NOTE. Avoid such crude errors as *if I was you, if he was in my place,* and similar illiterate expressions.

EXERCISES

I

In the following sentences point out, explain, and correct all errors in tense and mood:

1. Grandfather often assured me that youth was the best period in a person's life.

2. I had sank for the second time before I was rescued.

3. O that I was at home!

4. On graduation day I tried to recall how I spent my four years in college.

5. I swum two miles yesterday.

6. If he was not my guardian, I might ask his advice.

7. Roberts was our best track athlete last year, winning more points than all the other men on the team.

8. Losing his fortune in an investment in oil, he had begun life anew at the age of fifty.

9. I should not give the matter another thought if I was you.

10. Astronomers long ago proved that the sun was the center of our planetary system.

II

Write sentences using (1) the past tense and (2) the past-perfect tense of the following verbs: *begin, break, burst, choose, come, do, drink, eat, fall, freeze, ride, ring, run, see, sing, sink, speak, swim, take, tear, wear.*

E. *Participles, Verbal Nouns, and Infinitives*

159. Reference of participles. A participle, like a pronoun, must refer accurately to the noun or pronoun on which it depends for its meaning. The substantive must be within the sentence containing the participle, and the reference of the participle must be logical and immediately apparent. A participle that has no expressed substantive to which it can properly refer, or that has two substantives to which it may ambiguously refer, is called a *dangling participle.* (See section 121, rule 2.)

Do not use a participial phrase to introduce a sentence or a clause unless it logically modifies the *subject* of the sentence or clause.

Incorrect: Being in a cage, I was not afraid of the lion.
Correct: Since the lion was in a cage, I was not afraid of him.
Correct: The lion, being in a cage, did not frighten me.

Incorrect: Having returned from a visit to my aunt, my parents welcomed me home.

Correct: When I returned from a visit to my aunt, my parents welcomed me home.

Correct: Having returned from a visit to my aunt, I was welcomed home by my parents.

Notice that dangling participles may be avoided either by using a dependent clause instead of a participial phrase or by using as the subject of the sentence or clause the noun or pronoun to which the participal logically refers.

Do not end a sentence with a participial phrase that is made to refer to a vaguely implied substantive or to the entire thought of the preceding sentence or clause.

Incorrect: The water was impure, caused by bad drainage.

Correct: The impurity of the water was caused by bad drainage.

Correct: The water was impure as the result of bad drainage.

Incorrect: He speaks fluently many languages, thus aiding him in his travels.

Correct: He speaks fluently many languages; this ability aids him in his travels.

Correct: His ability to speak fluently many languages aids him in his travels.

160. Reference of verbal nouns. Do not use a verbal noun to introduce a sentence or clause unless it logically refers to the subject of the sentence or clause.

Incorrect: After inspecting my passport, I was permitted to go on board the boat.

Incorrect: In alighting from the car, my ankle was turned.

Errors of this kind may be avoided by using a clause instead of a verbal noun or by using as the subject of the sentence or clause the noun or pronoun to which the verbal noun logically refers.

Correct: After my passport had been inspected, I was permitted to go on board the boat.

Correct: After inspecting my passport, the official permitted me to go on board the boat.

Correct: In alighting from the car, I turned my ankle.

Correct: As I alighted from the car, I turned my ankle.

161. Reference of infinitives. Do not use an infinitive or an infinitive phrase to introduce a sentence or clause unless it logically refers to the subject of the sentence or clause.

Incorrect: To succeed, the process must be understood.

Correct: To succeed, you must understand the process.

Incorrect: To escape the heat, the trip should be made in April or October.

Correct: To escape the heat, you should make the trip in April or October.

162. Split infinitives. Avoid placing an adverbial modifier between an infinitive and its sign *to*.

Incorrect: The boat seemed to hardly move.

Correct: The boat seemed hardly to move.

EXERCISE

In the following sentences point out, explain, and correct all errors in the reference of participles, verbal nouns, and infinitives:

1. He has a large irrigation plant, thus assuring himself of a good crop every year.

2. Turning the corner suddenly, the motor cycle threw him down.

3. To obtain good seats, reservations should be made early.

4. Having recovered from his illness, the firm gave him his former position.

5. He is blind, caused by a wound that he received during the war.

6. After examining me and giving me a prescription, I paid the physician and left.

7. Coming out of the door, Forbes met a man as he entered.

8. To be sure that the dress will fit, a chart and form should be used.

9. Coming unexpectedly as it did, she was surprised at her election.

10. Being a guest, we were surprised at his rudeness.

11. Upon entering the hall, loud applause greeted him.

12. To play on the football team, your scholastic record must be good.

13. Having met her once before, she easily recognized me.

14. He approached, and, extending his hand, she took it.

15. In studying for his examination his eyes were strained.

F. *Prepositions and Conjunctions*

163. Prepositions. 1. *Object of a preposition.* A noun or a pronoun used as the object of a preposition should be in the objective case (see section 147, rule 4).

2. *Between and among.* *Between* should be used in speaking of two persons or things; *among*, in speaking of more than two.

3. *Ending a sentence with a preposition.* Since the end of a sentence is an emphatic position, it should usually be reserved for a more emphatic word than a preposition. This is the chief reason why reputable writers try to avoid placing a preposition at the end of the sentence. Often, in such a sentence as the following, the word preceding the preposition receives the necessary stress even when the preposition comes last.

America is a good country to live in, a good country to live for, and a good country to die for.

164. Conjunctions. Coördinate conjunctions should be used to connect words, phrases, or clauses that are coördinate in rank and alike in grammatical form (see sections 120, rule 3, and 121, rule 4; see also section 172).

Avoid the use of *like* as a conjunction to connect two clauses. Use *as* or *as if.*

> *Incorrect:* I did the work like he wanted it done.
> *Correct:* I did the work as he wanted it done.
> *Incorrect:* She cared for the child like it was her own.
> *Correct:* She cared for the child as if it were her own.

NOTE. *Like* is correctly used before a noun or a pronoun that is not the subject of a dependent clause.

1. He stands like a soldier at attention.
2. The wind blew like a hurricane.

G. *Miscellaneous Grammatical Cautions*

165. Improper omission of words. No essential word, unless it is clearly and correctly implied, should be omitted from a sentence.

1. *Omission of a verb.* Do not omit a principal verb in any part of a sentence unless the form expressed elsewhere in the sentence is grammatically correct and clearly implied at the point where it is omitted.

Incorrect: She has not and never will recover.
Correct: She has not recovered and never will recover.
Incorrect: I have not written, nor am I going to.
Correct: I have not written, nor am I going to write.

An auxiliary or a copulative verb should not be omitted unless the form expressed earlier in the sentence is grammatically correct and clearly implied in the latter part of the sentence.

Incorrect: The house was painted and the rooms papered again.
Correct: The house was painted and the rooms were papered again.
Incorrect: The garden has been prepared and all the plants set out.
Correct: The garden has been prepared and all the plants have been set out.
Incorrect: The first speaker was entertaining, but the others extremely boresome.
Correct: The first speaker was entertaining, but the others were extremely boresome.

NOTE. A single form of the verb *be* should not be made to serve as a copula and an auxiliary at the same time.

Incorrect: Miss Agnew was a successful teacher and loved by all her pupils.
Correct: Miss Agnew was a successful teacher and was loved by all her pupils.

2. *Omission of an article or of a demonstrative or possessive adjective.* Do not omit an article or a demonstrative or possessive adjective before any noun in a series unless the nouns designate the same person or thing or are self-distinguishing.

Incorrect: The three officers of our class are the president, vice president, and secretary and treasurer.
Correct: The three officers of our class are the president, the vice president, and the secretary and treasurer.
Correct: Last week I was the maid, cook, and nurse for our family.
Correct: His father and mother were born in Scotland.

3. *Omission of a preposition.* Do not omit a preposition that is either grammatically or idiomatically necessary in the sentence.

Incorrect: I have no understanding or interest in golf.
Correct: I have no understanding of, or interest in, golf.
Better: I have no understanding of golf and no interest in it.

Note. In formal composition many adverbial phrases of time, place, and manner regularly require a preposition.

> *Incorrect:* I never saw him act that way before.
> *Correct:* I never saw him act in that way before.
> *Incorrect:* I can be content any place.
> *Correct:* I can be content in any place.
> *Correct:* I can be content anywhere.

4. *Omission of the subordinate conjunction **that**.* (1) In formal composition the subordinate conjunction *that* should, as a rule, be expressed at the beginning of a noun clause that follows a verb of *saying, knowing, thinking, feeling, perceiving,* etc.

Incorrect: Do you realize by neglecting your present opportunities you are handicapping yourself for life?
Correct: Do you realize that by neglecting your present opportunities you are handicapping yourself for life?

(2) In formal writing *that* should not be omitted after *so* in the connective *so that* introducing a clause of purpose or of result.

Incorrect: The storm raged so violently no one slept.
Correct: The storm raged so violently that no one slept.

5. *Omission of other subordinate conjunctions.* Before an introductory participial phrase that is the equivalent of a dependent clause a subordinate conjunction is usually required.

Incorrect: Studying my lessons, I went to sleep.
Correct: While studying my lessons, I went to sleep.
Incorrect: Discouraged by his failure, he did not give up.
Correct: Though discouraged by his failure, he did not give up.

6. *Omission of the subject of a dependent clause.* Do not omit the subject of a dependent clause unless the same word serves properly as the subject of both the dependent and the independent clause.

Incorrect: When a small boy my father married again.
Correct: When I was a small boy, my father married again.
Correct: While still a youth, I resolved to become a missionary.

EXERCISE

In the following sentences supply all words that have been improperly omitted (see sections 151 and 186) and explain why the words that you have added are necessary:

1. We loved Aunt Clara better than anybody.
2. Traveling is so expensive nowadays.
3. The room was swept and the rugs placed in order.
4. Conroy had been a bank president and trusted by everybody.
5. He has acted just as anyone would.
6. I have no respect or confidence in such a man.
7. We applied early so we might secure desirable seats.
8. Waiting for the train, I read a magazine.

9. I have missed mother more than you.

10. We have always, and always shall have, high standards of honesty.

11. He knew in his condition he could not live very long.

12. A doctor, interne, and nurse stood by my bed.

13. The Morelands are such refined people.

14. While I was home I looked every place for my fountain pen.

15. A new constitution has been drawn up and new by-laws prepared.

166. Double subjects and double objects. In speech, as well as in writing, avoid the use of double subjects and double objects. Only illiterate and careless persons use such expressions as the following:

1. My uncle, he went home yesterday.
2. This paper, it says Lowry was elected.
3. That money you gave me, I lost it.

167. Double negatives. Do not use in the same sentence two or more negative words unless they are coördinate. Avoid using *hardly, scarcely, only,* and *but* (= *only*) with a negative. Guard against such double-negative expressions as *can't hardly, couldn't scarcely, hadn't only, cannot help but,* etc. Use instead *can hardly, could scarcely, had only, cannot help,* etc.

Incorrect: I can't hardly realize that Christmas is here.
Correct: I can hardly realize that Christmas is here.
Incorrect: I couldn't scarcely understand the child.
Correct: I could scarcely understand the child.
Incorrect: I hadn't met her only once.
Correct: I had met her only once.
Incorrect: I cannot help but sympathize with her.
Correct: I cannot help sympathizing with her.

168. *When* and *where* clauses wrongly used. Do not use a clause introduced by *when* or *where* in place of a predicate noun. Be particularly on your guard against this error when you are stating a definition.

Incorrect: Inflection is where you change the form of a word to indicate a change in its meaning.

Correct: Inflection is a change of form in a word to indicate a change in its meaning.

Incorrect: Narration is when you relate an experience or an event to someone else.

Better: Narration is the relating of an experience or an event to someone else.

169. *Because* clause wrongly used. Do not attempt to make an adverbial clause introduced by *because* perform the function of a noun clause either as the subject of a verb or as a predicate nominative. Do not say "The reason is because" etc. Say "The reason is that" etc.

Incorrect: Because your intentions were good proves nothing.

Correct: The fact that your intentions were good proves nothing.

Incorrect: The reason he failed in his examination was because he did not study.

Correct: The reason he failed in his examination was that he did not study.

Note. A clause introduced by *because* is correctly used as an adverbial clause of cause or reason.

Correct: He failed because he did not study.

II. Special Cautions in Sentence Structure

170. The *period fault*. The period fault consists in using a period to set off a phrase or a subordinate clause as if it were a complete sentence. Such a detached fragment of a sentence, since it is d*ependent* on some word outside itself, cannot stand alone or express a complete thought. In most instances the period fault is the result of carelessness. The writer thoughtlessly places a period where, perhaps, a comma or a semicolon is required. He then begins the next word with a capital letter and places a second period after the detached fragment.

In our informal everyday speech we employ many incomplete sentences. In all writing, however, we should carefully avoid the period fault, which is one of the most serious errors in composition that we can commit (see section 115, and review the exercise included in it; see also section 120, rule 2, and section 131).

Incorrect: Dalton sacrificed everything. His one aim being the attainment of his purpose.

Correct: Dalton sacrificed everything, his one aim being the attainment of his purpose.

Incorrect: He assured me that the attempt was useless. That better men than I had failed.

Correct: He assured me that the attempt was useless—that better men than I had failed.

Incorrect: I was surprised to learn of his prejudice. Because he had heretofore been very liberal in his views.

Correct: I was surprised to learn of his prejudice, because he had heretofore been very liberal in his views.

NOTE. Setting off an elliptical independent clause as a sentence does not constitute a period fault. In replying to a question we may rightly use such elliptical sentences as the following: *Yes. When? By all means. Certainly. Surely not. Very well, then. Not now. Good-by.* In each of these expressions the omitted words can be accurately supplied from the question or statement that has immediately preceded it.

> "Do you think that I should go to college?" I asked.
> "By all means [you should go to college]," my friend replied.

171. The *comma fault*. The use of a comma in place of a period, a semicolon, a colon, or a dash is termed the *comma fault*. This error is fully as serious as the period fault. Both errors are to be carefully guarded against. The person who is guilty of either of them proves that he does not yet know what constitutes a sentence. (See section 128, rule 7, and the caution that follows it; see also section 129, rule 1, and section 120, rule 1.)

Incorrect: I found him asleep in his bed, I had not heard him when he entered.

Correct: I found him asleep in his bed. I had not heard him when he entered.

Incorrect: Hanson always did his work a little better than the rest of us, that was what won him his promotion.

Correct: Hanson always did his work a little better than the rest of us ; that was what won him his promotion.

EXERCISE

In the following exercise point out, explain, and correct all comma faults and period faults:

1. Our guest entertained us with many interesting stories of adventure, he had been a newspaper correspondent during the World War.

2. Art museums have a great cultural value, they furnish the public an opportunity to develop a better æsthetic taste.

3. A freshman has much to learn. Never having been dependent on himself before. And not knowing how to study.

4. It was useless to argue with mother. Though Tom always tried to convince her that he was right.

5. This is an excellent novel. One which I am sure you will enjoy. Even if it is not a love story.

6. Blair won first place in three events. Thereby enabling us to win the meet.

7. When I left, I offered to pay him for his hospitality, he refused to accept a cent.

8. Toby has excellent table manners, I began training him when he was a small kitten, not even the smell of fish makes him forget to be polite.

9. As night approached I became uneasy. Because father had promised to return before six o'clock.

10. The manager of our ranch telephoned father that bandits had crossed the border and raided several towns. And that they had killed one of the rangers.

11. You may certainly depend on seeing me in Colorado this summer. If I can get away from this large family of mine. But not on keeping me more than a month.

12. I cannot understand the luck that some people have, last year our cook held the number that won an automobile, and now her uncle has made a fortune in oil.

172. Faulty coördination in compound sentences. The following cautions regarding the construction of compound sentences should be carefully observed:

1. *Unequal sentence elements wrongly coördinated.* Do not attempt to form a compound sentence by using a coördinate conjunction to join a phrase or a dependent clause to an independent clause. Omit the conjunction and express the thought properly in a simple or complex sentence; otherwise form a real compound sentence by recasting the dependent sentence element to make it coördinate with the other. (See section 120, rule 3, and section 121, rule 4.)

Incorrect: Clark failed in two subjects, and thus losing his position as captain of the team.

Correct: Clark failed in two subjects, and thus he lost his position as captain of the team. (A compound sentence)

Incorrect: The lecturer is a nerve specialist, and who was a classmate of my father's in college.

Correct: The lecturer is a nerve specialist, who was a classmate of my father's in college. (A complex sentence)

Better: The lecturer, who was a classmate of my father's in college, is a nerve specialist.

Incorrect: Skiing is an exciting sport, but which is rather dangerous.

Correct: Skiing is an exciting sport, but it is rather dangerous. (A compound sentence)

2. *Unequal sentence-thoughts wrongly coördinated.* Avoid overworking the compound sentence. Do not form the careless habit of expressing each part of a thought as an independent clause and then mechanically linking these clauses together with *and, but, or, nor,* or *for.* Very often the thought imperfectly expressed in a loosely constructed compound sentence could be much better expressed in a complex or simple sentence.

Subordinate portions of the sentence-thought should be given proper expression in phrases and subordinate clauses. (See section 120, rule 3.)

Incorrect: We are going to the country this summer, and we are going to visit my grandmother.

Correct: We are going to the country this summer to visit my grandmother. (A simple sentence)

Incorrect: My chum told me that I had won the scholarship, and I was overjoyed.

Correct: When my friend told me that I had won the scholarship, I was overjoyed. (A complex sentence)

NOTE. Try to break yourself of the "*so* habit." The thoughtless use of *so* as a connective between the members of a compound sentence is one of the chief causes of excessive coördination. Unless the relation of the second coördinate clause to the first is actually that of consequence, *so* is the wrong connective. As a rule, the clause preceding *so* should be subordinated and the *so* omitted. Avoid the slovenly habit of using *and so* as a connective.

Incorrect: The manager notified me yesterday of my appointment as secretary, and so I accepted the position at once.

Correct: When the manager notified me yesterday of my appointment as secretary, I accepted the position at once.

3. *Stringy compound sentences.* Do not allow yourself to write loosely constructed, or stringy, compound sentences. Devote a separate sentence to each sentence-thought. Place subordinate portions of the sentence-thought in subordinate sentence elements, either phrases or dependent clauses. (See section 120, rule 1.)

Incorrect: The old storekeeper had queer ways, but everyone was fond of him, and he certainly was a real friend to everyone, and I never knew a man who had a kinder heart.

Better: Though the old storekeeper had queer ways, I never knew a man who had a kinder heart. Everyone was fond of him, because each recognized in him a real friend.

4. *Careless choice of coördinate conjunctions.* In the construction of a compound sentence, determine the relation existing between the two clauses and then indicate this relation clearly by the use of the right connective or by proper punctuation (see section 120, rule 3).

Incorrect: It is time for the curtain to rise, and only a few of the audience have yet come.
Correct: It is time for the curtain to rise, but only a few of the audience have yet come.
Incorrect: Though you have failed, you have been given a fair trial; however, you should not blame your employer.
Correct: Though you have failed, you have been given a fair trial; hence you should not blame your employer.

173. Parallel construction. Ideas that are parallel in thought should likewise be parallel in grammatical expression (see section 121, rule 4). Observe the following cautions in conforming to this requirement:

1. *Infinitives, participles, and verbal nouns not parallel.* Do not attempt to make an infinitive and a participle, or an infinitive and a verbal noun, parallel in construction.

Incorrect: Clark tried to play football in the afternoon and studying his lessons at night.
Correct: Clark tried to play football in the afternoon and to study his lessons at night.
Correct: Clark tried playing football in the afternoon and studying his lessons at night.

2. *Infinitives, participles, and finite verbs not parallel.* Do not attempt to make an infinitive and a finite verb, or a participle and a finite verb, parallel in construction.

Incorrect: Last summer I had the choice of two trips: to accompany my parents to Maine, or I could go with my chum to California.
Correct: Last summer I had the choice of two trips: to accompany my parents to Maine or to go with my chum to California.

3. *Words, phrases, and clauses not parallel.* Do not attempt to make a word and a clause, or a phrase and a clause, parallel in construction (see section 121, rule 4).

Incorrect: I promised to take good care of the book and that I would return it promptly.

Correct: I promised to take good care of the book and to return it promptly.

Correct: I promised that I would take good care of the book and that I would return it promptly.

174. Shift in point of view. As a rule, avoid any shift in point of view within a sentence. It is desirable to employ the same subject and the same voice throughout the sentence. (See section 120, rule 4.)

Undesirable: The entire class attended the picnic, and an enjoyable day was spent by all.

Better: The entire class attended the picnic, and all spent an enjoyable day.

Undesirable: When you have selected a satisfactory pattern, the material may then be bought.

Better: When you have selected a satisfactory pattern, you may then buy the material.

GENERAL EXERCISE

In the following exercise point out, explain, and correct all errors in grammar and sentence structure:

1. Julia is not near so attractive as Jane.
2. These kind of days make everyone feel good.
3. When of high-school age, fate brought them together in the same town.
4. Returning home, I met him walking very slow.
5. Fatigued by his long walk, he insisted on accompanying me.
6. I cannot help but wonder where they have gone.
7. The great event of the game was when Faber made a touchdown.
8. Trent is a spectacular player, but who is not very dependable.

9. I spent a lonely summer. All my friends being away on their vacations.

10. Heavy rains came in August, and it was too late to benefit the crops.

11. We agreed to write regularly and that we would meet the next year as freshmen at Brighton College.

12. What sort of a vacation did you have?

13. Being a harsh man, we stood in awe of my father.

14. Neither of the men have been seen since Friday.

15. Whom do you think will be elected?

16. Mrs. Ralston, accompanied by her two nieces, have been spending the summer in Maine.

17. She would not consent to me going home alone.

18. Our state's governor has been impeached.

19. Each of us have had our pictures made.

20. I slept good last night, which is very unusual for me.

21. She wore a brooch in her hair which she bought in Paris.

22. She is one of those oil millionaires' wives.

23. We returned by the longest of the two routes.

24. They had better manners than any children I ever knew.

25. It don't seem that I have been laying in bed for ten hours.

26. I will be eighteen years old tomorrow.

27. We should have liked to have accompanied you.

28. If I was in your place, I would not answer his letter.

29. His ambitions are too high, but they will not be realized.

30. He spoke like he meant what he said.

31. She has not apologized, nor does she intend to.

32. Passengers should not enter or leave the car while moving.

33. In order to see the country at our leisure, a car was rented for three weeks.

34. He is a lecturer well worth hearing and who never disappoints his audiences.

35. A heavy rain fell during the night, and thus delaying our departure for several hours.

36. Naturalization is where a foreigner becomes a citizen of the country in which he intends to make his future home.

37. Where the Brents get their money is a mystery to me, that is the third car they have bought this year, and they take a trip every summer.

38. Someone told me that you are going away to school this fall. That you are going to study pharmacy.

39. The reason I am interested is because I thought once of studying pharmacy myself.

40. We have been admiring the shade for the lamp on the table that you recently bought.

41. Dr. Baldwin is one of the most reliable physicians who has ever practiced in our town.

42. All arrangements have been made and the date set for the contest.

43. I am not superstitious, but one could not live with grandmother very long without coming to believe in a few of them.

44. I always try to properly prepare my lessons.

45. She is prettier, but not so amiable as her sister.

46. To understand her character, her environment and training must be taken into consideration.

47. Upon consulting a chemist, the ore was found to contain small particles of gold.

48. Arson is when a person maliciously sets fire to a house.

49. She cares for me like I was her own child.

50. I wish that today was Sunday.

51. I have forgotten whom she said would lecture tonight.

52. Our class begun studying Latin in September.

53. Taking the child in her arms, she set down and sung him to sleep.

54. You shall miss us when we are gone.

55. I shall allow no one to criticize my action; I shall die first.

56. He sure was a gentleman, and acted real courteous.

57. You look badly since your illness.

58. She dances much more gracefully than him.

59. This is one of the best, if not the best, play that the young author has written.

60. In Aunt Ellen's girlhood they did not wear such sensible clothes.

61. Mother told sister that the doctor said she must get more sleep.

62. His investment made him a fortune, which surprised all the members of his family.

63. No one in our class but Tom had solved all their problems.

64. The monument's top was struck by lightning.

65. It was me who they blamed for the mistake.

66. He told him his books were on his desk.

67. Three new cases of pneumonia have been reported. Making forty-seven in all.

68. Neither the doctor nor the nurse were able to give him relief.

69. A person is known by the way they spend their leisure.

70. The clock struck ten, we had passed another hour in anxious suspense.

71. In order to enjoy good health, plenty of exercise should be taken.

72. The audience began hissing and to leave the theater.

73. There was not but one fault that he found in my drawing.

74. We live such a long way from the city.

75. Having been reared in the country, the city often oppresses me.

76. Our neighbors intended to have left for their vacation yesterday.

77. Today is some cooler than yesterday was.

78. She is more popular than any woman in town.

79. Farming entails great risk, for they never know when a frost or a drought may kill their crops.

80. Mother did not approve of us attending the dance. Unless we were chaperoned by Mrs. Gaston.

CHAPTER XII

THE CORRECT USE OF WORDS

175. Words. A word is a symbol that stands for an idea. When combined with other words to form a sentence, it helps to express a thought. Through use in communication it acquires meaning and currency. Later in the history of the language, however, it may gradually be supplanted by a word that is more expressive, or it may fall into disuse altogether as the idea for which it has formerly stood ceases to interest mankind. In every generation there are various attempts to add new words and to change the meanings of others, though comparatively few of these attempts prove successful. On the whole, language tends to be conservative and economical, and the fate of words is like that of living organisms: only the fittest survive.

176. The English language and its sources. The English language, according to the most recent unabridged dictionaries, contains more than four hundred and fifty thousand words. Of this total fully a third have either passed out of use altogether or are being gradually discarded. An even larger proportion consists of technical and trade words employed by scientists and other professional men and by business men in their various fields. The comparatively small remainder includes the words that constitute the vocabularies of the majority of persons.

The English language is descended from the Anglo-Saxon, but from that source it has derived not more than half its present store of words. The greater portion of the other half it has taken over and adapted from ancient and modern foreign languages. From the Latin and the French have come perhaps four fifths of these borrowed words. From the Greek and from modern languages other than the French have been acquired most of the words that make up the remaining fifth.

In addition to borrowing words liberally from other languages, English-speaking people are constantly coining new words. Scientists and inventors enrich the language with such words as *telephone, aëroplane, radio, vitamine, photostat,* and *synura.* From proper names come such words as *macadamize, babel, dahlia, volt,* and *bedlam.* From the names of animals are derived such verbs as *gull* and *ape,* and such adjectives as *sheepish, dogged,* and *henpecked.* Now and then, but usually after a long struggle, a slang word is admitted to legitimate use. Among words thus admitted may be mentioned *hoax, mob, banter,* and *gerrymander.*

EXERCISE

Bring to class a list of words that have recently come into the English language either through borrowing or through coinage. The World War and recent discoveries and inventions should afford you several examples.

177. Diction. By diction is meant the choice of words for the expression of our thoughts. Diction is based upon the usage of the best speakers and writers of the present time. Concerning such usage we can learn much from modern unabridged English dictionaries by observing the standing of various words that we use and that we hear others employ. We must remember, however, that an unabridged dictionary contains *all* the words in the language, including obsolete words and meanings as well as comparatively recent slang. The fact that a word appears in the dictionary does not warrant our using it, therefore, unless it is in good standing. We may also aid ourselves greatly in our choice and use of words by noticing the diction of the best speakers and writers with whom we associate.

178. Good use. Correctness of diction requires that each word chosen be in good use. Good use demands that words have a present, national, and reputable standing in the language. A word is in *present* use if it is used in modern speech or is found in contemporary literature. A word is in *national* use when it is employed not merely in certain professions and trades or in particular geographical sections but by a majority of the people throughout the nation. A word is in *reputable* use if it occurs in the speech of cultured persons and in the writings of the best authors. Unless a word satisfies all three of these requirements it is not in good use.

In respect to certain words and phrases English usage differs from American. *Lift* for *elevator*, *petrol* for *gasoline*, *barrister* for *attorney* or *lawyer*, *stop* for *stay*, *directly* for *immediately*, and *different to* for *different from* are a few examples of such variations. In the United States we should follow American usage.

179. Violations of good use. Since most of us employ daily in our speech and in our writing many words that violate one or more of the demands of good use, we need to have our attention called to the principal groups of words that offend against good use, in order that we may improve our diction. Everyone who desires to speak and write well must become intimately acquainted with the correct use of words.

Words that violate good use may be divided into six groups: (1) barbarisms, (2) solecisms, (3) improprieties, (4) slang, (5) obsolete and archaic words, and (6) technical words.

180. Barbarisms. A barbarism is a word that has not yet been approved by the best speakers and writers as a reputable English word. The following classes of words are regarded as barbarisms:

1. *Colloquialisms.* Words that are permissible in familiar conversation but that should be avoided in formal speech or writing are called colloquialisms. Such words as *cute, all right, folks, a raise* for *an increase, poor* for *thin,* and *reckon* or *guess* for *suppose* are colloquialisms.

2. *Dialectal and provincial words.* Words that are used and understood by only a small group of persons living in a particular section of a country are called provincial or dialectal words. Such words as *tote* for *carry, right smart* for *considerable amount, favor* for *resemble, redd up* for *put in order, lose a train* for *miss a train* are violations of national as well as reputable use.

3. *Vulgarisms.* Words peculiar to the speech of uneducated people are called vulgarisms. Such words as *enthuse, humans, anywheres, nowheres, everywheres, burgle, disremember, complected,* and *heaps* advertise the user as an illiterate person.

4. *Words of popular coinage.* Many words coined by newspaper writers, by workers in certain trades, and by the general public become national in their use, although not sanctioned by reputable use. To this class of words belong such coinages as *automobilist, autoist, typist, vulgarian, picturization, to picturize, to aviate,* and *to hooverize.*

181. Solecisms. An ungrammatical combination of words in a sentence is called a *solecism.* Solecisms include words and expressions that violate either idiom or the rules of syntax. The following illustrate this type of offense against good use: *these kind* and *those kind* for *this kind* and *that kind*; *between you and I* for *between you and me*; *he* (*she* or *it*) *don't* for *he* (*she* or *it*) *doesn't*; *different than* for *different from*; *treat on* for *treat of.* Solecisms are so serious an enemy of correct speech and writing that they should be included in our study of violations of good use in diction as well as in our study of errors in grammar. (In Chapter XI see section 144 and the following sections that deal with solecisms.)

182. Improprieties. An impropriety is a word wrongly transferred from its legitimate use as one part of speech to that of another, or employed with the meaning of some other word with which it is confused. Such words and expressions as *a combine, an invite, a defy, a buy, a steal, a win, a get-away, to gesture, to suspicion, learn* for *teach, raise* for *rear, effect* for *affect*, and *expect* for *suspect* are all improprieties.

183. Slang. Though slang consists of barbarisms and improprieties, it is such a grave offense against good use that it calls for separate consideration.

A peculiar kind of vagabond language, always hanging on the outskirts of legitimate speech, but continually straying or forcing its way into the most respectable company, is what we call *slang*. The prejudice against this form of speech is to be encouraged, though it usually rests on a misconception. There is nothing abnormal about slang. In making it, men proceed in precisely the same manner as in making language, and under the same laws. The motive, however, is somewhat different, for slang is not meant simply to express one's thoughts. Its coinage and circulation come rather from the wish of the individual to distinguish himself by oddity or grotesque humor. Hence slang is seldom controlled by any regard for propriety, and it bids deliberate defiance to all considerations of good taste.[1]

In general, as was stated above, slang words are either barbarisms or improprieties. Unauthorized popular coinages, such as *fake, flivver, flunk, skidoo,* and *spoof*, which have come to be used for their supposed comic suggestiveness, are vulgarisms. Many words and expressions in good use, such as *graft, pinch, kick, can, jug, cooler, cinch, swell, all in, cut out, on the side, take on,* and *up to*, have been given grotesque and incongruous,

[1] From "Words and their Ways in English Speech," by Greenough and Kittredge. Used by permission of The Macmillan Company, publishers. Read also the definition of *slang* in the paragraph quoted on pages 392-393.

FLOTSAM CASTLE (EXTERIOR AND INTERIOR VIEWS)

This dwelling was built from materials cast up by the sea

though often crudely picturesque, meanings that render them improprieties or barbarisms. Many other slang words result from the use of contractions, such as *exam*, *lab*, *gym*, *auto*, *prelims*, *prof*, *soph*, *ad*, and *caf*, derived from words in good use.

Though we may feel that slang occasionally lends vividness and life to everyday speech, we should guard against using it too frequently even in familiar conversation. In polite conversation, as well as in all writing, we should avoid its use altogether. Most slang words quickly pass out of use and are entirely forgotten, and even during their lifetime they have but a vague, general meaning. If we desire to speak and write with clearness and accuracy, we should never allow ourselves to become dependent upon slang, for by its use we limit our vocabulary and render ourselves incapable of expressing our ideas intelligibly in words that have a definite and permanent meaning.

184. Obsolete and archaic words. Words that have passed out of use or that are met with only in solemn discourse and in poetry are not in good use at present, unless a master of literary expression like Stevenson employs them for their suggestiveness and literary flavor. Rarely, if ever, shall we have occasion to use such obsolete and archaic words as *eke*, *dole*, *bedight*, *eftsoons*, *perchance*, *erstwhile*, and *yclept*. Modern authors sometimes employ such words, however, in mock-serious writing.

185. Technical words. Except in technical discussions of technical subjects, words that are peculiar to a certain art, science, profession, sport, or trade should not be used. In a discussion of a technical subject intended for the general public strictly technical terms should be avoided, if possible; otherwise those that must be used should be explained. Few persons having only a general education possess sufficiently accurate knowledge of such words as *perianth*, *chromoplast*, *caveat*, *aquarelle*, and *chiaroscuro* to be sure of their meaning.

186. A list of common errors in diction. The following list, though far from complete, contains a number of the more common barbarisms, solecisms, improprieties, slang terms, and archaic words, which we should avoid in our speech and writing. We should consult this list frequently and should make free use of an unabridged dictionary. (See section 225.)

Accept should not be confused with *except.* Consult a dictionary.

Accept of. Of is superfluous.

Affect (verb) should not be confused with *effect* (verb and noun). *To affect* means *to influence* or *change. To effect* means *to bring about* or *accomplish. Effect* (noun) means *result* or *outcome.* "The war affected prices." "The lawyer effected a compromise." "The effect of his speech was marvelous."

Aggravate should not be misused as a synonym of such verbs as *annoy, irritate,* and *vex.* Consult a dictionary.

Ain't. A vulgarism.

Allow means *permit.* It should not be misused for *admit, say, suppose,* or *think.*

Allude, mention, refer. Consult a dictionary.

Almost, most. Almost means *nearly. Most* is properly used to mean (1) *in the highest degree* or *to the greatest extent* and (2) *the greater portion* or *number*; as, "Most of the passengers drowned." *Most* used for *almost* ("I was most asleep when he came") is a puerility.

Alright. This word does not exist. Use *all right,* though even this is colloquial.

Among, between. Among should be used in speaking of more than two persons or things; *between,* in speaking of only two.

And, to. Avoid using *and* for *to. Incorrect:* "Try and come." "Try and be careful." *Correct:* "Try to come." "Try to be careful."

And etc. Etc. (the abbreviation for *et cetera,* meaning *and other things, and so on*) should never be preceded by *and.*

Any place, every place, no place, some place. These phrases are vulgarisms when used for *anywhere, everywhere, nowhere,* and *somewhere.* Used otherwise as phrases they are correct; as, "We could not find any place in which to camp."

Anyways, anywheres. These are vulgarisms for *anyway, anywhere.*

As, that, whether. Avoid using *as* for *that* or *whether. Incorrect:* "I don't know as I understood him." *Correct:* "I don't know whether (that) I understood him."

Aught, naught. Do not confuse *aught* (anything) with *naught* (nothing, zero).

Auto. Avoid this and similar abbreviations in formal writing.

Awful, awfully. Both are improprieties when used for *very, extremely.*

Bad, badly. In the expression "She feels bad" *bad* is colloquially permissible as a predicate adjective, indicating the person's state of health. (The adjective *ill*, not *bad*, is preferable usage.) In "She feels badly about making the error" the adverb *badly* is correctly used. (See section 152, rule 1.)

Badly. Often misused to mean *very much, greatly.*

Balance, remainder, rest. Consult a dictionary.

Because, that, the fact that. Avoid using *because* for *that* or for *the fact that* to introduce a noun clause. *Incorrect:* "Because you overslept does not excuse you." "The reason I am late is because I overslept." *Correct:* "The fact that you overslept does not excuse you." "The reason I am late is that I overslept." (See section 169.)

Beside, besides. Do not confuse the preposition *beside* (by the side of) with the adverb *besides* (in addition to).

Blame on. Avoid using *blame on* to mean *put the blame on* or *blame.*

Borned. A vulgarism for the past participle *born.*

Brainy. A vulgarism.

Bring, carry, fetch, take. These verbs are not synonymous. Consult a dictionary.

Bunch. A vulgarism when used to mean *crowd, company, group, assembly,* or *party.*

Bursted. A vulgarism for the past tense and past participle *burst.*

But that, but what. Avoid using these after the verb *doubt*. *That* alone should be used. *Correct :* "I do not doubt that he will come."

Calculate, believe, guess, reckon, think. These verbs are not synonymous. Consult a dictionary.

Can, may. Can implies power or ability ; *may* implies possibility or indicates permission.

Cannot help but. Often misused for *can but* and *cannot help* (followed by a verbal noun).

Can't hardly. Hardly implies negation in itself. To avoid a double negative, say *can hardly* (see section 167).

Can't seem. Misused for *seem unable.*

Caused by. Avoid using *caused by* for *because of, on account of. Caused* is correctly used in verb phrases and may then be followed by a prepositional phrase introduced by *by*; as, "His death was caused by accident."

Claim. Avoid using *claim* as a synonym of *assert* or *maintain.* Consult a dictionary.

Combine. An impropriety when used as a noun to mean *combination, trust, union, corporation.*

Common, mutual. Common implies joint interest or possession ; *mutual* implies a reciprocal relationship. Note the correct use of these words: "Mary's and Helen's letters contain many expressions of mutual admiration." "They have several tastes in common." "They have a common aversion to impressionistic art."

Complected. A vulgarism for *complexioned.*

Continual, continuous. Avoid using these as synonymous words. *Continual* implies repetition in close succession ; *continuous* implies action without cessation or interruption. "The continual dripping of the water became monotonous." "The continuous flow of the mighty stream impressed him."

Could of, may of, might of, must of, should of, would of, are all vulgarisms resulting from the careless pronunciation of *could have, may have, might have, must have, should have, would have.*

Cute. A colloquial word used to avoid mental effort. Use such definite adjectives as *amusing, dainty, engaging, pretty, alert, lively, vivacious,* but do not say *cunning,* which means *crafty, ingenious.*

Data, errata, phenomena, strata. All are plurals.

Date. Slang when used for *engagement* or *appointment.*

Deal. A colloquial and cant expression when used to mean *transaction, bargain, agreement, arrangement, trade.*

Demean, degrade. Consult a dictionary.

Depot. Not a railway station. Consult a dictionary.

Die with, sick with. Die of and *sick of* are preferable idioms.

Differ from, differ with. One object differs *from* another in a certain respect. A person differs *from* or *with* another person concerning an opinion or a belief.

Different than. A solecism. Use *different from.* Though *different to* is good usage in England, it is not so regarded in America.

Diner, sleeper, smoker. These words are still regarded as colloquialisms for *dining-car, sleeping-car,* and *smoking-car.*

Directly. Though *directly* for *as soon as* or *immediately after* is good usage in England, it is not so regarded in America.

Disremember. A vulgarism for *be unable to remember* or *fail to remember.*

Done. A solecism when used for *did.*

Don't. A solecism when used for *does not* or *doesn't. Don't* is the contraction for *do not* ; hence it is incorrect to say "He don't," "She don't," or "It don't." (See section 146, rule 8.)

Dope (noun and verb) and *dopey* (adjective). Slang. A substitute for mental effort. Consult a dictionary.

Doubt but. Use *doubt that.* See *But that.*

Dove. Colloquial and illiterate past tense of *dive.* Use *dived.*

Drownded. A vulgarism for *drowned.*

Due to. Misused for *on account of, owing to, because of. Due* may be correctly used as a predicate adjective followed by a phrase introduced by *to* ; as, "His illness was due to exposure." See *Caused by.*

Either, neither. Each requires a singular verb. Avoid using *either* for *any, neither* for *none.*

Elegant, grand, gorgeous, splendid, adorable, lovely, magnificent, exquisite, awful, horrible, terrible, etc. Such adjectives require intelligent use in order not to dull their meaning and effectiveness.

Enthuse. A vulgarism. Say *be enthusiastic, become enthusiastic, show enthusiasm, manifest enthusiasm.*

Except, without. When used for *unless, except* is archaic and *without* is a vulgarism.

Expect, suspect, suppose. Consult a dictionary.

Factor, feature, phase. Consult a dictionary for the correct use of these three nouns.

Fake, faker. Consult a dictionary.

Farther, further. *Farther* should be used to indicate distance or actual progress; as, "He walked two miles farther than I." *Further* should be employed to indicate figurative progress or degree; as, "He refused to aid us further."

Feature. Colloquial when used as a verb to mean *make a feature of, give especial prominence to.*

Fewer, less. *Fewer* should be used when numbers are considered; *less,* when quantities or amounts are thought of. "There were fewer than fifty men in the fort, and they had less than a cask of water."

Fine. Often carelessly used instead of a more definite adjective.

Firstly. A vulgarism. Use *first.*

First-rate. Correct as an adjective, not as an adverb.

Fix. A colloquialism when used as a verb to mean *repair* and as a noun to mean *plight, predicament, condition.*

Flee, flow, fly. Consult a dictionary for the principal parts.

Flivver. Slang.

Flunk. Slang.

Folks. A colloquialism for *family* or *relatives.* Consult a dictionary for the meaning and use of *folk.*

Funny, amusing, odd, peculiar. Consult a dictionary.

Gent, gentleman friend, lady friend. Vulgarisms.

Get. *Get,* meaning *find it possible,* is a provincialism when used with an infinitive; as, "I did not get to see him." "He did not get to prepare his lessons."

Go west. Euphemistic slang for *die.*

Got. Avoid the redundant use of *got* with forms of the verb *have* to denote possession. "I have (not *have got*) a new book."

Gotten. An obsolescent past participle. Use *got.*

Graft, grafter. Consult a dictionary for the slang and the colloquial uses of these words.

Had of. A vulgarism.

Had ought, hadn't ought. Vulgarisms. Use *ought* and *ought not.*

Hanged, hung. Consult a dictionary.

Hardly, scarcely. Not to be used with a negative. See *Can't hardly.*

Healthy, healthful. *Healthy* means *possessing* health; *healthful* means *causing* or *producing* health. "Children are healthy when they have fresh air and healthful food."

Heap, heaps. Vulgarisms when used to mean a *large amount, very much, a great deal, a great many.*

Heathens. The collective form *heathen* should be used.

Human, humans. Avoid using these words as nouns. *Humans* is a vulgarism. Say *human being* or *human beings.*

Hustle. Not to be used intransitively as a synonym of *hasten* or *hurry* or *bestir oneself.* *Hustle* may properly be used as a transitive verb; as, "He hustled us off to the station."

In back of. A vulgarism for *behind.*

Individual, party, person. Avoid using these words indiscriminately. Consult a dictionary.

Invite, invitation. *Invite* is a verb. When used as a noun to mean *invitation* ("I got an invite to the dance"), it is an impropriety.

Its, it's. *Its* is the possessive case of *it*; *it's* is a contraction for *it is.* Fix this distinction in mind.

Kind of, sort of. Colloquialisms when used for *somewhat* or *rather.*

Kind of a, sort of a, style of a, etc. Good use requires the omission of the article. "I enjoy this kind of day." "What style of dress did she wear?"

Lay, lie. *Lay* is a transitive verb meaning *place* or *put*; *lie* is an intransitive verb meaning *recline, rest,* or *occupy a position.* The principal parts of the two verbs are *lay, laid, laid; lie, lay, lain.* Practice using all these forms in sentences until you have mastered them. (See section 155.)

Learn, teach. Consult a dictionary.

Leave, let. *Leave* means *depart, abandon*; *let* means *permit, allow.* *Incorrect:* "She would not leave me see her."

Less, fewer. See *Fewer.*

Liable, likely, apt. Consult a dictionary.

Like. A vulgarism when used in place of *as* or *as if.* *Like* is not a conjunction. *Incorrect:* "He looks like he had seen a ghost." "Do like I tell you." *Correct:* "He looks as if he had seen a ghost." "Do as I tell you." *Like* may properly be followed by a noun or a pronoun, but not by a clause (see section 164).

Line. Grossly overworked in such phrases as *along this* (or *that*) *line, in the line of, in this* (or *that*) *line.* Seek a more definite and expressive word.

Listen, say. Inelegant when used as imperatives to preface or introduce a remark.

Literally. A colloquialism when used for *wholly, altogether.* Consult a dictionary for the correct use of *literally.*

Loan, lend. *Lend* is a verb. *Loan* should be used only as a noun.

Locate. A colloquialism when used for *settle.*

Look badly. See *Bad, badly* (see also section 152, rule 1).

Lose, loose. Do not confuse these verbs. Give their principal parts and use them in sentences.

Lot, lots. Colloquial when used to mean *a great amount of.*

Lovely. See *Elegant.*

Mad, angry, vexed, provoked. Consult a dictionary.

Mean. Properly used adjectivally as a synonym of *common, base, low.* A vulgarism when used for *vicious, unkind, brutal.*

Most. See *Almost.*

Mind, behave. Colloquialisms when used to mean *obey* or *act in accord with good manners.*

Mutual. See *Common.*

Myself. Correctly used as a reflexive or an intensive pronoun. Avoid using it interchangeably with *I* and *me.* *Correct:* "I hurt myself." "I myself saw him enter the house." *Incorrect:* "Mary and myself went to see Uncle Henry." "He told her and myself an interesting story."

Near by, near-by. Used colloquially as an adverb or a preposition to mean *near.* *Near-by* is often misused as an adjective to mean *adjoining, adjacent, contiguous, neighboring.*

Neither. See *Either.*

Nice. Colloquially used as an indefinite synonym of at least a score of adjectives. Select adjectives that accurately express the intended meaning. Learn from a dictionary the legitimate meanings of *nice*.

None. Grammatically singular, though well-established idiom warrants its use as a plural also; as, "None of the family was injured" or "None of the family were injured."

No sooner. Correct when followed by *than*; incorrect when followed by *when*.

Nowheres, everywheres, somewheres. Vulgarisms for *nowhere, everywhere, somewhere.* See *Anyways, anywheres.*

O, oh. Do not confuse *O*, the sign of direct address, with the interjection *oh.* *O* is correctly used in such exclamations as "O dear!" and "O my!"

Off of. *Of* is superfluous.

On the side. Slang when used to mean *in addition, besides, incidentally.*

Only, alone. Consult a dictionary for the distinction in meaning.

Onto. Not sanctioned by good use. Use *on, upon,* or *up on.* The phrase *on to* may be correctly used; as, "The tourists went on to the next town."

Out loud. Puerile. Say *aloud.*

Over with. *With* is superfluous. *Correct:* "The meeting is over."

Overly, muchly. Vulgarisms. Use *over* and *much.*

Party. See *Individual.*

Peeve, peeved. Slang. Say *provoke* and *provoked, exasperate* and *exasperated.*

Per cent, percentage. Avoid using these interchangeably. Consult a dictionary.

'Phone. A colloquial contraction for *telephone.*

Photo. A vulgarism.

Piano, violin, vocal, voice. Incorrect for *lessons on the piano, lessons on the violin, vocal culture, voice culture.*

Plan on. A solecism for *plan to.* *Incorrect:* "I plan on spending my vacation in Canada." *Correct:* "I plan to spend my vacation in Canada."

Plenty. *Plenty* (a noun) should not be used as a synonym of *plentiful* (an adjective) or as the equivalent of the phrase *plenty of*. *Incorrect:* "He has plenty money." *Correct:* "He has plenty of money."

Posted. A colloquialism for *informed.*

Present-day. *Present-day* should not be used as an adjective. Use *present* or *modern.*

Proposition. Colloquialism when used to mean *task, matter,* or *affair.*

Proven. An obsolescent past participle. Use *proved.*

Put in. Colloquial when used to mean *spend, employ, use.*

Put in an appearance. Colloquial. Say *appear.*

Put out. Slang when used to mean *disappointed, inconvenienced, discommoded, incommoded.*

Put over. Slang when used in such an expression as *put one over* to mean *accomplish, deceive, take advantage of.*

Put up with. Slang when used to mean *tolerate, endure, allow.*

Quite. Use *quite* only when it is properly a synonym of *entirely, wholly, altogether.* Avoid such colloquial phrases as *quite a few, quite a little, quite a lot, quite a number, quite a while.*

Raise, rear. Consult a dictionary for the distinction in the use of these words.

Raise, rise. *Raise* is a transitive verb meaning *lift* or *cause to rise*; *rise* is an intransitive verb meaning *ascend* or *assume an upright posture* (see section 155).

Rarely ever. A contraction of the phrase *rarely if ever.* *Ever* is superfluous.

Real. *Real* is an adjective, not an adverb. Avoid using *real* for *really* or *very.*

Reason is because. See *Because.*

Remember of. *Of* is superfluous.

Right away, right off. Colloquialisms for *at once, immediately.*

Right smart of. Provincialism for *a considerable amount of* anything.

Rise. See *Raise.*

Run. A colloquialism for *conduct, manage, operate.*

Same. *Same* is correctly used as an adjective to mean *identical.*

It is incorrectly used as a pronoun. *The same* should not be used to mean *also, likewise*. *Incorrect:* "He read the book and returned same promptly." "I am well, and hope you are the same." *Correct:* "He read the book and returned it promptly." "I am well, and hope that you also are well."

Says. Often misused by illiterate people to mean *said*.

Seldom ever. A contraction of the phrase *seldom if ever. Ever* is superfluous.

Set, sit. Set is a transitive verb meaning *place* or *cause to sit; sit* is an intransitive verb meaning *occupy a seat* or *assume a sitting posture* (see section 155).

Settle. Colloquial when used to mean *pay*.

Shall, will. See section 156.

Shape. Colloquial when used as a noun to mean *condition, circumstances, situation*.

Show. Colloquial when used as a noun to mean (1) *a theatrical performance, concert, opera;* (2) *chance, opportunity*.

Show up. A vulgarism for (1) *appear, attend, be present, come;* (2) *display;* (3) *expose, make a spectacle of;* (4) *appear to advantage*.

Sight, sight of. Colloquial when used to mean *a great quantity of, a considerable amount of, much, many, a great deal of*. See *Heap* and *Lot*.

Sit. See *Set*.

Size up. Slang for *estimate, judge*.

Smart. Colloquial when used to mean *mentally alert, quick-witted, clever, talented*.

Snap. Slang when used as a noun to mean *an easy task, bargain*.

So. Colloquial when used to mean *so that, in order that,* and when used as a synonym of *very. Incorrect:* "We went early so we could get a good seat." "I am so weary." *Correct:* "We went early so that we could get a good seat." "I am very weary." Or, "I am so weary that I must rest."

Some. A solecism when used to mean *somewhat*. "He is somewhat (*not* some) wiser because of this experience."

Some. Slang when used to mean *a genuine, a real, an excellent* person or thing.

Somewheres. See *Nowheres.*

Stand for. Slang for *permit, allow, countenance, tolerate.*

Start, begin, commence. Consult a dictionary.

Start in. Colloquial when used to mean *begin, enter upon, undertake.*

Start out. Colloquial when used to mean *set out, set off, leave.*

Stop. Though *stop* for *stay* is good usage in England, it is not so regarded in America.

Story. Colloquial when used to mean *lie, falsehood.*

Stunt. Slang when used as a noun to mean *feat* or *performance.*

Such. *Such* should not be used for *very.* Avoid also the vague and weak use of *such* without a result clause. A relative clause following *such* should be introduced by the relative pronoun *as.*

Suicide. A vulgarism when used as a verb; as, "He suicided." Say, "He committed suicide."

Sure. A vulgarism when used for the adverbs *surely* or *certainly.*

Suspicion. An impropriety when used as a verb; as, "I suspicioned there was something wrong." Say, "I suspected there was something wrong."

Swell. Slang when used as a noun to mean *a fashionable person, a fop,* or when used as an adjective to mean *stylish, fashionable.*

Take. Colloquial when used to mean *study*; as, "I am taking Spanish."

Take and. Usually superfluous, often crude; as, "Take and measure the flour." Say, "Measure the flour."

Take in. Colloquial when used to mean *attend, go to,* or when used to mean *deceive, cheat, dupe.*

These kind, those kind. Solecisms and vulgarisms for *this kind, that kind,* or *these kinds, those kinds.*

Thing. Avoid overworking this word.

This here, these here, that there, those there. Vulgarisms. Use merely *this, these, that, those.*

Through. Colloquial when used to mean *have finished*; as, "I am through studying my lessons."

Too, very. Usually neither *too* nor *very* should come immediately before a past participle. Use *too much, too greatly, very much, very greatly, too well, very well. Correct:* "He was too much astonished to move."

Transpire. Correctly used to mean *become known*; as, "In spite of all precaution the secret transpired." An impropriety when used to mean *happen, occur, take place.*

Try and. See *And, to.*

Turn up. A vulgarism when used to mean *arrive, appear.*

Two first, two last. Illogical. Say *first two, last two.*

Ugly. Colloquial when used to mean *vicious, uncivil, angry.*

Unique. Unique means *alone of its kind, single, sole.* Like *round, level, perfect,* it cannot be compared (see section 151, rule 5). Avoid *very unique, most unique. Unique* is often misused to mean *odd, strange, unusual.*

Unless. See *Except, without.*

Up. Not to be added unnecessarily to such verbs as *end, rest, pay, polish, open, finish, divide.*

Up to date. Correctly used as an adverbial phrase. Often misused as an adjective to mean *modern, stylish.*

Up to you. Slang for *for you to do* (or *to decide*), *incumbent upon you.*

Uplift. Colloquial when used as a noun meaning *betterment.*

Used to could. A vulgarism. Say *used to be able, could formerly, once could.*

Vamp, vampire. Consult a dictionary for the legitimate meanings of these words.

Very. See *Too.*

Viewpoint. Point of view is preferable.

Want in. Colloquial for *want to come in.*

Want to. Colloquial for *should, ought to, had better.*

Way. Colloquial when used for *away*; as, "Way up on the top shelf."

Ways. A solecism for the singular *way*; as, "He lives a long ways from here." Say, "He lives a long way from here."

When, where. Clauses introduced by *when* and *where* should not be used as predicate nouns. *Incorrect:* "A jail is where prisoners are confined." "Four o'clock is when I quit work." *Correct:* "A jail is a place where prisoners are confined." "Four o'clock is the time when I quit work." Exceptions occur when the subject of the sentence is some such noun as *question*; as, "The question is, When did he arrive?" (See section 168.)

Will, shall. See section 156.

Win out, lose out. Colloquial for *win* and *lose*.

Wire. Colloquial when used as a verb to mean *telegraph* and when used as a noun to mean *telegram*.

Worth while. Not to be used as an attributive adjective. *Incorrect:* "A worth-while concert." Say, "The concert was worth while."

Write up. Slang for the nouns *report* and *account*, or for the verb *write*.

You was. A solecism. *You were* is both singular and plural.

Yourself. Properly used as a reflexive and an intensive pronoun, but not as a substitute for *you*. "When did Mary and you (*not* yourself) arrive?" (See *Myself*.)

EXERCISES

I

In the following sentences (1) point out each violation of good use and name the class of violation to which each incorrect word or expression belongs; (2) express the thought of each sentence in words that are in good use; and (3) if the word or expression incorrectly used in this exercise has a correct use, make an original sentence in which you employ it correctly. Consult the list given above and an unabridged dictionary as often as it is necessary.

1. Everyone in the audience held his breath while the fearless aviator performed daring stunts in his aëroplane.

2. Your handwriting is awful, but your spelling is the worst.

3. I shall not budge a step without you go with me.

4. She was awfully put out because no one alluded to what had transpired.

5. I allowed it would aggravate her, alright.

6. Now, Helen, do try and behave like your sister does.

7. The reason I got mad was because the whole bunch claimed I told a story about 'phoning for an auto.

8. When they blamed it all on me, I sure got peeved; any guy would of.

9. I think it was real mean of them not to accept of my explanation, anyways.

10. During January and February I most froze, but the balance of the winter was some warmer.

11. Due to the storm, they calculated that nobody would put in an appearance, but quite a few finally showed up.

12. When the officer came in the room, he suspicioned that something was up.

13. She was a mutual friend of ours, and couldn't seem to get through telling us what a swell individual her gentleman friend was, especially when he got dressed up in them nifty glad rags of his.

14. Of course we enthused over him, but we couldn't hardly keep from laughing, for he's so different to her first husband, who suicided.

15. Just as I reached the depot, I saw father get off of the sleeper.

16. I disremember whether he died with the influenza or with the pneumonia.

17. She don't never have less than five dates a week.

18. Those kind of folks are funny.

19. They are nice and have got lots of pull socially, but they will never get an invite from Mrs. Rankin.

20. According to the write-up of his latest oil deal, I expect he is a grafter.

21. In back of the stove set a funny-looking human.

22. The teacher found it kind of a hard proposition to learn Stubbs any Spanish.

23. Myrtle and myself always take in everything in the motion-picture line.

24. Just between you and I, drawing sure is a snap; you want to be sure and take it.

25. I plan on having a lot of time to put in making money on the side.

26. Say, you have got plenty of nerve if you calculate to put that over.

27. He was not overly rich, but he raised a large family.

28. One of his daughters took vocal quite a while, and spent a sight of money, but she rarely ever sings in public.

29. While I was stopping with my aunt in the country, I met a very unique old party.

30. I sized up the situation right away and started out for a near-by house to try and get help.

31. I hustled as fast as I could, and 'phoned his wife and the doctor.

32. When I got back, he was laying on the grass and looked badly.

33. His wife seemed deeply effected when the doctor told her that her husband was in a bad shape.

34. We expected he would soon go west, but, due to a lot of physical pep, he upset all the dope and is now feeling fine.

35. He owes a heap, of course, to the healthy climate and the up-to-date doctor that he had.

II

In each blank left in the following sentences supply the right word. Use the rejected word correctly in a sentence of your own. Consult a dictionary to find the proper meaning of each word that you do not fully understand.

1. She refused to —— (except, accept) his apology.

2. Illness —— (effected, affected) his vision.

3. A mirage is an optical —— (allusion, illusion).

4. He —— (claimed, maintained) that he was right.

5. The earthquake on February 29, 1916, was an unusual —— (coincidence, happening).

6. I went to the lawyer for —— (council, counsel).

7. Marconi —— (discovered, invented) the wireless telegraph.

8. Twelve —— (disinterested, uninterested) men composed the jury.

9. His father —— (immigrated, emigrated) from Italy.

10. The —— (enormousness, enormity) of the task baffled him.

11. College offers —— (exceptionable, exceptional) opportunities to earnest students.

12. The prisoner was —— (hanged, hung) on Friday.

13. My mother is an —— (imaginative, imaginary) person.

14. My young cousin is a very naïve and —— (ingenious, ingenuous) girl.

15. Bronson's uncle was an upright, —— (notorious, notable) statesman.

16. He succeeded by close —— (observance, observation) of the golden rule.

17. Direct utilization of solar energy has not yet proved —— (practicable, practical).

18. A large —— (percentage, per cent) of the audience could not hear the speaker.

19. The summer house was almost concealed by a grove of —— (luxurious, luxuriant) tropical plants.

20. Our city is enlarging the —— (sewage, sewerage) system in order to dispose of the increased —— (sewage, sewerage).

21. This is a new —— (species, specie) of political dishonesty.

22. I received a letter written on blue —— (stationery, stationary).

23. The —— (statue, stature) was unveiled on Memorial Day.

24. I have been reading —— (a unique, an unusual) book.

25. Dr. Keller's —— (vocation, avocation) is training bird dogs.

III

With the aid of an unabridged dictionary learn the differences in meaning and use of the following words. Use each word correctly in an original sentence.

> admit, confess
> allude to, refer to, mention
> aware, conscious
> bring, carry, fetch, take
> character, reputation
> complement, compliment
> comprehensible, comprehensive
> conclude, decide
> contemptible, contemptuous
> credible, creditable, credulous
> custom, habit
> economic, economical
> expect, anticipate, presume, suspect
> hygienic, sanitary
> imply, infer
> insoluble, unsolvable
> majority, plurality
> official, officious
> oral, verbal

peculiar, odd, unusual
prescribe, proscribe
principal, principle
relation, relative
respectively, respectfully, respectably
scholar, student, pupil
secure, procure
various, varied, several
witness, observe, behold, see

IV

In your notebook make a list of all the slang words and expressions that you are able to recognize in your own vocabulary. For each of these slang expressions find one or more reputable expressions. Notice the superiority of the latter in accuracy and in elegance. By means of persistent self-cultivation and by the aid of your friends and the members of your family try to become independent of slang both in conversation and in writing.

V

During the coming week make a list of violations of good use that you recognize in your own speech and writing and in the speech and writing of others. Opposite each violation write words and expressions in good use that should have been employed. On the day that your teacher may assign submit your list for criticism and discussion.

VI

Read again "Self-Cultivation in English" and come to class prepared to discuss what the author says about the choice of words.

VII

Read again the schoolboy's composition "How we earned our Car," in Chapter V. Do you find any words not in good use?

VIII

In your notebook make a list of all the errors in diction that your teacher has indicated in your compositions thus far, and add to this list other errors that may be pointed out in the future. Opposite each word wrongly used write the word or expression that you should have used. Review this list frequently and try to avoid repeating any error.

187. Summary. A word is a symbol that stands for an idea. In every living language words that are no longer needed are discarded and new ones are added.

English is a composite language made up of words descended from the Anglo-Saxon and an equally large number borrowed from ancient and modern foreign languages. A relatively small proportion of words have been coined by English-speaking people.

Diction is the choice of words for the expression of our thoughts. It is based on the usage of the best modern English speakers and writers.

Correctness of diction requires that each word chosen be in good use.

To be in good use, a word must be in present, national, and reputable use.

In respect to certain words and phrases, usage in England differs from that in America. These differences should be noted, and American usage should be followed in the United States.

The principal violations of good use are (1) barbarisms, (2) solecisms, (3) improprieties, (4) slang, (5) obsolete and archaic words, and (6) technical words.

CHAPTER XIII

THE EFFECTIVE USE OF WORDS

188. Effectiveness of diction. In choosing our words we must first of all select words that are sanctioned by good use and avoid employing those that lack the approval of the best speakers and writers. But correctness of diction alone is not sufficient if we would express our thoughts not only with accuracy but also with clearness and force. Out of the large number of words in good use we should choose those that *best* convey our meaning. In making such a choice we should be guided by the principle of effectiveness. Effectiveness in diction requires that words be selected for their (1) exactness, (2) appropriateness, and (3) expressiveness. These three qualities we shall consider in the sections that follow.

189. Exactness. To be exact, a word must fit precisely the idea for which it stands. If we write "A man moved across the street" when what we have in mind to say is "An aged beggar tottered over the cobblestones," we vaguely suggest our meaning, but we do not definitely express it. *Man*, *moved*, and *street* are general words, whereas *beggar*, *tottered*, and *cobblestones* are specific words. Specific words are essential to exactness of expression. They are far more suggestive than general terms, in that they tend to arouse in the mind of the reader vivid mental pictures. Specific words are especially valuable in description and in narration, and they likewise add clearness and force to much expository and argumentative writing.

The groups of words on the following page illustrate the superiority of specific words over general terms in exactness and suggestiveness:

GENERAL	SPECIFIC
animal . . .	dog, horse, elephant, camel, lion, sheep, wolf, cow, hog, cat, mouse
vehicle . . .	carriage, wagon, cart, coach, chaise, buggy, omnibus, motor cycle, automobile, aëroplane
workman . .	plumber, painter, engraver, carpenter, chef, mason, shoemaker, designer
book	history, memoir, tradition, biography, romance, novel, diary, dictionary
receptacle . .	chest, box, casket, caddy, bureau, desk, cabinet, safe, vault, trunk, portmanteau, bag, valise
color	blue, orange, violet, green, red, yellow, crimson, scarlet, brown
write	copy, engross, transcribe, scrawl, scribble, indite, typewrite, engrave
good	pious, virtuous, patient, excellent, durable, palatable, beneficial, generous, self-sacrificing
said	stammered, stuttered, faltered, mumbled, muttered, drawled, croaked, screamed, roared, blustered, whined, whispered, lisped, pleaded, coaxed
move	crawl, creep, glide, fly, swim, walk, run, skip, hop, limp, totter, stride, stumble, pace, trip, waddle, whirl, dance, tumble, trot, canter, gallop

EXERCISE

For each of the general words given in the following list find as many specific words as you can:

building	utensil	flower	commodity	look	dark
sport	weapon	tree	recreation	ask	cold
school	tool	clothing	volume	deceive	hot
plant	science	periodical	stream	laugh	bright
insect	food	fish	occupation	consume	still

190. Appropriateness. Our diction is appropriate when it is properly adapted to our subject and to the understanding of our hearers and readers. Simple language is usually best, though in the discussion of technical subjects for educated persons we may rightly employ whatever technical words the subject may demand. In solemn discourse and in some forms of poetry archaic expressions are often fitting. Dialogue in narrative writing will properly contain colloquial words, and, if the characters are illiterate or speak somewhat carelessly, even slang terms. In public addresses and in formal writing, the subject under discussion, as well as the audience or the readers, will determine the speaker's or writer's choice of words.

EXERCISES

I

Read again a poem that you have recently studied in class and point out several good examples of the author's choice of appropriate words. What words do you find that would possibly not be used in expressing the same thought in prose? Did the author employ any archaic words?

II

What does the author of "Self-Cultivation in English" say about the effective use of words? For what three qualities of speech should you strive?

III

For what subjects, classes of readers, or kinds of writing would the following groups of words be appropriate?

1. Chassis, carburetor, spark plug, ignition system, steering-gear, tonneau, coupé, wind-shield, limousine.

2. Petal, pistil, stamen, perianth, pollen, stigma, corolla, calyx, ovule, cross-fertilization, chromoplast.

3. Tort, chancery, writ, *caveat*, jury, larceny, subpœna, appellate, habeas corpus.

4. Palette, easel, perspective, color harmony, pastel, sepia, chiaroscuro, aquarelle.

5. Links, cleek, mid-iron, niblick, putter, driver, tee, foursome, caddy.

6. Bias, flounce, French fell, accordion plait, kimono, hemstitch, tunic, blouse, organdie, voile, modiste.

IV

Make lists similar to those in Exercise III containing technical words that would be appropriate in a lecture, a talk, or an article on the following arts, sciences, professions, sports, and trades:

sculpture	carpentry	oil-refining	bee-keeping
music	plumbing	oil-drilling	pearl-fishing
photography	tailoring	glass-blowing	book-binding
zoölogy	radio	printing	rug-weaving
bowling	dairying	paper-making	interior decorating
billiards	assaying	geology	motion pictures

V

Come to class prepared to talk on some topic suggested by one of the subjects in Exercise IV. Explain any technical words that you think the class will not understand.

VI

In a letter to a friend explain clearly some technical subject that you understand thoroughly but that is not familiar to him. Give the meaning of each technical term.

191. Expressiveness. Many words have two degrees or levels of meaning. One meaning consists of what the word literally says. This we call its *denotation*. In addition, the word may have acquired through long use an implied, or associated, meaning, so that it suggests much more than it specifically denotes. This we call its *connotation*. The expressiveness of a word or phrase depends upon both its denotative and its connotative meaning. In expository and argumentative writing we desire specific words that are exact in their meaning and appropriate to the subject, to the understanding of the hearer or reader, and to the occasion; hence we choose words primarily for their denotation. In descriptive and narrative writing, on the other hand, we seek for expressive words that, by their power of suggestion and implication, will stimulate the feelings as well as the mind of the reader; we therefore select words that, besides being exact and appropriate, are rich in connotation. Poetry depends for its effectiveness largely upon the suggestive power of the words used.

The words *house* and *residence* denote the same object as does the word *home*, but they are far less expressive. *Home* means both *house* and *residence* and arouses within each of us associations and memories that cluster around it. Similarly *doubloons* and *pieces of eight* suggest not merely Spanish money but pirates' treasure. *Galleon* for *sailing-vessel*, *palfrey* for *saddle horse*, and *grail* for *cup* possess an archaic flavor and poetic connotation. For those who have had a vivid hospital experience the words *iodoform*, *anæsthetic*, and *interne* may call to mind varied associations.

EXERCISE

Read a poem and a short prose passage and make a list of as many connotative words as you can find. Note in each case what the author gained in expressiveness by their use. In the place of each connotative word substitute, if you can, a word that is merely denotative and observe the change in meaning that results.

192. The suggestive value of figures of speech. Figures of speech, which are variations from the literal or ordinary forms of expression, are highly effective, for they add vividness, vigor, and beauty to our utterances. A comparison of the following figures of speech with their corresponding literal equivalents will illustrate the suggestive value of figurative language as a means of effective expression.

LITERAL	FIGURATIVE
Misfortunes never come singly.	When sorrows come, they come not single spies, But in battalions.
Why can I not go to sleep?	O gentle sleep, Nature's soft nurse, how have I frighted thee?

In general, figurative language makes the expression of our thoughts more clear and forceful and at the same time renders them attractive to our hearers and readers. Though figures are the ornaments of speech, they should not be used unless they are natural and appropriate and increase the effectiveness of what we have to say.

In the sections that follow, the principal figures of speech are explained and illustrated.

193. Simile. A simile is a statement of the figurative resemblance of one person or thing to another, expressed in the form of a comparison. The best similes are those in which persons or things unlike in most respects are compared because they have one point of resemblance in appearance, qualities, or actions, or in the effect they produce. Usually this comparison is expressed by *like* or *as*. Not all expressed comparisons, however, are similes. "The automobile ran as fast as the train" is simply a comparison with no suggestion of figurative resemblance. Each of the sentences given below is a simile.

1. Our house swarmed with guests like a beehive.
2. He sat all the evening as silent as the Sphinx.
3. We spend our years as a tale that is told.
4. Thy soul was like a star.

194. Metaphor. A metaphor is a figure of speech in which the comparison is implied instead of being formally stated. As in a simile, the persons or things compared should be unlike in most respects. "That man is a hero" is not a metaphor. The following illustrations show the difference between a simile and a metaphor.

SIMILE	METAPHOR
Life lies between two eternities as an isthmus between two continents.	Life is an isthmus between two eternities.
Life is like a dome of many-colored glass.	Life is a dome of many-colored glass.
All the world is like a stage.	All the world 's a stage.
Her heart is like a garden fair.	The garden of her heart blossoms with kindness and love.

Each part of a metaphor should be consistent with every other part. Mixed metaphors, which constitute serious errors of composition, result from the confusion of different metaphors in the same sentence or from the joining of metaphorical with literal language.

He alone can steer the storm-tossed ship of state on its perilous march. (Confused metaphors)

He flung his powerful frame into the saddle and his great soul into the cause. (Literal joined with metaphorical language)

195. Personification. Personification is a figure of speech in which life is attributed to inanimate things or to abstract ideas. Personification is of three kinds:

1. That produced by raising an inanimate object to the rank of an animal or a human being.

The thirsty soil drank in the rain.
The wind howled and moaned.

2. That produced by raising an animal or a plant to the rank of a human being.

The dog laughed and said, "You don't deceive me that way."
The flowers nodded to her as she passed.

3. That produced by raising an abstraction to the rank of a human being.

> Justice lamented the deed.
> Freedom blushed for shame.

196. Apostrophe. Apostrophe is a figure of speech in which the absent are addressed as if they were present, the dead as if they were living, and inanimate objects as if they were human beings. Apostrophe is often combined with metaphor and personification.

> 1. Milton, thou shouldst be living at this hour.
> 2. O world, I cannot hold thee close enough!
> 3. Time, you old gypsy man,
>   Will you not stay?
> 4. My country, 'tis of thee,
>   Sweet land of liberty,
>   Of thee I sing.

197. Antithesis. Antithesis is a figure of speech made up of opposing or contrasted words or sentiments arranged in parallel construction in the same sentence. Antithesis is a figure based on unlikeness, and therefore always expresses contrast. Verbs should be contrasted with verbs, adjectives with adjectives, nouns with nouns, etc.

1. To err is human; to forgive, divine.
2. It is better to lose health like a spendthrift than to waste it like a miser.
3. Deeds show what we are; words, what we should be.

Often there is a double or even triple contrast in the same sentence.

> Silence is deep as Eternity; speech is shallow as Time.

Here *silence* and *speech, deep* and *shallow, Eternity* and *Time* are contrasted.

198. Epigram. An epigram is a brief, pointed saying that has the nature of a proverb. The best epigrams are those in which there is an apparent contradiction between the intended meaning and the form of the expression. Like antithesis, epigram is based on contrast. Puns are often expressed by epigrams.

1. The child is father of the man.
2. A little learning is a dangerous thing.
3. A new way to contract debts—pay them off.
4. The fastest colors are those that will not run.
5. If you have nothing to say, say it.

199. Metonymy. Metonymy is a figure of speech in which the name of one object is used for that of another which it clearly suggests.

1. The kettle boils (that is, the *water* in the kettle boils).
2. He chose a gun instead of a cap and gown (that is, he became a *soldier* instead of a *student*).
3. Have you read Shakespeare (that is, his *works*)?
4. Only the knife (that is, *a surgical operation*) can save him.
5. He addressed the chair (that is, the *presiding officer*).

200. Synecdoche. Synecdoche is a figure of speech in which a part is named for a whole, or a whole for a part.

1. The speaker beheld a sea of faces.
2. The world knows his worth.
3. He won her hand in marriage.
4. We have tea at six o'clock.
5. Give us this day our daily bread.

201. Hyperbole. Hyperbole is a figure of speech based on exaggeration. It is sometimes effective in descriptions of the grand and sublime. In general, except in humorous conversation or writing, exaggerations and extravagant comparisons should be avoided.

THE SKYSCRAPERS

1. We live the time that a match flickers.
2. I have looked all over creation for my book.
3. The tumult reached the stars.
4. Here [at Concord] once the embattled farmers stood,
   And fired the shot heard round the world.

202. Climax. Climax is a figure of speech in which a series of thoughts or statements is arranged in the order of increasing importance. In true climax a weaker or less important thought should never follow a stronger or more important one.

1. He sacrificed his business, his home, and his honor for political gain.
2. Since concord was lost, friendship was lost; fidelity was lost; liberty was lost—all was lost.

Anticlimax results when the climactic order is reversed. It is often used in humorous writing.

1. He lost his wife, his child, his household goods, and his dog at one fell swoop.
2. O dear! O dear! what shall I do?
   I've lost my beau and lip-stick, too!

203. Onomatopœia. Onomatopœia is a figure of speech in which the sound of a word or a group of words imitates the sound that it names or describes. The entire group of words that imitate natural sounds belongs to this class. All such words as *rumble, crash, splash, boom, whiz, hum, buzz, cackle, chirp, puff, gurgle, hiss, kiss, smack, tinkle,* and *chatter* are examples of onomatopœia. Poe's "The Bells" and Southey's "The Cataract of Lodore" are illustrations of the extensive use of onomatopœia.

204. Irony. Irony is veiled sarcasm. It consists in using expressions of commendation when the exact opposite is meant.

1. What a brilliant remark that was!
2. Brutus is an honorable man.
3. Such generosity as yours overwhelms me.
4. I assure you that I shall lose no time in reading your book.

205. Euphemism. Euphemism consists in stating a disagreeable truth in agreeable language. Often sarcasm is implied, but it is milder than in irony.

1. He and Truth are not on very intimate terms.
2. If only the good die young, he should live to a ripe old age.
3. He fed his family on bowls of sunshine.
4. She is the victim of an overactive imagination and is fond of romancing.
5. Her only son she gave to help make the world safe for democracy.

EXERCISES

I

In the following sentences point out and name all the figures of speech:

1. Wit is a dangerous weapon.
2. A wise man is never less alone than when alone.
3. And thrice the Saxon blade drank blood.
4. Books are the legacies that genius leaves to mankind.
5. Knowledge is proud that he has learned so much;
   Wisdom is humble that he knows no more.
6. And like the wings of sea birds
   Flash the whitecaps of the sea.
7. He worked hard to keep the wolf from his door.
8. Life is a leaf of paper white,
   Whereon each one of us may write
   His word or two, and then comes night.
9. She has as little cause for vanity as any woman I ever met.
10. God rest you, happy gentlemen,
    Who laid your good lives down,
    Who took the khaki and the gun
    Instead of cap and gown.
11. You, Four Walls,
    Wall not in my heart!
12. Like to islands in the seas
    Stand our personalities.

13. Oh, my heart is a little golden fountain;
   Through it and spilling over the brim
   Wells the love of you.
14. Earth is our mother, and our tent the sky.
15. And all the little streets reach out their arms
   To be received into the salt-drenched dark.
16. Behold where Night clutches the cup of heaven
   And quaffs the beauty of the world away!
17. And the bumblebee bass drums boomed beneath.
18. The bench, the pulpit, the press, and the stage—all exert a powerful influence.
19. The pen is mightier than the sword.
20. The factory employs fifteen hundred hands.
21. Some are too foolish to commit follies.
22. God made the country; man made the town.
23. O Nature, how wonderful are thy laws!
24. He raised a mortal to the skies;
   She drew an angel down.

II

Make a list of twelve figures of speech that you find in your reading or identify in conversation. After each sentence in your list name the figure or figures that it contains. Then write out a literal version of the same thought and note the loss in effectiveness.

206. Violations of effectiveness. Carelessness in our choice of words impairs the effectiveness of what we have to say. In our effort to make our diction exact, appropriate, and expressive we should do our utmost to avoid the following violations of effectiveness: (1) needless repetition, (2) exaggeration, (3) trite expressions, (4) hackneyed quotations, (5) overuse of figurative language, and (6) "fine writing."

207. Needless repetition. Conciseness, the use of one expressive word in place of several words, renders our diction more effective. We should therefore avoid *tautology*, which consists in the needless repetition of our meaning in other words, and *redundancy,* which consists in using superfluous words. Such expressions as *in plain sight and clearly visible, his own individuality and personality,* and *azure blue* illustrate what we mean by tautology. Phrases such as *advance forward, return back, join together, repeat again, finally at last,* and *rest up* are examples of redundancy. We should always be as concise as clearness will permit.

208. Exaggeration. The careless use of superlatives, as well as needless exaggeration of all other types, lessens rather than increases the effectiveness of our utterances. Many of us by overworking *very* and *most* have well-nigh destroyed the force that these words might otherwise have. Such modifying words as *adorable, awful, deadly, elegant, exquisite, fascinating, ghastly, gorgeous, grand, great, horrible, lovely, magnificent, splendid, stupendous, superb, terrible, weird, beautifully, gorgeously, horribly, magnificently, powerfully, splendidly, terribly,* and *wonderfully* should be used only when they express exactly the meaning intended. Our diction is weak and puerile when we use such expressions as "I was literally scared to death," "Look at that ghastly hole in my handkerchief!" or "Oh, I had the grandest, the most perfectly splendid trip you can possibly imagine!" Such expressions usually savor of insincerity, are felt to be lacking in accuracy and force, and are therefore ineffective.

209. Trite expressions. Within the limits of correct usage we should each strive to develop individuality in diction. This we cannot do if we lazily permit ourselves to continue to use trite expressions, such as *along this line, last but not least, green with envy, silence reigned supreme,* and *the handiwork of Mother Nature.* If we think clearly and choose words that say exactly and forcefully what we mean, we shall rarely find it necessary to use stale diction. Surely we can find fresher, more expressive phrases than the following:

the festive board
none the worse for wear
tired but happy
poor but honest
the fair sex
in our midst
the irony of fate
the moon in all its glory
order out of chaos

a worth-while life
the rippling waves
the velvety grass
the light fantastic
a long-felt want
consigned to earth
a few well-chosen words
an important factor
in all its phases

210. Hackneyed quotations. Quotations and proverbs that
have become hackneyed by too frequent use impair the effectiveness of our diction. We should avoid such threadbare expressions as the following:

method in his madness
he that runs may read
What's in a name?
sermons in stones
the straight and narrow way
far from the madding crowd
monarch of all I survey
where ignorance is bliss
A thing of beauty is a joy forever

the last rose of summer
There's no place like home
I could a tale unfold
Some have greatness thrust
upon them
Absence makes the heart grow
fonder
plain living and high thinking
Better late than never

211. Overuse of figurative language. Figures of speech, although they are valuable in increasing the effectiveness of what
we have to say, should never be far-fetched, forced, or inappropriate. They should be used instinctively, rather than as the
result of meditation and invention. They should not call attention to themselves as a device consciously used, but should in a
natural and unobtrusive manner contribute their share to the
force, vividness, and attractiveness of our expression. They are
a means, not an end in themselves. We should not abuse such
figures as hyperbole, apostrophe, epigram, irony, and euphemism. We should be on our guard also against overworked figur-

ative expressions such as *the grim reaper, the table groaned, brave as a lion, ran like a frightened deer, raven tresses,* and *marble brow.* We should make our own figures rather than accept them ready-made.

212. "Fine writing." "Fine writing" is "rich diction applied to a plain subject, or lofty words to a weak idea." Since its use indicates insincerity or affectation on the part of the speaker or writer, and since it distracts the attention of the reader, "fine writing" is one of the worst enemies of effectiveness. The boy who, during his school days, had written *sumptuous repast* for *meal, partake of* for *eat,* and *palatial residence* for *house* or *home,* later in life, as the editor of a small newspaper, wrote the following:

The lovely and elegant home of that crown prince of hospitality, the big-hearted and noble-souled Daniel Stone, was a radiant scene of enchanting loveliness, for Cupid had brought one of his finest offerings to the court of Hymen; for the lovable Miss Julia, the beautiful and accomplished daughter of Mr. Stone and his refined and most excellent wife, who is a lady of rarest charms and sweetest graces, dedicated her life's ministry to Dr. Howard K. Wortham, the brilliant and gifted and talented son of that ripe scholar and renowned educator, the learned Professor Wortham, the very able and highly successful president of the Female College.

EXERCISES

I

In the following exercise point out examples of tautology, redundancy, exaggeration, trite expressions, hackneyed quotations, and affected writing. Rewrite each sentence to improve its effectiveness.

1. We all returned back home, tired but happy, and none the worse for wear.
2. I absolutely adore lobster salad.
3. Then there came a dull thud that was clearly audible to our ears.

4. The work of Mother Nature in this secluded spot beggars description.

5. I just loathe and detest chemistry.

6. The gentlemen's cleansing-establishment was entirely devoured by the consuming element in our recent disastrous conflagration.

7. The lake stretched before us like a vast mirror of silver, while all around us the feathered songsters were caroling their morning matins.

8. I am terribly sorry that I have kept you waiting such an extremely long time, but haste makes waste, you know.

9. There she stood, divinely tall and most divinely fair, lost in maiden meditation, heart-whole and fancy-free.

10. On Easter Sunday our esteemed former citizen, Mr. Floyd Agnew Perkins, deserted the ranks of single blessedness and became a happy benedict, being united in the bonds of matrimony with Miss Eustacia Farley, one of our most talented musicians and the paragon of her sex. The happy pair will reside in Mortonville, where Mr. Perkins is at present engaged in commercial pursuits.

II

From your own vocabulary and from your observation of the speech of others make a list of tautologous, redundant, trite, exaggerated, and affected expressions.

213. Summary. Effectiveness of diction depends upon the use of exact, appropriate, and expressive words to convey our meaning.

To be exact, a word must fit precisely the idea for which it stands. Specific words, rather than general terms, are essential to exactness of expression.

To be appropriate, a word must be properly adapted to the subject and to the understanding of our hearers and readers.

To be expressive, a word should possess, in addition to its literal meaning, the power of suggestion that will stimulate the mind of the hearer or reader. What a word literally says is its denotation. What it suggests is its connotation.

Figures of speech intelligently employed have great suggestive value. The principal figures are simile, metaphor, personification, apostrophe, antithesis, epigram, metonymy, synecdoche, hyperbole, climax, onomatopœia, irony, and euphemism.

The six principal violations of effectiveness of diction are (1) needless repetition, (2) exaggeration, (3) trite expressions, (4) hackneyed quotations, (5) overuse of figurative language, and (6) "fine writing."

CHAPTER XIV

THE IMPORTANCE OF A LARGE VOCABULARY

214. Poverty in words and thoughts. Financially we are considered poor if we possess insufficient money—the symbol of value and the medium of commercial exchange—to live in keeping with the standards of the social group to which we belong. Intellectually and socially we are considered poor if we have insufficient words—the symbols of ideas and the medium of thought exchange—to express our thoughts clearly and effectively. And just as we cannot spend money that we do not have, so we cannot use words that are not in our vocabulary. Yet our mastery of English as a tool, as well as our mental growth, demands first of all that we have a large stock of words which we can use intelligently. The average educated person employs from three to five thousand words, whereas many of us "get along," as we say, with five hundred to a thousand. Surely we have need of a greater number.

215. Kinds of words a vocabulary should contain. In our efforts to enlarge our vocabulary we should make it a practice to add useful words common to the speech and writing of educated persons. Except in our study of special subjects, such as the sciences, we need not concern ourselves very much with learning technical terms or other words rarely encountered in conversation, in lectures, or in reading. We shall be aided in our endeavors if we understand some of the classes of words from which we may acquire additions to our vocabulary.

216. Anglo-Saxon words. Anglo-Saxon words, since they constitute a large proportion of the familiar words used in everyday life, contribute naturalness and force to what we say.

They include (1) words relating to the home, such as *mother, father, brother, sister, home*; (2) words expressing strong feeling, such as *gladness, sorrow, love, hate, fear, pride, shame*; (3) names of common things, such as *sun, moon, earth, hill, stone, sand, salt, tree, horse, cow, hand, arm, man, woman, day, night, cold, heat*; (4) a large number of our specific verbs, such as *slide, walk, run, leap, fly, swim*, as distinguished from general words like *move*; (5) many other words employed in the common affairs of life, such as *bring, fetch, sell, buy, work, play, rich, pretty, sweet*; and (6) most of the words in our familiar proverbs, such as "Haste makes waste."

217. Classical words. English words derived from either the Latin or the Greek are called classical words. We usually regard Anglo-Saxon words as *popular*, as distinguished from classical words, which we think of as *learned*, though a large number of classical words have become popular. In many cases words of this latter type are as familiar and as widely used as native English words. From the Latin have come such words as *animal, circus, contradict, describe, fact, graduate, junior, medicine, recess, suburb, vaccinate, ventilation, veto, victor, vote*. From the Greek we have derived such words as *athlete, atlas, biography, chemist, dialogue, encyclopedia, iodine, microscope, panic, photograph, skeleton, telegraph, zoölogy*. From modern foreign languages, particularly the French, we have obtained a considerable number of useful words.

218. Idioms. An idiom is a phrase that in its form of expression is peculiar to a given language. Usually it cannot be translated literally into another language. Many idioms cannot be justified by the strict rules of grammar, although long-continued and general usage has established them as reputable. They frequently possess a rugged, homely strength that adds greatly to the effectiveness of speech and writing. The following are a few examples of familiar English idioms:

hard put to it	*for*	in great extremity
get rid of	*for*	free oneself from
get used to	*for*	become accustomed to
get ready	*for*	prepare
pull through	*for*	succeed, recover, survive
put through	*for*	consummate

219. Synonyms and antonyms. Synonyms are words of similar meaning. Though several words may convey the same general idea, each word has its own particular force and application. A careful comparison of the precise meaning of such words as *aged, antique, antiquated, archaic, obsolete, ancient,* and *old* will illustrate this fact. Antonyms are words of opposite meaning, such as *plenty* and *want, pain* and *pleasure, honor* and *shame, weakness* and *strength.* English is unusually rich in synonyms and antonyms, owing to the fact that, in addition to Anglo-Saxon words, it has many equivalent and contrasting terms acquired from other languages. A study of synonyms and antonyms is one of the best ways of increasing our vocabulary and of enabling ourselves to speak and write with greater accuracy.

EXERCISES

I

Make a list of twenty idioms found in your conversation and in your reading.

II

Find in an unabridged dictionary the source and the exact shade of meaning of each word in the following pairs of synonyms, and use each word correctly in a sentence:

destroy, annihilate	learned, erudite
queer, eccentric	fire, conflagration
thin, emaciated	round, circular
play, drama	brave, valorous
sharp, acute	fat, corpulent

III

Find in an unabridged dictionary the exact shade of meaning of the synonyms in the following groups and use each word correctly in a sentence:

1. abandon, desert, forsake
2. avow, acknowledge, confess, admit
3. absolve, exonerate, acquit
4. account, report, narration, recital
5. sufficient, enough
6. pale, pallid, wan
7. opportunity, occasion
8. kill, murder, assassinate, execute, slaughter

220. How to acquire a large vocabulary. To obtain a large vocabulary we must possess or develop a lively and persistent interest in words. We should, moreover, be constantly on the alert for new ideas and new ways of expressing our thoughts. Such an interest and attitude will enable us to discover the best means of making new words our own.

There is great disparity between the number of words which we understand in conversation and in reading and the number which we ourselves use. This disparity is due in part to the narrow range of topics to which most of us confine our thinking and talking; in part, to the laziness which indisposes us to search for the most fitting expressions; and not infrequently to a foolish shame, which keeps us from using the best we know, for fear that we may be thought affected or bookish. Obviously, we may increase our active vocabulary by consciously making use of words that we understand but have heretofore avoided. Our ear-and-eye vocabulary is continually growing, so long as we associate with well-educated speakers and writers, and it should be our aim to make our active vocabulary keep pace with it.

Frequent conversation with persons better informed than we and attentive reading in the works of reputable authors will acquaint us with many new and useful words. A study of the dictionary and daily reference thereto will rapidly augment our stock of words. Translation from a foreign language and the use of synonyms for words already in our active vocabulary are two additional means of growth. Finally, by keeping in a small notebook all the new words we wish to acquire, and by using these words frequently in sentences, we may establish them permanently in our vocabulary. We should remember that not until we can use a word accurately and freely is it really our own.

EXERCISES

I

During the next week make a list of ten or more new words that you hear or find in your reading. Learn the correct meaning of each and use the word in a sentence.

II

What does the author of "Self-Cultivation in English" say about the importance of a large vocabulary? What suggestions does he give for acquiring new words?

III

Examine closely the following list of words and select for study those words that you are unable to use accurately in sentences of your own. Learn from an unabridged dictionary the meaning of each of these words and use the word in a sentence.

accelerate	derelict	facilitate	inert	redolent
charlatan	ductile	flaccid	lucid	requisite
chortle	emulate	frugal	mercenary	resilient
crafty	evolve	futile	meticulous	transient
cursory	expedite	gnome	nominal	valid

221. Summary. The mastery of English as a tool, as well as our mental growth, demands that we acquire a large stock of words which we can use intelligently. We should aim constantly at increasing not only the number of words that we understand but particularly the number of words that we actually use in speech and in writing. Our vocabulary will include both Anglo-Saxon and classical words. The study of idioms, synonyms, and antonyms will greatly augment our store of words.

The surest way of attaining a good vocabulary is to develop a lively and persistent interest in words and carefully to observe the usage of the best speakers and writers of the present time. Translation from a foreign language, the regular use of an unabridged dictionary, and the keeping of a list of new words in a notebook until we have mastered them we shall find particularly helpful in increasing our vocabulary.

CHAPTER XV

THE USE OF THE DICTIONARY

222. Importance of the study of the dictionary. Since a dictionary is not only a storehouse of words but also an authority as to the usage of the best authors, the study of it will help us to improve our diction. Many of us are not familiar enough with this valuable aid to English composition to understand its real worth. It may be well, therefore, for us to consider at this point the proper use of the dictionary.

223. Unabridged and abridged dictionaries. From our first year in high school throughout the remainder of our life we should have ready access to an unabridged dictionary that has been recently revised. The four principal English unabridged dictionaries now in common use are the following:

1. *Webster's New International Dictionary.* The latest revised edition contains four hundred thousand words and is especially practical in its arrangement. It is particularly useful for derivation and definition.

2. *The New Standard Dictionary.* This includes four hundred and fifty thousand words and contains, in addition to definitions, much encyclopedic material.

3. *The Century Dictionary and Cyclopedia.* Of the twelve volumes in which it is published, the first ten contain the dictionary material. Volume XI is a cyclopedia of names, and Volume XII an atlas of the world.

4. *A New English Dictionary.* When it is completed, this dictionary will include twenty volumes. It is comprehensive and scholarly and is considered the ultimate authority on correct English usage.

The New International and the Standard, each complete in one volume, we shall find adequate for our present use.

Though we may not individually own an unabridged dictionary, it is necessary that we possess a personal copy of an abridged edition. The four most satisfactory abridged dictionaries are the following:

1. Webster's Collegiate Dictionary.
2. The Concise Oxford Dictionary.
3. The High-School Standard Dictionary.
4. The College Standard Dictionary.

224. Arrangement of an unabridged dictionary. Not until we have made a careful examination of its system of arrangement and the character of its contents are we capable of using an unabridged dictionary most profitably. Preceding the dictionary proper, we find, are (1) a brief history of the English language, (2) a guide to pronunciation, (3) a discussion of the established rules for spelling, (4) a list of the abbreviations used throughout the volume, and (5) other explanations for our guidance. Following the dictionary proper, there are usually included (1) a pronouncing geographical dictionary, (2) a pronouncing biographical dictionary, (3) a list of the arbitrary signs used in writing and printing, and (4) a section of classified pictorial illustrations. In the dictionary proper, across the bottom of the pages facing each other, is given a key to vowel and consonant sounds. Printed in capital letters in the upper left-hand corner is the first word on the page; in the upper right-hand corner appears the last word on the page. By a glance at these words we can tell whether the word for which we are looking is included on the page before us. Webster's New International Dictionary has each page divided into two parts: the upper contains familiar words, and the lower contains, in small type, unusual, obsolete, and foreign words. If we fail to find a word in one division, we should look also in the other.

EXERCISES

I

Spend at least one hour becoming acquainted with the arrangement and system of the unabridged dictionary that you use.

II

Find the meaning of the following abbreviations:

a.	adv.	cf.	F.	D.	Gael.
n.	prep.	AS., A–S.	Sp.	Dan.	Teut.
v. t.	conj.	ME.	Slav.	Celt.	Pol.
v. i.	pron.	L., Lat.	It.	OF.	Icel.
p. a.	fr.	Gr.	G.	O.H.G.	Hind.

III

The most common marks used in indicating vowel sounds are the macron (*nātion*); the breve (*nĕt*); the diæresis (*zoölogy*); the dot (*ȧsk*); the wave (*fẽrn*); the circumflex (*ûrn*); the cedilla (*façade*). Make a neat list of all the vowel and consonant sounds properly marked, with a word to illustrate each.

IV

Find the pronunciation of the following proper names and any additional information about them that is available:

Beauchamp	Guadalajara	Medici	Ouida	Rouen
Benoit	Majori	Murillo	Rheims	San José

225. Information about words. In the dictionary proper of an unabridged dictionary we have access to the following useful information about words:

1. *Spelling.* If two or more forms of spelling are permissible, we should select the preferred form, which is placed first. In addition to the spelling of the basal words, we find also the spelling of (1) the remaining principal parts of verbs; (2) the

plurals and case forms of nouns and proncuns; (3) the comparative and superlative forms of adjectives and adverbs.

2. *Pronunciation.* If more than one pronunciation is permissible, the preferred form is placed first.

3. *Part of speech.* Immediately following the pronunciation comes an abbreviation indicating the part of speech to which the word belongs. Many words are used as different parts of speech. If we know the part of speech to which the word that we are looking for belongs, we should proceed immediately to the word so classified; otherwise we should examine various meanings of the word until we have found a meaning that seems consistent with the context in which the word stands.

4. *Derivation and history of words.* If this information is not given, look back to the first of the series of words derived from the root in question. A knowledge of the derivation of a word is usually an aid to precision of diction. Frequently, however, a word has had successive meanings in the course of its history and may at the present time be used in a sense not readily associated with its original meaning. Such words as *urbane, prevent, miser, impertinent, censure, reduce,* and *depart* illustrate changes in meaning.

5. *Various meanings.* These are systematically classified and are preceded by the figures 1, 2, 3, 4, etc. If a word has a technical use, this is indicated by a word or an abbreviation placed before the definition, such as *Law, Engin., Med., Astron., Arch., Pol. Econ.* These abbreviations are listed in the early pages of the dictionary.

6. *The standing of words.* Words that are not in good use or are restricted in use have this fact indicated by a word or an abbreviation placed after the definition. Such words and abbreviations include *Obs., Colloq., Dial., U.S., Rare, Cant, Slang.* If the standing of a word is not given, it may be assumed to be in good use.

7. *Illustrations of the use of words.* Many of the uses of words are illustrated by quotations from various writers.

8. *Synonyms and antonyms.* Frequently a list of synonyms, sometimes of antonyms also, is placed after the last definition.

9. *Reference.* Following the list of synonyms there is often a reference to a word or an illustration in another part of the dictionary. Such references are indicated by *See, Cf.,* and *q. v.*

10. *Combinations with other words.* Last of all, there is a list of established phrases in which the word in question is used. In the New International Dictionary the word *false* is followed by such phrases as *false action, f. analogy, f. cadence, f. face, f. perspective, f. representation.*

EXERCISES

I

Find the meaning of the following abbreviations:

Anat.	Class.	Geom.	Moham.	Pharm.	Sw.
Arch.	Dyn.	Jew.	Mus.	Psychol.	Theat.
Biog.	Eccl.	Math.	Ornith.	Relig.	Theol.
Biol.	Her.	Metal.	Paleon.	Surg.	Topog.
Bot.	Geol.	Micros.	Parl.	Surv.	Typog.

II

In an unabridged dictionary find the correct pronunciation of each of the following words. If two pronunciations are given, notice which is preferable. Make special note of those words that you are in the habit of mispronouncing.

acclimated	clique	disreputable	formidable
address	combatant	drought	genuine
adult	condolence	entire	hearth
almond	deference	express	hospitable
alternate	despicable	exquisite	idea
applicable	discourse	finance	illustrate

illustrative	irrelevant	precedence	salmon
incomparable	lamentable	precedent	sergeant
inexplicable	larynx	recess	sough
infamous	literature	resource	vagary
inquiry	medieval	rinse	vehemently
interesting	mischievous	romance	zoölogy

III

In an unabridged dictionary find the derivation, history, and standing of each of the following words:

alcohol	chortle	home	rathe
apron	churl	ingot	salary
artesian	dago	journey	siesta
atlas	dahlia	knave	silly
bedlam	disaster	madame	sincere
benefactor	doff	maize	sugar
biscuit	don	maudlin	taboo
bishop	doom	meander	tantalize
bombast	drink	mercerize	tawdry
boycott	echo	mermaid	tell
burglarize	explode	miniature	thug
cab	fain	mob	torture
candidate	feat	parasol	transpire
candy	fee	parson	trencher
casualty	fiasco	Pasteurize	umbrella
cathedral	focus	petulant	umpire
cavalier	garlic	piano	venison
cereal	gas	poet	villain
chaos	handkerchief	pyjama	walrus
cheese	hector	quixotic	welcome

226. Summary. Intelligent use of an unabridged dictionary requires that we learn its system of arrangement and the character of its contents. In consulting the dictionary we should avail ourselves of all the information given about each particular word. By so doing we increase our command over the word and quicken our interest in word study.

PART THREE

CHAPTER XVI

SIMPLE NARRATION

227. Simple narration defined. Simple narration is the recounting of an event or of a series of events. The incidents that compose a simple narration are arranged in the order of time; that is, they are related in the order of their occurrence. If, as in most simple narrations, the events are actual happenings in real life, we call the account a *narrative of fact*. But if, as in a few instances, the entire story is the product of the author's imagination, we call it a *narrative of fiction*.

Of all the forms of writing, simple narration is the easiest and most natural in composition. Like the rest of mankind, we enjoy relating our experiences and observations, as well as listening to or reading those of others. Moreover, we like to hear and to read accounts of romantic imaginary adventures that few, if any, human beings have ever experienced. For these reasons narration is more extensively written and more widely read than any other type of literature.

228. The three essentials of simple narration. A simple narrative answers four questions; namely, *When? Where? Who?* and *What?* In other words, the narrator, in order to relate an event or a series of events effectively, must inform his hearers and readers as to the time and the place at which the incidents occurred, the persons or the animals that took part in the action, and the series of incidents that constitute the narrative. This information is expected and demanded. Unless these questions

345

are satisfactorily answered either by statement or by implication, the narrative is vague and uninteresting.

The three essentials of simple narration are, therefore, *setting*, *characters*, and *action*. Usually at the beginning of his narrative the author answers the first two questions and adds any explanatory and descriptive details that he thinks are necessary to the proper understanding of the time and the place of the action. In answering the first two questions the narrator may partially or wholly answer the third question. That is, he may indicate one or more of the actors, or characters, in the narrative. If he does not mention all his characters at the beginning, he will introduce others later as they are needed. Generally the real narrative, which is the account of the characters in action and of the outcome of this action, begins with the mention of the first character. The story from this point to the end constitutes the answer to the fourth question.

Life and movement are vital elements in all narration. For this reason the narrator should avoid introducing any unnecessary explanation or description, since these tend to retard the movement of the story.

The following simple narrative illustrates very well the three essentials of simple narration that we have been considering.

WHEN BULL SNAKE AND RATTLER MEET

One evening in summer several years ago, while I was on my way to look at a trawling-line that I had set for whitefish in the North Platte River, I observed a commotion among my sheep, which were grazing near by. I knew at once that a rattlesnake was among them, for I could hear the rattles; but a moment or two later near the bank of the river I heard a noise of a different kind. On hurrying toward it I found a huge bull snake that was lashing his head hither and thither in a frenzied attempt to disgorge an overgrown toad.

Just then I remembered the rather common tradition that bull snakes and rattlers are deadly enemies, and, grabbing the big fellow and thrusting him into a burlap bag I had expected to put my fish into, I ran at top speed to the place where I had heard the rattler. I found him; he was a gigantic fellow, thickset, powerful of jaw, and at least six feet long.

I dropped my bag, and out came the bull snake, free from the toad. He advanced threateningly toward me, but in a moment the rattlesnake sounded his rattles, and like a flash the bull snake turned. Raising his head a foot or more, he remained quite motionless as if he were listening. Another buzz perhaps twenty feet away, and the bull snake knew where his enemy was. With a rush as if he were dropping from a height, he started for the rattler, which turned and fled. Fearing that he would disappear into a hole, I ran to head him off; but the precaution was not necessary. The bull snake quickly gained on him. When the snakes were perhaps six feet apart, they stopped and remained perfectly still. At the end of perhaps a minute the rattlesnake suddenly drew himself into a coil, and the bull snake started to circle the quarry, keeping about six feet from it. Gradually the bull snake moved faster and decreased the size of the circle, and all the while among the coils at the center there was a humming and a buzzing of rattles such as I had never heard before. The flat triangular head of the rattler was almost hidden and lifted only occasionally; whenever it did lift, the little eyes would blaze and scintillate.

When the bull snake had almost encircled his foe with his length, he suddenly drew himself together in a coil like that of his victim's, and from the midst of it raised and lowered his glistening, egg-shaped head. Never had I imagined so much fury, such terrible ferocity! The two writhing masses approached each other, and the hissing and the rattling ceased. The head of the rattlesnake began warily to emerge. Then the two heads lifted a foot and came together with an impact almost like that which a baseball bat makes when it strikes a baseball. For a time both snakes were so active that you could not see which had hold of the other. The two masses intertwined and lashed and tumbled and thrashed the earth too rapidly for the eye to follow.

Then the movements became almost imperceptibly less violent, and I could see that the bull snake had hold of his antagonist two inches behind the head. The rattler was vainly trying to embed his fangs in his adversary; both fangs, almost an inch long, were in plain sight. His head was almost flat; his beady eyes looked as if they would shoot out like his forked tongue.

Suddenly the bull snake made a terrific lunge, and his entire length shot to the other side of his enemy, which now lay stretched in the opposite direction. For a moment both lay outstretched; then the bull snake moved weakly away in the direction of the marsh. With his head bent back double, the rattler writhed in his last throes.

I followed the victor, but he had not gone far before he stopped and drew his whole length up into lumps almost like knots; then he turned on his back. By the fading light I could see many little pricks, dark with blood. The venomed fangs of the rattler had pierced him in many places. Before long he ceased to move. I returned to the scene of the fight, and there lay the rattler dead. The big toad, the unwitting cause of the struggle, was the sole survivor of the tragedy.—*Youth's Companion*

EXERCISE

In the simple narrative that you have read point out the three essentials explained above and show by reference to specific details how the narrator answered the four questions that all simple narration should answer.

229. Unity in simple narration. The principle of unity as applied to simple narration requires that in each narrative only one event or one series of events forming a single story be related. That is, the narrative that we relate, whether long or short, must be a unit, a single complete story. To satisfy this requirement, we should examine carefully the material that we contemplate using and should decide on the story that we intend to tell. In this preliminary process we shall find ourselves greatly aided by answering the following questions:

THE PIRATE

From an etching by Rodney Thomson

1. At what point should I begin this narrative?
2. At what point should I end it?
3. What incidents properly belong to my story?
4. What point of view should I select?

In answering the first and the second question we are establishing the boundaries of our narrative. Since life and movement are vital elements in narration, we should begin our story directly, with the first incident of the series of happenings that properly belong to our narrative. As soon as we have told our story we should bring it to a close. In simple narration, as in all other forms of writing, the beginning and ending should be natural and appropriate.

In answering the third question we should keep in mind the limits that we have set ourselves in choosing the points at which to begin and to end our story. Only the incidents falling within these limits, and only those essential to the effective telling of our story, should be selected. By means of a carefully prepared list of incidents we should be able to select those that are necessary.

The choice of the proper point of view we shall usually find easy and natural. If we are relating personal experiences in which we have been the principal actor, we shall generally choose the first-person point of view. But if we are narrating events in which we have played only a minor part, which we have observed at the time of their occurrence, or which we have merely heard of later, we shall adopt the third-person point of view. When, as the all-knowing author, we not only relate what we observed and what our characters did, but tell, besides, what they thought and how they felt, we employ the omniscient third-person point of view. We shall generally use the past or past-perfect tense. Our point of view, which will depend upon our relation to the story, should be consistently maintained throughout the narrative.

Show how the writer of the simple narrative given above satisfied the demands of unity. Did he limit himself to telling *one* and *only one* story? Note carefully the beginning and the ending. Point out the incidents that make up the narrative proper. From what point of view is the narrative written?

230. Coherence in simple narration. Coherence in simple narration requires that the incidents that make up the narrative be recorded in the order in which they happen. This does not mean that we are to include *all* the incidents composing the actual happening, but that we should arrange in chronological order those incidents which are really necessary in making our narrative clear and effective. All preliminary and intervening incidents that would hinder the movement and detract from the main point of our story should be omitted.

Show how the principle of coherence was applied by the writer of the simple narrative given above. Are the incidents arranged in strict chronological order? Show that your answer is correct.

231. Emphasis in simple narration. Since the beginning and the end are the most important parts of a composition, we should make the introduction and the conclusion of a narrative as interesting as possible. We are not able, however, to put in these places the chief event of the narrative, for that forms the body of the story. On account of this fact *proportion is highly important*. We should give the greatest amount of space to the principal incident and should allot space to the remaining incidents according to their relative importance.

Climax is an additional means of securing emphasis. In so far as the chronological order will permit, we should arrange

incidents in such a manner that the interest is continually increased until the highest point of the narrative is reached. We
should therefore subordinate earlier details, so that more attention may be later given to incidents of greater importance.
We should ask ourselves: What is the chief thing that the characters in this narrative are going to do? What is the real *point*
of my story? Having satisfactorily answered these questions,
we should model the narrative in such a way that due prominence will be given to this main point, which should come at the
end or very near the end of our story. *We should arouse the
curiosity of our hearer or reader early in the narrative and
should keep him in suspense as to the main point or the outcome
until the end is reached. We should at all times carefully avoid
revealing this point too early in the story.*

EXERCISE

Show how emphasis was secured by the writer of the simple narrative given above. Are the beginning and the end effective? Were
the incidents given their correct proportion of space? Comment on
the use of climax and suspense. Did the writer reveal the point of
his narrative too early?

232. Oral narration. In general, the principles governing
oral and written narration are identical. In both, carefully
chosen incidents, recorded in proper sequence and arranged
effectively, are essential. In both, life and movement are indispensable. Though most of us have had more practice in oral
narration than in any other form of composition, we should try
to improve our skill in telling a good story well. We should
give just as much consideration to choosing and arranging the
incidents in oral as in written narration. We ought to strive at
all times to enliven our narration by the use of concrete words,
vividly suggestive figures of speech, and direct conversation

whenever it seems natural and appropriate. We should never mar a good story by slovenly narration. (For suggestions as to the method of giving oral compositions see section 11.)

(For suggestions as to the method of giving oral compositions see section 11.)

ORAL EXERCISE

Come to class prepared to give an oral narration based on one of the following suggested subjects or on a subject of your own choice:

1. A Practical Joke.
2. The Greatest Scare I Ever Had.
3. An Animal Hero (or Heroine).
4. When I Almost Poisoned the Family.
5. A Novel Vacation Experience.
6. An Accident I Recently Witnessed.
7. My Most Costly Mistake.
8. The Consequences of a Lie.

233. Material for narration. The subject matter for narratives may be obtained from three principal sources; namely, first-hand experience, reading, and imagination.

1. *Experience.* Our experience includes not only events in which we have had some part, whether important or unimportant, but also events of which we have been spectators. Few of us have passed through romantic or exciting adventures, but we have taken part in athletic contests, or have had enjoyable or unpleasant experiences in the woods, on the road, and on fishing trips and hunting trips, besides scores of everyday adventures. We have observed many other persons in the midst of accidents or other novel experiences. All this material is available for our use in narration.

2. *Reading.* From our reading we may gain many useful suggestions for narratives. The reports of various events in the newspapers and on the motion-picture screen will yield us a large harvest of novel ideas. We shall often find it highly entertaining to expand some dull statement of fact into a lively

narrative by assuming the point of view of one of the characters and employing vivid conversation. The retelling of episodes from stories which are read at school or at home is useful practice. History and biography will often furnish us equally valuable material.

3. *Imagination.* At first our narratives may be little more than mere narratives of fact. With more experience, however, we shall be likely to add details from our imagination as a means of expanding and enlivening our stories. Occasionally we may be able to construct fictitious narratives out of incidents that we have invented by means of our imagination. We shall find the writing of both narratives of fact and narratives of fiction profitable and entertaining.

234. Dialogue in narration. Dialogue, or conversation, is often employed in narration to render the action more vivid and the characters more lifelike. In addition, it enables us to avoid the monotony of having the entire narrative related directly by the author. In writing dialogue we should be careful to paragraph and punctuate correctly what each speaker says (see section 83).

235. Principal types of simple narration. Incidents may be narrated in both verse and prose. In our present study of composition we shall consider, however, only narratives written in prose. If we exclude histories, the most comprehensive form of simple narration, there remain eight principal types for us to examine; namely, anecdotes, tales, news stories, letters, diaries, biographies, autobiographies, and travel sketches.

236. Anecdotes. The anecdote is the simplest and briefest type of simple narration. It relates concisely and pointedly a single event. As soon as this has been done it should end. Many of the best anecdotes record a humorous situation or a dramatic incident. The brief, simple narrative given on pages 346–348 is an anecdote.

Biographies, autobiographies, and other personal reminiscences include a large number of anecdotes, such as the following illustration chosen from the autobiography of Edward Bok:

Transportation, in those days [between 1870 and 1880] in Brooklyn, was by horse cars, and the car line on Smith Street nearest Edward's home ran to Coney Island. Just around the corner where Edward lived, the horse cars stopped to water the horses on their long haul. The boy noticed that the men jumped from the open cars in summer, ran into the cigar store before which the watering-trough was placed, and got a drink of water from the ice-cooler placed near the door. But that was not so easily possible for the women, and they, especially the children, were forced to take the long ride without a drink.

Here was an opening, and Edward decided to fill it. He bought a shining new pail, screwed three hooks on the edge, from which he hung three clean, shimmering glasses, and one Saturday afternoon, when a car stopped, the boy leaped on, tactfully asked the conductor if he did not want a drink, and then proceeded to sell his water, cooled with ice, at a cent a glass to the passengers. A little experience showed that he exhausted a pail with every two cars, and each pail netted him thirty cents. Of course Sunday was a most profitable day; and after going to Sunday school in the morning, he did a further Sabbath service for the rest of the day by refreshing tired mothers and thirsty children on the Coney Island cars—at a penny a glass!

But the profit of six dollars which Edward was now reaping in his newly found "bonanza" on Saturday and Sunday afternoons became apparent to other boys, and one Saturday the young ice-water boy found that he had a competitor; then two and soon three. Edward immediately met the challenge; he squeezed half a dozen lemons into each pail of water, added some sugar, tripled his charge, and continued his monopoly by selling "Lemonade, three cents a glass." Soon more passengers were asking for lemonade than for plain drinking-water!—EDWARD BOK, "The Americanization of Edward Bok"[1]

---

[1] Used by permission of Charles Scribner's Sons, publishers.

EXERCISES

I

Relate to the class orally a good anecdote that you have recently heard or read.

II

Relate to the class orally an original anecdote based on your own experience or observation. The following suggestions may help you to find a subject:

1. A Case of Absent-mindedness.
2. Judging by Appearances.
3. An Embarrassing Mistake.
4. When I Answered an Advertisement.
5. A Novel Method of Earning Money.
6. Too Obliging.
7. Heard on the Party Line.
8. An Instance of Mistaken Identity.

III

Write an anecdote of not more than three hundred words based on an incident observed

1. On the street.
2. At a public gathering.
3. In the park.
4. At home.
5. On the athletic field.

IV

Write an anecdote of not more than three hundred words suggested by one of the pictures in this book.

237. Tales. A tale consists of a series of incidents and is much longer than an anecdote. Most true stories are tales. The incidents form the stages, or steps, in the larger action which the tale as a whole recounts. Usually all the incidents concern the central character, or hero. A little skill in deciding where to begin and where to end the narrative, together with experience in choosing incidents, will enable us to observe accurately the principle of unity in this type of narration. Such writers as Irving, Hawthorne, and Jack London wrote many tales, as well as numerous short stories.

EXERCISES

I

Read three tales, one each from Irving, Hawthorne, and Jack London, or from some other writers of tales whom your teacher may recommend. Come to class prepared to relate one of these stories orally to the class. Explain how the tale differs from the anecdote.

II

Write a tale of five hundred words or more suggested by one of the following subjects. Before you begin to write, decide upon the best places to begin and end, and then make a list of the incidents that your narrative should include.

1. An Automobile Accident.
2. A Memorable Adventure.
3. Our Burglar.
4. My Uncle's Most Interesting Adventure.
5. A Narrow Escape.

238. News stories. The news story is a special form of simple narrative. In length it ranges from a brief paragraph to an account several columns long. Since the editor of a newspaper often finds it necessary because of lack of space to omit the latter part of a news-writer's story, the writer places the most important details of his account at the beginning, generally in the first paragraph. In the remainder of his narrative he gives the less important details arranged in the descending order of their importance. So well established has this practice become that the experienced reader feels that he has the essentials of a news item as soon as he has read the headlines and the first paragraph or two. Because of this peculiarity of structure, the news item is rarely constructed in strict accord with the principles of unity, coherence, and emphasis. Owing to the haste with which they must be written, news stories usually lack the organization and finish of other types of narrative.

The following selection illustrates the brief news story:

GIANT METEOR HITS VIRGINIA

BURIES TREES BENEATH IT IN DEPRESSION OF 500 SQUARE FEET

Had Orange Tail with Blue Tip

NORFOLK, Va., May 12.—The shock of a 20-ton meteor which crashed to the ground in an isolated spot in Nottaway county, 12 miles northwest of Blackstone, late last night, was felt for a radius of 50 miles, while the brilliant glare of the incandescent body illuminated the heavens over southern Virginia and sections of North Carolina.

The trail of light was visible in this city, at Richmond, and at points along the James river, creating general excitement among the negroes.

The meteor, composed of a metallic substance, crashed into a grove of oak trees with an explosive roar, some distance from any house, making a hole with an area of 500 square feet and burying several trees with it. Flames immediately shot up, which were visible for many miles, while trees caught fire.

A party of scientists and newspaper-men immediately left Richmond and this city for the scene, which is 120 miles west of Norfolk.

The shock of the fall was felt at Lawrenceville, Petersburg, Chase City, and other points. At Lawrenceville, 100 miles west of here, and at Chase City windows were rattled and houses shaken.

In Norfolk the meteor appeared to be about half the diameter of the full moon and much like a street arc light. Its tail, of orange brilliance, with a sharp blue flame fading out at the extreme end, apparently was about 10 or 12 times as long and fully as broad as the body. It fell diagonally from the zenith and at an angle of about 45 degrees. The downward course was leisurely.—*Boston Herald*

EXERCISES

I

Bring to class a good brief news story clipped from one of your state or local papers. Be prepared to explain its structure. Could you make a better simple narrative out of the incidents recorded than the news-writer made? If so, rewrite the news story and bring both versions of the event to class.

II

As a reporter for your school or town paper write a well-planned, interesting news story of about three hundred words based on one of the following topics:

1. An athletic rally.
2. A victory of a school athletic team.
3. An automobile accident.
4. A fire in your town.
5. A runaway horse.
6. A recently discovered crime.
7. An insignificant person who has become a hero (or heroine).
8. Some other event of local human interest.

III

Write a brief news story of a real or an imagined accident suggested by one of the following pictures:

1. Man's Conquest over Nature (facing page 198).
2. The Lights of Industry (facing page 402).
3. The Skyscrapers (facing page 324).
4. Harvesting Ice (facing page 258).

239. Letters. Most friendly letters contain a large portion of narration. Though the letter is not so distinct a type of narrative writing as it was in the seventeenth and eighteenth centuries, it still serves a very important narrative purpose. Those who travel write to friends and relatives accounts of interesting incidents connected with their trip. Those left behind relate to their correspondents what is going on at home. Writers have occasionally told entire stories by means of fictitious letters. It was thus that "Clarissa Harlowe," an early English novel, was written. "Daddy-Long-Legs" and "Marjorie Daw" are more recent stories narrated by means of letters. The four specimen letters (see Chapter VI) written by Theodore Roosevelt and by the two student writers are almost entirely simple narration.

EXERCISES

I

Read again the four letters mentioned above and come to class prepared to discuss them as examples of simple narration.

II

Read "Marjorie Daw," a short story by Thomas Bailey Aldrich, as an example of a story narrated by means of letters and telegrams.

III

Write one of the following letters, giving your correspondent a vivid, entertaining account of the incidents that you select:

1. A letter to a friend or a relative giving an account of the most interesting event that occurred on your trip last summer.
2. A letter to your family relating a thrilling experience you have recently had on a hunting, fishing, or camping trip.

3. A letter to your chum telling of an extraordinary event that has occurred since he or she left home.

4. A letter to a friend or relative recounting an act of bravery or intelligence on the part of a dog or a horse.

5. A letter relating some event of your own choice.

IV

Write a letter to a friend or a relative giving him a vivid, entertaining account of a real or imagined trip suggested by one of the following pictures:

1. Yosemite Falls (facing page 370).
2. Camping in Colorado (facing page 116).
3. The Dawn of a New Life (frontispiece).
4. The Lights of Industry (facing page 402).
5. Flotsam Castle (facing page 296).

240. Diaries. A diary is an intimate daily record of personal observations, experiences, and impressions. Its chief value for the writer, who is usually the sole reader, consists in the intimacy of style and the sincerity of expression with which it is written. One of the most famous and oft-quoted diaries is that of Samuel Pepys, an English government official, who, during the early years of the reign of Charles II, recorded in his diary not only incidents of his daily life but political and historical events as well. We shall find the keeping of a diary valuable training in composition if we put our best effort into the writing of each entry.

241. Biographies. A biography is the life history of one person written by another. A biography should give the events of a person's life; should show the influence of events on his character; should give an account of his ambition, desires, and purposes, and of the way he accomplished them; and should enable the reader to look at the man from different points of view and get an idea of his various qualities, good and bad.

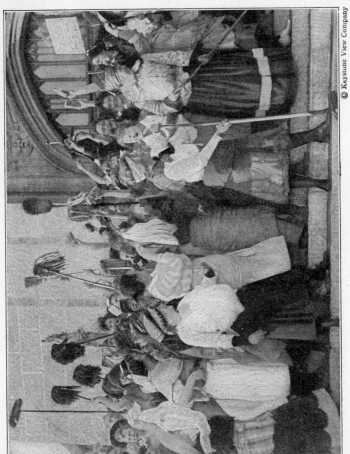

A MAY-DAY FROLIC

Since the life of every person is made up of a series of incidents, biography, which is the record of these incidents, is largely simple narration.

Some of the most interesting examples of biography are Boswell's "Life of Samuel Johnson," Lockhart's "Life of Sir Walter Scott," Forster's "Life of Dickens," Irving's "Life of Goldsmith," Morse's "Life of Lincoln," Cheney's "Life of Louisa May Alcott," and G. H. Palmer's "Life of Alice Freeman Palmer."

EXERCISES

I

Read some brief biography, such as "John Gilley," by Charles W. Eliot, or one that your teacher may assign you, and make a list of the chief incidents recorded. Show how the author applied the three principles of correct structure in writing this simple narrative. Are there any anecdotes included that are good brief narratives in themselves?

II

Write a brief biography of one of the following persons:

1. My Younger Sister (or Brother).
2. My Chum.
3. My Uncle (or Aunt).
4. Our Scout Master.
5. A person of your own choice.

242. Autobiographies. An autobiography is a life history written by the person himself. The writer frequently constructs the story of his life by relating as anecdotes the various significant incidents in his life. By adopting the first-person point of view he enables himself to write in an easy, conversational style and to relate personal anecdotes that would otherwise be out of place. A few autobiographers, like Edward Bok, have chosen the third-person point of view in order to speak more freely and naturally about their lives and experiences.

Familiar and interesting autobiographies are those of Benjamin Franklin, Joseph Jefferson, and Benvenuto Cellini. In recent years a number of other excellent autobiographies have been written, such as the following: "The Story of my Life," by Helen Keller; "The Promised Land," by Mary Antin; "The Making of an American," by Jacob Riis; and "The Americanization of Edward Bok," by Edward Bok.

EXERCISES

I

Within the limits of five pages relate the chief events in your life. Try to select incidents that will entertain your readers and afford them information as to your attainments, character, and ambition in life. Write naturally and observe proper proportion.

II

Write a brief fictitious biography or autobiography of a person represented in one of the following pictures:

1. The Pirate (facing page 348).
2. The Village Censor (facing page 382).
3. The Dawn of a New Life (frontispiece).
4. Flotsam Castle (facing page 296).

243. Travel sketches. Oral and written accounts of travels have from very early times been an interesting type of narrative. Such books as Stevenson's "An Inland Voyage" and "Travels with a Donkey," Mark Twain's "Innocents Abroad," and H. A. Franck's "A Vagabond Journey around the World" furnish delightful reading. Many magazines, such as the *Century* and the *National Geographic Magazine*, publish brief travel sketches monthly. In general, the travel sketch contains as much description as narration.

EXERCISES

I

Read in the *Century*, the *National Geographic Magazine*, or some other periodical one or two travel sketches. Note the use of description along with narration. Come to class prepared to give orally a brief summary of one of these sketches.

II

Write a travel sketch on one of the following topics, properly limited, and illustrate it with pictures if you have any appropriate photographs:

1. Historic New England.
2. The Spanish Missions of the Southwest.
3. Picturesque Mexico.
4. California, Florida, or Alaska.
5. A subject of your own choice.

III

Write a travel sketch of about five hundred words in which you might use one or more of the following pictures as illustrations:

1. Camping in Colorado (facing page 116).
2. Yosemite Falls (facing page 370).
3. The Sagebrush of Idaho (facing page 172).
4. Flotsam Castle (facing page 296).

GENERAL EXERCISES

I

Write a fictitious narrative telling how the pirate (facing page 348) lost his leg.

II

Retell a story that you imagine the village censor (facing page 382) is fond of telling. Try to make the incident related and the language used fit the character that his picture suggests.

III

Write a fictitious narrative suggested by the picture facing page 476.

244. Summary. Simple narration is the recounting of an event or of a series of events, either real or fictitious.

The three essentials of simple narration are setting, characters, and action. Life and movement are vital elements in all narration.

Unity in simple narration is secured by carefully selecting the points at which to begin and end, by choosing only relevant incidents, and by adopting and maintaining a definite point of view.

Coherence in simple narration is secured by relating events in the order of their occurrence.

Emphasis in simple narration is gained by means of an effective beginning and ending, by proper proportion, and by climax.

The principles governing oral and written narration are the same.

The three sources of material for narration are first-hand experience, reading, and imagination.

Dialogue renders the action in narration more vivid and the characters more lifelike.

The eight principal types of simple narration, exclusive of history, are anecdotes, tales, news stories, letters, diaries, biographies, autobiographies, and travel sketches.

CHAPTER XVII

DESCRIPTION

245. Description defined. Description is that form of composition by means of which we try to furnish our hearers and readers the same picture and the same impression that we ourselves derived from the place, object, or person described. By a skillful selection and arrangement of details of sight, sound, smell, taste, and touch we attempt to create for them an appropriate image, induce in them a fitting mood, or arouse a proper emotional response. Though description, both oral and written, may be used as an independent form of discourse, it is more frequently subordinate to narration, exposition, or argument. Almost every day we employ description to picture for others the scene of an event and to make them realize what our sensations were during the event. Writers of stories use description to make vivid the scenes, the characters, and the action of their narratives.

246. Expository description. If our aim in giving a description is to represent with photographic accuracy every detail in the appearance of a place, an object, or a person, so that our description may be used for purposes of identification, the result is an *expository description*. Such descriptions are found in catalogues, tourists' guidebooks, the stage setting of printed plays, textbooks on science, the files of courts and detective agencies, and brief classified advertisements in newspapers. The following passages are expository descriptions:

1. English Colonial house : ten rooms, tile bath, three fireplaces, hardwood floors throughout, Chamberlain metal weather strips, built-in bookcases in large living-room ; gas, electricity ; beautiful lawn with shade trees, shrubs, apple and quince trees. One acre in grounds ; more if desired.

2. The scene represents the Manton library. The room is furnished in walnut and is hung with rich draperies. At the center of the back wall is an open fireplace, in which a fire burns cheerily. To the left of the fireplace is a door opening into the dining-room. In the left wall is a wide door hung with heavy portières. In the right wall is a French window. A large brown velvet rug and two smaller rugs cover the floor. Bookcases line the walls. Several easy chairs, a library table covered with magazines, a floor reading-lamp, a smoker's stand, one or two pieces of statuary, and several framed etchings complete the furnishings.

247. Artistic description. If our aim in giving a description is to furnish others pleasure by stimulating their imagination, appealing to their sense of beauty, or arousing their emotions, the result is an *artistic description*. Descriptions of this kind are found in all forms of writing, both prose and poetry, that possess literary merit. To produce an artistic description we must decide upon the *single dominant impression* that we wish to emphasize and then select and arrange with skill the details that will most effectively convey this impression to others. Artistic description, like all other fine arts, depends upon the careful selection and right use of materials. It is not meant to be photographically accurate. Its chief purpose is to supply details that will stimulate our hearer's or reader's imagination and vividly suggest the impression and the emotions that we ourselves experienced. In this chapter we shall limit our discussion hereafter chiefly to artistic description.

248. Unity in description. The principle of unity in description demands first of all that we limit our subject definitely and include only relevant details. Let us examine the following description of the "house of the seven gables," to see how Hawthorne observed this first requirement of unity:

Maule's lane, or Pyncheon street, as it were now more decorous to call it, was thronged, at the appointed hour, as with a congregation on its way to church. All, as they approached, looked upward at the imposing edifice, which was henceforth to assume its rank among the habitations of mankind. There it rose, a little withdrawn from the line of the street, but in pride, not modesty. Its whole visible exterior was ornamented with quaint figures, conceived in the grotesqueness of a Gothic fancy, and drawn or stamped in the glittering plaster, composed of lime, pebbles, and bits of glass, with which the woodwork of the walls was overspread. On every side the seven gables pointed sharply toward the sky, and presented the aspect of a whole sisterhood of edifices, breathing through the spiracles of one great chimney. The many lattices, with their small, diamond-shaped panes, admitted the sunlight into hall and chamber, while, nevertheless, the second story, projecting far over the base, and itself retiring beneath the third, threw a shadowy and thoughtful gloom into the lower rooms. Carved globes of wood were affixed under the jutting stories. Little spiral rods of iron beautified each of the seven peaks. On the triangular portion of the gable, that fronted next the street, was a dial, put up that very morning, and on which the sun was still marking the passage of the first bright hour in a history that was not destined to be all so bright. All around were scattered shavings, chips, shingles, and broken halves of bricks; these, together with the lately turned earth, on which the grass had not begun to grow, contributed to the impression of the strangeness and novelty proper to a house that had yet its place to make among men's daily interests.—HAWTHORNE, "The House of the Seven Gables"

In this description we notice that the subject has been neatly limited to the appearance of the *outside* of the house. All details included are natural parts of the whole and are relevant. No details have been brought in which take our attention away from the house.

249. Point of view. A definite point of view, carefully chosen and consistently maintained, is an important requirement of a unified description. Our success in description, like an artist's success in painting, depends in a large measure upon our choice of a point of view. Our aim should be to choose a position that will enable us to view advantageously the scene or object that we are to describe. Experiment and practice will help us to select wisely. Having chosen our point of observation, we should let the reader know clearly where we are with respect to the scene or object. Unless completeness and naturalness of representation demand it, we should not change our point of view. In case a change is made, the new point of view should be mentioned or clearly implied. The point of view in the selection given above is that of the people in the street, and it remains fixed throughout the description.

In addition to the point of view in space, the point of view in time is often important. That is, if the time of day or night, the day of the week or month, or the season of the year affects the scene or object to be described, the time should be mentioned.

Furthermore, our personal point of view, which may depend upon age, previous environment, and special interests in life, may influence our observation, and hence our description, of a scene or an object.

250. Singleness of impression. In the description of the "house of the seven gables" we notice that Hawthorne dwelt on the *unusual appearance* of the house. This he did, not only by using the words "the imposing edifice" and "the impression of the strangeness and novelty," but also by choosing details which kept the impression in our minds and thus emphasized it. For example, he introduced such expressions as "quaint figures," "the grotesqueness of a Gothic fancy," "glittering plaster," "bits of glass," "seven gables pointed sharply toward the sky," and "threw a shadowy and thoughtful gloom into the lower rooms." This indicates that Hawthorne first decided on some *single impression* which he wished to make on the reader and then chose the best means of driving that impression home.

In observing a scene, an object, or a person that we intend to describe we should discover the dominant characteristic or most prominent quality. We should try to determine the effect or impression produced on us by this dominant characteristic. We should then seek to produce the same impression on our readers by means of our description. This we may be able to do if we are careful in choosing details that emphasize this one principal characteristic and if, with equal care, we avoid bringing in any details that detract from the single impression we wish to make. In the scene described below, the writer was most impressed by the *intense heat*, and this is the single impression that his description makes on the reader.

It was high noon, and the rays of the sun, that hung poised directly overhead in an intolerable white glory, fell straight as plummets upon the roofs and streets of Guadalajara. The adobe walls and sparse brick sidewalks of the drowsing town radiated the heat in an oily, quivering shimmer. The leaves of the eucalyptus trees around the Plaza drooped motionless, limp, and relaxed under the scorching, searching blaze. The shadows of these trees had shrunk to their smallest circumference, contracting close about the trunks. The shade had dwindled to the breadth of a mere line. The sun was everywhere. The heat exhaling from brick and plaster and metal met the heat that steadily descended, blanketwise and smothering, from the pale, scorched sky. Only the lizards—they lived in chinks of the crumbling adobe and in interstices of the sidewalk— remained without, motionless, as if stuffed, their eyes closed to mere slits, basking, stupefied with heat. At long intervals the prolonged drone of an insect developed out of the silence, vibrated a moment in a soothing, somnolent, long note, then trailed slowly into the quiet again. Somewhere in the interior of one of the 'dobe houses a guitar snored and hummed sleepily. On the roof of the hotel a group of pigeons cooed incessantly with subdued, liquid murmurs, very plaintive; a cat, perfectly white, with a pink nose and thin, pink lips, dozed complacently on a fence rail, full in the sun. In a corner of the Plaza three hens wallowed in the baking hot dust, their wings fluttering, clucking comfortably.—FRANK NORRIS, "The Octopus"[1]

[1] Used by permission of Doubleday, Page and Company, publishers.

In the paragraph above indicate the concrete details and the specific words used to convey the single impression of intense heat.

251. The fundamental image. If the dominant characteristic of a place, an object, or a person is shape, size, or color, we may often convey to the reader a quick general impression by the use of a fundamental image or by comparing the subject of our description to a more familiar object, place, or person. In the following passage observe how effectively the italicized expression suggests the outstanding characteristic of shape:

The Bay of Monterey has been compared by no less a person than General Sherman to *a bent fishing-hook*. . . . Santa Cruz sits exposed at the shank; the mouth of the Salinas River is at the middle of the bend; and Monterey itself is cozily ensconced beside the barb. Thus the ancient capital of California faces across the bay, while the Pacific Ocean, though hidden by the low hills and forest, bombards her left flank and rear with never-dying surf. In front of the town, the long line of seabeach trends north and northwest, and then westward to inclose the bay.—STEVENSON, "Across the Plains"[1]

252. Coherence in description. All effective description depends upon the orderly arrangement of the details selected. Such an arrangement we have already illustrated in the description of the "house of the seven gables." First, Hawthorne states the general appearance of the house: it is an "imposing edifice." Next, he gives the general aspect of the exterior. Then, as he views the house more closely, he fills in the minute details in the order in which they would probably attract our attention: the figures on the plaster, the gables, the lattices, the projecting stories, the carved globes of wood, the spiral rods of iron, the sundial, and finally, as the eye surveys the

[1] Used by permission of Charles Scribner's Sons, publishers.

© E. M. Newman

YOSEMITE FALLS

ground, the shavings and bricks. At the end he gives a sweeping impression of all the details in the words "strangeness" and "novelty." This kind of order—from the most striking to the less noticeable details, from the general to the particular —is very common in description. Other natural and useful orders of arrangement are (1) from far to near or near to far; (2) from right to left or left to right; (3) from top to bottom, from head to foot; and (4) from exterior to interior. The point that we should remember is that *some definite order must be followed.*

253. Emphasis in description. To secure emphasis in description we should place important details in prominent positions. If we can find a good fundamental image, we should place it first. All details chosen should be those that stand out prominently and are really important. It is neither possible nor desirable to include every detail. We should devote space to the parts of a description in proportion to their importance.

254. Vividness in description. Vividness is the essential quality in all descriptive writing. Unless a description furnishes the reader a well-defined picture or a distinct impression, it is lacking in effectiveness. We may enhance the vividness of our descriptions in three ways: (1) by using concrete details; (2) by employing both specific and connotative words; and (3) by appealing to other senses in addition to sight. The passage that follows illustrates these three ways:

The rain flashed across the midnight window with a myriad feet. There was a groan in outer darkness, the voice of all nameless dreads. The nervous candle flame shuddered by my bedside. The groaning rose to a shriek, and the little flame jumped in a panic, and nearly left its white column. Out of the corners of the room swarmed the released shadows. Black specters danced in ecstasy over my bed.—H. M. TOMLINSON, "Bed-Books and Night-Lights"[1]

[1] Used by permission of Alfred A. Knopf, Inc., publisher.

EXERCISES

I

Study the descriptions given below by means of the following directions: (1) Indicate the point of view in space and in time. (2) Explain the order of coherent arrangement of details. (3) Tell what the dominant impression of each description is. (4) If the writer used a fundamental image, point it out. (5) Find examples of specific words, concrete details, and appeals to the senses.

1. She was the central figure of a still landscape. The midday sunshine fell in broad effulgence upon it; the homely, dun-colored shadows had been running away all the morning, as if shirking the contrast with the splendors of the golden light, until nothing was left of them except a dark circle beneath the widespreading trees. No breath of wind stirred the leaves, or rippled the surface of the little pond. The lethargy of the hour had descended even upon the towering pine trees growing on the precipitous slope of the mountain, and showing their topmost plumes just above the frowning, gray crag—their melancholy song was hushed. The silent masses of dazzling white clouds were poised motionless in the ambient air, high above the valley and the misty expanse of the distant wooded ranges.—CHARLES EGBERT CRADDOCK, "The Mystery of Witch-Face Mountain"[1]

2. The room in which I found myself was very large and lofty. The windows were long, narrow, and pointed, and at so vast a distance from the black oaken floor as to be altogether inaccessible from within. Feeble gleams of encrimsoned light made their way through the trellised panes and served to render sufficiently distinct the more prominent objects around; the eye, however, struggled in vain to reach the remoter angles of the chamber or the recesses of the vaulted and fretted ceiling. Dark draperies hung upon the walls. The general furniture was profuse, comfortless, antique, and tattered. Many books and musical instruments lay scattered about, but failed to give any vitality to the scene. I felt that I breathed an atmosphere of sorrow. An air of stern, deep, and irredeemable gloom hung over and pervaded all.—EDGAR ALLAN POE, "The Fall of the House of Usher"

---

[1] Used by permission of Houghton Mifflin Company, publishers.

3. There was no dust in the cañon. The leaves and flowers were clean and virginal. The grass was young velvet. Over the pool three cotton-woods sent their snowy fluffs fluttering down the quiet air. On the slope the blossoms of the wine-wooded manzanita filled the air with springtime odors, while the leaves, wise with experience, were already beginning their vertical twist against the coming aridity of summer. In the open spaces on the slope, beyond the farthest shadow reach of the manzanita, poised the mariposa lilies, like so many flights of jeweled moths suddenly arrested and on the verge of trembling into flight again. Here and there that woods harlequin, the madrone, permitting itself to be caught in the act of changing its pea-green trunk to madder red, breathed its fragrance into the air from great clusters of waxen bells. Creamy white were these bells, shaped like lilies of the valley, with the sweetness of perfume that is of the springtime.— JACK LONDON, "All-Gold Cañon"[1]

4. A wet Sunday in a country inn! Whoever has had the luck to experience one can alone judge of my situation. The rain pattered against the casements; the bells tolled for church with a melancholy sound. I went to the windows in quest of something to amuse the eye; but it seemed as if I had been placed completely out of the reach of all amusement. The windows of my bedroom looked out among tiled roofs and stacks of chimneys, while those of my sitting-room com-manded a full view of the stable yard. I know of nothing more calculated to make a man sick of this world than a stable yard on a rainy day. The place was littered with wet straw that had been kicked about by travelers and stableboys. In one corner was a stagnant pool of water, surrounding an island of muck; there were several half-drowned fowls crowded together under a cart, among which was a miserable, crest-fallen cock, drenched out of all life and spirit; his drooping tail matted, as it were, into a single feather, along which the water trickled from his back; near the cart was a half-dozing cow, chewing her cud, and standing patiently to be rained on, with wreaths of vapor rising from her reeking hide; a wall-eyed horse, tired of the loneliness of the stable, was poking his spectral head out of a window, with the rain dripping on it from the eaves; an unhappy cur, chained to a doghouse hard by, uttered something every now and then between a bark and a yelp; a drab of a kitchen wench tramped backwards and forwards through the yard in pattens, looking as sulky as the weather itself; everything, in

[1] From "Moon-Face and Other Stories." Used by permission of The Mac-millan Company, publishers.

short, was comfortless and forlorn, excepting a crew of hardened ducks, assembled like boon companions round a puddle and making a riotous noise over their liquor.—IRVING

5. There was a heavy odor in the little house which quite blighted the soft spring air as it blew in through the half-open window. For supper there had been onions and sausage, and the fried potatoes had burned. The smells which had risen from the kitchen stove had mingled with the raw, soapy fumes which gave testimony that Monday was washday in the Black family. Now the smoking of the kerosene lamp on the center-table seemed to seal in hermetical fashion the oppressive room against the gentle breeze of the May evening.—LUCY HUFFAKER, "The Way of Life"[1]

II

From your reading select and bring to class three brief, vivid descriptions. Be prepared to analyze them according to the directions given in Exercise I, page 372.

III

In a composition of not more than two hundred words write a description, in terms of two or more of the senses, based on one of the following topics:

1. Mother's Kitchen on Baking Day.
2. The Dairy at Milking Time.
3. Early Morning in the City.
4. The Night before Christmas.
5. A Railway Lunch Room between Trains.

IV

Write a description of not more than three hundred words in which you set forth vividly the dominant impression that you gain from studying one of the following pictures:

1. Camping in Colorado (facing page 116).
2. The Sagebrush of Idaho (facing page 172).
3. Yosemite Falls (facing page 370).
4. The Lights of Industry (facing page 402).
5. Flotsam Castle (facing page 296).

[1] From the *Atlantic Monthly*. Used by permission of the publishers.

255. How to describe a place. Descriptions of places include descriptions of landscapes and other outdoor scenes, as well as those of buildings, both exterior and interior. In describing a place we shall find the following directions helpful:

1. Select a place which you already know or which you can easily visit before you write the description. The scene should be limited, as a picture is limited, to a definite portion of space. The place should be one that has genuine interest for you because of its beauty, its novelty, or its association.

2. Choose an advantageous point of view, and early in your description state or clearly imply what this point of view is.

3. Observe the place closely and try to discover the best natural order of arranging the details (see section 252).

4. Select *essential* details. Try to make your description as clear and as vivid as a picture.

5. Concentrate your efforts on making the dominant characteristic of the place stand out as the dominant impression that you wish the reader to get from your description.

6. Use specific words and try to appeal to more than one sense. Make the reader *experience* the place—not merely see it.

The following brief passages illustrate how a place may be described:

A FARMHOUSE

The rain was still falling, sweeping down from the half-seen hills, wreathing the wooded peaks with gray garments of mist, and filling the valley with a whitish cloud.

It fell around the house drearily. It ran down into the tubs placed to catch it, dripped from the mossy pump, and drummed on the upturned milk pails, and upon the brown-and-yellow beehives under the maple trees. The chickens seemed depressed, but the irrepressible blue jay screamed amid it all, with the same insolent spirit, his plumage untarnished by the wet. The barnyard showed a horrible mixture of mud and mire, through which Howard caught glimpses of the men slumping to and fro without more additional protection than a ragged coat and a shapeless felt hat.

In the sitting-room where his mother sat sewing there was not an ornament, save the etching he had brought. The clock stood on a small shelf, its dial so much defaced that one could not tell the time of day; and when it struck, it was with noticeably disproportionate deliberation, as if it wished to correct any mistake into which the family might have fallen by reason of its illegible dial.

The paper on the walls showed the first concession of the Puritans to the Spirit of Beauty, and was made up of a heterogeneous mixture of flowers of unheard-of shapes and colors, arranged in four different ways along the wall. There were no books, no music, and only a few newspapers in sight—a bare, blank, cold, drab-colored shelter from the rain, not a home. —HAMLIN GARLAND, "Up the Coulée"[1]

THE LISTS AT ASHBY

The scene was singularly romantic. On the verge of a wood, which approached to within a mile of the town of Ashby, was an extensive meadow, of the finest and most beautiful green turf, surrounded on one side by the forest, and fringed on the other by straggling oak trees, some of which had grown to an immense size. The ground, as if fashioned on purpose for the martial display which was intended, sloped gradually down on all sides to a level bottom, which was inclosed for the lists with strong palisades, forming a space of a quarter of a mile in length and about half as broad. The form of the inclosure was an oblong square, save that the corners were considerably rounded off in order to afford more convenience to the spectators. The openings for the entry of the combatants were at the northern and southern extremities of the lists, accessible by strong wooden gates, each wide enough to admit two horsemen riding abreast. At each of these portals were stationed two heralds, attended by six trumpets, as many pursuivants, and a strong body of men-at-arms for maintaining order and ascertaining the quality of the knights who proposed to engage in this martial game.—SCOTT, "Ivanhoe"

[1] Used by permission of Harper and Brothers, publishers.

I

From your reading select and bring to class three good descriptions of places.

II

Write a brief description of one of the following pictures:

1. Camping in Colorado (facing page 116).
2. The Sagebrush of Idaho (facing page 172).
3. Flotsam Castle (facing page 296), either exterior or interior.
4. Man's Conquest over Nature (facing page 198).
5. The Lights of Industry (facing page 402).
6. Yosemite Falls (facing page 370).

III

Give an oral description of one of the following places:

1. A street corner where an accident has recently occurred.
2. An attractive spot where you are trying to persuade the class to hold its spring picnic.
3. Your mother's flower garden.
4. A public park.
5. An old wharf.

IV

Describe in a single paragraph one of the following places:

1. The front yard of your home.
2. The back yard of your home.
3. A farmyard.
4. A street corner.
5. A scene of your own choice.

V

Describe one of the following buildings, both exterior and interior. Keep your reader informed of every change in point of view.

1. Your home.
2. Your father's garage (barn).
3. The school building.
4. The courthouse.
5. The country club house.
6. A building of your own choice.

VI

Write a description, of about three hundred words, of one of the following scenes:

1. An Attractive View from my Window.
2. A Public Square.
3. A Beautiful Picnic Spot.
4. The School Grounds.
5. Some other scene of local interest.

256. How to describe an object. In describing objects which appeal chiefly to the sense of sight we should avoid making a mere list or catalogue of details. We should avoid, too, using a series of sentences introduced by such expressions as "I can see" and "There is." We should try to gain variety of expression by employing various sentence forms. The following directions we shall find helpful:

1. Select an object that is interesting and that you know something about.

2. Keep one point of view.

3. Note the most striking things about the object, such as general features, shape, size, color, and the dominant characteristic. If possible, have the object before you as you describe it.

4. Select *essential* details, which distinguish the object from others in its general class.

5. Arrange the details according to the best natural order.

6. Use specific words.

7. When you have finished your description, compare it with the object itself, to see whether your description is clear and accurate.

The passages given below illustrate simple descriptions of objects:

1. In the center stood a magnificent column, the remains of which is now known as the "burnt pillar." It was originally composed of ten pieces of porphyry, bound together by bands of copper. Each block of porphyry was ten feet high and eleven feet in diameter, and the column thus composed was mounted on a pedestal of white marble twenty feet high. On the top of this column was a colossal bronze statue of Apollo. The god, crowned with glittering rays, held a globe in one hand and a scepter in the other.—CLARA ERSKINE CLEMENT, "Constantinople"

2. The Faun is the marble image of a young man, leaning his right arm on the trunk or stump of a tree; one hand hangs carelessly by his side; in the other he holds the fragment of a pipe, or some such sylvan instrument of music. His only garment—a lion's skin, with the claws upon his shoulder—falls halfway down his back, leaving the limbs and the entire front of the figure nude. The form, thus displayed, is marvelously graceful, but has a fuller and more rounded outline, more flesh, and less of heroic muscle, than the old sculptors were wont to assign to their types of masculine beauty. The character of the face corresponds with the figure; it is most agreeable in outline and feature, but rounded and somewhat voluptuously developed, especially about the throat and chin; the nose is almost straight, but very slightly curves inward, thereby acquiring an indescribable charm of geniality and humor. The mouth, with its full yet delicate lips, seems so nearly to smile outright that it calls forth a responsive smile. The whole statue—unlike anything else that ever was wrought in that severe material of marble—conveys the idea of an amiable and sensual creature, easy, mirthful, apt for jollity, yet not incapable of being touched by pathos. It is impossible to gaze long at this stone image without conceiving a kindly sentiment towards it, as if its substance were warm to the touch and imbued with actual life.

It comes very close to some of our pleasantest sympathies.—HAW-
THORNE, "The Marble Faun"

Note the superiority of the second passage over the first in its
suggestiveness and in its power to stimulate the imagination.

EXERCISES

I

Select from your reading and bring to class two good descriptions of objects. Analyze them according to the directions given in
Exercise I, page 372.

II

Describe orally one of the following objects:

1. A gate.	6. A kitchen utensil.
2. A beehive.	7. A sewing-cabinet.
3. A bookcase.	8. A ticket booth.
4. A monument.	9. A window seat.
5. An armchair.	10. An unusual signboard.

III

Write a description, of about two hundred words, of one of the
following objects:

1. A flower bed.	6. A farm implement.
2. A motor boat.	7. A bird house.
3. A windmill.	8. An old-fashioned desk.
4. A street car.	9. A street-vender's stand.
5. The postman's cart.	10. An object of your choice.

257. How to describe an animal. In describing animals, as
in describing objects, we should select the most striking details
of form, color, and size. In addition, we may include such
details as manner of movement, facial expression, disposition,
and any other details that individualize the animal. The following selections show how animals may be described:

1. The Tailless Tyke had now grown into an immense dog, heavy
of muscle and huge of bone: a great bull head; undershot jaw,

square and lengthy and terrible; vicious, yellow, gleaming eyes; cropped ears; and an expression incomparably savage. His coat was a tawny lionlike yellow, short, harsh, dense; and his back, running up from the shoulder to the loins, ended abruptly in a knoblike tail. He looked like the devil of a dog's hell, and his reputation was as bad as his looks. He never attacked unprovoked; but a challenge was never ignored, and he was greedy of insults.— OLLIVANT, "Bob, Son of Battle"[1]

2. El Rayo shone like burnished copper, his silver mane and tail glittering as if powdered with diamond dust. He was long and graceful of body, thin of flank, slender of leg. With arched neck and flashing eyes, he walked with the pride of one who was aware of the admiration he excited.

Vitriolo was black and powerful. His long neck fitted into well-placed shoulders. He had great depth of girth, immense length from shoulder points to hips, big cannon bones, and elastic pasterns. There was neither amiability nor pride in his mien; rather a sullen sense of brute power, such as may have belonged to the knights of the Middle Ages. Now and again he curled his lips away from the bit and laid his ears back as if he intended to eat of the elegant Beau Brummel stepping so daintily beside him. Of the antagonistic crowd he took not the slightest notice.— GERTRUDE ATHERTON, "The Splendid Idle Forties"[2]

EXERCISES

I

Give an oral description of some pet or domestic animal.

II

Write brief descriptions of two of the following animals:

1. A horse.   4. A cow.   7. A guinea pig.
2. A dog.   5. A pig.   8. A prairie dog.
3. A cat.   6. A peacock.   9. A beaver.

[1] Used by permission of Doubleday, Page and Company, publishers.
[2] Used by permission of Frederick A. Stokes Company, publishers.

258. How to describe a person. To be successful in describing a person we must possess or develop the power of keen observation. In our efforts to write personal descriptions we shall find the following directions valuable:

1. Select a person sufficiently striking in appearance to be interesting and easily differentiated from other persons.

2. Pick out the prominent characteristics of form, features, facial expression, posture, dress, and manner. Do not, however, exaggerate· peculiarities unless you intend to give a caricature.

3. Arrange the parts of your description logically and effectively. Often you may begin by giving a general impression of the person. You may then introduce prominent details in the order in which they impress you as you look at the person. Sometimes it may seem advisable to describe the person in detail first and then sum up your general impression at the end of your description.

4. Reference to a person's environment, his habits of life, and his manner of moving and speaking will often add vividness and completeness to a personal description.

The following passages contain brief descriptions of persons:

1. On a high chair beside the chimney, and directly facing Denis as he entered, sat a little old gentleman in a fur tippet. He sat with his legs crossed and his hands folded, and a cup of spiced wine stood by his elbow on a bracket on the wall. His countenance had a strongly masculine cast; not properly human, but such as we see in the bull, the goat, or the domestic boar; something equivocal and wheedling, something greedy, brutal, and dangerous. The upper lip was inordinately full, as though swollen by a blow or a toothache; and the smile, the peaked eyebrows, and the small, strong eyes were quaintly and almost comically evil in expression. Beautiful white hair hung straight all round his head, like a saint's, and fell in a single curl upon the tippet. His beard and mustache were the pink of venerable sweetness. Age, probably in consequence of inordinate precau-

THE VILLAGE CENSOR

From an etching by Sears Gallagher

tions, had left no mark upon his hands; and the Malétroit hand
was famous. It would be difficult to imagine anything at once
so fleshly and so delicate in design; the taper, sensual fingers were
like those of one of Leonardo's women; the fork of the thumb
made a dimpled protuberance when closed; the nails were perfectly shaped, and of a dead, surprising whiteness. It rendered
his aspect tenfold more redoubtable, that a man with hands like
these should keep them devoutly folded like a virgin martyr—
that a man with so intent and startling an expression of the face
should sit patiently on his seat and contemplate people with an
unwinking stare, like a god, or a god's statue. His quiescence
seemed ironical and treacherous, it fitted so poorly with his looks.
—STEVENSON, "The Sire de Malétroit's Door"[1]

2. Today he looked ten years younger. His kinky gray hair,
generally knotted into little wads, was now divided by a well-
defined path starting from the great wrinkle in his forehead and
ending in a dense tangle of underbrush that no comb dared pene-
trate. His face glistened all over. His mouth was wide open,
showing a great cavity in which each tooth seemed to dance with
delight. His jacket was as white and stiff as soap and starch could
make it, while a cast-off cravat of the Colonel's—double-starched
to suit Chad's own ideas of propriety—was tied in a single knot, the
two ends reaching to the very edge of each ear. To crown all, a red
carnation flamed away on the lapel of his jacket, just above an outside pocket, which held in check a pair of white cotton gloves
bulging with importance and eager for use. Every time he bowed
he touched with a sweep both sides of the narrow hall.—F. HOP-
KINSON SMITH, "Colonel Carter of Cartersville"[2]

3. Ysabel glanced with some envy at the magnificent jewels
with which the Governor of the Californians was hung, but did
not covet the owner. An uglier man than Pio Pico rarely had
entered this world. The upper lip of his enormous mouth dipped
at the middle; the broad, thick underlip hung down with its own
weight. The nose was big and coarse, although there was a certain spirited suggestion in the cavernous nostrils. Intelligence

---

[1] Used by permission of Charles Scribner's Sons, publishers.
[2] Used by permission of Houghton Mifflin Company, publishers.

and reflectiveness were also in his little eyes, and they were far apart. A small white mustache grew above his mouth ; about his chin, from ear to ear, was a short stubby beard, whiter by contrast with his copper-colored skin. He looked much like an intellectual bear.

And Ysabel? In truth, she had reason for her pride. Her black hair, unblemished by gloss or tinge of blue, fell waving to her feet. California, haughty, passionate, restless, pleasure-loving, looked from her dark green eyes; the soft black lashes dropped quickly when they became too expressive. Her full mouth was deeply red, but only a faint pink lay in her white cheeks; the nose curved at bridge and nostrils. About her low shoulders she held a blue rebozo, the finger tips of each slim hand resting on the opposite elbow. She held her head a little back, and Pio Pico laughed as he looked at her.
—Gertrude Atherton, "The Splendid Idle Forties"[1]

EXERCISES

I

From your reading select and bring to class three good descriptions of persons. Be prepared to explain how the author has described each person.

II

In a single sentence give a description of each of the following persons in terms of his chief characteristic:

1. A traffic policeman.
2. Your postman.
3. A dressmaker.
4. Your family physician.
5. A newsboy.
6. A local character.

III

Describe in a single paragraph a person in one of the following pictures:

1. Robinson Crusoe Opens his Chest (facing page 26).
2. A Fight in the Rigging (facing page 54).
3. The Pirate (facing page 348).
4. The Village Censor (facing page 382).
5. The End of the Trail (facing page 476).

[1] Used by permission of Frederick A. Stokes Company, publishers.

IV

Describe orally one of the following persons:

1. A person whom you have recently met.
2. A friend whom your brother has never seen but whom he is to meet for you at the station.
3. The athletic coach.
4. A relative.
5. A local character.

V

Write a description, of about two hundred words, of one of the following persons:

1. Your grandfather (or grandmother).
2. Your small brother (or sister).
3. The milkman (or iceman).
4. A clerk at a cold-drink stand.
5. A person included in Exercise II, above.

259. Description by effect. In some cases a useful method of describing a place, an object, or a person is to tell the effect produced upon the observer. In such description we are seeing through the describer's eyes and often observing through his other senses. We instinctively put ourselves in his place. This method is particularly valuable in describing impressions, as the following selection shows:

During the whole of a dull, dark, and soundless day in the autumn of the year, when the clouds hung oppressively low in the heavens, I had been passing alone, on horseback, through a singularly dreary tract of country; and at length found myself, as the shades of the evening drew on, within view of the melancholy House of Usher. I know not how it was—but, with the first glimpse of the building, a sense of insufferable gloom pervaded my spirit. I say insufferable; for the feeling was unrelieved by any of that half-pleasurable, because poetic, sentiment with which the mind usually receives even the sternest natural images of the desolate or terrible. I looked upon the scene before me—upon the mere house, and the simple landscape features of the domain, upon the bleak walls, upon the vacant eyelike windows, upon a few rank sedges, and upon a few white trunks of decayed trees—with an utter depression of soul which I can compare to no earthly sensation more properly than to the after-dream of the reveler upon opium: the bitter lapse into everyday life, the hideous dropping-off of the veil. There was an iciness, a sinking, a sickening of the heart, an unredeemed dreariness of thought which no goading of the imagination could torture into aught of the sublime. What was it—I paused to think—what was it that so unnerved me in the contemplation of the House of Usher?—POE, "The Fall of the House of Usher"

EXERCISE

Find in your reading and bring to class a passage in which an author has made use of description by effect. Point out the concrete details and the specific words used.

260. Principal aids in writing descriptions. The fundamental principles of description that have been discussed in the preceding sections may be briefly stated as follows:

1. Unify by singleness of impression.

2. Clarify by point of view.

3. Individualize by concrete details.

4. Vivify by range of sense appeal and by the use of specific and connotative words.

5. Combine details, for coherence, according to the most effective natural order.

GENERAL EXERCISES

I

Guided by the five aids mentioned in section 260, write a vivid description of one of the pictures in this book that you have not previously described.

II

Study one of the following pictures carefully and then write a description in which you set forth the dominant characteristic of the scene:

1. A May-Day Frolic (facing page 360).
2. A City Market (facing page 146).
3. The Skyscrapers (facing page 324).
4. Man's Conquest over Nature (facing page 198).

III

Write a vivid description of a scene or a building of your own selection. Make the dominant characteristic so clear that the reader will get the single impression that you aim to give him.

261. Summary. Description is that form of composition by means of which we try to furnish others the same picture and the same impression that we ourselves derived from the place, object, or person described. Descriptions may be either expository or artistic, according to the purpose of the writer.

Unity in description requires the proper limitation of the subject, the choice of relevant details, a consistent point of view, and singleness of impression. A fundamental image is often helpful in giving the single impression of shape, size, or color.

Coherence in description requires that the parts and the details be arranged in the most effective natural order.

Emphasis in description demands that only essential details be chosen, that these be placed in emphatic positions, and that the parts of the description be given space in proportion to their importance.

Vividness, the essential quality in all description, is obtained by using concrete details, by employing both specific and connotative words, and by variety in sense appeal.

Description by effect is sometimes a useful method of making an impression vivid and of creating the desired atmosphere.

CHAPTER XVIII

EXPOSITION

262. Exposition defined. Whenever we define a word, tell our companions how to play a game, recommend a book to a friend, discuss the character of our favorite heroine in fiction, or explain a law of science, we employ exposition. We may define exposition, then, as that form of composition by means of which we give explanations of facts, ideas, methods, and principles. The purpose of exposition is to make our meaning clear to the understanding of our hearers and readers. It appeals chiefly to the mind, rarely to the feelings. Next to narration, exposition is the most common form of discourse. The practice of exposition develops observation, judgment, orderly thinking, and accurate expression. It is of the utmost importance that we learn to explain to others exactly what we mean.

263. The importance of clearness. Our first object in all exposition should be to make our meaning entirely clear to others. But clearness, we must understand, is a relative quality. It depends primarily on the nature of the subject and on the amount of information possessed by the persons to whom we are explaining the subject. If we should attempt to explain baseball to a Chinese boy who had never seen the game played, we should find our task far more difficult than it would be to make the process clear to our younger brother who has already some knowledge of the game. In the case of the Chinese boy we should be obliged to explain not only the purpose of the game but also the use of the ball and bat, the meaning of *infield* and *outfield*, the duties of each player, and the method of scoring. At every moment we should need to interpret the baseball

388

language, the technical terms of the sport. The point of view and the information of the Chinese boy would differ from those of our younger brother.

In giving an exposition we should therefore put ourselves in the place of our hearers and readers and should try to realize their point of view and the amount of information that they possess about our subject. In this way we can properly adapt our explanation to their particular demands and thus make our exposition clear. The nature of our subject, then, and the needs of those for whom our explanation is intended must determine the minuteness and thoroughness of our exposition.

In order that our explanation may be clear and effective, it should be constructed in accordance with the laws of unity, coherence, and emphasis. Every exposition should be thoughtfully planned. Having chosen a sufficiently limited subject, we should select our material according to its demands and according to the needs of our hearers and readers. We should then make a complete outline, which must be tested and revised until it represents our best effort at logical arrangement. Only by such thorough preparation as this can we hope to make our exposition clear and effective.

EXERCISE

Make a systematic review of Chapter IV. Come to class prepared to discuss (1) the choice and limitation of subjects, (2) the making of an outline, and (3) the laws of unity, coherence, and emphasis as they apply to exposition.

264. Oral exposition. In oral exposition we have two advantages that we do not have when we write: first, we can talk directly to our audience and can judge from its attitude whether our point of view is the proper one; secondly, we are often able to use, for illustration, objects and diagrams which in writing we cannot so easily employ. Though it is true that a diagram may accompany a piece of written exposition, it is seldom so clear as the diagram which we construct and explain while we talk. Since oral exposition has these natural advantages, we should not fail to make the most of them. We should take great care to adapt our point of view to our audience and to avail ourselves of illustrative material. (For suggestions as to the method of giving oral compositions see section 11.)

265. Methods of exposition. The methods used in developing the subject of an extensive exposition and those employed in developing the topic of a paragraph are often the same. Frequently we shall employ two or more of these methods in the course of our exposition. In addition, we sometimes make use of portions of description and narration as a means of increasing the vividness and interest of our explanation.

EXERCISE

Come to class prepared to tell which of the paragraphs included in sections 92–97 and in Exercise I following these sections are expositions, and be able to explain which methods were used in each.

266. Kinds of exposition. Though the purpose of all exposition is the same, there are several recognized types with which we should become familiar. The most common of these are (1) definitions, (2) explanations of processes, (3) discussions of facts and ideas, (4) essays, (5) expository biography, (6) reviews and criticisms, (7) editorials, and (8) expository letters. These eight types we may consider in order.

267. Definitions. The explanation of what a word means is exposition reduced to its lowest terms. To define a word is to restrict, or set a limit to, its meaning. A definition should be as accurate as it is possible to make it and as concise in statement as clearness will permit. Let us consider the following definitions of a square:

1. A *square* is a *geometrical figure* | having four equal sides, the opposite sides being parallel and the four angles being right angles.

2. A *square* is a *parallelogram* | having four equal sides and four right angles.

3. A *square* is a *rectangle* | having equal sides.

All these definitions are accurate, but the third is to be preferred because of its conciseness.

The making of a definition involves a twofold process. The first step is the *identification* of the unfamiliar object or idea by stating that it is a member of a larger class of objects or ideas with which we are familiar. This larger class we call the *genus*; the smaller class, represented by the object or the idea to be defined, we call the *species*. Thus, the genus in the first definition given above is *geometrical figure*; in the second, *parallelogram*; and in the third, *rectangle*. The species in all three is *square*. By stating that the unfamiliar object *square* is included in any one of these larger classes of familiar objects, we give the word preliminary identification and partially restrict its meaning. This we have done in the portion of each definition that precedes the vertical line.

The second step in the process of definition is the accurate *differentiation* of the particular species to be defined from other species included in the genus. The portion of each definition following the vertical line sets forth the *particulars*, or *details*, that distinguish a square from other kinds of geometrical figures, parallelograms, or rectangles.

In order to make our definitions as concise as possible, we should carefully choose the smallest genus that we can find. By so doing we diminish the number of particulars required and frequently make our statement more accurate. The large genus *geometrical figure* calls for three distinct particulars; *parallelogram* demands two; whereas *rectangle*, the smallest genus, requires only one.

In formulating a definition we should observe two cautions. First, we should avoid using a cognate form of the word to be defined.

Incorrect: Narration is something that is *narrated*.
Correct: Narration is the recounting of an event or a series of events.

The words used in defining another word should be more familiar than the word to be defined.

Secondly, we should not attempt to define a word by the use of a *when*-clause or a *where*-clause.

Incorrect: A *lie* is *when* a person tells a falsehood.
Correct: A *lie* is a falsehood.

A noun should be defined by means of a noun, a verb by means of a verb, and so on.

We shall often find it impossible to give an adequate exposition of the meaning of a word in a single concise statement. In such cases it will be necessary to employ more elaborate exposition by means of one or more of the other methods. Frequently we shall find the method of comparison and contrast useful in expanding our definition. In other instances we may make our meaning more clear by repetition, by details, by examples and illustrations. The passage that follows illustrates the more elaborate form of definition:

Although the term *slang* is sometimes used with more or less intentional inexactness, and has often been carelessly defined, the notion to which it corresponds in general use seems to be tolerably precise. There are two principal characteristics which, taken in conjunction, may serve to distinguish what is properly called slang from certain other varieties of diction that in some respects resemble it. The first of these is that slang is a conscious offense against some conventional standard of propriety. A mere vulgarism is not slang, except when it is purposely adopted, and acquires an artificial currency, among some class of persons to whom it is not native. The other distinctive feature of slang is that it is neither a part of the ordinary language nor an attempt to supply its deficiencies. The slang word is a deliberate substitute for a word of the vernacular, just as the characters of a cipher are substitutes for the letters of the alphabet, or as a nickname is a substitute for a personal name. The latter comparison is the more exact of the two; indeed, nicknames, as a general rule, may be accurately described as a kind of slang. A slang expression, like a nickname, may be used for the purpose of concealing the meaning from uninitiated hearers, or it may be employed sportively or out of aversion to dignity or formality of speech. The essential point is that it does not, like the words of ordinary language, originate in the desire to be understood. The slang word is not invented or used because it is in any respect better than the accepted term, but because it is different. No doubt it may accidentally happen that a word which originates as slang is superior in expressiveness to its regular synonym (much as a nickname may identify a person better than his own name does), or that in time it develops a shade of meaning which the ordinary language cannot convey. But when such a word comes to be used mainly on account of its intrinsic merit, and not because it is a wrong word, it is already ceasing to be slang. So long as the usage of good society continues to proscribe it, it may be called a vulgarism; but unless the need which it serves is supplied in some other way, it is likely to find its way into the standard speech.—BRADLEY, in Encyclopædia Britannica

EXERCISES

I

Without the aid of a dictionary formulate the most accurate definitions that you can of the following words. Come to class prepared to give your definitions orally as sentences or to write them on the blackboard in the form illustrated below:

SPECIES	GENUS	DIFFERENTIA
pen	an instrument	used in writing with ink
to speak	to utter sounds	for the purpose of communication

angle	circle	hexagon	opaque	triangle
awl	dairy	ice	printer	umbrella
bicycle	diary	knife	rhombus	walk
bird	drum	money	sister	weed
bolt	fish	newspaper	tent	window

II

Point out the methods of exposition used by Bradley in the passage printed above.

III

Define in a paragraph one of the following pairs of words, using any of the methods of exposition that will enhance the clearness and accuracy of your definition:

1. plant, animal.
2. artist, artisan.
3. scholar, student.
4. education, culture.
5. opera, oratorio.

6. open shop, closed shop.
7. monument, statue.
8. work, play.
9. patience, stupidity.
10. bravery, ignorance.

IV

In others of your textbooks find and bring to class three good definitions. Be prepared to analyze them according to the form given in Exercise I.

268. Explanations of processes. The most common type of exposition is that employed in explaining how to do something. We are constantly telling people how to play a game, perform a task, or make some article. The various steps in any process should be explained in the order in which they naturally come; that is, in the order of time. In longer expositions of processes the chronological order may be supplemented by some other logical order. Each of the following passages is an explanation of how to play a game:

SCOUT'S NOSE

Prepare a number of paper bags, all alike, and put in each a different-smelling article, such as chopped onion in one, tan in another, and, in others, rose leaves, leather, aniseed, violet powder, orange peel, etc. Put these packets in a row a couple of feet apart, and let each competitor walk down the line and have five seconds' sniff at each. At the end he has one minute in which to write down or to state to the umpire the names of the different objects smelled, from memory, in their correct order.—ERNEST THOMPSON SETON, "Boy Scouts of America: Official Handbook"[1]

HAT–BALL

The players (about a dozen) put their hats in a row near a house, fence, or log (hollows up). A dead line is drawn ten feet from the hats; all must stand outside of that. The one who is "it" begins by throwing a soft ball into one of the hats. If he misses the hat, a chip is put into his own, and he tries over. As soon as he drops the ball into a hat, the owner runs to get the ball; all the rest run away. The owner must not follow beyond the dead line, but must throw the ball at someone. If he hits him, a chip goes into that person's hat; if not, a chip goes into his own.

As soon as someone has five chips, he wins the booby prize; that is, he must hold his hand out steady against the wall, and each player has five shots at it with the ball, as he stands on the dead line.—ERNEST THOMPSON SETON, "Boy Scouts of America: Official Handbook"[1]

EXERCISES

I

Find in Chapters II and V of this book selections that are explanations of processes. Is the student's composition "How we earned our Car" exposition or narration? Explain your answer. How does exposition differ from narration?

[1] Used by permission of the author and the publishers.

II

Explain orally one of the following processes, using objects or sketches as illustrations whenever they will render your explanation more effective. Plan your exposition carefully by means of an outline, which you will place on the blackboard before you give your talk.

1. How to Make and Set a Trap.
2. How to Remove Stains.
3. How to Weave a Basket.
4. How to Install a Wireless Telephone.
5. How to Change an Automobile Tire.
6. How to Detect Impure Milk (or Water).
7. How to Clean Old Lace.
8. How to Combat — (some insect enemy).
9. How to Make a Bird House.
10. How to Revive a Partially Drowned Person.
11. How to Build a Fire without Matches.
12. How to Perform a Card Trick.
13. How to Catch and Mount Butterflies.
14. How to Make a Butterfly Tray.
15. A process of your own choice.

III

Write from a carefully prepared outline (which you will hand in with your composition) an exposition of one of the following processes:

1. How to Train a Dog.
2. How to Fill a Silo.
3. How to Plan and Serve a Meal.
4. How to Get Advertisements for a School Paper.
5. How to Memorize Poetry.
6. How to Organize and Conduct a Canning Club.
7. How to Make Molasses (or Maple Syrup).
8. How to Exterminate Weeds.
9. How to Reclaim Exhausted Soil.
10. How to Plan and Conduct a Community Social.

11. How to Learn the Touch System of Typewriting.
12. How to Perform an Experiment in Domestic Science.
13. How to Make a Beaded Bag.
14. How a Newspaper is Printed.
15. A process of your own choice.

IV

Explain orally or in writing a process suggested by one of the following pictures:

1. The Dawn of a New Life (frontispiece).
2. The Skyscrapers (facing page 324).
3. The Lights of Industry (facing page 402).
4. Putting the Shot (facing page 94).
5. Off! (facing page 220).
6. A Marble Tournament (facing page 72).

269. Discussions of facts and ideas. A third kind of exposition consists of explanations of facts and discussions of ideas, theories, and opinions. Whenever we explain or discuss a topic of scientific, economic, political, religious, or literary interest, we employ this type of exposition. The range of subjects and the variety of treatment are much greater in this type than in definitions and in explanations of processes. Frequently description and narration are employed as a means of making the exposition more vivid and entertaining. The following selection is a discussion of facts and ideas:

THE NEW POSITION OF WOMEN

The new position of women is not a matter of suffrage or of "rights." It is not a matter of argument. It is a fact. Women are now entering new fields of economic and political life. They are earning their living in ways once thought improper; they are sharing in the responsibilities of the community in ways once thought impossible. Argument as to the right and wrong of the new position of women does not alter the fact that it is here, and that it has become a matter to reckon with in any attempt to understand the complex organization of modern life.

The new generation cannot know wholly the barriers of custom and tradition, which women had to break down before they attained their new position. They cannot fully realize how an apparently resistless movement was preceded by a long period of advocacy of bitterly fought principles. They cannot fully visualize the organization of the old society, where the position of women was so different from what it is now.

And yet they are faced with a hundred new problems, which are the legacy from those old conditions. It is true that these problems face mature men and women with more insistence than they do young people. Still, young people can prepare for the experiences which are to come later. They can try to re-create in their minds a picture of the old society and the share that women had in it. They can form that picture from their reading and from talks with their parents. They can try to understand the revolt from the old conditions. They can come to know the vigorous personalities who led that revolt. They can try to understand the principles and programs of the new movement as it developed: how people fought over questions of woman suffrage, and hardly noticed the silent change that was taking place in economic life. They can find out what work women are doing today, what influence they have, what movements they are engaged in, what they intend to do, to what degree they consciously plan group action. And with some of this information in hand, they can attempt to weigh good and bad, to try to find out to what extent the new is desirable and better than the old. What have women lost by the change? What have they gained? What things are good? What are bad?

Most important of all, students will have to decide their own attitude toward this part of life. Every girl will have to take a share in new responsibilities, powers, and opportunities; every young man will have to understand that in the coming years women will not quietly follow men, but will insist upon as free and genuine a partnership with men as they can command.— RALPH PHILIP BOAS, "Youth and the New World"[1]

[1] Used by permission of the Atlantic Monthly Press, publishers.

EXERCISES

I

What methods of exposition are used in the preceding discussion? (See sections 91–97.)

II

From your reading select and bring to class a discussion of some scientific, economic, political, or literary topic. Make an outline showing the paragraph topics, and be prepared to explain the methods of exposition that the author uses in developing his ideas.

III

Discuss orally one of the following topics. Plan your talk carefully by means of an outline, which you will place on the blackboard before you give your exposition. Illustrate your discussion by concrete instances and by anecdotes if they will make your talk more effective.

1. My Idea of School Spirit.
2. The Importance of the Gasoline Engine on the Farm.
3. The Greatest Problem in Cotton Growing.
4. Reasons for the Localization of Industrial Plants.
5. My Idea of a True Sportsman.
6. What Society Expects of Educated Men and Women.
7. Conservation in the Packing Industry.
8. Qualities Most Necessary for Success in Life.
9. Why People Leave the Country to Live in the City.
10. Advantages and Disadvantages of Free Textbooks.
11. What we Owe the Advertisers in our School Paper.
12. Some Advantages of Co-education.

IV

From a carefully prepared outline (which you will hand in with your composition) write an exposition of three hundred words on one of the following topics:

1. The Importance of Bacteria.
2. The Abuse of Athletics.
3. Advantages of Membership in the Interscholastic League.
4. The Value of Physical Training.
5. The Economic Balance between Animals and Plants.
6. The Meaning of Agricultural Conservation.
7. The Importance of Concrete.
8. Why Scott's Characters are Interesting.
9. Why I Like (or Do Not Like) Modern Poetry.
10. The Value of Community Socials.
11. The Importance of Fire in Civilization.
12. What Should an Education Include?

V

From a carefully prepared outline discuss orally or in writing a topic suggested by one of the following pictures:

1. Man's Conquest over Nature (facing page 198).
2. The Lights of Industry (facing page 402).
3. A City Market (facing page 146).
4. The Dawn of a New Life (frontispiece).
5. The Sagebrush of Idaho (facing page 172).

VI

In an exposition of about two hundred words interpret one of the following pictures:

1. Thrift and Prosperity (facing page 424).
2. The Dawn of a New Life (frontispiece).
3. The Skyscrapers (facing page 324).
4. The End of the Trail (facing page 476).

270. Essays. An essay is an exposition of an author's thoughts or reflections on some subject of human interest. It differs from the usual discussion of facts and ideas in that it is more deliberately composed and gives evidence of greater originality in respect both to the author's thought and to his manner of expression. It frequently contains narrative and descriptive

passages used as illustrations of the ideas that the writer is setting forth. Essays are of two kinds: the formal essay and the
informal essay.

Formal essay. It is the purpose of the formal essay to give
information and instruction. It is rather brief in scope, is usually impersonal in tone, and is addressed primarily to the intellect. It may deal with a great variety of subjects, such as
literature, art, history, biography, science, ethics, economics,
or philosophy. It must give evidence of greater care in structure, method of development, and manner of expression than
does the informal essay. Among the most noted formal essayists
in English and American literature are Macaulay, Carlyle,
Huxley, and Emerson.

Informal essay. The informal essay, as the name suggests,
is more free in its method than the formal essay. It does not
attempt to discuss a subject exhaustively, nor does it deal with
subjects that call for elaborate explanation. It is personal in
tone and point of view and is written in familiar style, such as
we use in easy, polite conversation and in well-written friendly
letters. It reveals the writer's personality, his whims and fan-
cies, sympathies and antipathies, grave moods and gay.

The chief purpose of the informal essay is to entertain,
though the thoughtful reader may often derive instruction as
well. From the delightful familiar essays of Addison and
Steele we gain information as to the manners and customs of
English life in the early eighteenth century. Charles Lamb, in
such essays as "A Dissertation on Roast Pig," "Poor Relations," "Old China," "Dream Children," and "A Bachelor's
Complaint of the Behavior of Married People," wrote purely
for his own enjoyment and our entertainment. Robert Louis
Stevenson wrote for much the same purpose in such essays as
"Talk and Talkers," "An Apology for Idlers," and "The Char-
acter of Dogs." In such essays as "El Dorado," "Aes Triplex,"

and "Pulvis et Umbra" Stevenson may have had a slightly more serious purpose. The reading of a few informal essays from such English writers as Addison, Steele, Lamb, Hazlitt, Stevenson, John Galsworthy, and E. V. Lucas, and from such American authors as Irving, Holmes, John Burroughs, Samuel McChord Crothers, and Robert Haven Schauffler, will add to our understanding of this type of expository writing.

The range of subjects on which informal essays may be written is as wide as the interests of mankind. The essayist may entertain us with familiar discussions of his personal experiences, his observation of other people, comments on life and the peculiarities of human nature, interesting discoveries he has made in his study of plants and animals, or any other subjects that appeal to him strongly and that he has the ability to present interestingly. It is the personality of the essayist and his treatment of a subject, more than the subject itself, that makes the informal essay enjoyable.

The following selection is a simple, informal essay:

ON GETTING UP IN THE MORNING

It is said that one can become accustomed to anything, even hanging, if the act is repeated often enough. As I grow older I believe this assertion less and less. I have been getting up every morning for a little more than nineteen years, and I am not used to it yet. It was quite as hard for me to arise this morning as it was a year ago, or, for that matter, ten years ago. I have little hope that time will make this daily task easier for me, and I have even imagined that I shall want to lie in my coffin for just a few minutes on that glorious morning after Gabriel blows his horn.

I have often wondered why it is so hard for me to get up in the morning. Why should I wish to lie in bed until the last minute? I am no bed-loving sluggard. A bed in itself holds no attractions for me. After I once get up, I am not anxious to lie down again. I once asked a good friend of mine to solve this problem for me,

THE LIGHTS OF INDUSTRY
Courtesy of *The Nation's Business*

and he said that the seat of the trouble was in the manner in which I was awakened. He advised me to buy a good alarm clock, and said that if I were awakened suddenly and regularly every day, the habit of wishing to stay in bed late could be easily overcome. I bought the clock and used it, but without success. If I put it close to my bed at night, I would reach out the next morning and cut the alarm off when it rang, and then go peacefully back to sleep. On the other hand, if I put it out of reach, I would lie still in bed and wait patiently for the spring to run down, and then turn quietly over and begin another snooze.

After the alarm-clock episode, I tried the oldest way known in the world; that is, having some hardy soul who gets up early to wake me. For nearly a month various friends of mine volunteered to do this service for me, but not one of them ever succeeded in getting me up on the instant. Even their threats and their blows failed to rouse me. I would open my eyes, smile sweetly, and go back to sleep again.

One of my father's friends heard of my malady in some way and delivered me a long lecture on the subject. He appealed to my ambition, but my ambition refused to be stirred. In vain did he call to my mind the early-rising habits of Washington, Franklin, and Jefferson. I looked innocent and asked him if it were not a fact that Burr and Arnold also were early risers. I ventured to ask him if it were not likewise true that at least a million and a half other men who had lived during the Colonial period and got up early every morning had in the end died unknown. After this I was even emboldened to inquire if Doctor Johnson did not make it a habit to stay in bed till two o'clock in the afternoon. Before he could reply, however, I had left the room.

The next time I saw him he told me a story about an early bird's catching a worm. I was not as much impressed with his narrative as I should have been. I felt too sorry for the unfortunate worm. If that worm had stayed in bed a little longer, he would not have been caught by the bird. But, after all, it was wasted sympathy, because the worm had no one to blame but himself.

It makes no difference what the season of the year is, I always rise late. In the winter the bed is warm, and the room is cold.

Why should I suddenly change from the warm and comfortable to the cold and uncomfortable? Dante would have us believe that lost souls are effectively punished by such sudden changes in temperature as these. Is it meet that a man should suffer punishment before dying?

In the summer how cool and comfortable it is in my bed with just a suggestion of a breeze blowing across my face, while on the world outside the fierce sun is shining! When finally I get up on summer mornings, how different I must appear from the early risers, who impress me as hot and tired and dusty!

I am afraid I shall never relinquish my habit of late rising. For, after all, is there any advantage in getting up early? A chicken obeys the adage of "early to bed and early to rise" all his life, and finally his head is cut off and he is made into a pie; while the owl, reputed to be the wisest of birds, stays up all night, sleeps all day, lives to a ripe old age, and is never eaten.

Again, are they that rise early any happier than I? Do they enjoy life more? If they do, their happiness must be supreme.

EXERCISES

I

As a means of becoming better acquainted with the informal essay, read three or more essays in the "Contributors' Club" of the *Atlantic Monthly* or in the "Point of View" of *Scribner's Magazine*.

II

Write an informal essay on one of the following subjects. Put as much originality into the thought and as much naturalness and ease into the expression of your thought as possible.

1. On Waiting for the Postman.
2. Garden Friends.
3. Human Parasites.
4. The Monotony of Being Good.
5. The Pleasures of Loafing.
6. On Being Small (or Large).
7. On Being the Youngest (or Oldest) Child.
8. People who Give Advice.

9. What "Central" Must Think of our Family.
10. On Answering Advertisements.
11. Curiosity in Animals.
12. Winter Joys.
13. Company Manners.
14. Personality in the Handshake.
15. A subject of your own choice.

271. Expository biography. Biography, since it contains an account of the chief events in a person's life, is properly classified as narration. The character sketch, in which is briefly set forth an interpretation and estimate of the life of a person, is primarily expository. Personal description and narrative passages used for illustration are often found, however, in an exposition of character. The subject of a character sketch may be a real person whom we know or a character in literature.

The following biographical sketch is a brief estimate of a character in literature:

In Portia, Shakespeare seems to have aimed at a perfect scheme of an amiable, intelligent, and accomplished woman. The result is a fine specimen of beautiful nature enhanced by beautiful art. Eminently practical in her tastes and turn of mind, full of native, home-bred sense and virtue, Portia unites therewith something of the ripeness and dignity of a sage, a mellow eloquence, and a large, noble discourse; the whole being tempered with the best grace and sensibility of womanhood. As intelligent as the strongest, she is at the same time as feminine as the weakest of her sex: she talks like a poet and a philosopher, and she talks, for all the world, just like a woman! She is as full of pleasantry, too, and as merry "within the limit of becoming mirth," as she is womanly and wise; and her arch sportiveness always has a special flavor as the free outcome of perfect moral health. Nothing indeed can be more fitting and well placed than her demeanor, now bracing her speech with grave maxims of practical wisdom, now unbending her mind in sallies of wit, or of innocent, roguish banter.—The New Hudson Shakespeare, "The Merchant of Venice," p. xxx.

The following biographical sketch is an informal exposition of character in which narration serves to make the person of the sketch vivid and natural:

AN UNUSUAL VISITOR

I know an old lady who spends most of her time in visiting her friends and relatives. "Grandma" never comes to stay, but is always "just passing through."

Upon her arrival she unpacks her suitcase, makes herself at home, and begins to gossip about her friends and relatives, especially those whom she has last visited. People whom she likes are beautiful or handsome, clever, rich, and brilliant. Her daughter's new clothes are lovely and attractive. John, her son, is plainly an object of pity as she tells of his family troubles: his wife hires a cook; plays cards; pays thirty dollars for a hat; drives her own car; and, most shocking of all, dances until three o'clock in the morning. Here "Grandma" folds her hands and shakes her head as if to say, "Before John married I told him what kind of girl Carrie was, but he would not listen to one word I said."

While eating she tells how well she used to cook. She serves herself the choicest food with the excuse that her teeth are not good. She never cares for the way a dish is prepared; nevertheless, she eats three hearty meals every day. In the summer she complains of thirst until the hostess is compelled to offer her an iced beverage.

If she wishes to buy something, her purse is never at hand; accordingly, she asks someone to pay until it is convenient for her to get her bag.

Her night habits are most peculiar. She often sleeps several hours during the day and is unable to sleep at night. She gets out of bed, turns on the fire, if the weather is cool, and writes letters which often cover twenty pages. In these letters she tells her imaginary troubles and ailments. After writing her letter she goes back to bed and sleeps until after breakfast the next morning. In the summer, she gets up at the break of day to "rest a while," before the other members of the household awaken. She usually seats herself in a rocker on the gallery and begins a slow, regular rocking back and forth. The sound thus produced, together with her footfall on the bare floor, is enough to make the late morning nap of even the hardiest sleeper anything but sweet.

Her attitude is that of a martyr. No one is kind to her or cares for her. "Last time I was at John's house Carrie was simply awful. I was so sick I could not sit up; I wanted her to talk to me. And do you know, she left me and went to a club meeting. I might have died, but Carrie didn't care." This is her old story of the way in which she is abused.

Finally, when the excitement of coming has passed, and all the news has been told, she leaves for another place, where she doubtless follows the same program.

EXERCISES

I

Write a short expository sketch of some character in a novel or a play that you have recently studied. Make your sketch an explanation of the qualities the character possesses, not a condensed narration of the part he or she plays in the story.

II

Write an informal character sketch of one of the following persons. Make the subject of your sketch vivid and lifelike.

1. The Town Oracle.
2. The Neighborhood Gossip.
3. The Cook.
4. The Hired Man.
5. The Postmaster.
6. The Choir Leader.
7. A person of your own choice.

272. Reviews and criticisms. Reviews and criticisms are a form of exposition. They are usually published in newspapers and magazines and are written on a large variety of subjects, such as books, plays, music, painting, and sculpture. We shall here consider only the book review.

An important aim of the book review is to estimate the value of recently published books. Good reviews are helpful in two respects: (1) they guide the reader in his selection of books and (2) they give him knowledge *about* books, as distinguished from knowledge *of* books, which is just as legitimate as knowledge about anything else.

A book review, as a rule, suggests enough as to the contents of the book to arouse the interest of the reader, yet not enough to make him feel that it is unnecessary for him to read it. Preceding the review are usually given the name of the author, the name and address of the publisher, and the price of the book.

The following book review illustrates this type of exposition:

The Story of Mankind, by Hendrik Van Loon. New York: Boni and Liveright. 1921. 8vo, xxviii+479 pp. $5.00.

"The Story of Mankind" is a book primarily for children, but even grown-ups will find it interesting. It begins with the beginnings of the earth, describes the rise of mankind to supremacy over all other living creatures, traces the general sequence of human progress, and touches the high spots of history down to the present day. All this is done in a series of sixty-three narrative chapters, each chapter forming a short story which is complete in itself. No attempt is made, of course, to cover all the events in every land: the author has confined his narration to those things which, in his judgment, have left a permanent impression upon the course of history. Even at that, there is an abundance of material with which to fill his galloping chapters, most of which fairly swirl with action and romance.

It is unfortunate that Mr. Van Loon comes so closely on the heels of Mr. H. G. Wells. Many will imagine, no doubt, that the "Story of Mankind" is merely a child's edition of the "Outline of History," which is far from being the case. There is no resemblance between the two books, whether in plan, purpose, workmanship, style, or illustrations. Mr. Van Loon has set himself to the less pretentious task and has performed it with more originality. He travels down the ages at a much more rapid pace, passing by those personalities who happen to have no direct connection with his story and spending none of his precious space in pointing morals. He is not trying to revamp history: he is concerned only with the outstanding facts and forces. His aim has been to weave these into a succession of short stories which, by their wealth of action, can be trusted to catch the interest of young readers. In the realization of this aim he has succeeded remarkably well.

But with all due respect to Mr. Van Loon's facility in storytelling, the pictures are the best feature of his book. The author makes for them no claim to artistic excellence, but their usefulness no one will deny. They are intelligible to the average child—which most of the illustrations in historical textbooks are not. This is because they are home-made drawings, which seek to convey ideas or impressions rather than to portray events. Some of them look a bit primitive, to be sure, but so do the products of a child's own pencil. They are the sort of pictures that a child would draw if his hand were cunning enough. Mr. Van Loon is right in believing that few children ever forget what they have drawn, while most of them easily forget what they have read. Setting youngsters to express their ideas in pictures, no matter how crude, is one of the most useful things in the whole educational process. Mr. Van Loon has done a real service by demonstrating the great possibilities that lie in this direction. Taking the text and illustrations together, it would be difficult to imagine a better book from which to give children their first lessons in history.—WILLIAM BENNETT MUNRO, in *Atlantic Monthly*, April, 1922

EXERCISES

I

Bring to class a good book review that you have read in a newspaper or a magazine. Be prepared to enumerate the items of information given about the book.

II

Write a short review of some novel, play, volume of poetry, or collection of short stories that you have recently read. Try to make the members of the class want to read the book, but avoid telling them too much. Do not resort to a summary.

III

Explain orally why you like or dislike one of the following. Plan your explanation by means of a simple outline. You may illustrate your talk by reading or quoting passages that enforce what you say.

1. A story in a recent magazine.
2. A poem in a recent magazine.
3. A recent novel.
4. A poem studied in class.
5. A selection of your own.
6. A selection suggested by your teacher.

273. Newspaper editorials. Editorials in newspapers are in reality brief expositions in which the editor explains the meaning of events in various parts of the world. Editorials differ from news items in several ways. News items are generally narratives. Editorials are usually expositions. News items are hurriedly written accounts; they give merely the facts, or what are supposed to be the facts at the hour the reports are written. Editorials comment on facts, show which are more important than others and why, and help readers to form opinions about them. News items record events which take place from hour to hour every day. Editorials often place these present events in relation to the past and, by referring to experiences of men in political, business, or social affairs, point out what the present events may lead to.

Consequently the newspaper editor does much to mold public opinion regarding politics, education, and social conditions.

The editor must be a man of wide knowledge and of great accomplishments; he must keep abreast of all the news if he is to understand promptly the full force of any particular item of it; he must watch every rising cloud in the political sky and calculate what its effect will probably be. His knowledge comes not only from books about history and government but from close contact with men and affairs. Editorials should be fair and honest in judgment. They should be written clearly and vigorously, but the attempt to gain force in style should not lead the writer to distort the facts.

In our ordinary school life we shall not have occasion to write editorials as important as those of a newspaper editor. We may have occasion, however, to write editorially for a school paper or for some similar publication, and then we should follow the methods of a good editorial writer in so far as they apply to our case.

The following editorial illustrates this type of exposition:

SCIENCE VERSUS CRIME

A great advance in the means for discovering and suppressing crime came in when telephone, telegraph, and ocean cable made possible almost instant communication over land and sea routes. But for city work even the telephone left something to be desired. At some critical moment, with time of supreme importance, an officer might find himself far out of reach of a receiver; under similar circumstances a whole squad of police might be in danger from the onslaught of a desperate mob. But in these latter days the "resources of civilization," as Gladstone once called them, are less than ever "exhausted," and wireless, their latest yield, now lends its help for coping with both the single offender and the law-breaking crowd. The authorities in Paris are already using automobiles equipped with wireless apparatus, enabling the police charged with the care of the French capital to cruise about the city in constant touch with headquarters. It is also proposed to employ airplanes similarly provided as a means of dealing with riots or "demonstrations" that threaten peril to the public peace.

Much nearer than Paris, the city of Chicago now is resorting to wireless for the protection of that community from the criminal class. Preparations are under way to equip every policeman with a miniature wireless telephone small enough to be carried in the pocket, as well as to provide within the lining of the officer's clothes the "antennæ" for receiving messages. Headquarters will thus be able to call up any policeman in the service, in whatever part of the city he may happen to be. A buzzing sound will announce the call, and by placing a small receiver to his ear the officer will get his instructions as easily and distinctly as if he were connected by ordinary telephone. At present the apparatus does not serve for sending, but its completion for use both ways is promised at an early date, with the result that the central station will then be within speaking-distance of the whole force.

Meanwhile the Chicago patrol wagons and rifle squads are already employing wireless telephones for both receiving and sending; only the other day each police station in the city was furnished with a portable bullet-proof shield for use when desperate criminals defending themselves have to be approached and overpowered. Add the fact that the police department of New York City is now asking sanction for an expenditure on "tear bombs" to be used for dispersing mobs or ousting gunmen from cellars in which they may hide, and it will be seen that in these scientific days the way of the transgressor is indeed becoming hard.— *Boston Herald*

EXERCISES

I

Clip from newspapers and bring to class two editorials that seem to you to possess the characteristics mentioned above.

II

After reading several editorials in your school or town paper, write a short editorial on some topic connected with one of the following subjects:

1. School Spirit.
2. Better Schools.
3. A New Gymnasium (Athletic Field).
4. Interscholastic Athletics.
5. Civic Improvement.
6. Motion-Picture Shows.
7. The Consolidated High School.
8. Agricultural Conservation.
9. Better Roads.
10. A subject of your own selection.

274. Expository letters. Most business letters and many social letters are short expositions. An application for a position explains the applicant's preparation and fitness for the place desired. Letters from business concerns setting forth the merits of their commodities, as well as letters from customers ordering particular articles, are expository. A large number of friendly letters are written to inform our correspondents as to what we are doing, what we desire and plan to do, or why we cannot carry out some previously made plan. Formal and informal notes of explanation or apology are also expository in character.

EXERCISE

Write specimens of the following types of exposition: (1) a business letter, (2) a friendly letter, and (3) an informal note. The following subjects may furnish you suggestions:

1. The advantages of owning a home in a recently developed section of your town.

2. The inability of your school team to play a scheduled game with the team of another school.

3. A statement to the registrar or the secretary of the Y.M.C.A. employment bureau of the college which you hope to attend, indicating your desire for a college education and your willingness to work for your expenses, and asking for suggestions as to how you may accomplish your desire.

4. The superiority of a summer resort of which you know over one that a friend of yours is considering.

5. An introduction of an intimate friend to another friend in a distant city.

6. An application for some responsible position.

7. A recommendation of a book you have read or of a play you have seen.

8. A comment to a friend on the significance of some recent happening in your school, community, or town.

9. A reply to the letter of a friend who has written you asking for your opinion of the car your father has recently bought.

10. In a letter to the editor of your home paper discuss some civic improvement that you regard as necessary.

275. Summary. Exposition is that form of composition by means of which we give explanations of facts, methods, ideas, and principles.

Clearness, the essential quality of all exposition, depends on our fully recognizing the nature of the subject and the amount of information that our hearers and readers possess about the subject. Every exposition should be constructed according to the laws of unity, coherence, and emphasis.

The principal methods of exposition are often the same as those employed in developing the topic of a paragraph.

The most common types of exposition are (1) definitions, (2) explanations of processes, (3) discussions of facts and ideas, (4) essays, (5) expository biography, (6) reviews and criticisms, (7) editorials, and (8) expository letters.

CHAPTER XIX

ARGUMENT AND DEBATING

276. Argument defined. If we tell a friend how to swim, or explain to him the value of a college education, we employ exposition. But if we try to persuade him to go swimming some afternoon or to convince him that he should obtain a college education, we employ argument. The chief difference between exposition and argument is this: exposition is an explanation of facts or of the way in which something is done, to make other people *understand*; argument is an attempt to lead other people to *believe* that our opinion about something is the correct one and to induce them to adopt this opinion as their own. In other words, argument is a course of reasoning designed to convince others of the truth or falsity of something in dispute. We are often arguing without realizing it: at home, at school, at work, and at play we are constantly trying to make others think and act as we would have them.

In many respects exposition and argument are closely related. All argument contains a large amount of exposition, for we must make our hearers and readers understand before we can really convince them that our opinion is the right one. Often we are able merely by the clearness and logic of our explanation to lead people to believe as we do. Both exposition and argument are addressed primarily to the intellect, though argument is sometimes reënforced by an appeal to the emotions. In both exposition and argument we may frequently see fit to employ narration and description for the purpose of illustration or greater vividness. In both types of composition, clearness is of primary importance.

415

277. Conviction and persuasion. The preceding definition of argument calls our attention to the twofold purpose of this form of composition. Its first aim is to *convince* another person's reason; this we call *conviction*. Its second aim is to *persuade* another person to act in accordance with the truth which he has been led to believe; this we call *persuasion*. Both are important in argument. If Antony, in Shakespeare's "Julius Cæsar," had merely proved to the people that Cæsar was their friend and had not deserved death, he would simply have convinced them. But when, by appealing to their emotions and passions, such as love of military glory and self-interest, he aroused the mob to drive Cæsar's murderers from the city, he persuaded them to act.

278. Kinds of argument. All arguments may, with a fair degree of accuracy, be classified as either *formal* or *informal*.

Formal argument is an attempt, by means of systematic reasoning and direct proof, to convince persons of the truth or falsity of a given proposition. It demands that all important contentions be supported by material evidence in the form of proof and that this evidence be arranged and presented according to a fixed logical plan, called a *brief*. Formal argument may be a plea, a defense, or a debate.

Informal argument is closely akin to logical exposition. In general, it is a sort of discussion, such as frequently develops in everyday conversation or in animated correspondence. Like any other type of composition, informal argument is more successfully constructed by means of an outline, but such an outline is much simpler than the elaborate brief of formal argument. In informal argument, moreover, there is not the same necessity as in formal argument to cite material evidence for every statement made.

Because of our greater familiarity with informal argument, we shall consider this type first.

I. Informal Argument

279. Uses of informal argument. Informal argument we employ daily, in speech if not in writing. In our homes we often appeal to our parents to reverse a decision they have made restricting our actions, and many of us attain considerable skill in supporting our appeals. In conversation with our friends differences of opinion are constantly arising, and we instinctively defend our own beliefs. In our classes questions that provoke lively informal discussions are always coming up. In our letters we frequently attempt to alter our correspondent's views or effect a change in some plan of his by pointing out reasons for such changes. Editors of newspapers and magazines in many of their editorials seek to convince the public that their interpretation of certain questions of the day is the correct one. Lecturers and writers on political, economic, scientific, literary, and religious subjects often employ informal argument as a means of presenting their theories and opinions convincingly. Though informal argument lacks the elaborate structure and the exhaustive treatment of formal argument, it is often very effective. Persuasion naturally plays an important part.

In informal argument are employed many of the methods used in developing the topic of a paragraph (see sections 91–97). Usually we begin with a general statement of our opinion and then give reasons to support our belief. Frequently we supplement this method by giving details and by citing specific examples as illustrations of our discussion. In some cases we find comparison and contrast helpful.

To be effective, informal argument must conform to the laws of unity, coherence, and emphasis. A carefully prepared outline will help us to observe these laws, which are sometimes more difficult to obey in argument than in other, simpler kinds of writing.

In the following passage the writer has presented his opinion more effectively by means of informal argument than he could have done by exposition alone. He begins with a general statement of his opinion and then presents details in support of his statement.

SELECTING IMMIGRANTS

Better than exclusion would be a plan of restriction which would select those who were capable of entering the well-paid occupations and exclude those who would crowd into occupations where wages are already too low. The best way to do this would be to reverse our present contract-labor law and admit only such immigrants as could present contracts, signed by responsible employers, guaranteeing employment at five dollars a day for at least a year. (It is not necessary that the wage should be exactly five dollars. That figure is named because it is about the minimum on which a family can be supported in comfort and decency in any large city in this country. It is essential that there be some minimum wage attached to these contracts.) This would admit all the laborers who were really needed. No employer can say, with a straight face, that he needs men so very badly unless he is willing to pay them five dollars a day. At the same time it would prevent the coming of hordes of cheap laborers whose influence is to depress the wages of unskilled labor. It would make the lower grades of labor so scarce as eventually to make five dollars a day the actual minimum wage without the difficulty of enforcing a minimum-wage law. This would automatically take care, also, of the distribution of our immigrants, because they would go only to those places where they were badly needed. This would be very much better than any immigration commission could distribute them, besides saving for useful work the man-power that would be wasted upon the commission.

The literacy test as a means of selecting immigrants is vastly better than no test at all. This is said with a full recognition of the fact that literacy is not an invariable test of character. Neither is it an invariable test for fitness for the civil service nor for entrance to college. It is believed, however, that if all literate immigrants are arranged in one group and illiterates in another, the *average* of the literates would be above that of the illiterates. Excluding illiterates would therefore improve the average quality of our immigrants.

Again, the illiterates go predominantly into the unskilled trades where wages are low. The exclusion of illiterates therefore tends to make unskilled labor scarce, while the admission of literates would permit us to get the skilled labor we need; that is, to increase our supply of any kind of labor which can in any sense be said to be scarce.

Whatever immigration policy is adopted we must not lose sight of the fact that the essential thing is to restrict. Unless the number of unskilled laborers is materially reduced, the immigration policy will do nothing for labor. If the number of unskilled laborers is materially reduced, it will tend to make unskilled labor scarce and hard to find. Our democratic institutions, under which every human being is encouraged to rise in the economic scale, and our system of popular education, which makes it easy for the rising generation to avoid the unskilled and poorly paid and to enter the skilled and highly paid occupations, will combine to thin out the unskilled laborers. These democratic institutions, however, will not relieve the oversupply of unskilled labor if we continue to import it in unlimited quantities. Any kind of restriction, therefore, is better than no restriction. In addition to the literacy test, any other test which will actually reduce the numbers imported and permit us to select the more desirable applicants is a good proposal, though some may be better than others.—CARVER, "Principles of National Economy"

EXERCISES

I

Come to class prepared to give orally an informal argument on one of the following subjects. After you have studied both sides of the question make a simple outline of the points that you intend to bring out in your talk. Try to convince the members of the class of the correctness of your opinion by your logical reasoning and effective presentation.

1. Civilized man is being mastered by his own inventions.
2. A lie is sometimes justifiable.
3. All gasoline stations should be closed on Sunday.
4. Motion-picture theaters should be kept open on Sunday.
5. Milliners should be prohibited from trimming hats with birds and feathers.
6. Manual training and domestic science should be made compulsory throughout the four years of high school.
7. The study of science is more valuable as a preparation for life than the study of languages.
8. Women voters have improved conditions in this state.
9. A subject suggested by your teacher.
10. A subject of your own choice.

II

Write one of the following letters, in which you make use of informal argument. State your opinion and set forth your reasons clearly and forcefully.

1. A letter to your state senator or representative urging him to propose or vote for a certain measure.
2. A letter in reply to one you have received from a "self-made" relative who insists that in getting a college education you will be wasting both time and money.
3. A letter to a friend defending a book that he has vigorously condemned in his last letter.
4. A letter to your aunt defending "these modern girls."
5. A letter to a friend urging him to change his plans and attend the same college that you expect to enter next year.
6. A letter to your friend's mother, in which you try to persuade her to allow your friend to join you at a summer camp.
7. A letter on a subject of your own choice.

III

Write one of the following editorials for your school, town, county, or state paper, in which you employ informal argument. Limit yourself to one or two important points and then set forth your opinion and reasons clearly and forcefully.

1. An editorial favoring the establishment of a junior high school in your town.

2. An editorial opposing the election of a certain candidate to a school or town office.

3. An editorial proposing and urging some improvement in local agricultural conditions.

4. An editorial urging a more liberal salary for county demonstration agents.

5. An editorial recommending an increase in the local tax rate for school support.

6. An editorial recommending free textbooks for the public schools of your state.

7. An editorial censuring the recent misconduct of an athlete or an athletic team.

8. An editorial proposing a "tag day" for the local Boy and Girl Scouts.

9. An editorial on a subject of your own choice.

10. An editorial on a subject suggested by your teacher.

II. FORMAL ARGUMENT

280. The value of debating. One of the most profitable forms of argument is debating. To the interest of the subject discussed is added the interest of a game. A debate is carried on by two sets of speakers, called teams. Each team tries to show the weakness or falsity of its opponent's side, as well as to maintain or establish the truth of its own. Consequently each team, spurred by the desire to win, not only prepares its arguments carefully but takes delight in presenting its case in a lively and forceful manner. But more important than the mere winning of the debate is the development of confidence in ourselves, which comes as the result of the practice that debating affords us in clear thinking, quick and accurate judgment, foresight, and facile expression.

281. Subjects for debate. The best subjects for debate are those which concern present and future conditions, and which, furthermore, we and our audience already have some knowledge of and some interest in. The questions that we choose should arise out of our information and experience. They should also be definitely limited and properly suited to our ability to discuss them and to our audience's capacity to understand them.

282. Wording the question. Before we can prepare an argument, we must know exactly what we are to argue about. This means that we must use great care in wording the statement which we are to prove or disprove. This statement is called the *question.* We may take, for example, the topic "Should military drill be maintained in our school?" The question must be a complete sentence, with subject and predicate, as above, and it must be a simple sentence, not a compound one. The reason why the question must be a sentence is that there may be two sides to the argument: the affirmative, which upholds the answer "yes," and the negative, which upholds the answer "no." The question should be worded with brevity, exactness, and impartiality. It should not include words which at once cause people to make up their minds on one side or the other. The following question causes prejudice at once: "Should the town license motion-picture shows which present scenes of brutality and crime?" Does not the clause "which present scenes of brutality and crime" indicate that the debater is prejudiced toward one side of the question? Could there be any argument if the motion-picture shows gave such scenes?

EXERCISES

I

Examine the following questions and tell why they are incorrectly worded:

1. The United States Senate, already growing to have too much power, should be nominated and elected by the direct vote of the people.

2. The people of the Philippine Islands should be speedily granted the self-government for which they are fitted.

3. Military drill should be taught in the common schools, and all able-bodied citizens should be required to serve a term in the army.

4. Baseball, the best sport for boys, is better exercise than football.

5. Highways should be built and maintained by the state, and all owners of property bordering them should plant trees by the wayside.

II

Prepare five correctly worded questions for debate and show how they are correctly worded.

283. Exposition of the question. Some preparation is necessary before we begin to debate, in order that we may learn just what the question means and find out the *special questions* on which the argument turns. For instance, suppose two boys are arguing the question "Shall we go swimming this afternoon?" Their minds are at once busy over a number of special questions which have to be settled before they decide on the main one. These special questions may be: "Will the swimming pool be too crowded?" "Can we use Mr. Brown's car to go out to the pool?" "Can we get back before supper?" It is necessary to find out what the special questions are before we can argue at all. We may find these by means of *definition of terms* and by examining all points about which there is a *conflict of opinion*.

284. Definition of terms. In order that we may proceed logically and consistently in preparing a debate, we must clearly define all terms in the main question that call for more exact limitation in meaning. Such definitions must be satisfactory to persons supporting both the affirmative and the negative side and should be made easily intelligible to readers or to an audience. For instance, in the question "Should the comic supplement of the Sunday newspaper be discontinued?" an exact explanation of what is meant by *comic supplement* must be given, so that a certain definite kind of pictures may be argued about — not newspaper pictures in general. Again, in the question "Is the treatment of the Indians by the United States unjust?" we must know exactly what *treatment* means and what *unjust* means. In other words, we must know what the present treatment of the Indians is and in what particular way it has been unjust.

Sometimes a dictionary will give the needed definition. This source, however, is often insufficient, and we must seek a better definition in books and periodicals. In many questions, on the other hand, all terms are simple, and we need only show in what particular sense we use them in our question. Again, the terms may be too obvious in their meaning to need any definition.

285. Conflict of opinion. Suppose we have as our topic for debate the question Should state censorship of motion pictures be adopted in the United States? A comparison of the affirmative and negative sides of the argument will reveal certain points about which there is no difference of opinion. For example, both sides will doubtless agree (1) that the standards of motion pictures are low and (2) that, to raise the standards, regulation and review are necessary. Such points as these may therefore be disregarded. On several other points, however, the two sides will disagree. For instance, the affirmative side may maintain (1) that the existing methods of censorship are not satisfactory, (2) that state censorship would improve present conditions, and (3) that state censorship is constitutional; whereas the negative may contend (1) that the existing methods of censorship are reasonably satisfactory and (2) that state censorship is unconstitutional. Out of this conflict of opinion will arise such special questions as the following: (1) Are existing methods of censorship satisfactory? (2) Would state censorship improve existing conditions? (3) Would state censorship be constitutional? These special questions will form the subject for debate.

THRIFT AND PROSPERITY

Find out the special questions in dispute in the following subjects for debate. First define the terms, if necessary; then make a list of opinions of the affirmative and the negative and compare them.

1. Should military drill be maintained in our school?
2. Are interscholastic athletics a benefit to our school?
3. Should our town adopt the commission form of government?
4. Should studies in high school be elective?
5. Should members of school athletic teams be required to maintain a passing grade in their studies during the playing season?

286. Proof. When we have found the special questions, we choose one side, affirmative or negative, and bring forward all the facts we can in support of our side. These facts are called the *proof*. We cannot make people believe in our side if we merely say or assert that things are thus and so. *Assertion is not proof.* We must support our arguments by facts and figures or by the statements of persons who know the subject. Such persons are called *authorities*. The best sources of authoritative information on questions which are interesting to the public are the reviews and magazines, such as the *American Review of Reviews*, the *World's Work*, the *Outlook*, the *Literary Digest*, the *Nation*, the *New Republic*, and the *Independent*. By the aid of such a reference work as *Poole's Index* or the *Reader's Guide* we may find the titles of numerous magazine articles dealing with a great variety of subjects. We must be sure, however, that the person whom we quote *is* an authority and that he is honest. We must not believe everything we see in print simply because it is in print. When we quote the words of an authority, or even when we make reference to one, we must be accurate. Furthermore, we must be ready to give the sources, even to the date and page of a periodical, or the volume, chapter, and page of a book.

287. Refutation. It is not enough to prove our side of the question. We must try to disprove the argument of our opponent. This is called *refutation*. We may refute his arguments by showing that the facts he states are not true. Unless we give due attention to refutation we weaken our own statements; for even when these are sound, our contention is stronger if we can show that the assertions of our opponent are wrong. Refutation may be introduced at any place in the course of the proof where it will be effective in weakening our opponent's argument.

288. Burden of proof. The proposition for debate should be so phrased that what is called the *burden of proof* will rest upon the affirmative side. The burden of proof is "the obligation resting upon one or other of the parties to a controversy to establish by proofs a given proposition before being entitled to receive an answer from the other side." Now this burden, or chief responsibility, rests on the side which advocates some change in existing conditions. If the proposition is phrased affirmatively,—as, "The city of Milwaukee should be governed by commission,"—the responsibility rests on the affirmative side. In this case the affirmative must convince us that the change in question should take place. The negative has a *presumption* in its favor; that is, it supports that side of the case which may be logically assumed to be correct until it is disproved. Thus the defense has the advantage of position.

289. Persuasion. The purpose of persuasion is to make people believe as we do about a question and to get them to act on their belief. By persuasion we make appeals to the emotions, imagination, sentiments, and interests which lead people to take action. We can stir the feelings of our audience by specific language, by forceful sentences, by anecdotes, and by facts which enforce our argument. We should always appeal to the nobler motives of people, such as their love of justice or of fair play, their patriotism, and their sympathy. Our manner of delivery is important. Distinct enunciation, sincerity in our way of speaking, and a natural, upright posture will all be of great advantage to us.

EXERCISE

From your class select two debating-teams of three members each who will debate one week hence a question that they or the class may select. The rules for the conduct of a debate will be found fully explained in Gregg's "Handbook of Parliamentary Law" or Cushing's "Rules of Proceeding and Debate in Deliberative Assemblies." In case a better question cannot be found, one of the following may be chosen:

1. Should our school publish a paper?
2. Should reports of murder trials be printed in newspapers?
3. Should the publication of the comic supplement to the Sunday newspaper be discontinued?
4. Should the manufacture and sale of chewing-gum be prohibited?
5. Should prices of the necessities of life be limited by Federal law?
6. Should our school provide a free clinic?
7. Should our town maintain a night school for persons who work in factories?
8. Should our state become fully self-supporting?
9. Should every person be allowed to spend Sunday as he pleases?
10. Should students who know of the dishonesty of others in school work report all such cases?
11. Should a boy or girl who is going into business have a college education?
12. With the teacher's assistance frame a proposition dealing with some problem of local or school interest.

290. The brief. In preparing to debate a question before the members of our class, we may find that brief notes and a simple outline will enable us to collect and arrange our material adequately. But when we have become more experienced debaters and take part in formal public debates or write a formal argument, we shall find it necessary to construct a logical outline that will satisfy the three fundamental principles of structure. An outline for a formal argument we call a *brief*.

In written argument the question to be argued is placed as the title; as, "Should School Fraternities be Abolished?" The question also appears later in the form of a statement (usually affirmative) at the beginning of the argument proper; as, "School fraternities should be abolished." In a debate the question is stated as a resolution; as, "*Resolved:* That school fraternities should be abolished."

After we have stated the question accurately in concise form, we may begin our outline, or brief. The three divisions of the brief, corresponding to the three parts of the argument, are *introduction, brief proper*, and *conclusion*.

1. *Introduction.* The introduction, which is expository in character, usually includes six main parts arranged in the following order: (1) a statement of the nature and importance of the question; (2) a statement of the history of the question; (3) a definition of terms; (4) an enumeration of the points on which both sides agree; (5) an enumeration of conflicting arguments; and (6) an enumeration, in interrogative form, of the special questions to be argued.

2. *Brief proper.* At the beginning of the brief proper the main question is stated affirmatively. Following this, each special question contained in the last section of the introduction is expressed as a declarative sentence and forms one of the main divisions of the argument proper. Under each special question are arranged the facts that go to prove or refute it.

3. *Conclusion.* This final division consists of a brief summary of the argument, followed by a formal statement that the main question has been proved.

The following student brief of a formal written argument will illustrate the form and contents of this special kind of outline. Notice that each numbered or lettered main division, together with its subdivisions, is a complete sentence and that each heading contains only a single assertion. Note also that, in the brief proper, each subordinate assertion is connected with the one on which it depends by the conjunction *for*.

SHOULD STATE CENSORSHIP OF MOTION PICTURES BE ADOPTED IN THE UNITED STATES?

Introduction

I. Public interest in the question of state censorship of motion pictures arises from the fact that the public throughout the country is protesting against the alleged unrestricted methods of the motion-picture industry and against the ineffectiveness of the National Board of Review.

II. The history of the question is as follows:

    A. During the year 1919 measures proposing the enactment of laws for the censorship of all motion pictures prior to their public exhibition were introduced in the legislatures of twenty-three states and in Congress.

    B. Four states—Kansas, Maryland, Ohio, and Pennsylvania—and every province in Canada already have censorship of motion pictures by state officials.

III. The following explanations will facilitate the discussion of the question and prevent misunderstanding:

    A. The National Board of Review is a self-appointed, unpaid group of about one hundred and twenty-five men and women, with New York City as its headquarters, which has set itself up as the only authority capable of impartially judging films and of controlling the industry.

        1. It has been in existence since 1909.

        2. It is not a Federal board, as its name might indicate.

    B. The underlying principle of state censorship, as practiced in Kansas, Maryland, Ohio, and Pennsylvania and in every province in Canada, is the examination and licensing of every film by an official board with power to debar films or parts of films which are deemed vicious.

    C. Vicious films may be defined as films which debase and corrupt
        morals by showing methods of committing crime; films
        which are sexually exciting or which depict marital infidelity
        as though it were a normal thing; pictures of cruelty, bru-
        tality, and inhuman acts; and pictures which are sacri-
        legious, obscene, or indecent.

IV. Both sides agree
    A. That the standards of motion pictures are low.
    B. That to raise the standards, regulation and review are necessary.
    C. That to regulate motion pictures effectively it is necessary to
        have a careful examination of every film by capable per-
        sons before it is released for exhibition.

V. The conflicting arguments on the question are as follows:
    A. Those in favor of state censorship believe
       1. That the existing methods of censorship are not satisfactory.
       2. That state censorship would improve present conditions.
       3. That state censorship is constitutional.
    B. Those opposed to state censorship believe
       1. That the existing methods of censorship are reasonably
          satisfactory.
       2. That state censorship is unconstitutional.

VI. From this conflict of opinion it appears that the special questions
    to be determined are
    A. Are existing methods of censorship satisfactory?
    B. Would state censorship improve existing conditions?
    C. Would state censorship be constitutional?

Brief Proper

State censorship of motion pictures should be adopted, for
I. The existing methods of censorship are unsatisfactory from the
    point of view of the public, for
    A. The National Board of Review is ineffective, for
       1. It has no legal power to enforce its decisions.
       2. It is merely a tool of the association of motion-picture
          producers, by whom it is supported.
       3. A very considerable percentage of the pictures approved by
          this unofficial board have been declared by local and state
          censorship boards unfit for exhibition.

B. Present laws do not meet the need, for
  1. They require complaint from the public in order to have a film withdrawn from exhibition at a theater.
  2. They fix the responsibility for showing vicious pictures on no person or group of persons.
  3. They punish offenders only after a vicious picture has been shown and seen by thousands of people.

II. State censorship would improve existing conditions, for
  A. It would save great sums of money spent in the maintenance of local and municipal censorship boards.
  B. It would create a board of officers responsible to the people of the state.
  C. It would create a uniform standard of judging films for the entire state.

III. State censorship would be constitutional, for
  A. It has become implied in the Constitution that the Supreme Court, with the consent of Congress, may infringe upon the liberty of the people when such an infringement results in benefit to the whole people.
  B. The Federal government has already established a precedent by enacting the Eighteenth Amendment, which makes illegal the manufacture and sale of alcoholic liquors.
  C. If state censorship were not constitutional, the Supreme Court would already have declared it unconstitutional in Kansas, Maryland, Ohio, and Pennsylvania.

Conclusion

I. Since the present methods of censoring motion pictures are unsatisfactory;

II. Since state censorship would improve existing conditions; and

III. Since state censorship would be constitutional,—

  Therefore, state censorship of motion pictures should be adopted in the United States by all states that are now without it.

291. Developing the brief into an argument. When we have collected all the necessary material and have made a logical brief, our work is more than half completed. The final step in the construction of our argument is the elaboration of the brief. This we accomplish by developing each division and sub-division by means of specific details and references to authorities on our subject. Great care should be used to make the transition from one heading to another perfectly clear. Though we should follow the brief closely, we should avoid making the argument too mechanical and stilted in expression. This we can do by writing with earnestness and sincerity and by skillfully combining persuasion with conviction.

EXERCISE

Make as complete a brief as you can of one of the following questions and then write the argument:

1. Should motion pictures be used in school work?
2. Should our school have a new gymnasium?
3. Should all students be required to study at least one foreign language throughout high school?
4. Should high-school students be permitted free election of courses?
5. Should the honor system in examinations be adopted by the students of our high school?
6. Should capital punishment be abolished?
7. Should students be allowed to participate in assembly exercises?
8. Should cartoons of public officials be published in newspapers and magazines?
9. Should all members of the fire department be paid?
10. A question of present local interest.

292. Summary. Argument is that form of composition by means of which we attempt to convince others of the truth or falsity of something in dispute. Argument has a twofold purpose: to convince and to persuade.

Arguments are of two kinds: formal and informal. Formal argument is an attempt, by means of systematic reasoning and direct proof, to convince persons of the truth or falsity of a given proposition. All details of evidence and proof must be arranged according to a fixed logical plan, called a *brief*. Informal argument, which is closely akin to exposition, is usually a discussion, and depends on a course of general or theoretical reasoning rather than on systematic proof.

Debating is valuable practice in oral composition, for it teaches us not only to support our arguments by evidence and persuasion but also to think more clearly and quickly and to express our thoughts more effectively.

The question for debate should be carefully chosen and accurately worded. The special questions that constitute the points at issue should be discovered by defining all terms in the main question that are not clear and by examining all points about which there is a conflict of opinion.

Every step in our argument must be supported by proof. In addition to proving each point on our side of an argument, we must try to refute the argument of our opponent. Every proposition should be so worded that the burden of proof will rest upon the affirmative side. Persuasion and a good oral delivery will greatly enhance the effectiveness of our argument.

In preparing a formal argument for public presentation, either in debate or in writing, we should arrange our material in logical order by means of a well-constructed brief. In elaborating the brief into the finished argument, we should develop each division and subdivision adequately and should make the transition from one heading to another perfectly clear. We should write with earnestness and sincerity and combine persuasion with conviction.

CHAPTER XX

THE SHORT STORY

293. The short story defined. A short story is a brief complex narrative composed of a series of causally related incidents skillfully arranged by means of a plot to present effectively a struggle and its outcome. The incidents that make up a simple narrative are related one to another merely in the order of time, whereas the incidents composing a short story must be arranged according to their cause-and-effect sequence, even though this sequence may violate the time order. By *plot* is meant the *plan* which the author devises as a means of telling his story more effectively. In making this plan the writer is guided by his purpose in relating the story and by the nature of its outcome, which he must foresee from the very beginning. Since in the majority of short stories there are two opposing forces which result in conflicting lines of action, a struggle of some kind forms the basis of the story action. This struggle may be either serious or humorous, physical, mental, or emotional. As a means of heightening the reader's interest the author of a short story, by arranging incidents in such an order as to lead up to a point of greatest interest, called the *climax*, creates suspense as to the outcome of the struggle. For this reason most short stories are the product of the writer's invention and are therefore fictitious, whereas simple narratives are usually true accounts of actual happenings. Imagination is a most important asset of the short-story writer.

294. Characteristics of the short story. In addition to the definition given above, let us consider some of the more noticeable characteristics of the short story.

Length. Though many narratives that are brief are in no sense short stories, comparative brevity is an external characteristic of the short story. The majority of short stories are included between the limits of 2000 and 7500 words. Very few exceed 20,000 words.

Number of characters. Because of the small compass in which he has chosen to work, the writer of the short story carefully avoids bringing in any character that is not absolutely essential to the effective telling of his story. Rarely do we find more than six characters who are really concerned with the action of the story, and often the number is much smaller.

Time covered by the action. It is desirable to limit the time covered by the action of a short story to as brief a period as possible. Skill in selecting a point of beginning near the intended climax will often enable the narrator to compress the action of his story into a few hours, as in Poe's "The Cask of Amontillado," given below. In other instances the writer will choose two or more significant portions of action that concern his plot and his characters, and pass over the unimportant intervals of action between these, as in Bret Harte's "Tennessee's Partner" and in Mrs. Mary E. Wilkins Freeman's "A Gala Dress." By such careful choice and relating of incidents the narrator gives the reader the impression that the time covered by the action is relatively short.

295. Essentials of the short story. According to two modern critics,[1] there are five essential elements in a properly constructed short story. These they enumerate in the following order: (1) singleness of impression; (2) well-defined plot; (3) a dominant incident; (4) a preëminent character; and (5) a complication and its resolution.

Since Edgar Allan Poe, the father of the modern short story, admirably illustrated all five of these essentials in "The Cask

---

[1] Esenwein and Chambers, The Art of Story-Writing.

of Amontillado," it will be well for us to read this story, which will be used as a model in the discussion of these essentials in the sections that follow.

THE CASK OF AMONTILLADO

By Edgar Allan Poe

The thousand injuries of Fortunato I had borne as best I could, but when he ventured upon insult, I vowed revenge. You, who so well know the nature of my soul, will not suppose, however, that I gave utterance to a threat. *At length* I would be avenged; this was a point definitely settled—but the very definiteness with which it was resolved precluded the idea of risk. I must not only punish, but punish with impunity. A wrong is unredressed when retribution overtakes its redresser. It is equally unredressed when the avenger fails to make himself felt as such to him who has done the wrong.

It must be understood that neither by word nor deed had I given Fortunato cause to doubt my good will. I continued, as was my wont, to smile in his face, and he did not perceive that my smile *now* was at the thought of his immolation.

He had a weak point—this Fortunato—although in other regards he was a man to be respected and even feared. He prided himself on his connoisseurship in wine. Few Italians have the true virtuoso spirit. For the most part their enthusiasm is adopted to suit the time and opportunity—to practice imposture upon the British and Austrian millionaires. In painting and gemmary Fortunato, like his countrymen, was a quack; but in the matter of old wines he was sincere. In this respect I did not differ from him materially: I was skillful in the Italian vintages myself and bought largely whenever I could.

It was about dusk, one evening during the supreme madness of the carnival season, that I encountered my friend. He accosted me with excessive warmth, for he had been drinking much. The man wore motley. He had on a tight-fitting party-striped dress, and his head was surmounted by the conical cap and bells. I was so pleased to see him that I thought I should never have done wringing his hand.

I said to him: "My dear Fortunato, you are luckily met. How remarkably well you are looking today! But I have received a pipe of what passes for Amontillado, and I have my doubts."

"How?" said he, "Amontillado? A pipe? Impossible! And in the middle of the carnival!"

"I have my doubts," I replied; "and I was silly enough to pay the full Amontillado price without consulting you in the matter. You were not to be found, and I was fearful of losing a bargain."

"Amontillado!"

"I have my doubts."

"Amontillado!"

"And I must satisfy them."

"Amontillado!"

"As you are engaged, I am on my way to Luchesi. If anyone has a critical turn, it is he. He will tell me—"

"Luchesi cannot tell Amontillado from Sherry."

"And yet some fools will have it that his taste is a match for your own."

"Come, let us go."

"Whither?"

"To your vaults."

"My friend, no; I will not impose upon your good nature. I perceive you have an engagement. Luchesi—"

"I have no engagement—come."

"My friend, no. It is not the engagement, but the severe cold with which I perceive you are afflicted. The vaults are insufferably damp. They are incrusted with niter."

"Let us go nevertheless. The cold is merely nothing. Amontillado! You have been imposed upon. And as for Luchesi, he cannot distinguish Sherry from Amontillado."

Thus speaking, Fortunato possessed himself of my arm. Putting on a mask of black silk, and drawing a roquelaure closely about my person, I suffered him to hurry me to my palazzo.

There were no attendants at home; they had absconded to make merry in honor of the time. I had told them that I should not return until the morning, and had given them explicit orders not to stir from the house. These orders were sufficient, I well knew, to insure their immediate disappearance, one and all, as soon as my back was turned.

I took from their sconces two flambeaux, and giving one to Fortunato, bowed him through several suites of rooms to the archway that led into the vaults. I passed down a long and winding staircase, requesting him to be cautious as he followed. We came at length to the foot of the descent and stood together on the damp ground of the catacombs of the Montresors.

The gait of my friend was unsteady, and the bells upon his cap jingled as he strode.

"The pipe," said he.

"It is farther on," said I; "but observe the white webwork which gleams from these cavern walls."

He turned towards me, and looked into my eyes with two filmy orbs that distilled the rheum of intoxication.

"Niter?" he asked at length.

"Niter," I replied. "How long have you had that cough?"

"Ugh! ugh! ugh!—ugh! ugh! ugh!—ugh! ugh! ugh!—ugh! ugh! ugh!—ugh! ugh! ugh!"

My poor friend found it impossible to reply for many minutes.

"It is nothing," he said at last.

"Come," I said, with decision, "we will go back; your health is precious. You are rich, respected, admired, beloved; you are happy, as once I was. You are a man to be missed. For me it is no matter. We will go back; you will be ill, and I cannot be responsible. Besides, there is Luchesi—"

"Enough," he said; "the cough is a mere nothing; it will not kill me. I shall not die of a cough."

"True—true," I replied; "and, indeed, I had no intention of alarming you unnecessarily—but you should use all proper caution. A draught of this Médoc will defend us from the damps."

Here I knocked off the neck of a bottle which I drew from a long row of its fellows that lay upon the mold.

"Drink," I said, presenting him the wine.

He raised it to his lips with a leer. He paused and nodded to me familiarly, while his bells jingled.

"I drink," he said, "to the buried that repose around us."

"And I to your long life."

He again took my arm, and we proceeded.

"These vaults," he said, "are extensive."

"The Montresors," I replied, "were a great and numerous family."

"I forget your arms."

"A huge human foot *d'or*, in a field azure; the foot crushes a serpent rampant whose fangs are embedded in the heel."

"And the motto?"

"*Nemo me impune lacessit.*"

"Good!" he said.

The wine sparkled in his eyes and the bells jingled. My own fancy grew warm with the Médoc. We had passed through walls of piled bones, with casks and puncheons intermingling, into the inmost recesses of the catacombs. I paused again, and this time I made bold to seize Fortunato by an arm above the elbow.

"The niter!" I said; "see, it increases. It hangs like moss upon the vaults. We are below the river's bed. The drops of moisture trickle among the bones. Come, we will go back ere it is too late. Your cough—"

"It is nothing," he said; "let us go on. But first, another draught of the Médoc."

I broke and reached him a flagon of De Grâve. He emptied it at a breath. His eyes flashed with a fierce light. He laughed, and threw the bottle upward with a gesticulation I did not understand.

I looked at him in surprise. He repeated the movement—a grotesque one.

"You do not comprehend?" he said.

"Not I," I replied.

"Then you are not of the brotherhood."

"How?"

"You are not of the masons."

"Yes, yes," I said; "yes, yes."

"You? Impossible! A mason?"

"A mason," I replied.

"A sign," he said.

"It is this," I answered, producing a trowel from beneath the folds of my roquelaure.

"You jest," he exclaimed, recoiling a few paces. "But let us proceed to the Amontillado."

"Be it so," I said, replacing the tool beneath the cloak and again offering him my arm. He leaned upon it heavily. We continued our route in search of the Amontillado. We passed through a range of low arches, descended, passed on, and, descending again, arrived at a deep crypt, in which the foulness of the air caused our flambeaux rather to glow than flame.

At the most remote end of the crypt there appeared another, less spacious. Its walls had been lined with human remains, piled to the vault overhead, in the fashion of the great catacombs of Paris. Three sides of this interior crypt were still ornamented in this manner. From the fourth the bones had been thrown down, and lay promiscuously upon the earth, forming at one point a mound of some size. Within the wall thus exposed by the displacing of the bones we perceived a still interior recess, in depth about four feet, in width three, in height six or seven. It seemed to have been constructed for no especial use within itself, but formed merely the interval between two of the colossal supports of the roof of the catacombs, and was backed by one of their circumscribing walls of solid granite.

It was in vain that Fortunato, uplifting his dull torch, endeavored to pry into the depth of the recess. Its termination the feeble light did not enable us to see.

"Proceed," I said; "herein is the Amontillado. As for Luchesi—"

"He is an ignoramus," interrupted my friend, as he stepped unsteadily forward, while I followed immediately at his heels. In an instant he had reached the extremity of the niche, and finding his progress arrested by the rock, stood stupidly bewildered. A moment more, and I had fettered him to the granite. In its surface were two iron staples, distant from each other about two feet, horizontally. From one of these depended a short chain, from the other a padlock. Throwing the links about his waist, it was but the work of a few seconds to secure it. He was too much astounded to resist. Withdrawing the key, I stepped back from the recess.

"Pass your hand," I said, "over the wall; you cannot help feeling the niter. Indeed it is *very* damp. Once more let me *implore* you to return. No? Then I must positively leave you. But I must first render you all the little attentions in my power."

"The Amontillado!" ejaculated my friend, not yet recovered from his astonishment.

"True," I replied; "the Amontillado."

As I said these words I busied myself among the pile of bones of which I have before spoken. Throwing them aside, I soon uncovered a quantity of building-stone and mortar. With these materials and with the aid of my trowel, I began vigorously to wall up the entrance of the niche.

I had scarcely laid the first tier of the masonry when I discovered that the intoxication of Fortunato had in a great measure worn off. The earliest indication I had of this was a low moaning cry from the depth of the recess. It was *not* the cry of a drunken man. There was then a long and obstinate silence. I laid the second tier, and the third, and the fourth; and then I heard the furious vibrations of the chain. The noise lasted for several minutes, during which, that I might hearken to it with the more satisfaction, I ceased my labors and sat down upon the bones. When at last the clanking subsided, I resumed the trowel, and finished without interruption the fifth, the sixth, and the seventh tier. The wall was now nearly upon a level with my breast. I again paused, and holding the flambeaux over the masonwork, threw a few feeble rays upon the figure within.

A succession of loud and shrill screams, bursting suddenly from the throat of the chained form, seemed to thrust me violently back. For a brief moment I hesitated—I trembled. Unsheathing my rapier, I began to grope with it about the recess; but the thought of an instant reassured me. I placed my hand upon the solid fabric of the catacombs, and felt satisfied. I reapproached the wall. I replied to the yells of him who clamored. I reëchoed—I aided—I surpassed them in volume and in strength. I did this, and the clamorer grew still.

It was now midnight, and my task was drawing to a close. I had completed the eighth, the ninth, and the tenth tier. I had finished a portion of the last and the eleventh; there remained but a single stone to be fitted and plastered in. I struggled with its weight;

I placed it partially in its destined position. But now there came from out the niche a low laugh that erected the hairs upon my head. It was succeeded by a sad voice, which I had difficulty in recognizing as that of the noble Fortunato. The voice said:

"Ha! ha! ha!—he! he! he!—a very good joke indeed—an excellent jest. We will have many a rich laugh about it at the palazzo—he! he! he!—over our wine—he! he! he!"

"The Amontillado!" I said.

"He! he! he!—he! he! he!—yes, the Amontillado. But is it not getting late? Will not they be awaiting us at the palazzo—the Lady Fortunato and the rest? Let us be gone."

"Yes," I said, "let us be gone."

"*For the love of God, Montresor!*"

"Yes," I said, "for the love of God!"

But to these words I hearkened in vain for a reply. I grew impatient. I called aloud,—

"Fortunato!"

No answer. I called again,—

"Fortunato!"

No answer still. I thrust a torch through the remaining aperture and let it fall within. There came forth in return only the jingling of the bells. My heart grew sick—on account of the dampness of the catacombs. I hastened to make an end of my labor. I forced the last stone into its position; I plastered it up. Against the new masonry I reërected the old rampart of bones. For the half of a century no mortal has disturbed them. *In pace requiescat.*

296. Singleness of impression. Now that we have read "The Cask of Amontillado," if we ask ourselves what single impression the story made on us, we shall very likely agree that it was one of *horror*. This seems to have been the one effect that Poe was trying to produce. Here, stated in Poe's own words, is the principle by which he devised his stories:

A skillful literary artist has constructed a tale. If wise, he has not fashioned his thoughts to accommodate his incidents; but having conceived, with deliberate care, a certain unique or single *effect* to be wrought out, he then invents such incidents—he then combines such events—as may best aid him in establishing this preconceived effect. If his very initial sentence tend not to the out-bringing of this effect, then he has failed in his first step. In the whole composition there should be no word written of which the tendency, direct or indirect, is not to the one preëstablished design.

Singleness of impression is the principal device for securing unity in the short story. The one predetermined effect must be produced in the briefest possible space by means of careful selection and arrangement of incidents. The story should be told with the greatest amount of compression and emphasis.

The *motivating idea* of a story should not be confused with singleness of impression. The motivating idea of "The Cask of Amontillado" (that is, the idea that is the mainspring of the action and the motive which drives Montresor on) is *revenge*, whereas the impression produced on the reader is *horror*. In almost every short story a little study will enable us to detect both the single impression and the motivating idea.

EXERCISE

Read again "The Cask of Amontillado" and point out the incidents and details used to produce the impression of horror. Can you discover a single sentence that does not help to establish this effect? Read some other story of Poe's and point out the single impression and the motivating idea.

297. Plot. The plot of a short story, as explained above, is the plan by means of which the writer arranges the incidents of his story in the most effective order to produce the single impression that he intends his story to make on the reader. In every plot there are three elements: a cause, a result, and a series of incidents that link the two together logically. Let us illustrate these three elements by reference to "The Cask of Amontillado."

The *cause* is stated in the first sentence: "The thousand injuries of Fortunato I had borne as best I could, but when he ventured upon insult, I vowed revenge."

The *result* is seen in the outcome of the story: Montresor has accomplished his revenge by walling Fortunato up in a niche and leaving him there to die. He has carried out his resolution to punish with impunity and to make himself felt as the avenger.

The *series of incidents that link the two together logically* is as follows: (1) Montresor encounters the intoxicated Fortunato on the street late one evening during the carnival season, greets him cordially, and tells him that he has just bought a cask of Amontillado, but that he doubts that it is genuine Amontillado. (2) Fortunato, whose weakness is his connoisseurship in wine, insists on going immediately to taste the Amontillado, and Montresor makes him all the more eager to go by telling him that he is then on his way to get Luchesi to taste it. (3) Having lured Fortunato into his family burial vaults, Montresor intoxicates him still further, all the while goading him on by the mention of Luchesi. (4) Having finally lured Fortunato into the niche previously prepared for him, Montresor chains him fast. (5) Fortunato, sobered by fright as he is being walled in, realizes Montresor's motive and pleads in vain to be spared.

A skillfully devised plot can usually be stated in one sentence. Such a statement should include the three elements of the plot. The following sentence indicates the plot of "The Cask of Amontillado": Montresor, having been insulted by Fortunato, vows revenge, and, after luring the intoxicated Fortunato into the burial vault of the Montresors, walls him up in a niche to die. The ease with which such a plot statement can be formulated is evidence that the story has a well-defined plot.

The following passage will add to our understanding of plot:

The plot is the nucleus of the story, the bare thought or incident upon which the narrative is to be builded. . . . A plot implies action—that is, something must happen; at the conclusion of the story the characters must be differently situated, and usually differently related one to another, from what they were at the beginning. The event need not be tragic, or even serious; but it must be of sufficient importance, novelty, and interest to justify its relation in narrative form. In general, the plot of a short story involves an incident or a minor crisis in a human life, rather than the supreme crisis which makes or mars a man for good. . . . Yet the short story may be a supreme crisis and a tragedy, as are Stevenson's "Markheim," Hawthorne's "The Ambitious Guest" and "The Birthmark," and many of Poe's tales; but these are stories of an exceptional type, in which the whole life of the chief actor comes to a focus in the crisis which makes the story.[1]

In the short story the action usually consists in a well-defined struggle of some sort. Rarely does the writer follow the precise sequence of events as they occur in actual life. Thus not until almost the end of the story does Poe tell of Montresor's having prepared the niche for Fortunato. More often, by means of his plot, the author selects and arranges real and fictitious incidents in such a way as to produce the impression desired and lead to an effective ending. A skillfully devised plot should prepare the reader for the outcome, but should not foreshadow its exact nature too plainly.

298. Dominant incident. By dominant incident is meant the main action that constitutes the story, as contrasted with any minor incidents that may be brought in as a means of making the story more vivid and natural. In "The Cask of Amontillado" the dominant incident is the action of Montresor in avenging himself on Fortunato for the insult. The brief compass of

[1] C. R. Barrett, Short Story Writing. Used by permission of Doubleday, Page and Company, publishers.

the short story restricts the writer to *one* main action or dominant incident. Every plot statement, such as that given in the preceding section, should indicate the dominant incident.

299. Characters. The characters are the persons in the story. Usually in the short story one person stands out more prominently than the rest. Indeed, some stories, such as Stevenson's "Markheim" and Jack London's "To Build a Fire," deal with but one principal character in some moment of great excitement, peril, or passion. The person who dominates the story and but for whom the action would not take place is the preeminent, or leading, character. In "The Cask of Amontillado" Montresor dominates the story. Frequently the title, as in "Markheim," "Tennessee's Partner," and "A New England Nun," indicates the most important character.

In most short stories there are, in addition to the preëminent character, other principal characters and usually a few necessary minor characters. In almost every story, as in "The Cask of Amontillado," at least two characters, representing the opposing forces, are necessary.

The persons in a short story may be characterized by two different methods. The *direct* method consists in allowing each person to characterize himself (1) by his actions, (2) by his speech and his manner of speaking, (3) by his thoughts and his emotions, and (4) by his reactions when he is associated with other persons. The *indirect* method includes the writer's (1) description of the person, (2) description of the setting or environment in which the person finds himself, (3) biographical details, and (4) analysis and explanation of character. Though the direct method is preferable in most short stories, both methods are often employed in the same story.

300. The complication and its resolution. In plot narrative the conflict of characters representing two opposing lines of action gives rise to a complication, or plot problem, to be solved in the course of the story. Something happens at the beginning of the story, or has previously happened, that brings about the conflict. This event is called the *complicating incident*. The writer, having shown us the complication and acquainted us with his plot problem, proceeds to develop the latter with proper suspense up to an effective climax, and then gives us the solution in the outcome of the struggle. In "The Cask of Amontillado" the insult suffered by Montresor is the complicating incident. The plot problem consists in enabling Montresor to avenge himself on Fortunato with impunity and to make himself felt as the avenger. The climax comes with Fortunato's final cry of terror and despair: "*For the love of God, Montresor!*" The outcome is given in the few remaining sentences of the story.

That portion of the action of a story that precedes the climax is called the *rising action*; that which follows it is termed the *falling action*. The outcome of the action is often called the *dénouement*.

301. Setting. To the five essentials that we have been discussing we should add *setting*. By *setting* is meant the scene of the action and the time of its occurrence. Both the place and the time should be appropriate to the action. Often writers find places so interesting in themselves that they write stories to present the peculiar quality or atmosphere of such places. Narratives of particular settings and environments are called *local color* stories. Many of the stories of such authors as G. W. Cable, who wrote of old New Orleans, or of Sarah Orne Jewett, who wrote of New England, are of this type. The experienced writer always tries to limit the setting of his story to one place as well as to a single occasion.

302. Point of view. If one of the characters tells the story, as in "The Cask of Amontillado," it is narrated from the first-person point of view. If a person outside the story is the narrator, as in "Tennessee's Partner" and "A Gala Dress," it is related from the third-person point of view. When the author tells not only what the characters did and said but what they thought and imagined as well, he adopts the omniscient point of view. Sometimes point of view is spoken of as the *angle of narration*.

303. Where to begin a short story. In general practice, writers of short stories begin as near the point of climax as possible. The nature of their story will lead them to adopt one of three orders of narration: (1) the chronological order, if it closely parallels the cause-and-effect order; (2) a modified chronological order, where the story opens in the midst of the action, as in "The Cask of Amontillado," with the necessary details of antecedent action supplied as the story progresses; and (3) the inverted order, as in detective stories, such as Poe's "The Gold-Bug" and "The Purloined Letter."

304. How to begin a short story. Since the writer must depend upon the opening of his story to induce people to read what follows, the beginning should receive special consideration. A good beginning must be clear and must interest the reader. In addition, it should be appropriate to the particular type of story that it introduces. A story presenting local color or some specific mood, such as Poe's "The Fall of the House of Usher," may begin with description of the setting and its effect on the narrator. A story emphasizing plot, such as "The Cask of Amontillado," may open with exposition. A story of character, such as "Tennessee's Partner," may begin with general narration leading up to the story proper. Other stories, such as Jack London's "Love of Life," may begin at once with vivid narration of the immediate action of the story. Often a beginning of this last type is rendered more attractive and concise by the use of conversation, as in such stories as "A Gala Dress," Stevenson's "Markheim," and Kipling's "Without Benefit of

STROLLING PLAYERS

© M. G. Abbey. From a Copley Print, © Curtis and Cameron

Clergy." As near the beginning as possible the writer should inform the reader where and when the action takes place, who the principal characters are, and in what unstable situation they find themselves. Brevity, directness, clearness, and attractiveness constitute the chief characteristics of a good beginning.

305. The title. If a person is to be induced to read even the beginning of a story, he must usually first have his interest aroused by the title. Brevity and attractiveness are the two primary qualities of a good title. Brevity demands that the title be either a single word or a short phrase, as "Markheim," "Ethan Brand," "The Piece of String," and "The Sire de Malétroit's Door." Attractiveness is attained by choosing a title that is suggestive and original, as "The Lady, or the Tiger?" "The Monkey's Paw," "A Lodging for the Night," and "Pigs is Pigs." Though a title often suggests the general character of the story, it should never reveal the outcome. Euphony, as in "Marjorie Daw," "The Luck of Roaring Camp," and "The Fall of the House of Usher," is a desirable quality in a title, though it is not so important as the other two qualities.

306. Aids in writing a short story. In addition to the elements and requirements of the short story thus far discussed, there are a few important aids that the writer employs to make his narrative more vivid and interesting.

Contrast. Characters that are unlike are individualized and better understood because of the contrast. Contrast in setting, too, as the gay street scene of the carnival and the somber gloom of the burial vaults in "The Cask of Amontillado," is also very effective in emphasizing both action and character.

Enveloping action. By *enveloping action* is meant the larger general action of which that of the story is a related incident or part, or against which the latter is placed for contrast or proper perspective. Life in a California mining camp in the days of forty-nine in "Tennessee's Partner," the carnival celebration in "The Cask of Amontillado," and life in Paris during the Hundred Years' War in "The Sire de Malétroit's Door" illustrate enveloping action. In serving as the background of action it often helps to contribute atmosphere to the story.

Suspense. Suspense is an invaluable aid in arousing and increasing the reader's interest as the story advances. Since the climax should come as near the end of the story as possible, the writer arranges his incidents in an ascending series of minor climaxes that result in rapid movement and a growing eagerness on the part of the reader to reach the turning-point, or main climax, of the action. Frequently the author inserts slight anticipatory hints that furnish the observant reader suggestive clues as to the turn that the action may take, as well as foreshadow its final outcome. The experienced writer is always careful not to tell too much by such hints, for suspense is destroyed the moment the reader feels certain of the exact nature of the outcome. In "The Cask of Amontillado" we find such anticipatory hints as Montresor's reply, "True—true," to Fortunato's statement "I shall not die of a cough"; the motto on the coat of arms of the Montresors; and the trowel which Montresor draws from under his roquelaure.

Dialogue. Dialogue contributes animation and variety to stories. It is, as we have noticed, one of the most natural and effective methods of characterization, but characters should be individualized by *what they say* as well as by *how they speak.* Care in the choice of synonyms of the verbs *said, asked,* and *replied* will aid the writer in suggesting a person's manner of speaking. In writing conversation the author must indicate the person who utters each speech, unless the identity is clearly implied. Besides characterizing, dialogue should be made to advance the action of the story. Conversation that does not serve one or both of these purposes, but is merely clever or attractive in itself, should be excluded.

307. Sources of short stories. In general, a writer seems to derive the working-suggestion for his story from one of four sources, the first three of which Stevenson enumerated and discussed.

1. "*You may take a plot and fit characters to it.*" Such stories as Poe's "The Gold-Bug" and "The Purloined Letter," Thomas Hardy's "The Three Strangers," Stevenson's "The Sire de Malétroit's Door," and Stockton's "The Lady, or the Tiger?" all seem to have had plot as their initial source.

2. "*You may take a character and choose incidents and situations to develop it.*" It seems probable that such stories as Bret Harte's "Tennessee's Partner," Mary E. Wilkins Freeman's "A Gala Dress," Henry James's "The Real Thing," and Stevenson's "Will o' the Mill" were developed from characters that the writers had known, though they adapted them freely to meet their artistic needs.

3. "*You may take a certain atmosphere and get actions and persons to realize and express it.*" Poe's "The Fall of the House of Usher," Stevenson's "The Merry Men," and Joseph Conrad's "The Lagoon" may have been suggested by this source.

4. *You may take a theme or dominant idea and choose a situation, necessary characters, and an appropriate setting to present it.* Such stories as Hawthorne's "The Minister's Black Veil," "Ethan Brand," "The Birthmark," and "Doctor Heidegger's Experiment," Kipling's "Without Benefit of Clergy," Guy de Maupassant's "The Piece of String," and O. Henry's "An Unfinished Story" were probably written to present a theme effectively.

On the basis of their source or their prevailing element we may classify stories as (1) stories of plot, (2) stories of character, (3) stories of setting or atmosphere, and (4) stories of theme or idea.

EXERCISES

I

Study by means of the questions given in Appendix A two short stories that your teacher may assign.

II

Read ten or more short stories that your teacher may recommend,[1] and analyze them by means of the questions given in Appendix A.

[1] If a book of short stories is desired for class study, any of the collections mentioned below will provide useful material:

Short Stories Old and New. Edited by C. Alphonso Smith. Ginn and Company.

Short Stories for High Schools. Edited by Rosa M. R. Mikels. Charles Scribner's Sons.

Modern Short Stories. Edited by Frederick H. Law. The Century Co.

Types of the Short Story. Edited by B. A. Heydrick. Scott, Foresman and Company.

A Book of Short Stories. Edited by Stuart P. Sherman. Henry Holt and Company.

A Book of Short Stories. Edited by Blanche C. Williams. D. Appleton and Company.

Short Stories. Edited by Leonard B. Moulton. Houghton Mifflin Company.

Americans All. Edited by B. A. Heydrick. Harcourt, Brace and Company.

The Short-Story. Edited by W. P. Atkinson. Allyn and Bacon.

Short Stories of America. Edited by Robert L. Ramsay. Houghton Mifflin Company.

Representative Short Stories. Edited by Hart and Perry. The Macmillan Company.

Modern Short Stories. Edited by Margaret E. Ashmun. The Macmillan Company.

The Short-Story. Edited by Brander Matthews. American Book Company.

Elements of the Short Story. Edited by Hale and Dawson. Henry Holt and Company.

Atlantic Narratives, First and Second Series. Edited by Charles Swain Thomas. Atlantic Monthly Press.

Selected Stories from Kipling. Edited by William Lyon Phelps. Doubleday, Page and Company.

Selected Stories from O. Henry. Edited by C. Alphonso Smith. Doubleday, Page and Company.

III

Write one of the following stories:

1. Read carefully Irving's "Legend of Sleepy Hollow," and then tell the story from the point of view of Brom Bones, who has devised a scheme to get even with his rival, Ichabod Crane. Alter the present story as you see fit and add any necessary new material.

2. Tell the story contained in Hawthorne's "The Minister's Black Veil" from the point of view of Elizabeth. Will your story extend beyond the death of the minister? Can you use the same title?

3. Tell the story contained in Guy de Maupassant's "The Piece of String" from the point of view of M. Malandain, the harness-maker.

4. In Guy de Maupassant's "The Necklace," suppose that Madame Forestier lends Mathilde a necklace, which she has an accomplice steal from Mathilde and return to her, though she makes Mathilde believe that it is lost. Invent a motive for Madame Forestier's action, and tell the story from her point of view.

5. In Stockton's "The Lady, or the Tiger?" have the semibarbaric princess tell the story after her lover has opened one of the two doors. Add any other characters that you may need, and give the story a definite, logical outcome.

IV

Work out a plot and write a story suggested by one of the following situations:

1. A boy in his freshman year at college is invited by his wealthy aunt, whom he has never seen, to spend the week-end with her at her home in a neighboring city. A conflicting engagement causes him to persuade his roommate to impersonate him and go in his stead. Decide upon an appropriate outcome. Will the aunt discover the deception? If so, how? What will happen to the roommate? to the nephew?

2. A tall brick chimney stands alone in a large inclosure overgrown with weeds. The house was burned years ago, and an unsolved mystery surrounds the utter disappearance of the occupants. Why was the house burned? What became of the inmates? Why has another house not been erected on the spot? Can you solve the mystery?

3. A man who stammers tries to warn some tourists of danger ahead of them. They laugh at his comical efforts to speak, and drive on before he can deliver his warning. What happens?

4. A family is greatly embarrassed by the terms of a legacy bequeathed by an eccentric relative. What is the legacy? What was the relative's motive in bequeathing it on such unusual conditions? Will the family forfeit it, or will they find a way out of the difficulty?

5. Two burglars meet in a house that has been closed for the summer. Each tries to make the other believe that he is the owner. Will another character be needed? What will be the outcome?

6. A situation, plot, character, or setting suggested by your teacher.

V

Devise a story to illustrate one of the following themes:

1. Nothing venture, nothing have.
2. Ambition often overleaps itself.
3. Do people profit by experience?
4. Murder will out.
5. He who hesitates is lost.
6. Earth gets its price for what Earth gives us.
7. If you wish a secret kept, keep it.
8. Sudden wealth is a dangerous thing.
9. A guilty conscience needs no accuser.
10. It pays to advertise.
11. It is an ill wind that blows no one good.
12. The best-laid schemes o' mice an' men
      Gang aft a-gley.

VI

Study the two pictures of Flotsam Castle (facing page 296). The house is built on a rocky seacoast. Who are the people in the lower picture? What could happen to them that would result in material for a short story? Would other characters be needed? What would be the outcome of the action of the story? Write the story if you can.

VII

Write a short story suggested by any other picture in this book.

308. Summary. A short story is a brief, complex narrative composed of a series of causally related incidents skillfully arranged by means of a plot to present effectively a struggle and its outcome. In length a short story may range from 2000 to 20,000 words, though the average story rarely exceeds 7500 words. The characters are few—seldom more than six. The time covered by the action is generally short.

The five essentials of a short story are (1) singleness of impression, (2) well-defined plot, (3) a dominant incident, (4) a preëminent character, and (5) a complication and its resolution.

The plot of a short story is the plan by means of which the writer arranges the incidents in the most effective order to produce the single impression that he intends the story to make on the reader.

The persons of a story may be characterized (1) directly by their actions, speech, manner of speaking, thoughts, and reactions when associated with other persons; and (2) indirectly by the author's description of them and of their environment, by his account of their lives, and by his analysis of their character. Contrast between the persons of a story is often an effective means of characterization.

Each short story presents the development and the solution of a plot problem which comes into existence as the result of a complicating incident that initiates the struggle. The action which precedes the climax is called the *rising action*; that which follows the climax is termed the *falling action*. The final outcome of the action of the story is called the *dénouement*.

The setting of a short story should be limited, if possible, to one time and place. Stories that emphasize particular place settings and environments are called *local color* stories.

Short stories may be narrated from either the first-person or the third-person point of view, according to the nature of the story and the judgment of the writer.

The beginning of a short story should be brief, direct, clear, and attractive.

A short story should begin as near the point of climax as possible.

A short story may begin with description, exposition, general narration, vivid narration of action, or dialogue. Whatever the beginning may be, it must be clear and must interest the reader.

The title of a short story should be brief and attractive.

Four valuable aids in writing the short story are (1) contrast in characters and in setting; (2) an enveloping action to furnish background and proper perspective for the immediate action of the story; (3) suspense as a means of arousing the reader's interest; and (4) dialogue, to add life and variety to the story and to aid in characterization.

On the basis of their source or their dominant element short stories may be classified as (1) stories of plot; (2) stories of character; (3) stories of setting or atmosphere; and (4) stories of theme or idea.

PART FOUR

CHAPTER XXI

A REVIEW OF GRAMMAR

309. Purpose of this chapter. The present chapter is not intended to take the place of a textbook in English grammar.[1] It contains merely a brief grammatical review, which is designed to supplement Chapter VIII, "The Sentence Grammatically Considered," and Chapter XI, "Special Cautions in Grammar and Sentence Structure."

I. THE PARTS OF SPEECH

310. Definition and enumeration. Words, according to the office they perform in the sentence, are divided into the following eight classes, which are called the *parts of speech*: nouns, pronouns, adjectives, adverbs, verbs, prepositions, conjunctions, and interjections.

A. *Nouns*

311. Kinds of nouns. A noun is the name of a person, place, or thing. Nouns may be divided into two great classes: proper nouns and common nouns.

1. A *proper* noun is the name of a particular individual of a class.

Marjorie, Los Angeles, Sunday, Easter, France

---

[1] Kittredge and Farley's "Concise English Grammar" or "Advanced English Grammar," published by Ginn and Company, may be used if a more detailed treatment of grammar is desired.

2. A *common* noun is a name applicable alike to a class and to each individual of the class.

girl, city, day, holiday, country

Common nouns include three special classes of nouns: collective nouns, abstract nouns, and verbal nouns.

a. A *collective* noun is the name of a collection or group of persons or things.

family, army, school, class, audience, flock, herd

b. An *abstract* noun is the name of a quality, an attribute, or a general idea.

beauty, neatness, elegance, eternity, patience, health

c. A *verbal* noun is the name of an action (see *Verbals,* p. 477).

312. Properties of nouns. The three properties of nouns are gender, number, and case. The inflection of a noun is called its *declension.*

Gender. Gender is the quality of nouns and pronouns which distinguishes sex. There are three genders: masculine, feminine, and neuter. Nouns such as *child, bird, cat,* which may be used to denote members of either sex, are of *common* gender.

The gender of masculine and feminine nouns may be shown in the following ways:

1. By the use of different words.

husband	wife	salesman	saleswoman
king	queen	manservant	maidservant

2. By the addition of an ending to the masculine, sometimes to the feminine, form.

hero	heroine	bride	bridegroom
actor	actress	widow	widower

Number. Number is the inflectional change of a substantive to show whether it indicates one person, place, or thing or more than one. A noun is in the *singular* number when it denotes one person, place, or thing, and in the *plural* when it denotes more than one.

The plural number of nouns may be formed in the following ways:

1. Most nouns form their plural regularly by adding *s* or *es* to the singular.

boy, boys   hero, heroes   piano, pianos   church, churches

2. Many nouns form their plural by change of vowel within the word.

man, men   foot, feet   goose, geese   mouse, mice

3. A few nouns form their plural in *en*.

ox, oxen   child, children

4. Most nouns ending in *f* or *fe* form their plural by changing the *f* to *v* and adding *es* or *s*.

leaf, leaves   wolf, wolves   wife, wives

5. Common nouns ending in *y* preceded by a consonant change the *y* to *i* and add *es*.

sky, skies   army, armies   lady, ladies

NOTE. If the final *y* is preceded by a vowel, the plural is formed regularly, as indicated in rule 1: *alley, alleys; way, ways; alloy, alloys.*

6. Many nouns adopted from foreign languages have retained their original plural form, though several have acquired English plurals.

datum, data   radius, radii   crisis, crises
beau, beaux *or* beaus   formula, formulæ *or* formulas

7. Letters, figures, signs, and words regarded merely as words form their plural by adding *'s*.

> Your *u's* resemble your *n's*.
> Your *and's* and *but's* are too numerous.

8. Compound nouns usually form their plural by pluralizing the principal word, though there are exceptions to this rule.

> son-in-law, sons-in-law   maidservant, maidservants

NOTE. Such words as *cupful, spoonful,* and *armful* are regarded as simple nouns and add the *s* at the end of the word.

9. Proper nouns usually form their plural by adding *s* or *es*.

> The Johns and Marys in the class are all present.
> The Misses Brown are visiting the Thomases.

NOTE. Usage favors the addition of the plural sign to the title, but the addition of the plural sign to the name is permissible in some cases.

> the Misses Lathrop (Reputable usage)
> the Miss Lathrops (Permissible usage)

10. A few nouns have the same form in both numbers.

> deer, sheep, trout, cannon

Case. Case is the inflectional change of a substantive to indicate the grammatical relations of the substantive to verbs, prepositions, or other substantives. There are three cases in the English language: nominative, possessive (or genitive), and objective (dative or accusative). Nouns have the same form in the nominative and objective cases. In nouns the possessive case alone is inflected.

The following rules govern the formation of the possessive case of nouns:

1. The possessive case singular of most nouns is formed by adding *'s*.

the boy's cap, the bird's wing, Burns's poems, Mr. Fox's last story

NOTE. Nouns of more than one syllable ending in *s* or an *s*-sound and not accented on the last syllable may form their possessive singular by adding *'s* or by the use of the apostrophe alone.

Dickens's (*or* Dickens') novels, conscience' sake

2. The possessive case plural of most nouns ending in *s* is formed by placing an apostrophe after the *s*.

girls' sweaters, the cooks' union, the boys' study hall

NOTE. If the plural of a noun does not end in *s*, the possessive plural is formed by adding *'s*.

men's gloves, sheep's wool, children's games

3. The possessive case of compound nouns is formed by adding the proper possessive sign to the last word only.

my sister-in-law's home, the Adjutant General's opinion

NOTE. The possessive case of a phrase or of a combination of names is formed according to the rule just stated.

the Queen of England's crown, Peter the Great's reign

If several nouns modify the same noun, the possessive sign is placed after the last noun only, if the possession is common.

Mary, John, and Blanche's mother

If the possession is individual, the possessive sign follows each noun.

Mary's, John's, and Blanche's mothers

313. Uses of nouns. In the nominative, possessive, and objective case, nouns have the following uses:

NOMINATIVE CASE

1. The *wind* blew the dust. (Subject of a finite verb)
2. You, *Helen*, may recite next. (Nominative of direct address)
3. Julia is my *cousin*. (Predicate nominative)
4. Poor *man*! A *fire*! a *fire*! (Nominative of exclamation)
5. Jack Groves, our *pitcher*, is ill. (In apposition)

POSSESSIVE CASE

My *father's* health is poor. (Modifier of a substantive)

OBJECTIVE CASE

1. He has painted his *house.* (Direct object of a verb)
2. I gave my *mother* a present. (Indirect object)
3. We elected Dan *captain.* (Predicate objective)
4. She laughed a scornful *laugh.* (Cognate object)
5. She sat in a *chair* by the *fire.* (Object of a preposition)
6. We walked a *mile.* (Adverbial objective)
7. I met my friend *Noyes* in the elevator. (In apposition)
8. They believed the *stranger* to be a detective. (Subject of an infinitive)

(See Noun Phrases, section 106; Noun clauses, section 110.)

314. Directions for parsing nouns. In parsing a noun classify it according to kind, tell its gender, number, and case, and state how it is used in the sentence.

B. *Pronouns*

315. Kinds of pronouns and their properties. A pronoun is a word that is used instead of a noun. The substantive for which a pronoun stands is called the *antecedent* of the pronoun.

Pronouns are of four kinds: (1) personal pronouns, (2) adjective pronouns, (3) relative pronouns, and (4) interrogative pronouns.

The properties of pronouns are person, number, gender, and case. The inflection of a pronoun is called its *declension.*

1. *Personal pronouns.* A personal pronoun is one which shows by its form whether it represents the person speaking, the person spoken to, or the person, place, or thing spoken of. This distinction in form is called *person.* Pronouns are said to be of the first, the second, and the third person.

The pronoun of the first person (*I*) is declined as follows:

SINGULAR		PLURAL	
Nominative	I	*Nominative*	we
Possessive	my *or* mine	*Possessive*	our *or* ours
Objective	me	*Objective*	us

The pronoun of the second person (*you* or *thou*) is declined as follows:

SINGULAR			PLURAL	
Nominative	you	(thou)	*Nominative* you (ye)
Possessive	your *or* yours	(thy *or* thine)	*Possessive* your *or* yours
Objective	you	(thee)	*Objective* you (ye)

The pronoun of the third person (*he, she, it*) is declined as follows:

	SINGULAR			PLURAL
	Masculine	*Feminine*	*Neuter*	*Masculine, Feminine, and Neuter*
Nominative	he	she	it	they
Possessive	his	her *or* hers	its	their *or* theirs
Objective	him	her	it	them

Thou, thy, thine, thee, and *ye* are archaic forms used chiefly in poetry and in solemn discourse.

The compound personal pronouns are *myself, yourself, thyself, himself, herself, itself, ourselves, yourselves*, and *themselves*. The compound indefinite **oneself** (or *one's self*) may also be included.

2. *Adjective pronouns*. An adjective pronoun is one that may be used as either a pronoun or an adjective. Adjective pronouns include (1) demonstrative pronouns and (2) indefinite pronouns.

The *demonstrative* pronouns *this* and *that* (plural *these* and *those*) direct special attention to particular persons, places, or things. They may be used either as adjectives or as pronouns.

AS ADJECTIVES	AS PRONOUNS
This book is a novel.	*This* is a novel.
I saw *that* man yesterday.	Who is *that* coming yonder?
I like *these* chocolates.	*These* are fine autumn days.
Those people are tourists.	You will like *those*.

Demonstrative pronouns are inflected for number only.

The *indefinite* pronouns direct attention to persons, places, or things less clearly or definitely than do demonstrative pronouns. The indefinite pronouns include such words as the following: *any, both, each, either, neither, every, each other, another, one another, one, none, such, some.*

None and *one* (except in its use as a numeral adjective) are used only as substantives, and *every* is used only as an adjective. *Each other* and *one another* are compound pronouns. The remaining indefinites may be used as pronouns or as adjectives.

Such words as *all, few, many, several,* which may be used either as pronouns or as adjectives, are often classed as indefinites.

Such words as *anybody, anything, everybody, everything, aught, naught, somewhat, anyone, each one, everyone, someone, no one,* are often classed as indefinite nouns.

None of the indefinites, when used as adjectives, are inflected.

The following indefinites, when used as pronouns, have partial inflection: *one, one's, the ones*; *another, another's*; *other, other's, others', the others*; *each other, each other's*; *one another, one another's.*

3. *Relative pronouns.* A relative pronoun introduces a clause, and not only refers to some noun or pronoun as its antecedent but also connects the clause in which it stands with that antecedent.

> This is a book *that* I can recommend.
> She is the woman *whom* you saw this morning.

The simple relative pronouns are *who, which, that, as, what* (=*that which*), and *but* (=*that not*). Only *who* and *which* have inflectional forms, and these are alike for the singular and the plural.

Nominative	who	which
Possessive	whose	whose
Objective	whom	which

In *that which*, the equivalent of the relative pronoun *what*, *that* is regarded as the antecedent and *which* is the relative. *What* should always be resolved into its component parts before it is parsed.

The compound relative pronouns are made by adding the words *ever* and *soever* to the simple relatives *who, which*, and *what* and their inflected forms.

4. *Interrogative pronouns.* The interrogative pronouns (*who which*, and *what*) are used in asking questions.

Who and *which* the interrogatives have the same inflection as *who* and *which* the relatives. *What* has no inflection.

Who is either masculine or feminine. *Which* and *what* are of all three genders.

Which and *what* are frequently used as interrogative adjectives.

> *Which* seat do you prefer?
> *What* play did you see last night?

What is often used as an adjective to introduce an exclamatory sentence. It may also serve as an interjection.

> *What* a fine day this is!
> *What!* Has the man lost his reason?

316. Uses of pronouns. In general, pronouns may be used in all the constructions in which nouns are used, except as a cognate object, a predicate objective, and an adverbial objective.

The following uses of personal pronouns should be noted:

The possessive forms *my*, *our*, *your*, *her*, and *their* are used as adjectives followed by a noun. The forms *ours*, *yours*, *hers*, and *theirs* are used as possessive pronouns and cannot be followed by a noun. *His* may be used either as an adjective or as a pronoun.

It often stands in the place of the subject of a verb which has for its real subject a word, phrase, or clause coming later in the sentence. In this use *it* is called an *expletive*.

It is difficult to understand his conduct (To understand his conduct is difficult).

It may also be used impersonally, without an antecedent.

It rains. *It* is ten o'clock.

The compound personal pronouns may be used (1) emphatically and (2) reflexively.

We *ourselves* heard him speak. (Emphatically)
He hurt *himself*. (Reflexively)

The uses of indefinite, relative, and interrogative pronouns have been adequately explained in section 315.

317. Directions for parsing pronouns. To parse a pronoun classify it according to kind, point out its antecedent if it is a personal or a relative pronoun, state the person, number, and gender, and tell how the pronoun is used in the sentence.

C. *Adjectives*

318. Kinds of adjectives. An adjective is a word used to modify a substantive, which it describes or limits.

Adjectives are of two principal kinds: (1) descriptive adjectives and (2) limiting adjectives.

1. *Descriptive adjectives*. Descriptive adjectives, which constitute much the larger class, are either proper or common.

A *proper* adjective may be either a proper noun used as an adjective or an adjective derived from a proper noun.

an *Edison* phonograph, an *English* poet, the *American* eagle

All descriptive adjectives that are not proper adjectives are classed as *common*.

a *bright* day, a *purple* flower, a *dusty* road

Most participles may be used as common adjectives.

a *deserted* house, a *moving* train, the *rising* sun

2. *Limiting adjectives*. Limiting adjectives may be divided into three classes: (1) pronominal adjectives, (2) numerals, and (3) articles.

a. Pronominal adjectives are pronouns used as adjectives. They include the following:

(1) *Possessives*; as, *my, your, thy, his, her, its, our, their*.

(2) *Demonstratives*; as, *this, these, that, those*.

(3) *Indefinites*; as, *any, every, each, some, such*.

(4) *Relatives*; as, *which, whose, what*.

(5) *Interrogatives*; as, *which, whose, what*.

b. An adjective designating number is called a *numeral* adjective. Numeral adjectives are of two classes:

(1) *Cardinal* numerals (*one, two, three,* etc.) answer the question How many?

(2) *Ordinal* numerals (*first, second, third,* etc.) indicate order or position in a series.

c. The *articles* are *a* (or *an*) and *the. An* is generally used before words beginning with a vowel or silent *h*, and *a* is used before other words.

I have eaten *an* apple. He is *an* honorable man. He is *a* doctor.

319. Comparison of adjectives. The inflection of an adjective is called its *comparison*. There are three degrees of comparison; namely, the positive, the comparative, and the superlative.

The *positive* degree merely names the quality without **expressing** or implying any comparison.

> My brother is *tall*.

The *comparative* degree indicates that the quality named exists in the object described in a higher degree than it does in some other object.

> My brother is *taller* than my father.

The *superlative* degree indicates that the quality named is possessed in the highest degree by the object described.

> My brother is the *tallest* member of my family.

Adjectives are compared in the following ways:

1. Many adjectives are compared by adding to the positive degree the terminations *er* to form the comparative and *est* to form the superlative.

> cold colder coldest   happy happier happiest

2. Many other adjectives are compared by prefixing the adverbs *more* and *most* to the positive degree.

> gracious   more gracious   most gracious

3. Several adjectives are irregularly compared.

POSITIVE	COMPARATIVE	SUPERLATIVE
good, well	better	best
bad, evil, ill	worse	worst
little	less	least
much, many	more	most
near, nigh	nearer	nearest, next
old	older, elder	oldest, eldest
far	farther	farthest
———	further	furthest
late	later, latter	latest, last

4. A few superlatives end in *most*. Often the positive or the comparative degree is lacking.

hind	hinder	hindmost
top	——	topmost
——	nether	nethermost

In general, only descriptive adjectives have comparison. (For the use of the comparative and superlative degrees of adjectives see section 151.)

320. Uses of adjectives. According to their position in the sentence, adjectives may be classified as attributive, appositive, and predicate adjectives.

An *attributive* adjective uniformly precedes its noun.

> The *blind* beggar had a *white* beard.

An *appositive* adjective follows its noun and, like an appositive noun, is usually set off by commas.

> A beggar, *blind* and *old*, sat on the curb.

A *predicate* adjective completes the meaning of the predicate verb and modifies the subject (see section 152).

> The beggar was *blind* and *old*.

An adjective standing in the predicate and completing the meaning of verbs of *making, believing, calling*, and *thinking* serves as a predicate objective (see section 152).

> I think him *rude*. I call his conduct *insulting*.

(See Adjective Phrases, section 106; Adjective clauses, section 111.)

321. Directions for parsing adjectives. To parse an adjective, state whether it is descriptive or limiting, tell its degree of comparison, point out the substantive to which it belongs, and explain whether it modifies the substantive attributively, appositively, or predicatively.

D. *Adverbs*

322. Kinds of adverbs. An adverb is a word which modifies a verb, an adjective, or another adverb.

Adverbs may be classified as (1) simple adverbs, (2) interrogative adverbs, and (3) relative, or conjunctive, adverbs.

1. *Simple adverbs.* According to its meaning, a simple adverb belongs to one of the following classes:

a. Adverbs of *place*; as, *here, there, forward, thence, thither.*

b. Adverbs of *time*; as, *then, now, soon, first, already.*

c. Adverbs of *manner*; as, *quickly, abruptly, eagerly, industriously.*

d. Adverbs of *degree*; as, *much, hardly, somewhat, entirely.*

A number of adverbs have the same form as adjectives.

> He came *early.*   We have traveled *far.*

There is often used unemphatically to introduce a sentence in which the subject follows the verb. In this use it is called an *expletive.*

> *There* were twenty people in the yacht.

The words *yes* and *no* are classified as adverbs.

2. *Interrogative adverbs.* An interrogative adverb is used to introduce a question. The six interrogative adverbs are *how, when, where, whence, why, whither.*

> *When* did you arrive?   *How* long shall you stay?

3. *Relative, or conjunctive, adverbs.* Relative, or conjunctive, adverbs are used to introduce dependent clauses. The chief relative adverbs are *how, when, where, whence, whither, while, why, as, after, until, till, before, since, whenever, wherever.*

> I know *where* he has gone. (Noun clause)
> The reason *why* he left is not known. (Adjective clause)
> He greeted me *as* I entered the room. (Adverbial clause)

323. Comparison of adverbs. The inflection of an adverb is called its *comparison*. Adverbs, like adjectives, have three degrees of comparison; namely, the positive, the comparative, and the superlative. Adverbs are compared in the following ways:

1. Most adverbs are compared by means of *more* and *most*.

slowly more slowly most slowly

2. Several adverbs are compared by means of the endings *er* and *est*.

fast faster fastest early earlier earliest

3. A number of adverbs are irregularly compared.

POSITIVE	COMPARATIVE	SUPERLATIVE
far, forth	farther, further	farthest, furthest
ill, badly	worse	worst
much	more	most
little	less	least
well	better	best

(See Adverbial Phrases, section 106; Adverbial clauses, section 112. See also section 152.)

324. Directions for parsing adverbs. To parse an adverb, state the class to which it belongs, tell whether it is an adverb of place, time, manner, or degree, and point out the verb, adjective, or adverb that it modifies. If it is a relative, or conjunctive, adverb, state what clauses it connects.

E. *Verbs*

325. Kinds of verbs. A verb is a word or a group of words that asserts action, being, or state.

The rain *falls*. God *is*. The house *stands* vacant.

A group of words that is used as a verb is called a *verb phrase*.

You *may go*. They *have gone*. We *should have been told*.

Certain verbs, when they help to form verb phrases, are called *auxiliary* verbs. The auxiliary verbs are *be* (in its various forms), *can, could, do, did, have, had, may, might, must, shall, should, will, would*.

The verb with which an auxiliary is used to form a verb phrase is called the *main* or *principal* verb.

Verbs are classified as either transitive or intransitive.

1. *Transitive verbs.* Verbs that are followed by a substantive designating the receiver of an action or the product of the action are called *transitive*.

A substantive that denotes the receiver or the product of the action and at the same time completes the meaning of the verb is called the *direct object*.

> The player *struck* the *ball*.   Helen *made* a *dress*.

A substantive that indicates the person for whom some action is performed is called the *indirect object*.

> We gave the *beggar* alms.   She painted *me* a picture.

Certain verbs of *making, naming, choosing, electing*, and *appointing* often take, in addition to the direct object, a second object. A substantive thus used to complete the meaning of the verb, and to denote the same person or thing as the direct object, is called a *predicate objective*, or an *adjunct accusative*.

> We chose John *president*.   They named the child *Ruth*.

2. *Intransitive verbs.* All verbs that are not transitive are called *intransitive*. An intransitive verb is not followed by a substantive denoting the receiver of the action or the product of the action, though it often requires a word or a group of words to complete its meaning.

> The judge *rose*.   The snow *falls*.   She *is* my *sister*.

Many transitive verbs may be used intransitively.

> The clock *struck*.   Helen *recited*.   The wind *blows*.

A verb that merely connects, or links, its subject with a substantive or an adjective in the predicate is called a *copulative* (or *linking*) verb. The substantive or adjective thus used to complete the meaning of the verb and to define or describe the subject is a *predicate nominative* or a *predicate adjective*.

That man *is* our *mayor*. The sailor *became* a *pirate*.

The principal copulative (or linking) verbs are *be* (in its various forms), *seem, become, appear, prove, look, taste, sound, smell, feel, grow, turn, stand, remain*.

326. Conjugation of verbs. The inflection of a verb is called its *conjugation*. Verbs are conjugated to show differences in *person, number, tense,* and *mood*. By means of verb phrases distinction of voice is indicated.

Person and number. Verbs, like substantives, have inflectional changes to show whether the speaker, the person spoken to, or the person spoken of is meant.

Furthermore, verbs, like substantives, have inflectional changes to indicate whether the speaker or writer means to designate one person, place, or thing or more than one.

The small number of inflectional forms by means of which verbs may indicate person and number makes it necessary, as a rule, to determine their person and number by noting the person and number of the subject.

I come. You come. We come. They come.

Tense. The inflectional change of a verb to indicate present, past, or future time is called *tense*. The six tenses are classified as (1) primary tenses and (2) secondary tenses.

1. *Primary tenses.* There are in English three primary tenses; namely, the present, the past, and the future.

a. The *present* tense represents an action that occurs, or a condition that exists, at the present time.

I *go*. She *sings*. He *turns* pale.

b. The *past* tense represents an action that occurred, or a condition that existed, at some past time.

I *went.* She *sang.* He *turned* pale.

c. The *future* tense represents an action that will occur, or a condition that will exist, at some future time. The auxiliaries of the future tense are *shall* and *will*.

I *shall go.* She *will sing.* He *will turn* pale.

(For an explanation of the uses of *shall* and *will* see section 156.)

2. *Secondary tenses.* There are in English three secondary tenses; namely, the perfect (or present perfect), the past perfect (or pluperfect), and the future perfect. These are sometimes called the *complete* or *compound* tenses.

a. The *perfect* tense represents an action that is complete, or a condition that has already come to pass, at the time of speaking. The auxiliary of the perfect tense is *have* in the present tense.

I *have gone.* She *has sung.* He *has turned* pale.

b. The *past-perfect* tense represents an action that was completed, or a condition that had come to pass, at some point in past time. The auxiliary of the past-perfect tense is *have* in the past tense.

I *had gone.* She *had sung.* He *had turned* pale.

c. The *future-perfect* tense represents an action that will be completed, or a condition that will have come to pass, at some point in future time. It is formed by prefixing the future tense of *have* (*shall have,* etc.) to the past participle.

I *shall have gone.* She *will have sung.* He *will have turned* pale.

Other verb phrases. In addition to the verb phrases formed in the future, the perfect, the past-perfect, and the future-perfect tenses, there are other verb phrases that are made by using certain auxiliary verbs with the infinitives or participles of the main verb.

1. *Conditional* verb phrases are formed by the use of *should* and *would* as auxiliaries.

> I *should accompany* you if I had time.

2. *Potential* verb phrases are formed by the use of *may* and *might, can* and *could,* as auxiliaries.

> I *may leave* soon. He *can speak* French. They *might return.*

3. *Obligative* verb phrases are formed by the use of *must* and *ought* as auxiliaries.

> We *must work.* You *ought to have listened* closely.

4. *Emphatic* verb phrases are formed in the present tense and the past tense by the use of *do* and *did* as auxiliaries.

> I *do know* it is true. He *did eat.*

Progressive forms. In addition to the common forms already enumerated, progressive forms for all tenses of the verb in the active voice and for the present and past tenses in the passive voice may be made by using as auxiliaries the various forms of the verb *be* with the present participle.

I *am giving*	I *have been giving*
I *was giving*	I *had been giving*
I *shall be giving*	I *shall have been giving*
I *am being given*	I *was being given*

Mood. Mood is the inflectional change of a verb to indicate the manner in which an action or a state is expressed. There are three principal moods; namely, the indicative, the imperative, and the subjunctive.

1. The *indicative* mood is used chiefly in statements of fact and in questions.

> I *enjoy* traveling. *Have* you *found* your book?

2. The *imperative* mood is used in commands and requests.

> *Come* home at nine o'clock.   *Help* us win the fight.

3. The *subjunctive* mood, though many of its functions have been usurped by the indicative mood, is still used in English in the following constructions:

a. To express a wish.

> The Lord *prosper* your undertaking.

b. To express a condition.

> If he *be* at home, give him this letter.
> If I *were* at home, I should be happy.

c. To express concession not as a fact but as supposition.

> Though he *implore* me, yet will I refuse him.

d. To express what would be or would have been the case instead of what is or was the case.

> It *were* better not to yield the point.
> You *had been* successful had you studied harder.

e. To express an exhortation.

> "Now *tread* we a measure," said young Lochinvar.
> Somebody *lend* a hand.

f. To express a command in the third person.

> Everybody *report* at the office before five o'clock.

(For the various mood forms see the synopses given on pages 478–483.)

Voice. Voice is that distinction in verbs which shows whether the subject acts or is acted upon. There are two voices; namely, the active and the passive. The *active* voice designates the subject as acting, whereas the *passive* voice indicates that the subject is acted upon.

> The pitcher *threw* the ball.   (Active voice)
> The ball *was thrown* by the pitcher.   (Passive voice)

© Fraser

THE END OF THE TRAIL

The verb phrases that constitute the passive voice are made by using various forms of the verb *be* with the past (passive) participle. (For the various passive verb phrases see the synopses given on pages 482–483.)

Verbals. Verbals are forms of the verb that do not have inflection for person and number. They include infinitives, participles, and gerunds (or verbal nouns in *ing*).

The *infinitive* is a form of the verb that may perform, in addition to its office as a verb, the function of a noun.

> *To deceive* him was not my intention.

The infinitive has two tenses; namely, the present and the perfect.

> to deceive, to have deceived (Active voice)
> to be deceived, to have been deceived (Passive voice)

The *participle* is a form of the verb which may perform, in addition to its office as a verb, the function of an adjective.

> The *rising* sun dispelled the fog. *Overpowered*, he yielded.

There are three participles; namely, the present, the past, and the perfect.

> deceiving, ——, having deceived (Active voice)
> being deceived, deceived, having been deceived (Passive voice)

The *gerund* is a verbal noun in *ing*. Like a verb, it may take an object or be modified by an adverb. It may also serve as a noun and be modified by an adjective.

> *Growing* tulips is his avocation. (Followed by a direct object)
> *Driving* recklessly cost him his life. (Modified by an adverb)
> Reckless *driving* cost him his life. (Modified by an adjective)

(For an explanation of the principal parts of a verb and for a list of verbs with their principal parts see section 154.)

Regular and irregular conjugations. Verbs are divided into two great classes according to the manner in which they form their past tense and past participle.

If a verb forms its past tense and past participle by adding *ed*, *d*, or *t* to the present, it is called a *regular* verb, because it belongs to the *regular conjugation* (also called the *new* or *weak* conjugation).

play, played, played ; trade, traded, traded ; mean, meant, meant

If a verb forms its past tense and past participle in any other way, it is called an *irregular* verb, because it belongs to the *irregular conjugation* (also called the *old* or *strong* conjugation).

run, ran, run ; speak, spoke, spoken ; swim, swam, swum

Below are given synopses of the verbs *be, have,* and *give,* illustrating the conjugation of irregular verbs. From these the conjugation of regular verbs will be apparent.

I. IRREGULAR CONJUGATION

Synopses of the Verbs *Be* and *Have*

Principal Parts: *be, was, been; have, had, had*

INDICATIVE MOOD

Present Tense

Singular	*Plural*	*Singular*	*Plural*
I am	We are	I have	We have
Thou art	You are	Thou hast	You have
He is	They are	He has	They have

Past Tense

I was	We were	I had	We had
Thou wast	You were	Thou hadst	You had
He was	They were	He had	They had

FUTURE TENSE

Singular	*Plural*	*Singular*	*Plural*
I shall be	We shall be	I shall have	We shall have
Thou wilt be	You will be	Thou wilt have	You will have
He will be	They will be	He will have	They will have

PERFECT TENSE

I have been, etc.   I have had, etc.

PAST-PERFECT TENSE

I had been, etc.   I had had, etc.

FUTURE-PERFECT TENSE

I shall have been, etc.   I shall have had, etc.

SUBJUNCTIVE MOOD

PRESENT TENSE

(If) I be	(If) we be	(If) I have	(If) we have
(If) thou be	(If) you be	(If) thou have	(If) you have
(If) he be	(If) they be	(If) he have	(If) they have

PAST TENSE

(If) I were	(If) we were	(If) I had	(If) we had
(If) thou wert	(If) you were	(If) thou had	(If) you had
(If) he were	(If) they were	(If) he had	(If) they had

PERFECT TENSE

(If) I have been, etc.   (If) I have had, etc.

PAST-PERFECT TENSE

(If) I had been, etc.   (If) I had had, etc.

IMPERATIVE MOOD

be (thou, you, *or* ye)   have (thou, you, *or* ye)

PRESENT INFINITIVE

to be   to have

PERFECT INFINITIVE

to have been   to have had

GERUND

being   having

PRESENT PARTICIPLE

being   having

PAST PARTICIPLE

been   had

PERFECT PARTICIPLE

having been   having had

SYNOPSIS OF THE VERB *GIVE*

PRINCIPAL PARTS : *give, gave, given*

ACTIVE VOICE

Common Form   *Progressive Form*

INDICATIVE MOOD

PRESENT TENSE

I give, etc.   I am giving, etc.

Past Tense

I gave, etc.   I was giving, etc.

Future Tense

I shall give, etc.   I shall be giving, etc.

Perfect Tense

I have given, etc.   I have been giving, etc.

Past-Perfect Tense

I had given, etc.   I had been giving, etc.

Future-Perfect Tense

I shall have given, etc.   I shall have been giving, etc.

SUBJUNCTIVE MOOD

Present Tense

(If) I give, etc.   (If) I be giving, etc.

Past Tense

(If) I gave, etc.   (If) I were giving, etc.

Perfect Tense

(If) I have given, etc.   (If) I have been giving, etc.

Past-Perfect Tense

(If) I had given, etc.   (If) I had been giving, etc.

IMPERATIVE MOOD

give   be giving

PRESENT INFINITIVE

to give   to be giving

PERFECT INFINITIVE

to have given   to have been giving

GERUND

giving

PRESENT PARTICIPLE

giving

PERFECT PARTICIPLE

having given   having been giving

PASSIVE VOICE

INDICATIVE MOOD

PRESENT TENSE

I am given, etc.   I am being given, etc.

PAST TENSE

I was given, etc.   I was being given, etc.

FUTURE TENSE

I shall be given, etc.

PERFECT TENSE

I have been given, etc.

PAST-PERFECT TENSE

I had been given, etc.

FUTURE-PERFECT TENSE

I shall have been given, etc.

PRESENT TENSE

(If) I be given, etc.

PERFECT TENSE

(If) I have been given, etc.

PAST TENSE

(If) I were given, etc.

PAST-PERFECT TENSE

(If) I had been given, etc.

IMPERATIVE MOOD: be given.

INFINITIVE : *Present*, to be given ; *Perfect*, to have been given.

PARTICIPLES : *Present*, being given ; *Past*, given ; *Perfect*, having been given.

327. Directions for parsing verbs. To parse a verb tell its kind (transitive or intransitive), name its conjugation (regular or irregular), give its principal parts, state its person, number, tense, mood, and voice, and explain its agreement with the subject.

To parse an infinitive, a participle, or a gerund tell from what verb it comes, state its voice and tense, and explain how it is used in the sentence.

F. *Prepositions*

328. Kinds of prepositions. A preposition is a word that is placed before a substantive to show its relation to some other word in the sentence. The substantive before which the preposition is placed is called its object and is in the objective case.

A prepositional phrase consists of a preposition and its object. Such a phrase may be used either as an adjective or as an adverb. (See section 106.)

Prepositions, which include a small group of about a hundred words, may be classified as (1) simple and (2) compound.

1. *Simple prepositions*. The principal simple prepositions are *at, by, but, in, of, for, on, to, up, with, down, near, off, since, from, ere, over, under, through, till, after.*

2. *Compound prepositions.* Among the more common compound, or derived, prepositions are *above, beyond, into, upon, about, across, against, around, before, below, beneath, among, between, during, beside, outside, inside, toward, towards, until, without, within, concerning, regarding, notwithstanding.*

There are also a number of phrases, such as *in spite of, with respect to, out of, as to, for the sake of, instead of, according to, in addition to, apart from, by means of,* which are usually classified as compound prepositions.

Prepositions have no inflection.

329. Directions for parsing prepositions. To parse a preposition, state its kind, tell what word it governs, and explain the relation that it shows between its object and some other word in the sentence.

G. *Conjunctions*

330. Kinds of conjunctions. A conjunction is a word that connects words or groups of words. Conjunctions are classified as (1) coördinate and (2) subordinate.

1. *Coördinate conjunctions.* A coördinate conjunction connects words, phrases, or clauses of equal rank. The principal coördinate conjunctions are *and, but, for, or, nor, then, yet, still, however, moreover, therefore, nevertheless, notwithstanding, either . . . or, neither . . . nor, both . . . and, not only . . . but also.*

2. *Subordinate conjunctions.* A subordinate conjunction connects a subordinate, or dependent, clause with the clause on which it depends. The principal subordinating conjunctions are *as, as if, because, although, though, if, than, lest, since* (= *because*), *unless, that, whereas, whether, but that, in order that, so that, provided that, in case that, even if, as though.*

(For relative, or conjunctive, adverbs see section 322.)

Conjunctions that are used in pairs are called *correlative* conjunctions. The following correlative conjunctions are co-ordinate: *both . . . and, either . . . or, neither . . . nor, not only . . . but also.* The following conjunctions are subordinate: *although . . . still, though . . . yet, if . . . then, since . . . therefore.*

Conjunctions have no inflection.

331. Directions for parsing conjunctions. To parse a conjunction, state its class (coördinate or subordinate) and point out the words, phrases, or clauses that it connects. If it is a conjunctive adverb, explain its use in the clause which it introduces.

H. *Interjections*

332. Nature and use of interjections. An interjection is a word or exclamatory sound used to express surprise, pleasure, sorrow, anger, pain, or some other emotion or feeling.

> oh, ah, alas, hush, fie, aha, hist, pshaw, bravo

Interjections, since they usually have no grammatical relation to the sentences in which they stand, are considered as independent elements. In parsing an interjection, therefore, it is sufficient to point it out and tell what feeling or emotion it expresses.

II. Sentence Analysis

333. Directions for analyzing sentences. The analysis of a sentence consists in separating it into its component parts and in explaining the construction of each of these parts.

The steps in the analysis of a sentence are as follows:

1. Tell whether the sentence is simple, compound, complex, or compound-complex.

2. Unless the sentence is simple, resolve it into its clauses and classify each clause as independent or dependent.

3. Divide the simple sentence or each independent clause into its complete subject and complete predicate.

4. Point out the unmodified subject and the unmodified predicate. (These form the base of the simple sentence or clause.)

5. Name all the modifiers of the subject, with their modifiers (if they have any).

6. Name all the modifiers and complements of the predicate, with their modifiers (if they have any).

7. Unless the sentence is simple, analyze each remaining clause according to steps 3, 4, 5, and 6, state the relation of each clause to the rest of the sentence, and indicate each connective.

8. Point out independent elements (if the sentence contains any).

CHAPTER XXII

SPELLING

334. Importance of learning to spell correctly. No person, regardless of the extent of his knowledge and the admirable qualities of his speech, is considered truly educated unless he spells correctly all the words that he uses. Though we may find it necessary throughout life to consult a dictionary now and then to verify our spelling of certain unusual words, we shall save ourselves much precious time and later embarrassment if, during our school days, we hold ourselves responsible for the correct spelling of all the words that we use. Such a habit early formed will be of inestimable value throughout life. Unfortunately no set of simple rules for spelling can be formulated. If, however, we make use of the rules and the suggestions given in this chapter as they apply to the various words we are called upon to spell, we shall find our difficulties decreasing. Frequent drill in the spelling of the words included in the lists that follow will greatly increase our efficiency. But never shall we be wholly independent of the dictionary.

RULES FOR SPELLING

Rule 1. Words of one syllable ending in a single consonant preceded by a single vowel double the final consonant before a suffix beginning with a vowel.

lag	lagged	lagging	laggard
stop	stopped	stopping	stopper
beg	begged	begging	beggar
sin	sinned	sinning	sinner

Rule 2. Words of more than one syllable, accented on the last syllable, ending in a single consonant preceded by a single vowel, double the final consonant before a suffix beginning with a vowel.

occur	occurred	occurring	occurrence
control	controlled	controlling	controller
remit	remitted	remitting	remittance
demur	demurred	demurring	demurrer
propel	propelled	propelling	propeller

Exception: unforgetable.

Words of more than one syllable, *not* accented on the last syllable, ending in a single consonant preceded by a single vowel, do *not* double the final consonant before a suffix beginning with a vowel.

profit	profited	profiting	profitable
marvel	marveled	marveling	marvelous
conquer	conquered	conquering	conqueror

A few words may be spelled according to either division of Rule 2.

travel	traveled	traveling	traveler
	travelled	travelling	traveller
worship	worshiped	worshiping	worshiper
	worshipped	worshipping	worshipper
revel	reveled	reveling	reveler
	revelled	revelling	reveller
kidnap	kidnaped	kidnaping	kidnaper
	kidnapped	kidnapping	kidnapper

Rule 3. Words ending in silent *e* drop the *e* before a suffix beginning with a vowel.

advise	advising	advisable
elevate	elevating	elevator
oppose	opposing	opposite
incline	inclining	inclination
secure	securing	security

NOTE I. Words ending in silent *e* following *c* or *g* retain the *e* before a suffix beginning with *a* or *o*, in order to preserve the soft sound of *c* and *g*.

change	changeable	notice	noticeable
manage	manageable	outrage	outrageous
damage	damageable	advantage	advantageous
peace	peaceable	umbrage	umbrageous
service	serviceable	courage	courageous

NOTE 2. Words ending in *ie* drop the *e* and change the *i* to *y* before a suffix beginning with *i*.

lie	lying	tie	tying
die	dying	vie	vying

NOTE 3. A few words retain the final *e* before the suffix *ing*.

dye	dyeing	singe	singeing
hoe	hoeing	tinge	tingeing
shoe	shoeing	toe	toeing

Rule 4. Words ending in silent *e* usually retain the *e* before a suffix beginning with a consonant.

arrange	arrangement	nine	ninety
divine	divinely	late	lateness
rue	rueful	safe	safety

Judgment and *acknowledgment* are preferably spelled without the final silent *e* of the primitive form.

NOTE. A few words drop the final *e* before a suffix beginning with a consonant.

argue	argument	due	duly
awe	awful	true	truly

Rule 5. In words containing *ei* or *ie* put *i* before *e* when the combination is pronounced as *ee*, except after *c*.

believe	reprieve	conceive	receipt
brief	yield	conceit	deceive
chief	grief	ceiling	deceit
niece	wield	receive	perceive

Exceptions: either, neither, leisure, species, weird, seized, plebeian.

NOTE. When the combination of the two vowels has the sound of long *a*, long *i*, or short *e* or *i*, *i* generally follows *e*.

neigh	weigh	veil	heifer
inveigh	freight	sleight	foreign
sleigh	neighbor	height	counterfeit

Exceptions: friend, sieve, ancient.

Rule 6. Words ending in *y* preceded by a consonant usually change *y* to *i* before a suffix.

busy	business	pity	pitiful
easy	easily	envy	enviable
harmony	harmonious	merry	merriment

NOTE. Final *y* is retained before the suffix *ing*.

worry	worrying	amplify	amplifying
pacify	pacifying	hurry	hurrying

Rule 7. The final letter of a word or prefix is generally retained before the same letter in the suffix or root.

legible	illegible	satisfied	dissatisfied
equal	equally	spent	misspent
prove	approve	sudden	suddenness

Rule 8. A word ending in *ll* generally drops one *l* when used as a prefix or suffix.

already	fulfill	almost
fearful	skillful	altogether

335. Helps in learning to spell. 1. Pronounce words accurately. Do not slur either internal vowels or consonants: *separate*, not *seperate*; *laboratory*, not *lab'ratory*; *government*, not *gover'ment*. Be sure that the word is properly accented.

2. In spelling derivative and compound words think of the root, or simplest form of the word, and the prefix or suffix (see section 337) : in spelling *separation* think of *separate*; in spelling *professor* think of *profess* and *or*; in spelling *government* think of *govern* and *ment*; in spelling *dissatisfied* think of *dis* and *satisfied*.

3. In the case of words that have slight resemblances either in appearance or in sound, think of what each word means. By this method you can distinguish such words as *dining* and *dinning*; *rain, reign,* and *rein*; *aisle* and *isle*.

4. In a notebook keep a list of the words that you misspell. Study the list at regular intervals until you have mastered each word. If a word is particularly difficult, write it several times, dividing it into syllables, and spell it aloud as you write it.

336. Syllabication. In both oral and written spelling we need an accurate knowledge of the syllabication of words. In dividing a word at the end of a line we should make the division between syllables, not elsewhere. A hyphen should be used to indicate the division. The rules given below we should observe in all our writing.

1. Never divide a word of one syllable.

2. In general, prefixes and suffixes should be treated as separate syllables.

de-fine   un-skill-ful   co-in-ci-dence   pre-em-i-nent

3. In words containing double consonants the syllabic division almost always comes between the consonants.

plan-ning   oc-cur   cool-ly   com-ma   clean-ness

NOTE. Derivative words containing a simple word ending in a double consonant are divided according to Rule 2 if the suffix begins with a vowel.

cross-ing   will-ing   pass-a-ble

4. Never divide two consonants which together constitute a single sound. Combinations of this kind are *gn, ng, gh, ch, rch, tch, th, ph.*

con-sign-ment   thith-er   haugh-ty   syc-o-phant

5. In writing do not separate a syllable of one or two letters from the remainder of the word.

337. Prefixes and suffixes. A knowledge of prefixes and suffixes, as well as familiarity with their meaning, we shall find helpful not only as an aid to correct spelling but often as a guide to the proper use of words.

The following list contains the principal prefixes used in the formation of derivative words:

a, ab (from, away) : avert, abnormal, absolve, abrupt

a, an (not, without) : anæmic, atonic, anæsthetic

ad (to), with its combining forms *ac, af, ag, al, an, ap, ar, as, at*: adhere, accede, affect, aggressive, alleviate, annex, appoint, array, assign, attract

ambi (around, both): ambient, ambiguous, ambidextrous

ante (before): antedate, antecedent, anteroom

anti (against, opposite): antidote, antagonist, antimacassar

auto (self) : automobile, automatic, autobiography

bene (well) : benefit, benefactor, benediction

bi, bis (two, twice) : biped, bigamy, biennial, biscuit

circum (around, about) : circumference, circumscribe

com, con, co, col, cor (together, with): compare, conference, convene, coöperate, collision, correspondent

contra (against, opposite): contradict, contraband

de (from, down, away): defend, dethrone, depose, deflect

dia (through): diameter, diagram, diagonal, dialogue

dis, dif, di (away, apart, not) : dismiss, discard, disobey, differ, difficult, digress, diminish

e, ex, ef (from, out, out of, off, beyond) : emit, emigrate, expel, expatriate, effeminate, efface

epi (on, in, besides) ; epitaph, epigram, epidemic, epilogue

eu (well) : eugenic, euphemism, euphony, eulogy

in, en (in, into, among) : inspire, inquest, entangle
in (not) : insincere, innocent, inorganic, inopportune
inter (between, among) : interrupt, intervene, intermittent
intro (within, against) : introspective, introduction
mono (single, one) : monarch, monopoly, monogamy, monoplane
non (not, without) : nonsense, nonresident, nonpartisan
ob (in the way of, against) : obviate, obstruct, obstinate
per (through, for, by) : perspire, perpetual, perennial
post (after) : postscript, postpone, posterior, post-mortem
pre (before) : prearrange, prelude, prefix, premeditated
pro (before, instead of) : proceed, prologue, pronoun
re (again, back) : report, retell, retract, reflect
retro (backward) : retrospective, retroactive, retrograde
se (aside, apart) : secede, seclude, separate, selective
sub (under, beneath) : subordinate, subscribe, substitute
super (above, over) : superlative, superannuate, superintend
syn (together with) : synonym, synopsis, syndicate, synod
tele (afar) : telephone, telegraph, telescope, telepathy
trans (across, beyond) : translate, transmit, transpose, transpire
tri (three, thrice) : triangle, tripod, trisect, triune
un, uni (one) : unanimous, unison, universe, unicorn
un (not) : unequal, unsafe, unfamiliar, unnecessary

The following list includes the principal suffixes used in the formation of derivative words:

able, ible (capable of being) : readable, discernible
ace, acy, ance, ancy (condition, state of being) : menace, illiteracy, disturbance, buoyancy, constancy
age (condition, state) : marriage, bondage, dotage
al, eal, ial (pertaining to) : dismissal, ethereal, cereal, filial, cordial, celestial
an, ean, ian (pertaining to, one who) : Alaskan, epicurean, physician, musician
ant (relation, quality) : servant, dependant, discordant
ar (pertaining to) : stellar, lunar, solar, vulgar
ary (pertaining to, one who, place where) obituary, secretary, dictionary
ate (state, condition, one who, to make) : fortunate, desolate, vindicate, facilitate, illuminate

ee (one who is) : employee, trustee, payee, patentee
eer (one who does) : auctioneer, engineer, profiteer
ence, ency (condition, state) : permanence, transparency
ent (condition, one who) : affluent, despondent, resident
fy, ify (to make) : terrify, pacify, simplify, rectify
hood (state, condition) : knighthood, manhood, falsehood
ic (made of, resembling) : plastic, tragic, anthropomorphic
ile (pertaining to) : senile, puerile, juvenile, servile
ion (state of being, act) : completion, expulsion, creation
ise, ize (to make) : familiarize, civilize, organize
ist, ite (one who) : artist, organist, suburbanite
ity, ty (state, quality) : vicinity, purity, veracity
ive (pertaining to) : creative, selective, administrative
less (without) : helpless, valueless, worthless
ment (state of being) : employment, encouragement, development
or, er (one who, that which) : sailor, employer, adviser, founder, binder
ory, ery (place where, pertaining to) : factory, reformatory, crematory, bindery, inquisitory, congratulatory
ose, ous (full of, abounding in) : verbose, otiose, jocose, plenteous, adventurous, courageous
some (full of) : quarrelsome, mettlesome, troublesome
tude, itude (quality of, condition) : gratitude, servitude, longitude, latitude
ure (act, condition) : procedure, tenure, indenture
ward (in the direction of) : windward, forward, westward, homeward
wright (maker of) : wheelwright, shipwright

338. Spelling-list. The following list contains the majority of words that give students trouble:

abbreviate	acquainted	alley	analogous
absence	acquitted	allotted	analysis
absurd	across	ally	anecdote
academy	addressed	already	annual
accept	adviser	altogether	antecedent
accidentally	aëroplane	alumnus	anxiety
accommodate	affects	always	apartment
accumulate	aggravate	amateur	apparatus
accustom	all right	among	appearance

appropriate
arctic
argument
arising
arithmetic
arrange
arrival
ascend
ascertain
asks
athletic
audience
auxiliary
awkward

balance
banana
baptize
barbarous
baring
barring
baseball
based
bearing
becoming
before
beggar
begging
beginning
believing
benefited
bicycle
biscuit
boundaries
brilliant
Britain
Britannica
buoyant
bureau

business
busy

calendar
candidate
can't
cemetery
certain
changeable
changing
characteristic
chauffeur
chiffonier
choose
chose
chosen
colloquial
column
coming
commission
committee
comparative
compel
compelled
competent
concede
conceivable
conferred
conquer
conqueror
conscience
conscientious
considered
continuous
control
controlled
coolly
coöperate
country

courteous
courtesy
cruelty
cylinder

daily
dealt
debater
deceitful
decide
decision
deferred
definite
derived
descend
describe
description
desirous
despair
desperate
destroy
dictionary
difference
digging
dilemma
dining-room
dinning
dirigible
disappear
disappoint
disavowal
discipline
disease
dissatisfied
dissipate
distinction
distribute
divide
divine

doctor
doesn't
don't
dormitories
drudgery
dying

ecstasy
effects
eighth
eliminate
elliptical
embarrass
emigrate
eminent
encouraging
enemy
equipped
erroneous
especially
etc.
everybody
exaggerate
exceed
excellent
except
exceptional
exhaust
exhilarate
existence
expense
experience
explanation

facilitate
familiar
fascinate
February
fiery

fifth
finally
financier
foreigner
forfeit
forty
frantically
fraternity
freshman
friend
furniture

gallant
gambling
generally
goddess
government
governor
grammar
grandeur
grievous
guard
guess
guidance

harass
haul
having
height
hesitancy
holloed
huge
humorous
hundredths
hurriedly
hygienic
hypocrisy

imaginary

imitative
immediately
immigration
imminent
imperative
impromptu
incidentally
incidents
incredulous
independence
indispensable
induce
infinite
influence
intellectual
intelligence
intentionally
intercede
invitation
irresistible
itself

judgment

knowledge

laboratory
ladies
laid
liable
library
lieutenant
lightning
likely
literature
loneliness
loosing
losing
lying

maintain
maintenance
manual
manufacturer
many
marriage
material
mathematics
mattress
meant
measles
messenger
mileage
miniature
minutes
mischievous
Mississippi
misspelled
momentous
month
mosquitoes
murmur
mysterious

necessary
negroes
neither
nickel
niece
nineteenth
ninetieth
ninth
noticeable
nowadays

oblige
obstacle
occasion
occasionally

occur
occurred
occurrence
occurring
o'clock
officers
omission
omitted
opinion
opponent
opportunity
optimistic
original
outrageous
overrun
owing

paid
pamphlet
pantomime
parallel
parliament
participial
particularly
partner
pastime
peaceable
perceive
perceptible
perception
peremptory
perform
perhaps
permissible
perseverance
perspiration
persuade
pertain
pervade

physical
picnic
picnicking
planned
pleasant
politician
politics
possession
possible
poultry
practically
prairie
precede
precedence
precedents
preference
preferred
prejudice
preparation
prevalent
primitive
principal
principle
prisoner
privilege
probably
procedure
proceed
prodigy
profession
professor
proffered
prohibition
promissory
prove
purchase
pursue
pursuit
putting

quantity
quizzes

rapid
ready
really
recede
receive
recognize
recommend
reference
referred
regard
region
religion
religious
repetition
replies
representative
reservoir
restaurant
rheumatism
rhythmic
ridiculous
righteous

sacrilegious
safety
sandwich
scarcely
schedule
science
scream
screech
seems
seize
sense
sentence
separate

sergeant
several
shiftless
shining
shriek
siege
similar
simultaneous
since
soliloquy
sophomore
speak
specimen
speech
statement
stopped
stopping
stops
stories
stretch
strictly
substantial
succeeds
successful
summarize
superintendent
supersede
sure
surprise
syllable
symmetrical

temperament
tendency
than
therefore
they're
thief
thorough

thousandths
till
together
track
tract
tragedy
tranquillity
transferred
translate
treacherous
treasurer
tries
trouble
truly
Tuesday
typical
tyranny

universally
until
using
usually

vacancy
vengeance
vigilance
vigor
village
villain
visible
volunteer

warring
weak
weather
weird
welfare
where
wherever

whether	wintry	world	yacht
which	wiry	wrath	yield
whole	within	wrist	
wholly	without	writing	zephyr
wield	women	written	zoölogy

EXERCISE

Go through the list of words slowly, noticing carefully the spelling of each word. Analyze each derivative word into its root and its prefix or suffix. Copy in your notebook all words that give you trouble. Study these words at frequent intervals until you have mastered them.

339. Words frequently confused. In addition to the list above, a brief supplementary list of words frequently confused is here given. Associate the spelling and the correct meaning of each word. Notice also the part of speech to which it belongs. Make free use of your dictionary in studying this list.

accept, except	Calvary, cavalry
access, excess	canvas, canvass
advice, advise	capital, capitol
affect, effect	censor, censure
all ready, already	chord, cord
all together, altogether	cite, sight, site
alley, ally	cloth, clothe, cloths, clothes
allude, elude	coarse, course
allusion, illusion	complement, compliment
altar, alter	confidant(e), confident
angel, angle	corps, corpse
ascent, assent	costume, custom
	council, counsel, consul
berth, birth	council(l)or, counsel(l)or
born, borne	
breadth, breath, breathe	dairy, diary
bridal, bridle	deceased, diseased
Britain, Briton	decent, descent, dissent

desert, dessert
device, devise
dew, due
dual, duel
dyeing, dying

elicit, illicit
emigrant, immigrant
emigrate, immigrate
envelop, envelope

fair, fare
finally, finely
formally, formerly
forth, fourth
freeze, frieze

hear, here
hoard, horde
holey, holly, holy, wholly
hoping, hopping
humerus, humorous

idle, idol, idyl
ingenious, ingenuous
instance, instants
irrelevant, irreverent
it's, its

knead, need
knew, new
know, no

later, latter
lead, led
lessen, lesson
lightening, lightning
loath, loathe
loose, lose

mantel, mantle
mean, mien
metal, mettle
muscle, mussel

of, off

pardoner, partner
passed, past
peace, piece
persevere, preserve
personal, personnel
plain, plane
pore, pour
practice, practise
precede, proceed
precedence, precedents
presence, presents
principal, principle
prophecy, prophesy

quiet, quit, quite

rain, reign, rein
rap, wrap
respectfully, respectively
rhyme, rhythm
right, rite, wright, write
ring, wring
road, rode

scene, seen
seize, siege
severally, severely
shone, shown
sing, singe
staid, stayed
stationary, stationery

statue, stature, statute
steal, steel
straight, strait
suit, suite

taught, taut
than, then
their, there
therefor, therefore
threw, through
throne, thrown
to, too, two

track, tract
troop, troupe

waive, wave
wander, wonder
ware, wear
weak, week
weather, whether
which, witch
who's, whose

your, you're

340. Proper names frequently misspelled. The following list contains proper names often misspelled. To it may be added other names that give you trouble.

Annapolis
Apollo
Burns's
Carlyle
Chesapeake
Coleridge
De Quincey
Dickens's
Eliot, George
February
Huguenots

Johnson, Samuel
Jonson, Ben
Macaulay
Macbeth
Massachusetts
Mediterranean
Mississippi
Odyssey
Parliament
Philippi
Philippines

Renaissance
Sir Roger de Coverley
Shelley
Spencer, Herbert
Spenser, Edmund
Tennessee
Thackeray
Ulysses
Waverley
Wednesday
Westminster

APPENDIX A

SUGGESTIONS FOR STUDYING THE PRINCIPAL TYPES OF LITERATURE [1]

The author's background. Before any piece of literature can be studied with profit, the age that produced the author must be understood. Acquaintance with the political, social, and literary history of the period may be acquired by studying such topics as the following: (1) important historical events of the period; (2) the status of literature; (3) means and extent of public education; (4) moral and religious standards; (5) social customs; (6) literary predecessors; (7) literary contemporaries.

The author and his work. Fully as important as a knowledge of the author's background is an intimate acquaintance with the author himself and his work. From a text in the history of literature, from a biography, and from biographical essays information on such topics as the following may be obtained: (1) the date and place of the author's birth; (2) the economic and social rank of his family; (3) his education; (4) his acquaintance with influential people; (5) other advantages that he enjoyed; (6) disadvantages that he overcame; (7) his chief interests in early life; (8) why he became a writer; (9) writers by whom he was most influenced; (10) his principal writings; (11) his purpose in writing the selection now being studied; (12) circumstances connected with his later years and death; (13) his place and influence in literature.

In addition to the biographical information concerning the author and his work, much may be learned of him from his writings, which constitute to a greater or lesser degree his mental and spiritual autobiography. In familiar essays and in lyric poetry the

---

[1] If more specific guidance in the study of the classics prescribed by the College-Entrance Examination Board is desired, Trent, Hanson, and Brewster's "Introduction to the English Classics" (Revised Edition), published by Ginn and Company, will prove helpful.

personality of the writer is a more evident, as well as a more essential, quality than it is in other types of literature, though in almost all it can be easily detected.

The study of prose fiction. The principal modern types of prose fiction are (1) the novel and (2) the short story. In the study of each of these there are five important items to consider: (1) the *plot*, or the plan by which the author arranges the incidents of his story with reference to the outcome; (2) the *characters*, or the people who take part in the action of the story; (3) the *setting*, or the place and the time of the action; (4) the *theme*, or the central idea that forms the basis of the story; and (5) the *author* and his *purpose* in writing the story.

I. THE NOVEL

Plot. 1. Is the plot well constructed? 2. Is it simple or complex? 3. Enumerate the plot incidents and show that they constitute the framework of the story. 4. Are the incidents arranged in the order of time, or is the action inverted? 5. Enumerate the most dramatic incidents and explain their bearing on the plot. 6. What incident furnishes the climax (the turning-point in the main action) of the story? 7. Draw a diagram representing the rising action and the falling action. 8. What incidents are indispensable to the plot? 9. Are there any episodes that might be omitted without impairing the plot? 10. Is the movement of the story as a whole swift or slow? 11. What incidents and scenes particularly impress you?

Characters. 1. Are the characters many or few? 2. Name the principal and the subordinate characters. 3. Does the author reveal his characters by analysis, by conversation, or by their influence on others? 4. What impression does the heroine make on first appearance? the hero? 5. Is the leading character unmistakable and well portrayed? 6. Are the characters real or conventional? 7. Which characters are the most natural? 8. Which (if any) seem overdrawn? 9. Who is the principal character in the main plot? in the subplot? 10. Which characters develop as the story advances? 11. Is the author sympathetic toward his characters? 12. How does he dispose of them at the end of the story?

Setting. 1. How much does the setting contribute to your interest in the story? 2. Is it an indispensable part of the story? 3. Is it simple or elaborate? 4. Does the background harmonize with the action and the characters? 5. In the introduction do you discover a dominant tone? 6. Does the setting lend atmosphere to the story? 7. Is the setting historical? Is it romantic? 8. Are the descriptions of nature numerous and long? 9. Are they closely connected with the plot? 10. Does the leading character's environment greatly influence his or her actions? 11. Does the author possess noticeable skill in writing description? 12. Mention scenes that impress you because of the vividness of the description.

Theme. 1. State in one sentence the theme, or central idea, of the story. 2. Are there any secondary themes? 3. Does the story teach, preach, or merely entertain? 4. Do you consider the central truth significant?

The author: his purpose, traits, and style. 1. Is the author's purpose definite and easily discoverable? 2. Is it a worthy purpose? 3. Does he write to entertain, to reform, or to stress a moral? 4. Does he give an essentially true representation of life? 5. Do you agree with the author in his way of looking at life? 6. Do you notice any peculiarities of style? 7. Does the author employ any special devices to secure effects? 8. Does he make effective use of dialogue? 9. Comment on the author's use of words. 10. How does he secure emotional response? 11. Does the author's style harmonize with his theme? with the character of his story? 12. Is the author a careful observer of nature? 13. Quote passages that illustrate beauty and clearness of style. 14. What have you learned about the author's skill in writing? 15. Find examples of vividness, contrast, directness. 16. Does the author impress you as being a particularly likable person? If so, why?

II. THE SHORT STORY

Plot. 1. State the plot of the story in a single sentence. 2. What single impression does the story produce? 3. What is the complicating incident that gives rise to the action of the story? 4. What is the plot problem that the author solves by means of the story?

5. What is the climax? 6. How near the end of the story does it come? 7. Show how the writer secures suspense. 8. Are the incidents arranged in chronological order? 9. Show the causal relation between the plot incidents of the story. 10. At the end of the story how have the situation and the relation of the characters changed from what they were at the beginning?

Characters. 1. How many characters are there? 2. Who is the preëminent character? 3. By what means of direct and indirect characterization has the author revealed his characters? 4. How early in the story does the author acquaint you with his principal characters? 5. From what point of view is the story told?

Setting. 1. What are the place setting and time setting? 2. Do they change in the course of the story? 3. How much time is covered by the action? 4. Does the author accurately describe his setting, or does he merely suggest it? 5. Does the setting lend atmosphere to the story? 6. Has the story an enveloping action? 7. Point out instances of contrast in setting and in character.

Theme. 1. What is the theme, or central idea, of the story? 2. Is this theme prominently brought out, or is it incidental? 3. Is the relation between the theme and the action of the story natural and convincing, or forced and weak?

The author: his purpose and his style. 1. Is the author's purpose to entertain, to teach, or to emphasize a moral truth? 2. Is he best in description, characterization, or vivid narration? 3. Does the dialogue seem natural? 4. Is his diction commonplace or striking? 5. Is the story, as told, worth telling? 6. Have you read a better story written by another author on the same theme?

The study of the drama. A drama may be written in either verse or prose. According to the author's purpose in writing a drama, it may be tragedy, comedy, melodrama, or farce. Since dramas are written to be presented before an audience by actors on a stage, they are usually briefer than novels and, in general, contain more action. In reading a drama, one is called upon to supply by means of his imagination what the novelist would furnish in the descriptions and explanations of his settings and his characters. In studying a play of one, three, four, or five acts, the following questions will prove helpful in making a general analysis of it:

Plot. 1. Has the play one plot only, or has it a main plot and one or more minor plots? 2. Enumerate the plot incidents that constitute the play. 3. Summarize the main action as briefly as you can. 4. What is the inciting force? 5. At what point does the rising action culminate and the falling action begin? 6. Draw a diagram of the plot. 7. Are there any unnecessary scenes? 8. What constitutes the struggle of the play? 9. Is the struggle mental, moral, or physical? 10. Is the climax well marked and effective? 11. Explain the author's use of suspense. 12. Is the action of the play swift or slow?

Characters. 1. Are the characters many or few? 2. Name the principal and the subordinate characters. 3. Who is the dominant character? 4. How are the leading characters introduced? 5. Do the characters talk naturally? 6. What is the author's method of revealing them? 7. Which characters develop and which remain the same during the course of the play? 8. Is the interest in characters greater than the interest in events? 9. How are the characters disposed of at the end of the play?

Setting. 1. Is the setting important? 2. Is the interest in setting greater than the interest in plot or characters? 3. What is the time setting of the play? 4. By what touches does the author suggest the place and time? 5. Does setting contribute atmosphere or a dominant tone to the play? 6. Does the plot depend in any way upon the setting? 7. How does the author give the impression that time is passing?

Theme. 1. What is the dominant idea of the play? 2. Does the play teach a lesson? reveal a human truth? present a problem? 3. Is the theme clearly defined and effectively illustrated by the action of the play? 4. Can you formulate the theme of the play in one sentence?

The author and his style. 1. Has the author any special distinction of style? 2. Is his style commonplace or striking? 3. Is his diction noticeably good? 4. Are there any effective figures of speech? 5. Does the play contain any especially beautiful passages?

The study of the essay. The study of an essay involves a consideration of the following points: (1) the *author's purpose*, (2) the *structure* of the essay, (3) the *theme*, or central idea, (4) the *author's personality*, (5) the *diction and allusions*, and (6) the *style*. (For a discussion of the essay see section 270.)

The author's purpose. 1. Is the author's purpose to instruct or to entertain? 2. Is the essay formal or informal?

Structure. 1. Does the essay give evidence of careful planning? 2. Are the paragraphs well constructed? 3. Make a topical outline of the essay. 4. What means of transition does the author use?

Theme. 1. What is the theme, or central idea, of the essay? 2. Is it presented convincingly? 3. Is it made more attractive by means of concrete illustrations? by humor? by the author's personality?

The author's personality. 1. Does the author seem to possess a pleasing personality? 2. Has he lofty ideals? 3. Is he sincere? sympathetic? critical? impartial? 4. Is he a great lover of books and people? 5. What are his hobbies? 6. Are his likes and dislikes very pronounced? 7. Has he a sense of humor? 8. Is he a close observer? 9. Has he a vivid imagination? 10. Should you enjoy having him for a friend?

Diction and allusion. 1. Has the essayist a wide range of words? 2. Is his diction precise? vivid? individual? vigorous? euphonious? 3. Has he any favorite words or expressions that you have discovered? 4. To what extent does he employ figurative language? 5. Are his illustrations well chosen? 6. From what principal sources are his allusions drawn?

Style. 1. Is the essayist's language simple or elaborate? 2. Is his style commonplace, striking, or brilliant? 3. Is the style well adapted to the subject matter and the theme? 4. Are the sentences clean-cut and direct, or ponderous and involved? 5. To what extent does the style contribute to your enjoyment of the essay? 6. Point out several passages that illustrate characteristics of the essayist's style. 7. Does the essay possess charm?

The study of poetry. Since the comprehension of the writer's thought is more difficult in poetry than in prose, the poem to be studied should be read and re-read until the author's purpose and thought are fully understood. The poem may then be studied by means of the following questions:

The approach to the poem. 1. Is the poem narrative, dramatic, lyric, descriptive, or didactic? (See pages xxiii–xxiv.) 2. Does it represent a special structural type, such as the sonnet? 3. What seems to be its purpose? 4. State as best you can its principal thought or incident. 5. What other poem that you have read contains the same thought or incident? 6. Is the chief appeal of the poem to your emotions or to your intellect? 7. Is the poem easy or difficult to read? (Try by reading it aloud to someone to interpret the thought accurately.) 8. Do you find the poem enjoyable?

Structure. (Study Appendix C.) 1. In what meter is the poem written? In what stanza form? 2. Scan the first six lines. 3. Test the rhythm by reading these lines aloud. 4. Is the structure of the poem well adapted to the thought or emotion expressed?

Vividness. 1. Point out examples of vividness gained by the use of figures of speech and identify each figure. 2. Do you find any appeals to the various senses? 3. Do the details that are included call up vivid pictures in your mind? 4. Does the poem produce in you a definite emotional response? 5. Does it recall vividly some memory? some mental or spiritual experience?

Diction and allusions. 1. Is the language of the poem simple or learned? 2. What archaic or obsolete words and expressions do you find? 3. Point out examples of well-chosen connotative words. 4. Do you find any onomatopœic words? 5. From what sources are the allusions drawn? 6. Point out any particularly melodious lines or passages.

The author's personality. 1. What characteristics of the author's personality are revealed in the poem? 2. Does he impress you as being buoyant, robust, and optimistic, or timid, delicate, and pessimistic? 3. Is he chiefly a man of action or of reflection? 4. Is he a close observer? 5. Is he intimately acquainted with nature? 6. Does he thoroughly understand and sympathize with people? 7. Is he a poet of books or of people? 8. What characteristic do you most admire in him? 9. Is his poem to any extent autobiographic? 10. Does he remind you of any other poet?

APPENDIX B

SUGGESTIONS FOR USING A SCHOOL LIBRARY

The library catalogue. Every modern school or public library
has a card catalogue of all the books and periodicals that it contains. On each card appear the title of a book, the letter or letters
indicating the library classification of the book, and a group of
figures showing in what section and on what shelf of the library the
book is to be found. Usually each book is represented by three different cards, arranged in one alphabetical series in the trays of the
filing-cabinet. That is, each book is classified according to (1) the
title, (2) the name of the author, and (3) the general subject. For
example, "One-Act Plays by Modern Authors," edited by Helen
Louise Cohen, would be represented by a card under the subject of
Drama, a card for the title, "One-Act Plays by Modern Authors,"
and a card for the name of the editor, Helen Louise Cohen. In
filling out a library slip requesting the loan of a book, you should
write down the following items: (1) the title of the book, (2) the
name of the author, (3) the classification letter or letters and the
call number, and (4) your name and address. If you need further
information concerning the use of the card catalogue, you may
obtain it from the librarian or an assistant.

EXERCISE

Consult the card catalogue of your school or public library to
see whether it has a novel, a collection of essays, or a book of poems
that you wish to read. Look for the three different cards representing the book.

Reference books. In every well-equipped school library, as
well as in many public libraries, the following reference books
should be available:

ENCYCLOPEDIAS

Encylopædia Britannica (eleventh edition, twenty-nine volumes, 1910; three supplementary volumes added in 1922). Very full; highly authoritative, but not for ready reference.

New International Encyclopædia (reëdited in 1916). Brief; good for contemporary biography.

Johnson's Universal Cyclopædia. Popular; full treatment of American biography, politics, and natural sciences.

Chambers's Encyclopædia. Brief and popular in character.

DICTIONARIES

Standard Dictionary. Useful for technical expressions in trade.

Century Dictionary. Full and authoritative; gives brief, clear account of subject; volume of proper names especially valuable.

Webster's New International Dictionary. New and enlarged edition, with copious and exact etymologies; especially good for definitions.

Roget's Thesaurus of English Words and Phrases. A standard book of synonyms.

Fernald's English Synonyms and Antonyms. Many illustrations and expositions of the differences in meaning.

BIOGRAPHICAL DICTIONARIES

Dictionary of National Biography. Confined to English biography and to persons dead at the date of publication. The articles are full and authoritative. In the index and epitome is a convenient summary of dates and facts.

Thomas's Comprehensive Dictionary of Biography. Brief, trustworthy accounts of great men of all countries.

Men and Women of the Time. Contemporary English and American men and women.

Who's Who. An annual publication; living persons of note, mostly English.

Who's Who in America. A biennial publication; noteworthy living Americans.

Selections from English and American Literature

Allibone's Dictionary. A brief account of British and American authors.

Harvard Classics. For selections.

Warner's Library of the World's Best Literature. For selections.

Stedman and Hutchinson's Library of American Literature. For selections.

Allusions and Quotations

Brewer's Reader's Handbook. Allusions, references, plots, stories.

Strong's Exhaustive Concordance. An index to every word in the Bible.

Bartlett's Concordance to Shakespeare. An index to the words in Shakespeare.

Bartlett's Familiar Quotations. An index to a large number of the quotations most frequently met with.

Brewer's Dictionary of Phrase and Fable. This explains a great quantity of common allusions expressed in words and phrases.

Century Cyclopedia of Names. This includes not only names of real persons but also those of many famous characters in fiction.

Lippincott's Universal Pronouncing Dictionary of Biography and Mythology.

Classical Dictionaries and Handbooks

Smith's Classical Dictionary. Greek and Roman biography and mythology.

Anthon's Classical Dictionary. Greek and Roman biography and mythology; full treatment of geography.

Bulfinch's Age of Fable. Greek and Roman mythology.

Gayley's Classic Myths in English Literature. Greek, Roman, and Norse mythology.

Hastings's Dictionary of the Bible.

Larned's History for Ready Reference.

CYCLOPEDIAS OF ARTS AND SCIENCES

Bliss's Encyclopedia of Social Reform.
Sturgis's Dictionary of Architecture and Building.
Grove's Dictionary of Music and Musicians.

REFERENCE BOOKS ON CURRENT TOPICS

The Statesman's Year-Book. Arranged by countries; contains a great mass of facts; a bibliography follows the section devoted to each country or state.

The World Almanac. Contains an enormous mass of facts, chiefly American.

Whitaker's Almanac. Much miscellaneous information about the British Empire and other countries.

The Annual Register and *The New International Yearbook.* These two books give information about the events of the year preceding publication.

Poole's Index to Periodical Literature. An index, by title and subject, to all the articles in important English and American periodicals from 1802 to 1908.

Readers' Guide to Periodical Literature. A continuation of Poole's *Index* since 1908; it is brought up to date each month.

MISCELLANEOUS WORKS

The Century Atlas. Contains classified references to places.
Library Atlas of the World. Excellent maps.
Lippincott's New Gazetteer. Useful for the spelling and the pronunciation of geographical names; condensed geographical information.
The Handy Reference Atlas. A useful book for the library table.
Ploetz's Epitome of Universal History. A compact epitome of history, with all the important dates.
Bibliographies issued by the Library of Congress.
Sonnenschein's The Best Books. A guide to about fifty thousand of the best available books in a variety of fields.

Spend at least two hours in finding out which of the reference books mentioned above are in your school or public library, and get acquainted with as many of them as you can.

Suggestions concerning the use of a library. If you observe the following simple suggestions for using a library, you will save yourself much time and labor and greatly add to your enjoyment of books.

1. Ascertain beforehand, as definitely as possible, what facts you are to look for and in what books these facts are to be found.

2. If you wish to collect material from several books and do not know what books are available, use the catalogue. Suppose your subject is "The Search for the North Pole." Under "North Pole" or "Exploration" you will probably find references to Nansen, Baldwin, Kane, Peary, and other explorers. If you look up these names, you will find a list of special books to be consulted.

3. If you wish to use magazine articles, as you will often have occasion to do when the subject is one of recent interest, consult *Poole's Index* and the *Readers' Guide to Periodical Literature*, a series of bound volumes which stand in the same relation to the best magazine articles as does the catalogue to the books of the library.

4. When you have ascertained what books and magazine articles are at your disposal, select those that seem most likely to be interesting and authoritative. If you need advice as to which are the best for your purpose, consult your teacher or the librarian.

5. Study carefully the table of contents and the index of a book to find out the author's development of the subject, his arrangement of the parts of that subject, and the chapters most likely to prove valuable for your purpose.

6. If time permits, saturate yourself with the subject; that is, read thoughtfully but rapidly to gain all the information possible. You need to know much more about the subject than you will have time or space to tell in your composition. There is danger of too general reading, but there is greater danger of gathering a few disconnected facts to be written down in a composition almost, if not quite, in the author's exact words.

7. Re-read the most important parts of the book or article and make the notes for your composition. Unless the article or the chapter has been fully outlined by the author at the beginning or by means of sideheadings, it will be necessary sometimes to search for the topic. This is not always a disadvantage, for it helps to show you what the relation of the parts was intended to be. After a time you will find it comparatively easy to take your notes in outline form at first; but since this is a matter of practice, and the outlines made thus far have been brief and simple, it may be easier to write the important facts in the form of catchwords. Occasionally you will want to use a sentence or a phrase in the exact words of the author. This is allowable if you *remember always to give full credit for it, either by the use of quotation marks or by the addition of the author's name.* You must take care not to present the ideas of another as if they were your own. Unless you give proper credit to the author, you are guilty of a form of dishonesty known as *plagiarism*, which is simply a type of stealing. As a rule, quotations should be few and brief, and should be used only when it seems impossible to express the idea in any other suitable way. Notes should contain, besides the outline and the quotations, any conclusions or impressions of your own. These will be particularly helpful later in expanding the notes and outlines into a composition.

EXERCISES

I

State exactly what books or magazines you would read to collect material for compositions on the following subjects.[1] Write out composition notes on any three of the subjects.

1. The Wireless Telegraph (Telephone). 2. The Making of Pottery. 3. The Roosvelt Dam. 4. Pasteur and his Work. 5. Haunts of Shakespeare. 6. Government by Commission. 7. Free Verse. 8. The Initiative and Recall. 9. Education of the Blind. 10. The Refining of Cottonseed Oil. 11. The Experimental Theater in America. 12. Excavations at Pompeii. 13. The Countries of Europe and their Present Form of Gov-

[1] To make this list you may consult the catalogue of the nearest library to see what books and magazines are available. Examine them carefully enough to know which of them contain really valuable material for your use.

ernment. **14.** The Romans as Road Builders. **15.** The Present Cabinet of the United States. **16.** Radium and its Uses. **17.** Luther Burbank and his Work. **18.** Halley's Comet. **19.** Petroleum By-Products. **20.** The Passion Play of Oberammergau.

II

Make a list of the reference books which contain information that will enable you to answer the following questions:

1. What is the prevailing religion in India? **2.** What is the Rosetta Stone? **3.** Name the colleges and universities of California. **4.** How is China governed? Who is the present ruler? **5.** Who was Prometheus? Dionysus? **6.** What are the principal exports of Jamaica? **7.** What state in the Union has the greatest railway mileage? **8.** What nations were represented at the Disarmament Conference at Washington? **9.** Who was Florence Nightingale? **10.** Who wrote "A little learning is a dangerous thing"? Give a brief account of the author's life. **11.** Who was Landseer? For what was he famous? **12.** What were the three types of ancient Greek architecture? **13.** Who were the Druids? **14.** To whom were the last Nobel Prizes awarded? For what achievements? **15.** Who were Jubal and Orpheus? **16.** Give a brief sketch of the life of Beethoven. **17.** What is the present center of population in the United States? **18.** What are the child-labor laws of your state? **19.** What are the restrictions on immigration in the United States? **20.** Who was Disraeli?

APPENDIX C

VERSIFICATION

Definition. The mechanical process of poetic composition is called *versification*. A single line of poetry is called a *verse*.

Rhythm. Each verse in a poetic composition is characterized by a uniform, measured movement which results from the regular recurrence of accented and unaccented syllables. This characteristic, the essential quality of all verse, is called *rhythm*. Rime, which we shall consider later, often occurs in verse, but it is not a really necessary element. Let us observe the difference in the movement of the two lines that follow:

And the sheen | of their spears | was like stars | on the sea.

Tell me | not in | mournful | numbers.

Each line, we notice, is divided into four groups of syllables. In the first line there are three syllables in each group; in the second, two syllables. Each group of syllables is called a *foot*.

Kinds of feet. The character, as well as the name, of a poetic foot is determined by (1) the number of syllables in the foot and (2) the position of the accented, or stressed, syllable. The four principal kinds of feet in English verse are the following:

The *iambic* foot, consisting of an unaccented syllable followed by an accented syllable, is represented thus: ◡ —. The following line contains iambic feet:

And thĕn | mȳ heărt | wĭth pleās|ŭre fīlls.

The *trochaic foot*, consisting of an accented syllable followed by an unaccented syllable, is represented thus: — ◡. The following line is composed of trochaic feet:

Līves ŏf | greāt mĕn | āll rĕ|mīnd ŭs.

The *anapœstic* foot, consisting of two unaccented syllables followed by an accented syllable, is represented thus: ◡ ◡ —. The following line contains anapæstic feet:

◡ ◡ — | ◡ ◡ — | ◡ ◡ — | — ◡ | ◡ —
For the moon | never beams | without bring|ing me dreams.

The *dactylic* foot, consisting of an accented syllable followed by two unaccented syllables, is represented thus: — ◡ ◡. The following line is composed of three dactylic feet with a trochaic foot at the end:

— ◡ ◡ | — ◡ ◡ | — ◡ ◡ | — ◡
Slowly the | mist o'er the | meadow was | creeping.

In addition to the four principal feet mentioned above, there are two other types, less frequently used:

The *spondaic* foot, consisting of two accented syllables, is represented thus: — —.

The *pyrrhic* foot, consisting of two unaccented syllables, is represented thus: ◡ ◡.

Spondaic and pyrrhic feet are comparatively rare and are practically never used alone.

Variations in rhythm. Certain regular variations in rhythm are likely to be found in verse, and unless we are prepared for them the verse may seem irregular and confusing. Often a line may contain two or more different kinds of feet. The following variations, in particular, should be noted:

1. *Iambic* and *anapœstic* feet are likely to occur in the same line:

◡ — | ◡ ◡ — | ◡ — | ◡ —
And this | was the rea|son that, long | ago,

◡ ◡ — | ◡ — | ◡ —
In this king|dom by | the sea.

These lines are from Poe's "Annabel Lee," the rhythm of which is chiefly anapæstic. Yet these two lines contain four iambic feet.

The following line is from Bryant's "The Death of the Flowers," the rhythm of which is chiefly iambic:

— — | ◡ — | ◡ — | ◡ — | — — | ◡ — | ◡ — | ◡
Till fell | the frost | from the clear | cold heav|en, as falls | the

— ◡ | —
plague | on men.

2. *Trochaic* and *dactylic* feet are likely to occur in the same line:

Bearded with | moss, and with | garments | green, indis|tinct in the |
    twilight.

How the | oriole's | nest is | hung.

3. In an *iambic* line the first foot is often *trochaic*:

Daughters | of time, | the hyp|ocrit|ic Days
Muffled | and dumb | like bare|foot der|vishes.

In addition to these regular variations, verse is often written with
lines ending in an additional unaccented syllable or in a foot of one
accented syllable.

The day | is done, | and the dark|ness
Falls from | the wings | of Night.

Laughed the | brook for | my de|light.
Through the | day and | through the | night.

Though a line frequently contains different kinds of feet, one
kind usually predominates and gives its name to the line.

Kinds of verse. Different lines contain different numbers of
feet. The number of feet in a line determines its meter, or measure.
English poetry includes the following eight kinds of lines:

Monometer line (one foot):

    I trust.

Dimeter line (two feet):

    The wild | winds weep.

Trimeter line (three feet):

    The au|tumn-time | has come.

Tetrameter line (four feet) :

He lives | to learn, | in life's | hard school.

Pentameter line (five feet) :

What might|y con|tests rise | from triv|ial things.

Hexameter line (six feet) :

This is the | forest pri|meval; the | murmuring | pines and the | hemlocks.

Heptameter line (seven feet) :

She is fair|er than earth, | and the sun | is not fair|er, the wind | is not blith|er than she.

Octameter line (eight feet) :

In the | Spring a | young man's | fancy | lightly | turns to | thoughts of | love.

A verse is named according to the number of feet it includes and the kind of foot that predominates. In describing a line, therefore, we should first tell the rhythm, or kind of feet, and then the meter, or the number of feet, thus: *iambic pentameter, trochaic tetrameter, dactylic hexameter*, and so on.

Scansion. The whole process of indicating the rhythm and the meter of a line of verse is called *scansion* or *scanning*. To *scan* a line is to divide it into its constituent feet, to mark the accented and the unaccented syllables, to count the number of feet and state their kind. In scanning a verse, therefore, we indicate its metrical structure. Scansion may be marked in either of the following ways:

If I | should die | think on|ly this | of me.

If I | should die | think on|ly this | of me.

Scansion is a mechanical process, but it is useful in helping us to appreciate the work of a poet; for poets, besides being spiritually gifted, are skilled in metrical composition.

Rime. When we come to consider groups of lines, we are brought immediately to the subject of rime. Rime may be defined as similarity of sound between words, especially words at the ends of lines. A perfect rime requires that the following conditions regarding riming words be fulfilled:

1. The vowel sounds bearing the verse stress should be the same.
2. The consonants, if any, preceding the vowels should be different.
3. The consonant sounds following the vowels should be the same.

The following groups of words meet these conditions and constitute perfect rimes:

park	greet	play	be	make	fate
lark	meet	gay	sea	break	late

Such groups as the following are sometimes rimed, but they are not perfect rimes:

blood	dove	pen
wood	move	been

Such groups as the following are not rimes at all:

then	bent	bless
send	bend	nest

Such identical sounds as the following are not considered rimes:

weigh	rain	break	scene
way	rein	brake	seen

Couplets and stanzas. A group of two consecutive riming lines is called a *couplet*. The commonest form of couplet is the iambic pentameter, often called the *heroic* couplet, or simply the *riming* couplet. It is the prevailing form of verse in the works of Pope and several other eighteenth-century writers. It is illustrated by the following lines from Pope:

> Know then thyself, presume not God to scan;
> The proper study of mankind is man.

Another common couplet is the iambic tetrameter:

> The stag at eve had drunk his fill,
> Where danced the moon on Monan's rill.

A third familiar couplet is the trochaic tetrameter:

> Blessings on thee, little man,
> Barefoot boy, with cheek of tan!

A group of more than two riming lines is called a *stanza*. There are a great variety of forms of the stanza in English verse, but we need consider only a few in this brief discussion. A common form is the *ballad stanza*, made up of four iambic lines, alternating tetrameter and trimeter, as follows:

> John Gilpin was a citizen
> Of credit and renown,
> A train-band captain eke was he
> Of famous London town.

It may be well at this point for us to learn the way of indicating the arrangement of the rimes in a stanza. Such an arrangement is called the *rime scheme*. It is indicated by the first letters of the alphabet, and the same letter is used to represent rimes, or riming words. Thus the preceding ballad stanza would be represented as follows: *abcb*, the *b*'s denoting the rime. Hereafter rimes will be indicated by means of the rime scheme.

A second familiar stanza is the iambic tetrameter, riming *abab*. It is illustrated by the following lines referring to Shakespeare:

> Yet 'twas the king of England's kings;   [a]
> The rest with all their pomp and trains,   [b]
> Are moldered, half-remembered things;   [a]
> 'Tis he alone that lives and reigns.   [b]

Another familiar stanza is the so-called *elegiac*, used in Gray's "Elegy Written in a Country Churchyard":

> Full many a gem of purest ray serene   [a]
> The dark unfathomed caves of ocean bear: [b]
> Full many a flower is born to blush unseen,   [a]
> And waste its sweetness on the desert air.   [b]

The foregoing stanzas are examples of the *quatrain*, or stanza of four lines riming alternately. Besides quatrains, there are stanzas of three, five, six, seven, eight, and nine lines. A good example of the five-line stanza is found in Lowell's "An Invitation":

You sought the new world in the old,   [*a*]
I found the old world in the new,   [*b*]
All that our human hearts can hold,   [*a*]
The inward world of deathless mold,   [*a*]
The same that Father Adam knew.   [*b*]

The stanza of six lines is used in Longfellow's "Village Blacksmith," and the seven-line stanza in "America." A stirring stanza of eight lines is illustrated by Longfellow's "Skeleton in Armor":

Bright in her father's hall   [*a*]
Shields gleamed upon the wall,   [*a*]
Loud sang the minstrels all,   [*a*]
    Chanting his glory;   [*b*]
When of old Hildebrand   [*c*]
I asked his daughter's hand,   [*c*]
Mute did the minstrels stand   [*c*]
    To hear my story.   [*b*]

The stanza of nine lines, known as the *Spenserian stanza*, Keats employed in his "Eve of St. Agnes."

Blank verse. A great deal of verse does not contain any rime at all. Rhythm is essential to verse, but rime is not. Neither "Evangeline" nor "Hiawatha" contains rime. Most of Shakespeare's works are not in rime; neither is Tennyson's "Idylls of the King," nor Bryant's "Thanatopsis." It is evident, therefore, that rime is not an essential of poetry. The term *blank verse* is used loosely to designate any unrimed verse, but strictly the term should be used in reference to *iambic pentameter* lines only. "Thanatopsis" is written in blank verse, though "Evangeline" is not. The following blank-verse lines are from Tennyson's "Morte d'Arthur":

So all day long the noise of battle rolled
Among the mountains by the winter sea,
Until King Arthur's table, man by man,
Had fallen in Lyonnesse about their lord.

Free verse. Free verse may be defined as rhythmical poetry composed without regard for meter or rime. The following lines from Walt Whitman illustrate free verse:

Sing on there in the swamp,
O singer bashful and tender, I hear your notes, I hear your call,
I hear, I come presently, I understand you,
But a moment I linger, for the lustrous star has detain'd me,
The star, my departing comrade, holds and detains me.

The sonnet. The sonnet is a complete poem consisting of fourteen iambic-pentameter lines. It includes two distinct types: the Italian, or regular, and the English, or Shakespearean. The Italian sonnet consists of two parts: the first eight lines constitute the *octave*, which is composed of two quatrains; the last six lines form the *sestet*. The rime scheme of the regular, or Italian, sonnet is *abba abba cde cde*, or the sestet may rime *cdcdcd*. The rime scheme of the English, or Shakespearean, sonnet is *abab cdcd efef gg*. The couplet at the end is felt to emphasize the thought or the emotion expressed in the preceding lines. Such poets as Spenser, Milton, Wordsworth, Keats, and Rossetti employed the sonnet in various modified forms.

The following sonnet by Longfellow, called "Nature," is a good example of the Italian, or regular, form:

As a fond mother, when the day is o'er,   [*a*]
    Leads by the hand her little one to bed,   [*b*]
    Half willing, half reluctant to be led,   [*b*]
And leave his broken playthings on the floor,   [*a*]
Still gazing at them through the open door,   [*a*]
    Not wholly reassured and comforted   [*b*]
    By promises of others in their stead,   [*b*]
Which, though more splendid, may not please him more;   [*a*]
So Nature deals with us, and takes away   [*c*]
    Our playthings one by one, and by the hand   [*d*]
       Leads us to rest so gently, that we go   [*e*]
Scarce knowing if we wish to go or stay,   [*c*]
    Being too full of sleep to understand   [*d*]
       How far the unknown transcends the what we know.   [*e*]

Kinds of poetry. There are five general classes of poetry; namely, narrative, dramatic, lyric, descriptive, and didactic.

1. The *narrative poem*, which tells a story, is of four general kinds:

a. The *epic* is a long narrative poem dealing impersonally with celebrated heroes and great events, usually of the distant past. Homer's Iliad and Odyssey, Virgil's Æneid, and Milton's "Paradise Lost" are the best-known epics.

b. The *romance* is also an extensive narrative poem, dealing with historical or mythical personages, such as Charlemagne, Alexander the Great, and King Arthur.

c. The *tale* is a narrative poem of moderate length. Scott's "Lady of the Lake" and Longfellow's "Tales of a Wayside Inn" are good examples.

d. The *ballad* is a short narrative poem. Ballads were originally chanted, and they are usually composed in a form suitable for musical accompaniment. "John Gilpin's Ride" and "The Wreck of the Hesperus" are good examples of the modern ballad. "Sir Patrick Spens" and the Robin Hood ballads illustrate the earlier type.

2. *Dramatic* poetry is also narrative, but it is designed to tell a story by means of action and speech and is therefore usually more vivid than nondramatic narrative. The play, or drama, is usually in verse, though modern plays are often written entirely in prose. There are two principal forms of the play—tragedy and comedy. In general, a tragedy is a play that ends unhappily, whereas a comedy is a play that ends happily (or, at least, not tragically). Shakespeare's "Macbeth" and "King Lear" are tragedies; his "As You Like It" and "A Midsummer Night's Dream" are comedies. Blank verse is the metrical form employed in most dramatic poetry.

3. *Lyric* poetry expresses the personality and the emotions of the author. The name is derived from the word *lyre*, and hence means "singable." Nearly all lyrics are short. Lyric poetry is of many types. All love songs, patriotic songs, and hymns are lyrics. So also are elegies, odes, sonnets, and many ballads. Burns's "Bonnie Doon," Newman's "Lead, Kindly Light," Gray's "Elegy Written in a Country Churchyard," and Bryant's "To a Waterfowl" are all lyric poems.

4. *Descriptive* poetry includes pastorals and idyls. Whittier's "Snow-Bound," Burns's "Cotter's Saturday Night," and Milton's "L'Allegro," "Il Penseroso," and "Lycidas" are primarily descriptive poems.

5. *Didactic* poetry includes verse compositions that are reflective and expository in nature. Criticisms, satires, and other poems that are addressed primarily to the intellect and have for their purpose the imparting of instruction belong to this class. Such poems as Pope's "Essay on Criticism," Cowper's "Task," Young's "Night Thoughts," and Wordsworth's "Excursion" are examples of didactic poetry.

USED IN CORRECTING COMPOSITIONS

ion marks. If a teacher's criticism of a composi-
f any value to us, we must know how to interpret
n correcting our paper and understand accurately
ch error. From the following list of marks and
sections of the text we shall be able to get this
ation.

GRAMMAR

of a rule of grammar.
nse of the verb.

SENTENCE STRUCTURE

balance in the sentence.
clearness.
ecified error in sentence construction.
fault (section 171): the use of a comma to separate two
nct sentences.
rd sentence structure.
fault (section 170): the unwarranted use of a phrase or a
endent clause as a complete sentence.
tion of parallel construction (section 173).
reference of a participle (section 159).
ation of point of view (section 174).
reference of a pronoun (section 150).
ation of sentence coherence (section 121).
ation of sentence emphasis (section 122).
lation of sentence unity (section 120).
pose a word, a phrase, or a clause to a better position in
e sentence.

A LIST OF COMMON ABBREVIATIONS

Use of abbreviations. As a general rule, abbreviations should
not be used in any kind of *formal* writing. A few exceptions to this
rule are such abbreviations as the following: *Mr.*, *Mrs.*, *Messrs.*,
M., *Mme*, *Mlle*, and *St.*, preceding proper names; *Esq.*, *Jr.*, *Sr.*,
M.D., *A.B.*, *D.D.*, *Ph.D.*, *LL.D.*, and other titles, following proper
names; *No.* before numerals; and B.C. and A.D., preceding or
following dates.

In *informal* writing recognized abbreviations may be used, but
they should always be limited to those that will be immediately
intelligible to the reader.

The following list contains the common abbreviations and their
meanings:

A.B. or *B.A.* (Latin *Artium Baccalaureus*): Bachelor of Arts.

A.D. (Latin *anno Domini*): in the year of our Lord.

ad. fin. (Latin *ad finem*): at the end.

ad. infin. (Latin *ad infinitum*): to infinity.

ad. lib. (Latin *ad libitum*): at pleasure.

æt. (Latin *aetatis*): aged.

A.L.A.: American Library Association.

A.M. (Latin *ante meridiem*): before noon.

A.M. or *M.A.* (Latin *Artium Magister*): Master of Arts.

Anon.: anonymous.

A.S.: Anglo-Saxon.

Bart.: Baronet.

bbl. (plural *bbls.*): barrel.

B.C.: before Christ.

B.C.L.: Bachelor of Civil Law.

B.D.: Bachelor of Divinity.

B.Mus. or *Mus.B.:* Bachelor of Music.

B.S. or *B.Sc.:* Bachelor of Science.

c. or *ca.* (Latin *circa*): about.

C.E.: Civil Engineer.

cf. (Latin *confer*): compare.

ch. or *chap.:* chapter.

C.O.D.: cash (*or* collect) on delivery.

con. (Latin *contra*): against.

c. p.: chemically pure; also candle power.

C. P. A.: Certified Public Accountant.

d. (Latin *denarius*): penny; pence.

D. A. R.: Daughters of the American Revolution.

D. C. L.: Doctor of Civil Law.

D. D.: Doctor of Divinity.

D. D. S.: Doctor of Dental Surgery.

do.: ditto.

Dr.: Doctor; debtor.

ed.: edition; editor.

E. E. T. S.: Early English Texts Society.

e. g. (Latin *exempli gratia*): for example.

Esq.: Esquire.

et al. (Latin *et alii*): and others.

et seq. (Latin *et sequens*): and the following.

etc. (Latin *et cetera*): and so forth.

f. or *ff.:* following.

Fahr.: Fahrenheit.

f. o. b.: free on board.

F. R. S.: Fellow of the Royal Society.

G. A. R.: Grand Army of the Republic.

Gen.: General.

Gov.: Governor.

H. M. S.: His Majesty's Service.

Hon.: Honorable.

h. p.: horse power.

ibid. (Latin *ibidem*): in the same place.

id. (Latin *idem*): the same.

i. e. (Latin *id est*): that is.

inc.: incorporated.

inst. (Latin *mense instante*): instant, the present month.

J. D. (Latin *Jurum Doctor*): Doctor of Laws.

J. P.: Justice of the Peace.

Jr.: Junior.

l. (plural *ll.*): line.

lb. (plural *lbs.*): pound.

l. c.: lower case (small letter).

L. H. D. (Latin *Litterarum Humaniorum Doctor*): Doctor of the Humanities.

Lit. D. or *Litt. D.* (Latin *Litterarum Doctor*): Doctor of Letters.

LL. B. (Latin *Legum Baccalaureus*): Bachelor of Laws.

LL. D. (Latin *Legum Doctor*): Doctor of Laws.

loc. cit. (Latin *loco citato*): in the place previously cited.

Ltd.: limited.

m. (Latin *meridies*): noon.

M. (French; plural *MM.*): *Monsieur.*

M. (Latin *mille*): thousand.

M. C.: Member of Congress.

M. D. (Latin *Medicinae Doctor*): Doctor of Medicine.

M. E.: Mechanical Engineer; Mining Engineer; Middle English; Methodist Episcopal.

Mgr.: Manager.

M. L. A.: Modern Language Association.

Mlle (French): *Mademoiselle.*

Mme (French): *Madame.*

M. P.: Member of

MS. (plural *MSS.*

M. S.: Master of S

N. B. (Latin *nota* well; take not mind.

N. E. A.: National E sociation.

N. E. D.: New Englis

non. seq. (Latin *non* does not follow.

N. P.: Notary Public.

O. E. D.: Oxford Engl ary.

op. cit. (Latin *opus c* work previously cit

Oxon. (Latin *Oxonia*):

oz.: ounce or ounces.

p. (plural *pp.*): page.

Ph. B. (Latin *Philosophi laureus*): Bachelor losophy.

Ph. D. (Latin *Philosoph tor*): Doctor of Philo

pinx. (Latin *pinxit*): he pa

P. M. (Latin *post meridie* ternoon.

P. M.: Postmaster.

P. P. C. (French *Pour t congé*): to take leave.

pro. tem. (Latin *pro temp* for the time being.

prox. (Latin *proximo*): month.

P. S. (Latin *post scriptum*): script.

MARKS

Use of correct tion is to prove o the marks used i the nature of ea from the proper necessary inform

Gr.	Violation
Tn.	Wrong t
Bal.	Lack of
Cl.	Lack of
Cst.	An unsp
C. F.	Comma dist
K	Awkwa
P. F.	Period dep
Pll.	A viola
Ptc.	Faulty
Pt. V.	A viola
Ref.	Faulty
S. C.	A viol
S. E.	A viol
S. U.	A vio
Tr.	Trans th

SPELLING

Sp.	An error in spelling (sections 338–340).
Syl.	Wrong syllabic division of a word (section 336).
⌣	Write as one word without a hyphen.
Dy.	Consult a dictionary (section 225).

DICTION

D.	An error in diction (sections 177 and 186).
Id.	A violation of idiom (section 218).
Wd.	Wordiness ; condense.
Wk.	Diction weak or colorless (section 206).
Coll.	Diction too colloquial (section 180, 1).
Rep.	Objectionable repetition (section 207).
Fig.	Faulty figure of speech (section 194).
F.W.	"Fine writing": affected or inappropriate diction (section 212).

PUNCTUATION

P.	An error in punctuation (sections 126–141).
Cap.	Use a capital letter (section 143).
l.c.	Use a small (lower case) letter.
Ital.	Use italics (section 142).

MISCELLANEOUS MARKS

MS.	Manuscript poorly arranged, untidy, or illegible.
C.I.	Consult the instructor.
U.	Lack of unity in the paragraph (sections 85–89).
C.	Lack of coherence in the paragraph (sections 90–98).
E.	Lack of emphasis in the paragraph (sections 99–100).
¶	Indent ; begin a paragraph here.
¶?	Should a paragraph begin here?
No ¶	Do not begin a new paragraph.
?	A doubtful statement.
X	An unspecified obvious error.
∧	Necessary word or words omitted (section 165).
δ	Omit unnecessary word or words.
/	Divide a word or a sentence.
#	Leave more space between words or sentences.

APPENDIX F

MARKS USED IN PROOFREADING

Proofreaders' marks. To call attention to errors in a printers' proof special marks and symbols are used in the margin at a point opposite the line in which the mistake occurs. Proofreaders' marks should never be inserted between the printed lines of a proof, but each should be accompanied by an appropriate mark in the printed line to show where the correction is to be made. The following marks are commonly used:

ℌ	Take out (Latin *dele*); omit.
℘	Turn an inverted letter to right position.
#	A space or more space between letters or words.
⌞	Carry a word or a line farther to the left.
⌟	Carry a word or a line farther to the right.
⌐	Raise a letter or a word sunk below the proper level.
⌎	Lower a letter or a word raised above the proper level.
∪	Push down the lead which shows with the type.
⌒	Take out space and close up.
℈	Take out a letter or letters and close up.
⌢	Print as a single character; as, a͡e = æ.
℘	Make a new paragraph.
No ℘	No paragraph needed here.
stet	Let the word or words crossed out remain as at first. (Dots are placed under these words.)
//	Type margin uneven; straighten it.
=	Straighten line or lines.
λ	A broken letter.
∧	Marks the point within the line where an insertion is to be made.
=	Insert a hyphen at point indicated by caret.
⊙	Insert a period at point indicated by caret.

APPENDIX D

A LIST OF COMMON ABBREVIATIONS

Use of abbreviations. As a general rule, abbreviations should not be used in any kind of *formal* writing. A few exceptions to this rule are such abbreviations as the following: *Mr.*, *Mrs.*, *Messrs.*, *M.*, *Mme*, *Mlle*, and *St.*, preceding proper names; *Esq.*, *Jr.*, *Sr.*, *M.D.*, *A.B.*, *D.D.*, *Ph.D.*, *LL.D.*, and other titles, following proper names; *No.* before numerals; and *B.C.* and *A.D.*, preceding or following dates.

In *informal* writing recognized abbreviations may be used, but they should always be limited to those that will be immediately intelligible to the reader.

The following list contains the common abbreviations and their meanings:

A. B. or *B. A.* (Latin *Artium Baccalaureus*): Bachelor of Arts.

A.D. (Latin *anno Domini*): in the year of our Lord.

ad. fin. (Latin *ad finem*): at the end.

ad. infin. (Latin *ad infinitum*): to infinity.

ad. lib. (Latin *ad libitum*): at pleasure.

æt. (Latin *aetatis*): aged.

A. L. A.: American Library Association.

A. M. (Latin *ante meridiem*) : before noon.

A. M. or *M. A.* (Latin *Artium Magister*) : Master of Arts.

Anon.: anonymous.

A. S.: Anglo-Saxon.

Bart.: Baronet.

bbl. (plural *bbls.*): barrel.

B.C.: before Christ.

B. C. L.: Bachelor of Civil Law.

B. D.: Bachelor of Divinity.

B. Mus. or *Mus. B.:* Bachelor of Music.

B. S. or *B. Sc.:* Bachelor of Science.

c. or *ca.* (Latin *circa*) : about.

C. E.: Civil Engineer.

cf. (Latin *confer*) : compare.

ch. or *chap.:* chapter.

C. O. D.: cash (*or* collect) on delivery.

con. (Latin *contra*): against.

c. p.: chemically pure ; also candle power.

C. P. A.: Certified Public Accountant.

d. (Latin *denarius*) : penny ; pence.

D. A. R.: Daughters of the American Revolution.

D. C. L.: Doctor of Civil Law.

D. D.: Doctor of Divinity.

D. D. S.: Doctor of Dental Surgery.

do.: ditto.

Dr.: Doctor ; debtor.

ed.: edition ; editor.

E. E. T. S.: Early English Texts Society.

e. g. (Latin *exempli gratia*) : for example.

Esq.: Esquire.

et al. (Latin *et alii*) : and others.

et seq. (Latin *et sequens*) : and the following.

etc. (Latin *et cetera*) : and so forth.

f. or *ff.:* following.

Fahr.: Fahrenheit.

f. o. b.: free on board.

F. R. S. : Fellow of the Royal Society.

G. A. R.: Grand Army of the Republic.

Gen.: General.

Gov.: Governor.

H. M. S.: His Majesty's Service.

Hon.: Honorable.

h. p.: horse power.

ibid. (Latin *ibidem*) : in the same place.

id. (Latin *idem*) : the same.

i. e. (Latin *id est*) : that is.

inc.: incorporated.

inst. (Latin *mense instante*) : instant, the present month.

J. D. (Latin *Jurum Doctor*) : Doctor of Laws.

J. P.: Justice of the Peace.

Jr.: Junior.

l. (plural *ll.*) : line.

lb. (plural *lbs.*) : pound.

l. c.: lower case (small letter).

L. H. D. (Latin *Litterarum Humaniorum Doctor*) : Doctor of the Humanities.

Lit. D. or *Litt. D.* (Latin *Litterarum Doctor*) : Doctor of Letters.

LL. B. (Latin *Legum Baccalaureus*) : Bachelor of Laws.

LL. D. (Latin *Legum Doctor*) : Doctor of Laws.

loc. cit. (Latin *loco citato*) : in the place previously cited.

Ltd.: limited.

m. (Latin *meridies*) : noon.

M. (French; plural *MM.*) : *Monsieur*.

M. (Latin *mille*) : thousand.

M. C.: Member of Congress.

M. D. (Latin *Medicinae Doctor*) : Doctor of Medicine.

M. E.: Mechanical Engineer ; Mining Engineer ; Middle English ; Methodist Episcopal.

Mgr.: Manager.

M. L. A.: Modern Language Association.

Mlle (French) : *Mademoiselle*.

Mme (French) : *Madame*.

M. P.: Member of Parliament.

MS. (plural *MSS.*): manuscript.

M. S.: Master of Science.

N. B. (Latin *nota bene*): note well; take notice; bear in mind.

N. E. A.: National Educational Association.

N. E. D.: New English Dictionary.

non. seq. (Latin *non sequitur*): it does not follow.

N. P.: Notary Public.

O. E. D.: Oxford English Dictionary.

op. cit. (Latin *opus citato*): the work previously cited.

Oxon. (Latin *Oxonia*): Oxford.

oz.: ounce or ounces.

p. (plural *pp.*): page.

Ph. B. (Latin *Philosophiae Baccalaureus*): Bachelor of Philosophy.

Ph. D. (Latin *Philosophiae Doctor*): Doctor of Philosophy.

pinx. (Latin *pinxit*): he painted it.

P. M. (Latin *post meridiem*): afternoon.

P. M.: Postmaster.

P. P. C. (French *Pour prendre congé*): to take leave.

pro. tem. (Latin *pro tempore*): for the time being.

prox. (Latin *proximo*): next month.

P. S. (Latin *post scriptum*): postscript.

pseud.: pseudonym; assumed name.

Q. E. D. (Latin *quod erat demonstrandum*): which was to be proved.

q. v. (Latin *quod vide*): which see.

R. F. D.: Rural Free Delivery.

R. G. S.: Royal Geographical Society.

R. S. V. P. (French *Répondez s'il vous plaît*): please reply; reply, if you please.

sc.: scene.

sc. (Latin *scilicet*): namely.

s. g.: specific gravity.

sic (Latin): thus.

S. P. C. A.: Society for the Prevention of Cruelty to Animals.

sq. (Latin *sequens*): the following.

Sr.: Senior.

st.: stanza.

S. T. D. (Latin *Sacrae Theologiae Doctor*): Doctor of Sacred Theology.

ult. (Latin *ultimo*): last month.

U. S. M.: United States Mail.

U. S. N.: United States Navy.

v. (plural *vv.*): verse.

vid. or *v.* (Latin *vide*): see, consult.

viz. (Latin *videlicet*): namely.

v. s. (Latin *vide supra*): see above.

vs. (Latin *versus*): against.

APPENDIX E

MARKS USED IN CORRECTING COMPOSITIONS

Use of correction marks. If a teacher's criticism of a composition is to prove of any value to us, we must know how to interpret the marks used in correcting our paper and understand accurately the nature of each error. From the following list of marks and from the proper sections of the text we shall be able to get this necessary information.

GRAMMAR

Gr.	Violation of a rule of grammar.
Tn.	Wrong tense of the verb.

SENTENCE STRUCTURE

Bal.	Lack of balance in the sentence.
Cl.	Lack of clearness.
Cst.	An unspecified error in sentence construction.
C. F.	Comma fault (section 171): the use of a comma to separate two distinct sentences.
K	Awkward sentence structure.
P. F.	Period fault (section 170): the unwarranted use of a phrase or a dependent clause as a complete sentence.
Pll.	A violation of parallel construction (section 173).
Ptc.	Faulty reference of a participle (section 159).
Pt. V.	A violation of point of view (section 174).
Ref.	Faulty reference of a pronoun (section 150).
S. C.	A violation of sentence coherence (section 121).
S. E.	A violation of sentence emphasis (section 122).
S. U.	A violation of sentence unity (section 120).
Tr.	Transpose a word, a phrase, or a clause to a better position in the sentence.

APPENDIX F

MARKS USED IN PROOFREADING

Proofreaders' marks. To call attention to errors in a printers' proof special marks and symbols are used in the margin at a point opposite the line in which the mistake occurs. Proofreaders' marks should never be inserted between the printed lines of a proof, but each should be accompanied by an appropriate mark in the printed line to show where the correction is to be made. The following marks are commonly used:

ℌ	Take out (Latin *dele*); omit.
ℊ	Turn an inverted letter to right position.
#	A space or more space between letters or words.
⌐	Carry a word or a line farther to the left.
⌐	Carry a word or a line farther to the right.
⌐	Raise a letter or a word sunk below the proper level.
⌐	Lower a letter or a word raised above the proper level.
⌣	Push down the lead which shows with the type.
⌒	Take out space and close up.
ℬ	Take out a letter or letters and close up.
⌢	Print as a single character; as, $\widehat{ae}$ = æ.
ℙ	Make a new paragraph.
No ℙ	No paragraph needed here.
stet	Let the word or words crossed out remain as at first. (Dots are placed under these words.)
//	Type margin uneven; straighten it.
=	Straighten line or lines.
λ	A broken letter.
∧	Marks the point within the line where an insertion is to be made.
=	Insert a hyphen at point indicated by caret.
⊙	Insert a period at point indicated by caret.

SPELLING

Sp.　　An error in spelling (sections 338–340).
Syl.　　Wrong syllabic division of a word (section 336).
⌣　　　Write as one word without a hyphen.
Dy.　　Consult a dictionary (section 225).

DICTION

D.　　　An error in diction (sections 177 and 186).
Id.　　A violation of idiom (section 218).
Wd.　　Wordiness; condense.
Wk.　　Diction weak or colorless (section 206).
Coll.　Diction too colloquial (section 180, 1).
Rep.　Objectionable repetition (section 207).
Fig.　Faulty figure of speech (section 194).
F. W.　"Fine writing": affected or inappropriate diction (section 212).

PUNCTUATION

P.　　　An error in punctuation (sections 126–141).
Cap.　Use a capital letter (section 143).
l. c.　Use a small (lower case) letter.
Ital.　Use italics (section 142).

MISCELLANEOUS MARKS

MS.　　Manuscript poorly arranged, untidy, or illegible.
C. I.　Consult the instructor.
U.　　Lack of unity in the paragraph (sections 85–89).
C.　　Lack of coherence in the paragraph (sections 90–98).
E.　　Lack of emphasis in the paragraph (sections 99–100).
¶　　　Indent; begin a paragraph here.
¶?　　Should a paragraph begin here?
No ¶　Do not begin a new paragraph.
?　　　A doubtful statement.
X　　　An unspecified obvious error.
∧　　　Necessary word or words omitted (section 165).
δ　　　Omit unnecessary word or words.
/　　　Divide a word or a sentence.
#　　　Leave more space between words or sentences.

⸴	Insert a comma at point indicated by caret.
ᵛ⸝	Insert quotation marks at point indicated by caret.
ᵛ	Insert apostrophe or single quotation at point indicated by caret.
cap	Use a capital.
s. caps.	Use small capitals.
l.c.	Use small (lower case) letters, not capitals.
wf.	Wrong font (wrong size or style of type).
tr.	Transpose word or words.
ital.	Use italic type.
rom.	Use roman type.
Out	Words omitted. See copy (author's manuscript).
lead	Insert a lead (a thin metal strip) to widen the space between lines.
?	A query as to spelling, exactness of quotation, etc.
≡	Print in CAPITAL letters.
══	Print in SMALL CAPITAL letters.
——	Print in *italic* letters.
﹏	Print in **bold-faced** type letters.
≣	Print in **BOLD-FACED** CAPITAL letters.
═	Print in **BOLD-FACED** SMALL CAPITAL letters.
﹋	Print in ***bold-faced italic*** letters.

Printed below is a specimen of corrected proof showing nearly all the proofreaders' marks.[1]

SHORTHAND UNDER THE CAESARS ⫽ *āe /center*

Plutarch mentions the speech on the con- *#*
spiracy of Catiline as the only one of Cato *e/tr.*
the Younger's speeches that has been pre *wf. /=/*
cap. served. on the day that Cato made it Cicero
had disposed in various parts of the Senate
several of the most expert rapid writers
m/ whom he had taught "to make figures com- *wf.*
prising numerous words in (few/a) short *tr.*

[1] The following passage was published in the *Youth's Companion.*

strokes. Plutarch adds that it was then tical use of the art.

But acording to a writer in the Century Magazine the earliest use an abbreviated form of writing goes back to 200 B.C., when the Roman poet Quintus Ennius used a system of eleven hundred signs that devised. Tiro the reporter the orations of Cicero, was in early life a slave, but, having acquired an education, he found favor with his master, who gave him his freedom and made him his secretary and confidant. Tiro was evidently a capable stenographer, for once during his absence from rome Cicero wrote to a friend complaining that his work was delayed because, whereas he had been to able dictate to Tiro in periods, he now had to dictate to others in syllables.

The System of pothooks that Tiro invented came to be known as the Tironian Notes and was the basis of all the shorthand used during the days of the Roman Empire and the dark ages. It was, however, merely a system of ideographs, hundred of different characters that had to be laboriously memorized. Shorthand Systems based on phonetic characters were not Invented until after the reformation.

INDEX

[*References are to pages. Roman numerals designate pages in the Appendixes.*]

Abbreviations, common, xxv–xxvii
Action, essential in narration, 346; rising, 447; falling, 447; enveloping, 449–450
Adjective clauses, 173–174
Adjective phrases, 161
Adjectives, 466–469; use, 259–262, 469; kinds, 466–467; comparison, 467–469; parsing, 469
Adverbial clauses, 174–176; misused for noun clauses, 281–282
Adverbial objective, 462
Adverbial phrases, 161–162
Adverbs, 470–471; conjunctive, 174–176, 470; kinds, 470; comparison, 471; parsing, 471
Analysis of a sentence, 485–486
Anapæstic foot, xvi
Anecdotes, 353–354
Antecedent, definition of, 462
Antithesis, 323
Antonyms, 335, 343
Apostrophe, in possessive, 238; in plural of letters and figures, 238; in contractions, 238–239
Apostrophe, figure of speech, 323
Apposition, noun clause in, 172; punctuation of appositive expressions, 212–213; case of appositive nouns and pronouns, 254, 461–462
Archaic words, 297
Argument, 2; definition of, 415; conviction in, 416; persuasion in, 416; kinds of, 416; informal, 417–421; formal, 421–432
As, 254, 260, 277, 299
As if, 277
Asterisks, 239
Atherton, Gertrude, 381, 383–384
Attention, devices for keeping, 28, 29
Author's background, i
Autobiography, 354, 361–362
Auxiliary verbs, 472

Bacon, Sir Francis, 5
Bailey, L. H., 146–147
Barbarisms, 294–295
Barnes, N. W., 4
Barrett, C. R., 445
Biography, 354, 360–361; expository, 405–407
Boas, Ralph Philip, 397–398
Bok, Edward, 354
Brackets, 234
Brief, 416, 427–432; model, 429–431; development into argument, 431–432
"Brooklyn Bridge at Dawn," 48
Brown, R. W., 4
Bruce, H. Addington, 146, 151
Burke, Edmund, 155
Burroughs, John, 58–60

Caldwell, Otis W., 12, 13
Capital letters, for first word of sentence, 242; first word of line of poetry, 242; first word of direct question, 242; proper nouns and proper adjectives, 242–243; names of days and months, 243; sections of country, 243; common nouns in proper names, 243–244; titles of honor or office, 244; titles of family relationship, 244; literary titles, 244; words naming or referring to Deity, 244–245; names of school classes, 245; *I* and *O*, 245; personification, 245
Caret, 239
Carver, Thomas Nixon, 418–419
Case, 253–255, 460–461
"Cask of Amontillado, The," 436–442
Clauses, in compound sentences, 166–167; noun, 171–172; adjective, 173–174; adverbial, 174–176; incorrect use of dependent, 182, 282–283

Clearness, of thought, 14–22; of speech, 22–24; importance of, in exposition, 388–389

Climax, in sentence, 202; figure of speech, 325; in short story, 434

Cognate object, 462

Coherence, law of, 75–78; in paragraph, 140–151; secured by connecting words and phrases, 150–151; in sentences, 195–199; in simple narration, 350; in description, 370–371

Colloquialisms, 295

Colon, in formal statements, 225; long quotations, 225; lists of items, 225; explanation or illustration, 225; formal salutations, 225

Comma, in direct address, 212; apposition, 212–213; series, 213; introductory words, phrases, clauses, 213–214; parenthetical expressions, 214; nonrestrictive phrases and clauses, 214–215; coördinate clauses, 215–216; quotations, direct and indirect, 216–217; omission of words, 217; limiting or identifying words, 217; mild interjections, 218; for greater clearness, 218

Comma fault, 191, 216, 283–284

Comparison, expressions of, 259–260; adjectives, 467–469; adverbs, 471

Composition, definition of, 1–2; units, 2; kinds, 2; sources of material, 2; essentials of effective, 2–3; reasons for studying, 3–4; original, 67; planning an original, 68; requirements of a good, 68; choice and limitation of subject, 68–69; choice of title, 69–70; point of view, 70–72; selection of material, 72–74; arranging material by means of outline, 74–79; unity, 74–75; coherence, 75–78; emphasis, 78–79; form of an outline, 79; development from outline, 86–91; beginning, 91–92; ending, 92–93; transitions between paragraphs, 94–95; revision, 95–98

Composition, oral: definition of, 1; importance of, 8; practice in, 8–9; qualities necessary for successful, 10, 14, 22, 24, 26; topics for, 10–11; compared with written, 32–33

Composition, written: definition of, 1; compared with oral, 32–33; proper form for, 33–36; requirements, 36–37

Condensation, 51–61

Conjugation, 473; regular, new, or weak, 478; irregular, old, or strong, 478

Conjunctions, 484–485; kinds, 484–485; parsing, 485

Conjunctive adverbs, 174–176, 470

Connectives, 150–151, 166–167

Connotation, 319

Coördination, in an outline, 79; in sentence, 198–199; faulty, 285–287

Copulative verbs, 473

Correctness of speech, 24–26

Couplet, xix–xx

Criticisms, 407–410

Dactylic foot, xvi

Dash, change in construction of sentence, 231; parenthetical expressions, 231; summarizing, 231; dramatic effect, 232; omissions, 232; with other marks, 232; references, 232

Debating, value of, 421; subjects for, 421–422; wording the question, 422; exposition of the question, 423; definition of terms, 423–424; conflict of opinion, 424; proof, 425; refutation, 426; burden of proof, 426; persuasion in, 426–427; brief for, 427–431; development of brief, 431–432

Definitions, 390–394

Denotation, 319

Dénouement, 447

Description, 2; definition of, 365; expository, 365–366; artistic, 366; unity in, 366–367; point of view, 367–368; singleness of impression, 368–370; fundamental image, 370; coherence, 370–371; emphasis, 371; vividness, 371; of a place, 375–378; of an object, 378–380; of an animal, 380–381; of a person, 382–385; by effect, 385–386

Dialogue, in narration, 353; in short story, 450

Diaries, 360
Diction, 293–294; common errors, 298–315; effectiveness, 316–332; exactness, 316–317; appropriateness, 317–318; expressiveness, 319–326; violations of effectiveness, 327–330
Dictionary, importance of study of, 339; unabridged, 339–340, 341–344; abridged, 340; information about words, 341–343
Different than, 301
Digressions, avoidance of, 138–139
Discussions of facts and ideas, 397–400
Don't, 252
Double negatives, 281
Double subjects and objects, 281
Drama, study of, iv–v

Editorials, newspaper, 410–413
Effectiveness of diction, 316–332; exactness, 316–317; appropriateness, 317–319; expressiveness, 319–327; violations of, 327–331
Eikenberry, W. L., 12, 13
Else, 259
Emphasis, law of, 78–79; in the paragraph, 152–153; in sentences, 201–203; in simple narration, 350–351; in description, 371
Emulation, value of, in improving composition, 37–38
English language, as a tool, 5; self-cultivation in, 6; sources of, 292–293
Epigram, 324
Errors in diction, 298–315
Essay, 400–405; formal, 401; informal, 401–404; study of, v–vi
Euphemism, 326
Euphony in sentences, 204–206
Exaggeration, 328
Examinations, 60–61
Exclamation mark, with words, 229; phrases, 229; sentences, 229; interjections, 230
Expansion, 62–63; value of, 63
Experience provides material for narration, 352
Explanations of processes, 394–397
Expletives: *it*, 466; *there*, 470
Exposition, 2; definition of, 388; importance of clearness in, 388–389;

necessity for outline, 389; oral, 389–390; methods, 390; kinds, 390–413; in letters, 413–414; in argument, 415

Fables, 19–20, 46–47
Feet, kinds of, xv–xvi
Fiction, types of prose, ii; study of, ii
Figurative language, overuse of, 329–330
Figures of speech, 321–326; suggestive value of, 320–321
"Fine writing," 330
Forbes, W. Cameron, 141, 147
Form, in written composition, 33–36; in letters, 104–106, 124–126
Franklin, Benjamin, 39–40
Fundamental image in description, 370

Gender, 256, 458, 465
Gerund, definition of, 477; reference, 275–276. *See* Verbal noun
Gerund phrase, 160, 196–197
Good form in composition, 3
Good use, requirements of, 294; violations of, 294–315
Grammar, cautions: agreement of subject with predicate, 249–253; compound subject, 249–250; nouns, 250–252; pronouns, 251–252; adjectives, 251–252; *don't* and *was*, 252; nouns and pronouns, 253–259; case, 253–255; number of nouns and pronouns, 255; agreement of relative pronouns, 256; reference of pronouns, 256–259; adjectives and adverbs, 259–263; comparison of adjectives and adverbs, 259–260; confusion in use of adjectives and adverbs, 260–261; demonstratives, 262; verbs, 263–274; principal parts of verbs, 263–264; transitive and intransitive verbs, 264–266; *shall, will, should, would*, 266–271; tense, 266–273; subjunctive mood, 273; participles, verbal nouns, infinitives, 274–277; split infinitive, 276; prepositions, 277; conjunctions, 277–278; miscellaneous, 278–282
Grammar, definition of, 2

Grammar, review: parts of speech, 457–485; nouns, 457–462; pronouns, 462–466; parsing, 462, 466, 469, 471, 483, 484, 485; adjectives, 466–469; adverbs, 470–471; verbs, 471–483; prepositions, 483–484; conjunctions, 484–485; interjections, 485; directions for sentence analysis, 485–486
Greenough, C. N., 135–136, 296
Guiterman, Arthur, 47

Hawthorne, Nathaniel, 366–367, 379–380
Hexameter, xviii
Hill, Howard Copeland, 57–58, 144, 145, 148
Holmes, Oliver Wendell, 149
Hyperbole, 324–325
Hyphen, 239

Iambic foot, xv
Idioms, 334–335
Imagination provides details for narration, 353
Imitation, value of, in improving composition, 37–38
Improprieties, 296
Infinitive, reference of, 196–197, 276; subject or complement of, 254; perfect for present, 272; split, 276; definition of, 477
Infinitive phrase, 160
Interjections, 485
Intransitive verbs, 472–473
Irony, 325
Irving, Washington, 153, 373–374
Italics, 239; in titles, 240; for emphasis, 240; sideheadings, 240; foreign words, 240; words, letters, and figures, 241; names of ships, 241

Johnson, Samuel, 187
Jordan, David Starr, 144–145

Kellogg, Vernon L., 144–145
Kipling, Rudyard, 43
Kittredge, George Lyman, 135–136, 296
Knowledge of subject, 10

Lamb, Charles, 134–135, 401
Lay, 264–265, 303

Le Gallienne, Richard, 48
Letters, kinds of, 104; form of, 104–106; parts of, 106–111; qualities of friendly, 111–112; subject matter of friendly, 112; paragraph arrangement in, 116–117; informal notes, 120–122; formal notes, 122–124; form of business, 124–126; qualities of business, 126–128; of application, 128; narration in, 359; expository, 413–414
Letter-writing, importance of, 104
Library, card catalogue, viii; reference books, viii–xi; use of, xii–xiii
Lie, 264–265, 303
Like, 277–278, 304
Lincoln, Abraham, 38–39, 114
Linn, James Weber, 136
London, Jack, 373

Macaulay, T. B., 151, 153
Marks, in correcting compositions, xxviii–xxix; in proofreading, xxx–xxxii
Mastery of English language as a tool, 5
Material, selection of, 72–73; for narration, 352–353
Matthews, Brander, 154
Merwin, Henry C., 137
Metaphor, 321–322
Meter, xvii–xviii
Metonymy, 324
Mills, Enos A., 134, 148–149
Mood, subjunctive, 273, 476; definition of, 475; indicative, 475; imperative, 476
Munro, William Bennett, 409
Myers, Philip Van Ness, 54

Narration, 2; simple, definition of, 345; essentials, 345–348; unity, 348–350; coherence, 350; emphasis, 350–351; oral, 351–352; material for, 352–353; dialogue, 353; types, 353; in letters, 359
Negatives, double, 281
Neilson, William Allan, 141–142
News stories, 356–358
Norris, Frank, 369
Notes, informal, 120; formal, 122–123
Note-taking, 53–55

Noun clauses, 171–172

Noun phrases, 161

Nouns, 457–462; kinds, 457–458; properties, 458–461; uses, 461–462; parsing, 462

Novel, study of, ii–iii

Number, 255, 459–460, 473

Object, direct, 472; indirect, 472

Obsolete words, 297

Omission of words, 278–281

Onomatopœia, 325

Other, 259

Outlines, 16–18, 74; value in planning a composition, 16; models, 17–18; importance of, in condensing, 56–57; form, 79; development into composition, 86–91; in exposition, 389

Painter, F. V. N., 134, 137, 143–144

Palmer, George Herbert, 7

Paragraphs, transitions between, 94–95; definition of, 131; indentation, 131; detailed study of, 131–153; length, 132; requirements of, 132–153; unity, 133–140; coherence, 140–151; emphasis, 152–153; transitional, 155

Parallel construction, 199, 287–288

Parentheses, in explanatory expressions, 233–234; with figures and letters, 234

Participial phrases, 160, 196–197, 274–275

Participles, reference, 196–197, 274–275; definition of, 477

Parts of speech, in dictionary, 342; definition of, 457; nouns, 457–462; pronouns, 462–466; adjectives, 466–469; adverbs, 470–471; verbs, 471–483; prepositions, 483–484; conjunctions, 484–485; interjections, 485

Pentameter, xviii

Pepys, Samuel, 360

Period, at end of sentences, 227; after abbreviations, 227; after letters and figures, 227; after sideheadings, 228; after topics, 228

Period fault, 182, 190–191, 227, 282–283

Periodic sentence, 186

Personification, 322–323

Phrases, definition of, 160–162; adjective, 161; adverbial, 161; noun, 161; absolute, 162; verb, 162; independent, 162; incorrect use of, 182, 282–283

Plagiarism, xiii

Plot, 434, 443–445

Poe, Edgar Allan, 205, 372, 385–386, 436–442

Poetry, study of, vi–vii; kinds of, xxiii–xxiv

Point of view, 70–72; in sentence, 193, 288; in description, 367–368; in short story, 447–448

Points, 239

Possessive case, 254–255, 461–462; wrong use of possessive sign, 255

Predicate adjective, 261, 469, 473

Predicate nominative, 172, 253, 473

Predicate objective, 172, 261, 472

Prefixes, 492–493

Prepositions, object of, 172, 254, 277; ending a sentence, 277; kinds, 483–484; parsing, 484

Pronouns, 462–466; reference of, 197–198, 256–258; agreement, 256; kinds, 462–465; properties, 462–465; uses, 465–466; parsing, 466

Proof, in debating, 425; burden of, 426

Proofreading, marks used in, xxx–xxxi; specimen, xxxi–xxxii

Prose fiction, study of, ii–iv

Provincialisms, 295

Punctuation, value of, 211; requirements of accurate, 211; general directions, 212; comma, 212–220; semicolon, 221–224; colon, 224–226; period, 226–228; question mark, 229; exclamation mark, 229–230; dash, 230–233; parentheses, 233–234; brackets, 234–235; quotation marks, 235–238; apostrophe, 238–239; hyphen, 239; caret, 239; points or asterisks, 239; italics, 239–241; capital letters, 241–245

Quatrain, xxi

Question mark, with direct question, 229; with doubtful statement, 229

Quotation marks, with direct quotations, 235; long quotations, 235–236; quotation within quotation, 236; titles, 236; with another mark, 236; miscellaneous, 237

Quotations, xiii; hackneyed, 329

Raise, 264–265, 306

Reading, value of, in improving composition, 37; provides suggestions for narration, 352–353

Redundancy, 328

Reference, of participles, 196–197, 274–275; of verbal nouns, 196–197, 275–276; of infinitives, 196–197, 276; of pronouns, 197–198, 256–258

Refutation in debating, 426

Repetition, needless, 327–328

Reproduction, as a means of self-cultivation, 41–42; as a means of cultivating accuracy, 42; three methods of, 42–65; by retelling closely, 42–51; by condensing, 51–62; by expanding, 62–65

Reviews of books, 407–410

Revision of a composition, 95–98

Rhetoric, definition of, 2

Rhythm, xv; variations in, xvi–xvii

Rime, xix

Rime scheme, xx

Rise, 264–265, 306

Roosevelt, Theodore, 115–116

Scansion, xviii

Scott, Sir Walter, 376

Self-cultivation in English, 6, 37, 41–42

Semicolon, with coördinate independent clauses, 221; with coördinate dependent clauses or phrases, 222; with introductory expressions, 222

Sentence analysis, 485–486

Sentence structure, special cautions concerning: period fault, 282–283; comma fault, 283–284; coördination in compound sentences, 285–287; parallel construction, 287–288; point of view, 288

Sentences, definition of, 159; kinds, 159, 181–182, 186–187; simple, 159–165; compound, 165–170; complex,

170–180; compound-complex, 180–181; loose, 186; periodic, 186; balanced, 186–187; effect of different kinds, 187; essentials of, 189; unity, 190–195; coherence, 195–200; emphasis, 201–204; euphony, 204–207

Set, 264–265, 307

Seton, Ernest Thompson, 395

Shall, 266–271

Short stories, collections of, 452

Short story, definition of, 434; plot, 434, 443–445; climax, 434; characteristics of, 434–435; essentials of, 435–436; singleness of impression, 442–443; dominant incident, 445–446; characters, 446; complication of plot, 446–447; resolution of plot, 446–447; setting, 447; point of view, 447–448; beginning, 448–449; title, 449; contrast, 449; enveloping action, 449–450; suspense, 450; dialogue, 450; sources, 451; study of, iii–iv

Should, 266–271

Simile, 321, 322

Singleness of impression, in description, 368–369; in short story, 442–443

Sit, 264–265, 307

Slang, 296–297, 392–393

Smith, F. Hopkinson, 383

Solecisms, 248, 295

Sonnet, xxii

Spelling, importance of correct, 487; rules, 487–490; syllabication, 491–492; prefixes, 492–493; suffixes, 493–494; troublesome words, 494–498; words frequently confused, 498–500; proper names, 500

Spondaic foot, xvi

Stanza, xx–xxi; ballad, xx; elegiac, xx; quatrain, xxi; Spenserian, xxi

Stevenson, Robert Louis, 27, 40–41, 43, 46, 112, 113–114, 121, 138, 143, 148, 149, 156, 205, 370, 382–383, 401–402

Strunsky, Simeon, 147–148

Subject, of composition, choice and limitation, 68–69

Subject, of sentence, compound, 159, 249

Suffixes, 493–494

Suspense, 450
Syllabication, 491–492
Synecdoche, 324
Synonyms, 335, 343

Tales, 355–356
Tautology, 327–328
Technical words, 297
Tenses, cautions regarding *shall* and *will*, 266–271; additional cautions, 271–273; definition of, 473; primary, 473–474; secondary, 474
Tetrameter, xviii
Than, 254, 260; *different than*, 301
Thomas, Edward, 47
Thorndike, A. H., 141–142
Title, choice of, 69–70; for short story, 449
Tomlinson, H. M., 371
Topic sentence, 133–138; logical development, 140–150; development by repetition, 140–141; development by details, 141–143; development by definition, 143–144; development by specific examples, 144; development by comparison and contrast, 144–145; development by reasons supporting statement, 146
Topics for composition, selection of, 10–11; sources, 10–11
Transition between paragraphs, 94–95
Transitional paragraphs, 155
Transitive verbs, 472
Translation, 49–50
Travel sketches, 362–363
Trite expressions, 328–329
Trochaic foot, xv

Unity, law of, 74–75; in paragraph, 133–140; in sentence, 190–193; in simple narration, 348–349; in description, 366–367
Usage, 294

Verb phrases, 161, 162, 266–270, 474; conditional, 475; potential, 475;

obligative, 475; emphatic, 475; progressive, 475; passive, 476–477
Verbal noun, reference of, 196–197, 275–276; definition of, 477. See Gerund
Verbal-noun phrases, 160
Verbs, principal parts of, 263–264; six troublesome, 264–266; *shall* and *will*, *should* and *would*, 266–271; kinds, 471–473; conjugation, 473–483; person and number, 473; tense, 473–474; phrases, 474–475; mood, 475–476; voice, 476–477; verbals, 477; regular conjugation, 478; irregular conjugation, 478; parsing, 483
Verse, definition of, xv; kinds of, xvii–xviii; blank, xxi; free, xxii
Versification, xv; rhythm, xv; kinds of feet, xv–xvi; variations in rhythm, xvi–xvii; kinds of verse, xvii–xviii; scansion, xviii; rime, xix; couplets, xix–xx; stanzas, xx–xxi; blank verse, xxi; free verse, xxii; the sonnet, xxii; kinds of poetry, xxiii–xxiv
Vividness, of speech, 26–28; in description, 371
Vocabulary, poverty of, 333; enlargement of, 333, 336–337
Voice, active, 476; passive, 476
Vulgarisms, 295

Was, 252
Will, 266–271
Words, definition of, 292; colloquial, 295; dialectal, 295; coined, 295; obsolete, 297; technical, 297; Anglo-Saxon, 333–334; classical, 334; spelling, 341–342, 487–500; pronunciation, 342; derivation, 342; history, 342; meanings, 342; standing of, 342; illustrations of use, 343; combinations, 343; syllabication, 491–492; prefixes, 492–493; suffixes, 493–494
Would, 266–271